THE GIFT OF KINDS

THE GIFT OF KINDS

THE GOOD IN ABUNDANCE

STEPHEN DAVID ROSS

an ethic of the earth

STATE UNIVERSITY OF NEW YORK PRESS

Published by
State University of New York Press, Albany

For information, address State University of New York Press,
State University Plaza, Albany, N.Y., 12246

Production by Marilyn P. Semerad
Marketing by Dana E. Yanulavich

Library of Congress Cataloging-in-Publication Data

Ross, Stephen David.
    The gift of kinds: the good in abundance : an ethic of the Earth
/ Stephen David Ross.
    p.   cm.
    Includes bibliographical references and index.
    ISBN 0-7914-4253-5 (alk. paper). — ISBN 0-7914-4254-3 (pbk. :
alk. paper)
    1. Ethics.   2. Philosophy of nature.   3. Categories (Philosophy)–
–Moral and ethical aspects.   I. Title.
BJ1031.R67   1999
171—dc21   99-17962
                                                                 CIP

10   9   8   7   6   5   4   3   2   1

Contents

The fourth of several volumes devoted to the good. Human, natural worlds filled with gifts. Nature the general economy of the good, earth's abundance. Resisting authority and totality. Plato's idea of the good beyond measure. Unlimiting every limit, interrupting authority. Gifts and giving. Exposure interruption, calling for responsiveness, responsibility. Cherishment exposure to the good everywhere in generosity. Sacrifice impossibility of fulfillment. Plenishment crossing cherishment and sacrifice: inexhaustible exposure to the good. Socrates' suggestion that the good grants authority to knowledge and truth. Anaximander and injustice in all things, demanding restitution. The good as ideality. Volumes projected in this project. Began with art in response to Nietzsche's interruption of authority in name of art. Continue within possibility that Western philosophic tradition has always given precedence to truth and being, neutralizing the good. This volume addresses kinds of the earth as ecstatic revelations of life and being, resistant to neutrality.

Spinoza and abundance of kinds. God and nature expressed in infinite numbers of infinite kinds. Nature composed of infinite individuals, each expressed through infinite kinds. *Conatus*, desire. Love of God, *Dei amor, beatitudo*, blessedness. *Kind\red\ness* and *kind\ness*. Tyranny of kinds: using other kinds in any way whatever. Interruption: essentialism and identity politics. Tyrannies of singularities and kinds. Heterogeneous differences among singulars and kinds. Good and evil. Profit and advantage. Two ethical discourses: good and evil, God and nature. *Natura naturans, natura* *naturata; potentia, potestas.* Infinity of kinds. Levinas. Infinity of infinite. Singularity. Wittig. Exaltation and universality. *Mimēsis.* *The Lesbian Body.* All human works and things given from the good, without neutrality. Cherishment, sacrifice, plenishment. Sacrificing sacrifice. In expression, the abundance of species and kinds.

women and animals, sacrifice and consumption. Griffin. Body vessel of death, in blood. Blood of our mother. Spilling and devouring blood. Derrida. *Geschlecht. Dasein's* sexuality. Heidegger's neutralization. Foucault. Genealogy. Nietzsche. *Ursprung, Entstehung, Herkunft, Abkunft, Geburt*: birth, origin, descent; emergence, *parousia*; family, stock, nation, kin, kind, propinquity, bonded by blood. Impurity of purity. Attached to bodies. Interruption: Irigaray. *Genre, genre humain.* Nature, neutrality, touch. Mark of gender in nature through language. Butler. Coding, citation, iterability, materiality. Derrida. *Geschlecht.* Gender in language. Man's hand, paws, fangs, claws. *Dasein's* friend never animal. Question of Heidegger. Rigor. Iterability, singularity and repetition. Examples. Immeasurability of responsibility and sacrifice. Cherishment, sacrifice, plenishment.

Eating well. Stockpiling. Impeding circulation of goods. Consumption, stockpiling, storing, owning, devouring the good. Derrida. Responsibility excessive. Affirmation. *Différance*, trace, iterability, ex-appropriation, not only human, well beyond humanity. Responsibility. Expression, *mimēsis*, representation. Interruptions: Griffin. Consumption. Abjection. Blood. Interruption: Adams. Absent referents. Violence against women and animals. Derrida. Humanism does not sacrifice sacrifice. Interruption: Foucault. Bodily inscriptions. Lateral effects. Bataille. Sacrifice. Sovereignty nothing. Extravagance and consumption without use. Humanity under the curse. Humans, animals, death, abjection. Gifts. Women. Sacrificing sacrifice. Derrida. Eating the good. State power, meat, and vegetarianism. Male dominance, virility, and meat. Political power. How to sacrifice sacrifice. *Mimēsis* without domination.

I am because we are. Sacrificing sacrifice. Animals, women, slaves. Stored, seized, classified as kinds. Heidegger. Standing-reserve. Domestication and mastery. Spinoza. Anything whatever can be used for human advantage. Aristotle. Slaves, women, animals subordinate by nature. Du Bois. Celebration of races. Interruption: Mingling and impurity of kinds. Value presupposes abundance. Chains and whips of slavery, animal domestication. Value. Between general and restricted economy. Sacrificing sacrifice. Racism, sexism, classism, speciesism as possession, consumption, in blood. Guidelines resistant to stockpiling kinds. Abundance, restriction, possession, mastery. Sacrificing sacrifice. Celebrating race. *Mimēsis.* Invisibleness. Senghor.

Negritude. Black feminism. Identity politics. Tyranny of kinds. Community fascism. Kindism. Appiah. Racialism, extrinsic racism, intrinsic racism. Outlaw. Critical theory and race. Delacampagne. Racism and Western rationality. Gates. Poststructuralist denial of subjectivity. Anti-universalist universalism. Balibar. Racism, kindism, universality, and humanism. Humanity menaced by animality. Jacoby. Slavery and domestication of animals. Spiegel. Comparing suffering of animals and suffering of slaves.

Kristeva. Strangers to ourselves. Foreigners and cosmopolitanism. So-called primitive societies. Threshold rituals. Liminaries. Simmel. Outsiders near and far, in danger. Interruption: Lyotard. Reality composed of *différends*. Genres. Nature and reality. Expression, *mimēsis*. Interruption: Jowett. Levinas. Responsibility in proximity. Lyotard. Politics threat of *différend*: no genre, takes place as genre. Foucault. Power and resistance. Kristeva. Nationality without nationalism. Strangeness in proximity. Subjection and abjection. Being-in-proximity. *Exposition*—exposure and expression. Nationality. Democracy without territory. Policing strangeness. Interruption: United States's naturalization law. Racism and strangers. Kristeva. Dialectic of master and slave. The curse. Interruption: African strangers. Liminaries. Exogamy. Women always strangers. Interruption: Jussawalla. *Missing Person*. Bhabha. Fanon. Hindi alphabet and silence. Repetitious desire to recognize ourselves doubly. Politics and *mimēsis*. The good as abundance.

Naess. Shallow and deep ecology. Without *mimēsis*. Without sacrificing sacrifice. Foucault. Power and resistance. Odd term. Two pervasive contingencies in ethical|political practice: insecurity of every ethical judgment; good is bad. Ethics requires sacrifice and its sacrifice. Power and resistance dispersed and incalculable. Shallow ecology may be more effective than deep. Deep ecological platform. Expressing impurity. Qualifications and reservations. Cherishment, sacrifice, plenishment. Ecosophy. Philosophy in exposure and proximity. In *mimēsis*. Rejection of total view. *Oikos*. Dominations of women, slaves, and children in the home. Propinquity. Responsibility as change. Ecosophy as excessive responsibility. Plenishment. Rights, human and natural. Economics. Without authority. Ecosophy as *mimēsis*, sacrificing sacrifice. Deep ecological platform without police. Too late to escape human presence everywhere. Politics. Resistance to neutrality. Gandhian rules of nonviolence. Guidelines to plenishment in the earth.

Total view. Endless questions of responsibility. Universal right to live and blossom. Rights. Over others. Right to sacrifice. Inclusive ethics of abundance. *Friluftsliv*: exuberance in nature. Touching the earth lightly. Guidelines for exuberance.

Goddesses. Weaving and ethical ecology. Griffin. Women and nature. Technology. Domination. Natural kinds. Impurity. Ecological feminism. Women's lived experience. Kheel. MacKinnon. Shiva. Feminine principle. Linking multiplicity, profusion, liminality, impurity. King. Activities of women absolutely social. Social and natural inseparable. Dirty little secret. The curse. Radical cultural feminists. Radical rationalist feminists. Essentialism. Overcoming dualisms, oppositions. Abundance of the earth. Heterogeneity, impurity, *différends*. Spiritual renewal. Interruption: Total earth view.

Ferry. Modern world rests on separation of humanity from nature. Animals instinctive, leave no legacy. All valorization human. Modernity formed under curse. All rights belong to subject. Nature has no rights. Foucault. Prose of the world. Ferry. Freedom absolute condition of ethics and law. Of democracy. Under the curse. Resistance to absolute distinction between human beings and animals, humanity and nature. Freedom as responsibility without authority, always qualified. Critique of universality. Ferry. Ethical superiority of humanity. Ethics for human beings. Humanism sacrifices nature to humanity. Serres. Natural contract. Jonas. Link of radical ecology with National Socialism. Kant. Man the final purpose of nature. Inequality. Ferry. Public torture of animals. politeness and civility toward animals, not ethics. Conflict between democracy and environmentalism. Democracy and responsibility toward all. Interruption: Postmodern radical ecology. Nature's expressiveness, *mimēsis*. Critique of humanism and anthropocentrism. Animistic cultures. Expressiveness of nature. Ecological humility. Gaia hypothesis. New sense of democracy and polity, including natural world. Wilderness spaces. Otherness as wildness. Beyond anthropocentrism.

Abundance and heterogeneity of kinds. Bhabha. Repetitions of *mimēsis* and desire. Ackerman. Heterogeneities. Culture, capitalism, world system. Ecological reflections from other cultures. China. One body with universe. As *mimēsis*. *Tao-te*. Jewel net of Indra. Hua-yen Buddhism. Ontological parity. *Nirvana*. Continuity of reality. Loving-kindness. Compassion. Sacrifice. Sacrificing sacrifice. Blake. World in grain of sand. Bodhi tree. Interdependence throughout nature. Endless *mimēsis*. Experiential reality. Emptiness as abundance.

Responsibility a call from nowhere. Abundance in the earth. Heterogeneity. Giving. Exposure. Expression and proximity. Propinquity. *Mimēsis*. Resisting neutrality. Cherishment, sacrifice, plenishment. Ethic of inclusion. Resisting humanism, mechanism, universalism. Program built on platform of deep ecology. Responsibility interruption in proximity. Resist neutrality! Sacrifice sacrifice! Resist injustice in the abundance of the earth. Abjection. Under the curse. Greater responsiveness and self-criticism. Exposure among different human beings and kinds. In propinquity. Promote female literacy. Beware the purity of the better. Resist every border. Undertake responsibility within exposure and proximity. *Mimēsis*. *Friluftsliv*. Normative model without normativity, with exclamation marks! Local determination! Abundance, heterogeneity, kinds, responsibility, cherishment, sacrifice, plenishment, intermediary movements, liminality, impurity, exuberance, interruption! Bhabha. Immeasurable ecology, ethics itself. Concluding examples. No one knows good for another. Struggle between global centralization and local determination. World condition. Democracy as heterogeneity. Capitalist economy as locally competitive economies. Democratic institutions institute homogeneity, capitalist economies widen disparities. Democracy discounts every authority in name of heterogeneity. Animal experimentation. Human experimentation. Conclusions: Become vegetarians? Of course. But . . . Animal experimentation? Of course. But . . . Ethics of *perhaps* and *but*. Feeding one's cats, other cats. Plenishment as love. Kindness. Endless crossings.

General Preface to the Project: Gifts of the Good*

This volume is the fourth of several devoted to the good,[1] understanding human and natural worlds to be filled with gifts,[2] exposing us everywhere to other individuals and kinds,[3] calling us and others to respond with endless movements in and out of every place.[4] The works we know, their precious ingredients, all dwelling places and natural kinds, come as gifts in the name of something other than themselves, unlike any thing, interrupting the limits of places and worlds, resisting authority. I speak of these local and contingent gifts as the giving in abundance everywhere in nature, understanding nature as the general economy of the good, the circulation of goods beyond expense, the earth's abundance, interrupting measure, resisting totality.[5] An ethic of inclusion, bearing responsibility to supplement the goodness of things everywhere, however impossibly, in memory of disaster.

I speak of the good in memory of Plato, who recalled Socrates' death as a disaster.[6] I read every word he wrote in memory of that and other disasters, echoes of the good. Yet we do not find it congenial today to speak of the good. We prefer to speak of value, or virtue, or the good life; and God.[7] We pursue being in the neuter as if it bore no ethical exposure.[8] I hope to rehabilitate the good in relation to each of these and more, as what calls us to them and what disturbs our relation to them, what impels them in circulation. But the good is not any of them, is not a thing, or event, or

---

*This general preface, with ensuing changes, begins each volume of the project, reaching out to those who may not have prior knowledge of the undertaking, to call their attention to the good. The first volume of the project is *The Gift of Beauty: The Good as Art;* the second *The Gift of Truth: Gathering the Good;* the third *The Gift of Touch: Embodying the Good.* I hope to trace gifts of the good in other places, multiplying their profusion.

Each volume may be read independently, in its terms. Each may benefit from other volumes. Here I address the ecology of human and natural worlds in the heterogeneous abundance of things and kinds, the immeasurable giving of the good.

being; does not belong to us, to human beings; and is not God—though many have spoken of the good in terms of the divine. It is neither in this world nor out, inhabits no immanent or transcendent place, but is giving in abundance, the unlimiting of every limit and the displacement of every place, exposing each creature and thing to others, incessantly moving them to respond. The good of which I speak is not a category, does not oppose the bad or beautiful, does not war with evil, but interrupts the authority of judgment, gives responsibility for making and unmaking categories, opposing evil, struggling to make things better, or worse. The good is not good opposed to bad, right opposed to wrong, justice opposed to injustice.[9] It expresses what is priceless, irreplaceable, lovely, in local, contingent, heterogeneous things and kinds, worth cherishing, in human beings and their works, and other creatures and kinds throughout nature, all born in immeasurable exposure to others, imposing a debt to foster them and to pursue ideality, instituting the good in place. It haunts the limits of individual things in their identities and relations and of the kinds and collectives of the earth, gives itself to nature everywhere, composing the circulation of goods beyond measure.[10]

To speak of the good is to speak of an exposure given from no place or thing, which circulates everywhere, in every place, a giving without a giver, without a receiver, everywhere in proximity. In this sense, it is impossible to speak of the good, impossible to fix its limits, not because the good is something we cannot know but because expressing it is endless interruption. My efforts here are endeavors in an ongoing struggle to understand and to participate in working to make things better where every such effort is a betrayal.[11] The struggle is to interrupt the flow of continuities and identities that do the work of the good in nature. It is a struggle to keep the gifts moving, not to let them come to rest in a better that denies its own betrayal, insisting on its authority.

I call exposure to the good everywhere in generosity *cherishment*; I call the impossibility of fulfilling conflicting demands everywhere *sacrifice*, wounding and disaster, without honor; I call work in response to the good *plenishment*, the crossing of cherishment and sacrifice, inexhaustible exposure to the good, filled with endless interruption, endless *mimēsis*. These make it possible to undertake and to resist binary divisions between good and bad, true and false, high and low, make it possible to give goods in circulation, unlimiting every limit, dwelling in and crossing every threshold, in the endless responsivity in which we do ethical work, calling us to work for justice and to resist injustice by struggling against the authority of every category and identity, including every authority that would justify sacrifice.

This thought pursues Socrates' suggestion that the good grants authority to knowledge and truth, gives the possibility of being to all things

and kinds: "This reality, then, that gives their truth to the objects of knowledge and the power of knowing to the knower, you must say is the idea of
the good, and you must conceive it as being the cause *[aitian]* of knowledge, and of truth in so far as known" (Plato, *Republic*, 508e), described by
Glaucon as "[a]n inconceivable beauty *[kallos]*" (509a). This beautiful idea
of the good, giving knowledge and truth, and more, meets and surpasses
the idea of the sacred as nature's expressiveness and beauty, as *mimēsis*:
sonance, radiance, and glory beyond neutrality.[12] Plato expresses it in
Diotima's voice as a "nature of wondrous beauty *[phusin kalon]*" (*Symposium*, 211). The sacred touches the mundane with beauty, disturbs the hold
of categories and distinctions, interposes ideality, ecstatically displaces every place, answers to the profane. The good touches the sacred with a call
to resist endless injustices perpetrated in the name of the good, and God.
For the good resists every authority, including the rule of the gods. In the
institution of authority, it resists authority.

Socrates' words evoke Anaximander, who understands all things to
bear the mark of the good, demanding restitution for endless injustices. All
things, "make reparation to one another for their injustice according to the
ordinance of time."[13] This debt incurred by being is remembrance of the
good, lacking any possibility of instituting justice, of inaugurating the good
without injustice. All things are charged by the good with their truth and
being, responsible for who and what they are, the sacrifices of their birth.
The sense of *aitia* here is *for the sake of which*, responsive and responsible
for and to, exposed in heterogeneity. Knowledge and truth are for the sake
of the good, demanding unlimited responsiveness everywhere and always.
The good is that within each thing, for the sake of which it is and for which
it moves, gives it ideality, interrupts the fixing of its identity.

This giving, as I understand it in Plato, does not measure up the goal
for which things strive, but undercuts the inescapable wound of measure.
I pursue Levinas's thought that the good does not rule over being, does not
reassemble being in its place together with the authority of identity and
difference, but interrupts the order of being. The giving interrupts the rule
of identity, undermines the domination of being and law, challenges the
authority of every rule, disrupts the totality of truths. In immeasurable
exposure. In proximity, in propinquity, in kind. Face to face with heterogeneity, with other beings of other kinds, touched everywhere with strangeness. The good is less encounter with the face of the singular other,
something that only humans may know, than touching another, exposure
to others in skin and flesh and kind, reaching beyond one's limits to others,
known to every thing in every place.

I believe that the forms of thought around which philosophy has traditionally coalesced have been sites of interruption, where the good displaces

the hold of work upon us. The work of human life, the promulgation of rules, the coercion of political powers, all institute excessive authorities against which life repeatedly struggles to recapture a freedom it never had. This mobilization against the claims of authority, legitimate and otherwise, fills the world of disciplines, including Western philosophy, themselves filled with clashes of authority, with coercion and exclusion. The possibility that an authority might claim legitimacy, or that it might be resisted, both draw sustenance from the good, not a good with overarching authority, preempting this clash of power and resistance, but a good that resists authority yet demands it for its work. The space of this ceaseless struggle with authority echoes the call of the good,[14] demands from us endless responses to the injustices of every authority.

Why did I begin this project with beauty and art, followed with truth, bodies, and kinds?[15] Why not speak at once, in general, of the good, throughout nature, specifying beauty and truth in their places? That would take more than one volume to answer, perhaps the entire ongoing project, in relation to the good. I respond that truth and beauty have no proper places, but come from the good as gifts, displaced, unplaced, in Heidegger's words, *ek-static*: out of place. The good ecstatically places things outside themselves, interrupts the hold of being everywhere in nature, in every kind. The forms of displacement are inexhaustible. Touch touches things with excess, expressed in every kind.

I began with beauty to address Nietzsche's challenge to the authority of the good, undertaken in the name of art. He interrupted the authority of truth in the name of the good. With this thought a radical possibility emerged that Nietzsche himself did not explore in its extremity, nor did Heidegger, who accepted Nietzsche's challenge in the name of Being. The thought of Being, however forgotten, remains gathered neutrally in truth under the sign of *legein*.[16] I understand Nietzsche to offer another possibility, that the challenge posed to truth by the will to power cuts to the heart of being and its authority. What if the Western philosophic tradition, from the beginning and nearly always, gave precedence to being and truth, precedence to gathering and assembling being; and what if that privilege gestured toward—betrayed—something that was neither truth nor being, but gave them forth as gifts, interrupting the gathering, resisting neutrality? What if the Western philosophic tradition, from the beginning and nearly always, gave precedence to spirit, to gathering and assembling being in a disembodied truth; and what if that privilege gestured toward and betrayed something that was neither truth nor being nor spirit, but gave them forth as corporeal gifts, interrupting the gathering? And again, what if the Western philosophic tradition, from the beginning and nearly always, insisted on subordinating singular things to kinds, ranking kinds from high to low, so that kinds betrayed singularity, as if that were extreme betrayal, as if without responsibility? Or if, in resistance, autonomous individuals found their freedom in a hierarchy of kinds, human and otherwise? The provocation I undertake in this volume is to explore the embodied kinds of the earth as ecstatic revelations of life and being, resistant to neutrality, including the neutralization of kinds in the singularities of beings, resistant to their authority.

If the Western tradition, from its beginning with the Greeks, followed the trajectory I have described, instituting the rule of spirit within the gathering of being, and if this sovereignty and rule are to be understood as I have suggested, as ethical|political,[17] in memory of the good, then this volume undertakes a critical movement of the project incongruous in many ways with traditional philosophy. Yet I hope to show that this departure can be understood from within that same tradition, that the most fervent defenders of the privilege of spirit, in their ardor, gesture toward the abundance of earthly kinds.

I pursue my task in each volume in the same movement, reading traditional Western philosophers to interrupt the hold of their authority and that of the tradition that has fixed their reading, to open them and others to abundance. I understand the call of the good, endless touch and responsiveness toward ideality, to release the authority of every category, including the categories of tradition, by reading traditional works in different ways, and by reading nontraditional works, both interrupting authority.

This book, however long, is shorter than the topic of natural kinds demands, which could be as long as the Western tradition. I have said much in framing this discussion here of gifts and generosity in other places, beginning with *The Ring of Representation* through *Injustice and Restitution: The Ordinance of Time* and *Plenishment in the Earth: An Ethic of Inclusion*. My project of generosity and abundance pursues this ethic of inclusion, an ethic that includes all things, mourning its impossibility. All these different works come together in the name of the good, remembering countless injustices, sorrows and joys.

With this immeasurability before us, I undertake the impossible project of working toward the good without impeding its circulation. Endless interruptions.

Introduction:
The Abundance of Kinds

By God I understand a being absolutely infinite, i.e., a substance consisting of an infinity of attributes, of which each one expresses an eternal and infinite essence.

... not infinite in its own kind; ... (Spinoza, *E*, I, D6)

From the necessity of the divine nature there must follow infinitely many things in infinitely many modes [*modus*: ways]. (I, P16)

If someone has been affected with Joy or Sadness by someone of a class, or nation, different from his own, and this Joy or Sadness is accompanied by the idea of that person as its cause, under the universal name of the class or nation, he will love or hate, not only that person, but everyone of the same class or nation. (IV, P46)

Apart from men we know no singular thing in nature whose Mind we can enjoy, and which we can join to ourselves in friendship, or some kind of association. And so whatever there is in nature apart from men, the principle of seeking our own advantage does not demand that we preserve it. Instead, it teaches us to preserve or destroy it according to its use, or to adapt it to our use in any way whatever. (IV, App26)

Spinoza speaks of an abundance of individuals and kinds given in infinite profusion and expression. God is expressed in infinite numbers of attributes, infinite kinds; nature is composed of infinite numbers of corporeal individuals, each of which expresses God and nature through infinite attributes and kinds.[1] Each individual is expressed as, defined by *conatus*— yearning, striving, desire, power.

Each thing, as far as it can by its own power *(potentia)*, strives to persevere in its being. (III, P6)

1

The striving by which each thing strives to persevere in its being is
nothing but the actual essence of the thing. (P7)

[W]e neither strive for, nor will, neither want, nor desire anything because
we judge it to be good; on the contrary, we judge something to be good
because we strive for it, will it, want it, and desire it. (P9n)

Desire is man's very essence, insofar as it is conceived to be determined, from any given affection of it, to do something. (Def Aff 1)

The natural world is filled with infinite numbers of individuals and kinds,
where individuals are members of infinite kinds, where the infinite kinds—
the attributes—express the essence of God in relation to each individual
thing, where the essence of individual things, their power to exist, is expressed as desire, and where desire defines good and evil. All are given in
the abundance of the natural world, the earth, in relation to God beyond
any profit or advantage, beyond decision and choice. All are given throughout the earth in an ethical relation beyond measure, of desire and love,
without neutrality. Infinite kinds, in infinite abundance, mark the ethical
side of Spinoza's *Ethics*, abundant generosity from God or nature, whose
love Spinoza describes as the highest good *(summum bonum)* (V, P20): a
love of God *(Dei Amor)* indistinguishable from infinite love in God: *beatitudo*,
blessedness, virtue itself (P42).

The Mind's intellectual Love of God is the very Love of God by which
God loves himself. (V, P36)

Blessedness is not the reward of virtue, but virtue itself; . . .
Dem.: Blessedness consists in Love of God. (P42)

God and nature, expressed in infinite numbers of infinite kinds, is filled
with infinite desire and love, expressed in each individual thing and place.
I understand this infinite desire as given in memory of the good, beyond
measure, expressed in infinite kinds. The good, in debt beyond measure,
takes place everywhere in kinds. Kinds are gifts from the good in abundance, resistant to neutrality.[2] The good is *kindness*, expressed in kinds,
permeated by love: *kind\red\ness* and *kind\ness*. More of this later.

To this remarkable understanding of nature's abundance, filled with
kinds as well as individuals, heterogeneous and multifarious corporeal kinds
permeated by excessive desire, Spinoza joins the hateful side of the thought
of kinds—*the tyranny of kinds*—that marks the ethical debt under which
philosophy has labored to mark a profusion of heterogeneous kinds in a
world filled with domination and oppression. Kinds are ranked from high
to low, where the lower are for the sake of the higher, expressed by Spinoza

to an extreme. Every other kind in the world may be used by Us, We Human Beings, by human kinds, *in any way whatever*! Every human being belongs to a class or nation or tribe or kind that humans love or hate in that kind. Spinoza speaks directly to a world in which Jews were tortured and expelled from Spain and Portugal *as Jews*, in which Germans later killed Jews *as Jews*, as belonging to another kin or kind, by blood; in which Turks killed Armenians because they were not Turks; in which Serbs killed Croats and Muslims, Europeans murdered Africans, Hutus slaughtered Tutsis; in which human beings kill other human beings in the kind to which they belong by blood, by family, nation, and kin; in which other human beings are ranked according to their proximity to Us, classifying them in kind beyond their singularity. In which every *We* marks a kind that threatens other kinds. Propinquity without intimacy.

I interrupt Spinoza to reflect upon the movements in our time that mark this hate and fear with two entwined names that together express one side of the project undertaken here: *essentialism* and *identity politics*. Two ugly names of opprobrium, profoundly linked, overlapping, pointing in opposing directions. *Essentialism* names the hierarchies and rankings in the name of essences and kinds that institute and authorize domination and exclusion. Members of other kinds—genders, races, nations, classes, any kinds whatever—are to be excluded or dominated as inferior in their kinds. Essentialism expresses the practices of domination and exclusion in the name of essences and kinds against which we may hope to foster resistance. To classify human beings by their essences is to threaten them with domination. To classify natural things by their essences, perhaps, is to rank them in a system of mastery or property. Essences are social constructions where human beings are too heterogeneous and abundant to be classified in their essences.[3] I take the kinds and species of the earth, human and otherwise, to be inexhaustibly complex, heterogeneous, and entwined, resisting hierarchies, rankings, domination, and exclusion, still the kinds they are.

Essentialism speaks more of those who classify singular individuals into kinds by stable essences, ranked and ordered, frequently to dominate them, sometimes to harm them, even destroy them. *Identity politics* speaks more of those who classify themselves by their kind, typically a single kind: we women, Americans, Jews, Serbs, Africans, African Americans: always *We*. Human beings hope to resist oppression in the name of a kind. Human beings claim allegiances, seek alliances, sometimes in the name of a single kind. *I Am Because We Are* is the striking name of a fine collection in African American philosophy, one whose guiding thought is of the possibilities and difficulties of identity politics. Yet whatever the difficulties, the title expresses a truth of irresistible importance for human beings, even those who do not know themselves well enough to say it. Individuals are who and what they are in virtue of the kinds in which they participate. Identity politics may insist too strongly for some to hear that a certain group identity defines its members, even those who would deny it, where perhaps the truth is that any of us is the individual we are in virtue of the many kinds, the many *We*'s, in which we participate, that every *we* is difficult, contested, multiple, and heterogeneous. To be an individual is to be a member of many different kinds. That is among the issues of kinds that underlie this project.

So that it may be clear from the outset, I resist the ideas of kinds and practices associated with them that are named *essentialism* and *identity politics*. I hope to resist the tyranny of kinds. Yet I resist as well the opprobrium associated with them, as if we no longer need to think of essences and identities, but of singular individuals only. Instead, I believe, the ethical|political obligation of our time, perhaps of every time, is toward individuals in their kinds, human and otherwise, unthinkable, unimaginable except in terms of essences and kinds, given identities as individuals in virtue of their multiple and heterogeneous kinds. An obligation to resist the restrictions, exclusions, and oppressions instituted in the name of essences and kinds, knowing that they are inescapable. *Essentialism* and *identity politics* are names of betrayals at the heart of any ethics|politics, which finds itself surrounded by inescapable responsibilities toward individuals in virtue of their kinds.

I think that we will not get rid of God until we get rid of the tyranny of individuals and kinds—not to abolish them but the tyranny. To understand the good to call from the abundance of kinds against every tyranny including the neutrality of individuals and kinds. To resist neutrality in kindness. Nothing is neutral; tyranny threatens everywhere, in the profusion and circulation of singulars and kinds. I return from this interruption.

Although every singular thing in Spinoza's world strives to endure as an individual thing, every thing participates in kinds, strives to benefit or harm other individuals in virtue of the kinds in which they participate; and every thing participates in nature, yearns for God, in multiple senses of desiring and participating. Individuals strive as individuals to preserve their essence as individuals; yet their essence pertains to God and nature infinitely composed of infinite kinds, and the essence of an individual thing is empowered or confined by other kinds. To be, here, is to be an individual composing and composed of kinds—always plural: a world composed of infinite numbers of singular individuals, each of which participates in infinite numbers of infinite kinds, from which each individual derives its essence, expressed inseparably as desire and power. Moreover, in relation to God and nature in the abundance of their kinds, there is no betrayal, no ranking and destruction in the name of use. Yet alongside this infinite participation in infinite kinds, fulfilling the essence of singularities, individuals find themselves classified and ranked according to kinds against which they must mobilize endless resistance.

As does Spinoza, who insists that human beings benefit each other collectively despite differences in kind. Though animals—who have feelings and emotions as much as human beings (Spinoza, *E*, IV, P37n1)—may be used by human beings in any way whatever, to human profit, human beings—who differ in their feelings and emotions as they differ in their essences—benefit each other collectively and strive to do so. Advantage shows that human beings benefit from associating with other kinds of human beings, but not other kinds than human. "The rational principle of seeking our own advantage teaches us the necessity of joining with men, but not with the lower animals, or with things whose nature is different from human nature" (P37n1). We might imagine that every thing, of every kind, might benefit us all the more as we understand us to share the earth together, that we might strive toward a good for all creatures and things in which hatred and use were replaced by love. That would lead us to an ecological ethic toward all natural things. Spinoza recoils from such an ethic. I hope to take this hesitation seriously as I insist on interrupting its authority.

I will not pursue the line of thought that those who divide the world into natural kinds that are advantageous to us and those that are not, which we may adapt to our use in any way whatever, typically fail to sustain the claim that human beings in general are like us and advantageous to us, that we are obligated to pursue their good as we pursue our own. It seems that those who judge according to their advantage judge other kinds of human beings—yellow, black, Jew, Christian, woman, stranger, barbarian—to be used, employed, bonded, enslaved, even destroyed where they are perceived to be a threat, different from others in kind. Spinoza's argument that we may use other kinds of things in any way whatever supports using other kinds of human beings in any way whatever—or not using them at all, hoping to rid the earth of them where they threaten what we take to be our advantage.[4]

What if we were to read Spinoza as speaking ethically of kinds in two voices, one ranging from the most hateful, heinous, yet historically truthful thought that the human world has been and is a world of profit, advantage, use, that ethics demands, imposes, insists that we use others to our own advantage: Europeans enslaving Africans, men dominating women, human beings owning and possessing animals, natural things and kinds, using them in any way whatever, regardless of their natures, essences, suffering or joy? Good and evil, justice and injustice, are what human beings—through the laws, rules, and governments that implement and define them—say what they are, extrinsic notions. Which we must acknowledge openly as conditions of human life in which ethical and political striving take place, but of which, perhaps, we must not say too much, must not commit ourselves too far, in the name of ethics. Perhaps this entire understanding and practice is what Spinoza calls *extrinsic*. Perhaps ethics|politics as we know it is in this sense extrinsic. Which is not to suggest that it can be replaced by what is intrinsic. Nor is it to deny that Spinoza speaks of what is intrinsic, still in an ethical voice, however strange.

For he speaks of God and nature in relation to humanity in a different register, still ethical, a voice of freedom, of which, perhaps, we can never say enough though everything is caused by necessity. "If men were born free, they would form no concept of good and evil so long as they remained free" (Spinoza, *Ethics*, IV, P68). What if we understood Spinoza to offer two ethical discourses together composing ethics? One a binary discourse of good and evil, truth and falsehood, justice and injustice, love and hatred. This is traditional ethical discourse, the ethical|political world we know ourselves to inhabit as finite creatures, where each individual thing participates in many kinds: nations, tribes, races, and families; genders, classes, ethnic groups. We may describe this ethical world as composed of individuals who differ among themselves in their kinds in countless ways, in their histories, memories, truths, and desires; who endlessly negotiate the difficult terrain of heterogeneous and multiple kinds where we may understand ourselves to be safer, benefited by, the production of agreement and similarity among kinds, all individuals members of a single family or kin or tribe. Even here, however, human life is filled with variety, and we may know that where all individuals share common kinship, then all become replaceable, one kin substituting for another. Heterogeneity, if that is valued, always looks to differences in kinds.

We may describe this ethical world as in part striving for agreement and commonality, yearning for community, among countless individuals differing in multiple ways. And we may understand it to occupy a space forever contested by multiply different kinds, where agreement among all human beings may perhaps be an ideal, a dream, filled with differences and betrayals. So we may occupy this space of heterogeneous individuals and kinds in endless mediation between one kind and another, one kind striving to dominate others, surrounded by dreams and practices that would foster agreement among all human beings: a universal ethics, a world government, a harmony of all human and natural individuals. In a world in which hatred of others passes from one individual to the entire kind of which the individual is a member, the entire nation of which the individual is a citizen, the entire tribe in which the individual participates by history, geography, or blood, we may seek a more comprehensive harmony based on the universality of reason, the commonality of human beings, or something else. In every case, we struggle among heterogeneous kinds to institute commonality. In every case, we institute commonality in a ranking of kinds, human or otherwise, in the name of agreement, that justifies our treating other creatures as present for our use in any way whatever, to be destroyed, or enslaved, or harmed. Sacrificed and cursed.[5] We take for granted that heterogeneity presupposes conflict, instituting domination—a presumption I would question—whether or not we ourselves participate in domination or struggle against it.

I understand this discourse and practice to be what most human beings understand by ethics, or ethics|politics. And I do not imagine that anything can replace this practice with something better. *Better* occupies a crucial place in this discourse, whether it is better to strive to benefit oneself, one's family, one's tribe, or all human beings—always at someone's or something's expense. This is an ethics that defines a good in opposition to evil, truth in opposition to falsity, a good that ranks and excludes. It is a binary ethics, even when given over to harmony and collectivity. And we may say that the kinds of the world, as we encounter them and as we classify, rank, and order them here, occupy the binary world of identities and oppositions.

A second ethical discourse found in Spinoza—inseparable from the first—pertains to God and nature, still ethical, still of kinds. God and nature are absolutely infinite, filled with infinite numbers of infinite kinds. God is *natura naturans*, the creative power, *potentia*, of the universe, present everywhere in things and kinds. The finite world is *natura naturata*, pervaded by finite powers *(potestas)* to accomplish, achieve, bring out, gain advantage. Freedom pertains to the infinite, creative power of things in participating in infinite kinds, a freedom that knows nothing of good and evil, but is pervaded by desire, by yearning for the absolutely infinite, again understood as the abundance of infinite kinds.

It is essential to emphasize as forcefully as possible that *natura naturans* and *natura naturata* do not compose a binary, that nothing of nature's productivity and of what is produced can be in opposition. Similarly, *potentia* and *potestas* compose no powers in opposition, as if power to seek advantage might be chosen over emergent productivity, or the reverse. To the contrary, power always occupies both sites together; *potestas* requires *potentia*; *potentia* takes form as *potestas*. When Spinoza speaks of emotion and *conatus*, it is in terms of the *potentia* of the body, not *potestas*, though finite bodies inevitably desire their own advantage. In advantage, in *potestas*, in the rankings and hierarchies of kinds of the world in which we hope to foster some at the expense of others, something infinite is always present, beyond ranking and hierarchy, beyond binarity,[6] still related to kinds. Conversely, something is present in the infinite, beyond binarity, that insists on exclusion, hierarchy, and rank, given in kinds.

This, perhaps, is the thought at the heart of my project related to the good, gathered from Spinoza. The thought is of the infinity of kinds—the infinite infinity of kinds—more vividly present in Spinoza than perhaps anywhere else in the Western tradition until recently, where identities—of women, African Americans, Asians, animals, forests, landscapes—are expressed in kinds, kinds in relation to other kinds, human and natural kinds in the earth. This thought of abundance in kinds is an ethical thought, the unbounded thought that ethics occupies an immensely difficult and contested space between finite, binary relations and something nonbinary, beyond measure, beyond neutrality. The debt, Levinas says, is beyond limit and identity. The responsibility increases to infinity.

> The infinity of the infinite lives in going backwards. The debt increases in the measures that it is paid. (Levinas, *OB*, 12)

> The more I answer the more I am responsible; the more I approach the neighbor with which I am encharged the further away I am. This debit which increases is infinity as an infinition of the infinite, as glory. (p. 93)[7]

Exalting singularity.[8] To which I respond in kind, remembering the abundance of kinds, evoking the possibility that endless, growing, inescapable responsibility is toward both individuals and kinds, toward individuals who participate in multiple kinds, where kinds know nothing of neutrality. Singularity can become empty abstraction. As can a kind without members, the universal alone. Kinds are not universals; the infinity of kinds is not their totality or immensity, but the unlimited responsivity that comes with kinds. The debt I owe to individuals who are members of kinds is to know the inescapability of domination and betrayal, all in the name of kinds. And to resist.

I imagine that to understand this rejection or transformation of singularity is to know it as the death of God in whom is present all infinity. God preserves infinity in each finite thing in God's own infinity. Which comes too close to totality for me, lacking every trace of heterogeneity. Yet the universality of kinds, the most famous way in which they have been gathered into the *logos*, is another totality, another neutrality. Which is to hope to understand and to live in the heterogeneous infinity of kinds, not totality, not universality, but something otherwise. Which is not to deny, but to admire, something of this thought elsewhere in the name of universality, something I understand in the name of the good. In interruption. Echoing essentialism and identity politics.

Wittig insists that writing (especially as a lesbian) is to reach toward universality, however strange that universality may be, related to subjectivity.

> When *elles* is turned into *the women* the process of universalization is destroyed. All of a sudden, *elles* stopped being *mankind*. (Wittig, *MG*, 86)

> [N]o woman can say "I" without being for herself a total subject—that is, ungendered, universal, whole. Or, failing this, she is condemned to what I call parrot speech (slaves echoing their masters' talk). (p. 80)

Whatever one's place, women or lesbians or others, to fix that place, one's essence or kind, is to subject oneself or others to domination, akin to slavery. Even under totality. Wittig's writing, in *le corps lesbien*, untranslated in *The Lesbian Body*, undertakes this task of universalization, freeing women from grammatical subjection to men as if incapable of universality.

> "I" *[Je]* conceals the fact that *elle* or *elles* are submerged in *il* or *ils*, i.e., that all the feminine persons are complementary to the masculine persons. The feminine "I" *[Je]* who writes is alien to her own writing at every word because this "I" *[Je]* uses a language alien to her; this "I" *[Je]* experiences what is alien to her since this "I" *[Je]* cannot be *"un ecrivain."* . . . If *I [J/e]* examine m/y specific situation as subject in the language, *I [J/e]* am physically incapable of writing "I" *[Je]*, I *[J/e]* have no desire to do so. (Wittig, *LB*, 10–11)

As I might put it, writing reaches toward infinity. As does being, in memory of the good. As expression, *mimēsis*, representation, responsivity. The memory of infinity is essential to writing, Wittig says. I insist it is given from the good, as responsibility. She also speaks of *exaltation*, still infinity.

> The bar in the *j/e* of *The Lesbian Body* [actually, *Le corps lesbien*] is a sign of excess. A sign that helps to imagine an excess of "I," an "I" exalted. "I" has become so powerful in *The Lesbian Body* that it can attack the order of heterosexuality in texts and assault the so-called love, the heroes of love, and lesbianize them, lesbianize the symbols, lesbianize the gods and the goddesses, lesbianize the men and the women. (Wittig, *MG*, 87)

Lesbianization is ethical|political, striving in the name of infinity—universality and exaltation—for a world in which lesbians and other people can assault, transform, a world hostile to them, resistant to neutrality. And Jews, reminding us of Spinoza. The ethical|political task is unbounded, in debt beyond any possibility of institution. Even so, we strive to institute, thereby to contain, regulate, and exclude. Our power to institute contains an infinite power within itself, not an unbounded power to institute, as if we were omnipotent, but an infinite power in every finite institution, under whose authority we are dominated.

I understand authority to bear this play of institution and excess within itself, with the terrible danger that institutions will always exceed their authority, trampling on some in the name of kinds. I understand ethics—always ethics|politics—to bear immeasurable responsibility toward authority and its excesses, always multiple: the excess authority bears within itself to become dominating, excluding, bearing down on its subjects, trampling them into abjection; the excesses authority bears within itself as authority, answering to something beyond measure. I understand this second excess of authority to recall the abundant generosity of the good, where the first authority may be understood as what is given, gifts. Authority answers to something beyond measure, is itself something beyond measure, always betraying it in its institutions. Authority repudiates neutrality yet works by claiming to institute it.

The task of the overarching project to which this volume is a contribution is to understand all human works and natural things as given from the good, without neutrality, occupying two economies: one a general economy beyond measure of generosity and excess, permeated by unlimited desire, infinitely resistant to neutrality; the other restricted economies of measure, institutions of control, regulating excess and desire, creating hierarchies of rank, domination, and exclusion, typically claiming neutrality. These economies are inseparable, are not two, compose no binary relation, can never be in conflict. Restricted economy presupposes general economy; every authority and measure exceeds itself; every authority and measure overwhelms neutrality. General economy circulates endlessly in restricted economies, institutions of authority and regulation. General economy interrupts the hold of every institution of authority with excessive desire; restricted economy interrupts the anarchic circulation of general economy with work, unable to escape the betrayals of hierarchy and exclusion. Neither of these can be avoided; nor can they be separated. Betrayal is unavoidable. So is excess, unlimit in every limit.

This story or picture is given in kinds. Always *mimēsis*. General and restricted economy are economies of kinds—as are all economies, and as is the struggle to institute or resist neutrality. Singularities participate in no economies, general or restricted, are nowhere we might say, vanish into neutrality. And perhaps we may think that that is what makes singulars the heart of ethics. I reply that it removes the most difficult aspect of heterogeneity from ethics, given from the good, the impossibility (and undesirability) of avoiding betrayal, always instituted in kinds and their domination, the authority of kinds. I reply that singulars participate in kinds, that singular essences are always kinds, even essences of individuals. This thought is difficult not in terms of being—the being of essences—but in terms of the good, essences yearning for the good without betrayal. Resistance to neutrality betrays betrayal everywhere in the kinds instituted in resistance.

The ethics of kindlredlness of which I speak here emerges from the links of domination and mastery among human and other kinds—genders, races, animals, plants, machines, and inorganic things; together with nationality, ethnicity, class, and more; repetitions of mastery and domination among different kinds, human and otherwise. Ethical responsibility demands that we resist such domination in memory of something beyond ranking, something infinite, perhaps neutral. Shall we imagine that kinds might be redeemed from domination into a neutral neutrality that does not write its laws in blood, does not hold other kinds for the use of some human kinds? My entire project is directed against this possibility, in resistance to neutrality. This resistance, however, does not speak against another possibility, also resistant to neutrality, that kinds might be celebrated in their heterogeneous identities and natures, in their multiplicity and profusion, welcoming the abundance of the earth, without neutrality and without ranking, for the ownership and use of none, not even the celebrative kind. Abundance beyond ranking and neutrality, in memory of kinds. Kindlness as ethics, the cherishment of kinds in the earth given from the good in immeasurable abundance. Exposure in kindness.

The reexamination of essences here begins with the ethical task of responsibility toward natural and human things, to act toward them for the sake of the good, where the good calls for infinite responsiveness toward things in heterogeneous abundance, in the endless variety of their kinds. Abundance in the earth gives itself in infinite species and kinds. Toward which human beings may respond, I believe, with *cherishment*, perhaps with love, the first condition of responsibility, exposed to things as individuals and kinds, responsive to them beyond measure. The second condition of ethicallpolitical responsibility is that individuals and kinds conflict, that not all can flourish without harm, that cherishment evokes *sacrifice*, inescapable loss, under the curse. Sacrifice without cherishment is ranking, exclusion, domination. Sacrifice joined with cherishment is endless mourning, memory of loss. And joy. In the conjunction is endless responsiveness through cherishment and sacrifice known as *plenishment*, the endless sacrifice of sacrifice in love and care. I believe that Spinoza's ethics is plenishment, infinite joy and infinite sorrow, infinite hatred and infinite love, all joined impossibly in the blessedness of a love beyond measure known to finite creatures who remain to betray, still to respond for the sake of the good. Always given in essences and kinds, beings and something otherwise. Expressive everywhere; nature's *mimēsis*; as the abundance and propinquity of kinds.

CHAPTER 1

Woman's Kinds

He says that woman speaks with nature. That she hears voices from under the earth. That wind blows in her ears and trees whisper to her. That the dead sing through her mouth and the cries of infants are clear to her. But for him this dialogue is over. He says he is not part of this world, that he was set on this world as a stranger. He sets himself apart from woman and nature. (Griffin, *WN*, 1)

Her body is a vessel of death. Her beauty is a lure. Her charm a trap. She is irresistible. Her voice is deceit. Her word a plot. Her gesture a snare. . . . She will eat the flesh she appears to love. Her hunger is never satisfied. . . . She is a plague. A disease. . . . The color of her blood is the color of calamity, of fire, of evil. The smell is offensive, the smell is a warning. She loves blood. . . . She devours even herself. Her passion is endless, without reason, without boundary, existing only for itself. . . . [S]he would consume herself; in her body is the seed of nothingness. (p. 83)

We know ourselves to be made from this earth. We know this earth is made from our bodies. For we see ourselves. And we are nature. We are nature seeing nature. We are nature with a concept of nature. Nature weeping. Nature speaking of nature to nature. . . . [A]s we speak to each other of what we know: the light is in us. (pp. 223–27)

If the rethinking of essences and kinds is demanded of us by a history that has instituted and justified the domination of kinds in the name of neutrality; if the task before us remains the debt ethical creatures face of undertaking endless responsibilities toward others in their kinds: then we may imagine that the thoughts and practices required of us—resistance to neutrality among heterogeneous kinds—may present incredible challenges and dangers. Not least, I might say again, what cannot be said too frequently,

13

the threats of every instituted *We*, instituted in law and rule, in every thought and practice. I speak to and with some *we* of ethics|politics, always hoping to interrupt the institution of a rule of domination, always risking institution in addressing any collectivity.

I add in challenge rather than threat that this responsiveness toward essences and kinds calls for something expressive in the possibility of writing, thinking, saying, acting, and perceiving: abundance in the earth as expression in kinds. Expression and interruption in natural kinds as resistance to neutrality.[1]

I begin this resistance with two works whose excessiveness is marked repeatedly despite every effort to tame them, extreme resistance to neutrality. Where the strangeness of their voices, the inexplicability of their ideas, reaches toward the expression of the abundance of kinds I understand as the impossible giving in which ethics is possible and exigent: between abundance beyond measure, beyond every opposition, and the divisions that delimit life and practice: general and restricted economy. I understand general economy to be no economy, interrupting the institution and authority of every restricted economy. I understand giving in abundance to interrupt the authority of every gift.

I have suggested that Spinoza understands the succession of *natura naturata* to be everywhere constituted and interrupted by *natura naturans*. Here I wish to explore a different kind of interruption of the rule of nature, another resistance to the authority of *natura naturata*. *Woman* constitutes and interrupts the rule and domination of nature, as Griffin understands them, expressed in an abundance of pronouns. The expression of abundance in kinds in pronouns.

He says. *She* hears. *We* know. Do *we*, whoever *we* are—readers, philosophers, people in the street, indigenous people, perhaps Griffin *herself*—know who *she* and *he* and *we* are, in *their* essences and kinds, in the pronouns that demarcate *them*? Unmistakably *they* are kinds. And unmistakably *they* mark essences—though perhaps not identifiable, stable essences, identities, and kinds. Perhaps not always essences and kinds instead of, distinguishable from, individual men, women, human beings, and other creatures, other *hes*, *shes*, *wes*, and *theys*. Women, nature, other kinds. Mixed, impure, ambiguous kinds.

I interrupt to think of pronouns in other places, recalling Wittig's claim concerning the vanishing of women as *elles* into *ils*, present in every *Je*, marked in *Le corps lesbien* as *J/e*. The plural pronouns *I*, *we*, and *they* refuse infinity to women, which perhaps they lack in a heterosexual economy, but also to lesbian women who, Wittig says, are the only women who can be *elles* together, fully themselves without men. In love. Wittig calls it *lesbianization*.[2]

It may seem strange that resistance to oppression could take place in pronouns, understanding oppression to include language, perhaps the structure of thought itself. In a gendered language:

> Sex, under the name of gender, permeates the whole body of language and forces every locutor, if she belongs to the oppressed sex, to proclaim it in her speech, that is, to appear in language under her proper physical form and not under the abstract form, which every male locutor has the unquestioned right to use. The abstract form, the general, the universal, this is what the so-called masculine gender means. . . . The universal has been, and is continually, at every moment, appropriated by men. (Wittig, *MG*, 79–80)

Wittig suggests reappropriating the pronoun *they* from men, who would thereby be denied appearance as *they*—as women have throughout history been so denied. I fear the possibility of neutralizing gender, sex, or kinds in memory of the oppressions carried out in their name. I lean toward exaltation rather than neutrality, toward infinity in kinds. I understand Wittig's insistence on *elles*, on a feminine *they*, to insist on infinity for women, impossible in a society dominated by men, where infinity is appropriated for a single kind. In the name of neutrality.

The pronouns express the rules of grammar Nietzsche associates with reason and God[3] and the systems of social hierarchy that institute domination. The rules of grammar, the institution of reason, are not neutral; nor is God. All define some kinds as having the right as kinds to dominate and rule over others, obscurely or covertly. Leading Irigaray to urge resistance as *mimēsis*:

> Turn everything upside down, inside out, back to front. *Rack it with radical convulsions.* . . . Reinscribe them hither and thither *as divergencies*, otherwise and elsewhere than they are expected, in *ellipses* and *eclipses* that deconstruct the logical grid of the reader-writer, drive him out of his mind, trouble his vision to the point of incurable diplopia at least. *Overthrow syntax* by suspending its eternally teleological order, by snipping the wires, cutting the current, breaking the circuits, switching the connections, by modifying continuity, alternation, frequency, intensity. (Irigaray, *ATS*, 142)

Perhaps we may, through pronouns, overthrow syntax, dislodge the rule of reason, God, and language without giving up meaning, truth, or sacred places, understanding pronouns to institute and mark oppression, but also to interrupt that institution. Pronouns mark individuals and kinds under a rule of grammar that opens onto interruption. They express the expressiveness of natural things and kinds, resist neutrality. *Mimēsis* as resistance, expressing abundance in kinds as nature's expression.

I return with this thought to Griffin's pronominal transformations. *He* says. *She* hears. *We* know. *Her* body. *Her* beauty. *She* is irresistible. *We* are nature. *We* are nature seeing nature. *We* are nature with a concept of nature. Nature weeping. Nature speaking of nature to nature. All that *I* know, *I* know in this earth. *She* and *I* and *we* are nature speaking in nature to nature. I hope to find something here in Griffin beyond a certain reading of Nietzsche and Irigaray, though both may be read beyond it. I am interested in the possibility that the rule of God, as Nietzsche describes it, the institution of the good into law, issues into reason and language, so that to seek to overthrow the tyranny of kinds is to strive to overthrow the rules and methods of language and reason that have historically defined the truth of kinds. On this understanding, Nietzsche and Irigaray hope to resist the tyranny of language—which, I would argue, repeats something of tyranny in resistance. Overthrow syntax but not, perhaps, think of replacing language with music—something Nietzsche strongly proposes.

In the context of these striking pronouns—how could they be anything but language?—I wonder if Griffin achieves something—in writing, in language—beyond or interrupting grammar, evoking the possibility that natural kinds neither belong to language nor fix identities in place in the order of nature. Especially the feminine pronouns *she* and *her*, and where feminine, *we* and *they*, interrupt the linking of woman and nature as an act of domination with another linking, resisting domination. This other liaison remains with kinds—women and nature, nature's kinds—against hierarchy and domination, against the classifications of neutrality. Griffin's pronouns resist neutrality in the feminine, in nature and natural kinds.

Ecological feminism emerges from the premise that the dominations of nature and of women are linked.[4] As kinds. Resisting neutrality. Griffin is an ecological feminist according to this definition, exposing and resisting these dominations as linked together. In the pronouns of her writing, these links are interrupted and transformed, but not dissolved. The pronouns mark links in kinds between women and natural kinds where it would be impossible to replace kinds by singulars and individuals: this woman, this animal, this natural creature—always kinds. Even in so ungendered a language as English, Griffin insists that we come face to face with gender everywhere, in human history and in nature, where these are inseparably conjoined, and where the pronouns mark that conjunction in a gendered voice, resistant to neutrality. The feminine pronouns link with nature in the feminine, multiply transforming that bond, inverting and diverting a relation that insists on nature's neutrality, insists on objectivity, so that nature's femininity is available to be mastered, like a woman, a cow, or horse.

As *he* insists, whoever *he* may be. The masculine pronoun appears in Griffin in its multiple ambiguities. *He* who sets himself apart from woman and nature, *her* and *elles*, is both *Man—mankind* and *men*—and some— but not all—individual men, together with the institutions, practices, and rules governed by the point of view gathered neutrally under these masculine pronouns. Some women speak of *patriarchy*, marking a kind that might better remain unnamed if it suggests that it might be abolished. The end of the kind of patriarchy. But perhaps not so plainly the end of men or of the institutions, language, and pronouns that have been put in play in the name of reason's objectivity. The masculine and feminine pronouns mark resistance to a neutrality that has been instituted in the name of one kind rather than another—the kinds that set themselves apart from woman and nature. If such kinds can be identified and named. Even so, what Griffin describes as falling under the masculine pronouns is easily recognizable as what (mostly) men have said historically about women and nature. She gives the history with dates. Two extended examples, first women as witches:

1468	The Pope defines witchcraft as *crimen exceptum*, removing all legal limit to torture....
1523	One thousand witches burn in a single year in the diocese of Como....
1583	Witch Burnings in two villages leave one female inhabitant each....
1581–91	Nine hundred burned in Lorraine. (That nature must be bound into service, he persuades.)...
1609	Galileo ... constructs a telescope (It is urged that nature must be hounded in her wanderings before one can lead her and drive her.)
1609	The whole population of Navarre is declared witches. (He says that the earth should be put on the rack and tortured for her secrets.)...
1619	The first black slaves are introduced in America.... (She is asked if she signed the devil's book. She is asked if the devil had a body. She is asked whom she chose to be an incubus.)...
1628	One hundred fifty-eight burned at Würzburg....
1738	Dean of Faculty of Law at Rostock demands that witches be extirpated by fire and sword.
1745	Witch trial at Lyons, five sentenced to death....
1778	Anna Maria Schnagel executed for witchcraft.... (Griffin, *WN*, 14–17)

And another, women and animals, not neglecting Spinoza:

> It is argued now that animals do not think. That animals move automatically like machines. That passion in animals is more violent because it is not accompanied by thought. That our own bodies are distinguished from machines only by "a mind which thinks without reference to any passion."
>
> And it is further argued that if animals could think, they might have immortal souls.
>
> But it becomes obvious that animals do not have immortal souls (and cannot think), since if one animal had an immortal soul, all might, and that "there are many of them too imperfect to make it possible to believe it of them, such as oysters, sponges, etc."
>
> And it is said the souls of women are small.
>
> It is decided that matter is dead. . . .
>
> Everything in the universe, it is perceived, moves according to the same laws: the earth, the moon, the wind, the rain, blood, atoms. . . .
>
> And it is decided that what makes God divine is his power. . . .
>
> And it is written in the law that "Women should be subject to their men." (Griffin, *WN*, 17–19)

Still with regard to the masculine pronouns, we may read Griffin to mark engagement, commitment, passion—resistance to neutrality—in the context of a historical insistence upon the neutrality of being and the dispassionateness of truth. In a world in which women are denied standing in virtue of their gender, a genderless, neutral world may offer a promise of something better. In a world in which God is taken as male, a neutral God may offer a promise of something better, something otherwise. Griffin's masculine pronouns are passionate, committed, masterful. *He* says *he* is not part of this world, that *he* was set on this world as a stranger. Her feminine pronouns are enraptured, ecstatic, enchanted: woman or nature, *roaring. "We are women. We rise from the wave. We are gazelle and doe, elephant and whale . . . we are girls. We are woman and nature. And he says he cannot hear us speak"* (p. 1). Griffin is not the first or last to speak of nature filled with ecstasy and enchantment.[5] Which is by no means to speak of joy. Woman and nature. Woman or nature. We do not know who *she, he, we* are speaking of.

Her body is a vessel of death. *Her* beauty is a lure. *Her* charm a trap. *She* is irresistible. *Her* voice is deceit. *Her* word a plot. *Her* gesture a snare. *She* will eat the flesh *she* appears to love. *Her* hunger is never satisfied. *She* is a plague. A disease.

She devours even *herself*. *Her* passion is endless, without reason, without boundary, existing only for itself.

Or who is speaking.

We know ourselves to be made from this earth. And *she* wrote, . . . all that I know, I know in this earth . . . *the light is in us.* In *us*, whoever *we* may be, whatever kind.

Gazelles and does, elephants and whales. Wild animals. Cows and horses. Domesticated animals. I add tigers, wolves, preying mantises, and wasps, where females know themselves to be made of this earth. And kill.

And we are reminded that we have brought death into the world (Griffin, *WN*, 7). As sin, the curse, which these other females do not know. Where males fight the battles, aim to conquer.

I would hope to think of the earth without recoiling from brutality, include pain and death in nature, even as I would respond to the debt, the call, the responsibility I take to be given to all human beings, perhaps to all things in the earth, to respond and cherish everywhere. It is worth pondering that Griffin does not allow *us in the earth* to harm. In contrast, Wittig does not recoil from violence in *The Lesbian Body.* I interrupt with a single example with archaic antecedents. I have considered more extreme examples elsewhere.[6]

> At m/y order the women prepare m/y severed limbs m/y arms m/y thighs m/y legs whose flesh is meticulously removed and boiled for a long time, they offer it to you surrounded by different sauces on glittering plates each plate bearing a different name to please you. You consume them readily their appellations do not strike you with astonishment. Bringing you a finger-bowl and crystallized fruits the women inform you of what and of whom you have eaten. Immediately you begin to vomit, a profuse perspiration appears on your cheeks on your temples without your shedding a tear, you fall flat on your face your stomach utterly revolted hiccups preventing you from resuming breathing. (Wittig, *LB*, 105)

This violence is human, social. Yet it speaks of love and the earth. Without death and violence, could there be love, could we live together in the earth? What of the violences we must violently resist?

I have interrupted Griffin twice to recall Wittig and *The Lesbian Body;* perhaps a third time would not be amiss. Interruption is the advent of the good, which has nothing better to offer, but disturbs every best; which reminds us of the good, which gives all kinds to the world in profusion, touches all creatures and things with generosity, giving a debt that cannot be paid, that has no name, but echoes endless demands before the heterogeneity of the other, given in kinds. Griffin reminds us of women, interrupting the voice in which we speak of human beings indifferently as if all were men; reminds us of nature and natural things, gendered in language, possibly gendered beyond language, nature and natural kinds. I interrupt to think of Wittig once more, who like Griffin expresses the profusion of kinds in the confusion of pronouns, who unlike Griffin, still pronominally, reminds us of women who offer lesbianization to a world in which women are expected to give their bodies up to reproduction; who unlike Griffin speaks pronominally of violence beyond the violence done to women by men, speaks of violence in the earth without which we could not be, without which violence toward women would be impossible. And love.

Her body is a vessel of death. *She* is a plague. A disease.

Nature. The Earth. The lesbian lover. The woman.

And man. And men. Who also harbor death, whose honor is a snare, who lie, and kill, and devour; who kill the women they love.

A statistic not mentioned by Griffin: the leading cause of death of women at work in the United States is homicide, by men. Men kill women. Another statistic. Abusive men kill women who are about to leave or have just left the abusive relationship. Men kill women who resist domination.

If Griffin retrieves something miraculous in nature, something of the wonder of being, of the earth, through the confusion, the wild circulation of pronouns that do not stabilize into identities, then perhaps we can retrieve something miraculous and wonderful beyond that circulation by multiplying it into more confusing pronouns. Still in mind of love. Lesbianization, understood in Wittig's terms as a marginalized and dominated kind striving toward exaltation, universalization, infinity, unbounding the bonds of kinds but not their kindliness, not kindness, still kinds. Lesbianization as the abundance of women released from their role as the subordinate kind so that they may be *elles*, may be *they*, in a world without men, in a world containing men. Seeking kindlness.

Woman, nature, the earth as the abundance of women and nature under the subordination of kinds—to mastery, neutrality, perhaps to men, perhaps in the very possibility of limit. Woman, nature, the earth as general economy, beyond measure, nature's abundance interrupting every restricted economy, resisting every limit, sometimes by violence, sometimes in love, interrupting every interruption. Always, in Griffin and Wittig, circulating as kinds. Every individual, every singularity in general economy circulates in the abundance of kinds.

I return to where we paused before the body—women's, nature's, men's, and animals' bodies—filled with violence, disease, death, deceit, blood, and plague. All perhaps pervasive qualities of nature, dangerous and evil everywhere. All perhaps pervasive qualities of women, dangerous and deceitful everywhere. So Nietzsche says, in a difficult voice. So Griffin says as well, in a resistant voice. Women and nature are the plagues of humanity, without which humanity—possibly men, possibly all humans under the social contract—could not be humanity. Bataille calls it the *curse*. In a difficult, contaminated voice. Humanity defines itself as "nature transfigured by the *curse*" (Bataille, *AS*, I, 78). Humanity is *the accursed share* at the same time that some—the victims—are chosen to be destroyed. Humanity separates itself from things by singling out some as victims. Another interruption.

> The victim is a surplus taken from the mass of *useful* wealth. And he can only be withdrawn from it in order to be consumed profitlessly, and therefore utterly destroyed. Once chosen, he is the *accursed share [part maudite]*, destined for violent consumption. But the curse tears him away from the *order of things*; it gives him a recognizable figure, which now radiates intimacy, anguish, the profundity of living beings. (p. 59)

This curse, in Griffin's voice, singles women out. Men can be men, can be human, only under a curse that curses them by victimizing others, destroying women and others. I know this curse as abjection, the double movement at the heart of the subject, who throws *himself* down into subjection in the act of expulsion that constitutes *his* subjectivity.[7] It is a curse that curses humanity's victims—women, animals, children, everything whose domination and destruction institutes the figure of the human subject; curses man; and curses nature. "[M]an sets himself essentially apart from nature; he is even vehemently opposed to it, and the absence of prohibition would have only one meaning: that *animality* which men are conscious of having left behind, and to which we cannot aspire to return" (Bataille, *AS*, II, 23).

Women, nature, animals are cursed, excluded and destroyed, along with countless other victims, in the institution of the subject who reigns over nature, who is himself accursed, abject, before the law. I understand this transmigration as an extreme example, a generalization, of Foucault's principle of lateral effects, where "the penalty must have its most intense effects on those who have not committed the crime" (Foucault, *DP*, 95). All the effects of the institution of the curse have their most intense effects on those who implement them, who are themselves accursed. This does not make them victims. The agonizing truth of the curse is that those who are most influenced by the curse, who are most abject, impose the curse on others as destruction. Women and natural creatures are cursed with destruction. Men are cursed as the destroyers. Both curses diminish, reduce abundance, curse nature's abundance with restriction, with destruction, domination, and exclusion.

I deny that women, or animals, or people of other nations, races, and classes bear responsibility as victims for the curse. I pursue Bataille's thought that humanity as a kind defines itself as The Human Kind as and through a curse that expresses the demand to own nature, to restrict nature's abundance in the production of restricted economies. I think of nature as abundant, as general economy, always circulating in restricted economies, circulating as accursed. The curse is human, The Human Kind, that reigns as master or owner in its own abjection. In the destruction of others.

This is a strange and difficult thought, inseparable from violence. I began this interruption wondering at the neglect of violence in Griffin's portrayal of women and nature. *We who are of the earth* seems to deny or minimize nature's violence, to deny nature's curse for women. Wittig denies neither violence nor the curse. The beloved is accursed. Not just accursed, not made hateful by the curse, but loving|beloved in the curse, in erotic violence, which can perhaps be resisted but cannot be avoided.

I am exploring the curse of kinds, kinds as accursed: above all, the curse that some kinds dominate, rule, destroy other kinds, in the name of their kind: human, men, European, African. One family, one kin, strives to enslave, destroy, other families, other kin and kinds. Lovers strive in the midst of their love, their passion, to conquer their beloved. *Erōs* is dangerous. None of which is to diminish the passion, the glory, the joy and goodness of love. Or the goodness of participating in a tribe, a community, a human kind.

For it is a double curse. And perhaps I mean to suggest that Griffin, in her wonderful multiplication of the multiplicities of natural kinds may not multiply violences to abundance, may refrain from insisting on the abundance of the curse, the curse of the curse, the violence of violence, of which Foucault speaks so powerfully in memory of Nietzsche:

> Humanity does not progress from combat to combat until it arrives at universal reciprocity, where the rule of law finally replaces warfare; humanity installs each of its violences in a system of rules and thus proceeds from domination to domination.
> The nature of these rules allows violence to be inflicted on violence and the resurgence of new forces that are sufficiently strong to dominate those in power. (Foucault, *NGH*, 150–51)

I do not imagine that the violence against violence of which Foucault and Nietzsche speak can be mobilized as a concept or a ground of practice. I hope instead to think of this violence as the inescapable curse toward which we may hope to respond with love, responsibility, resistance, and care, still accursed. The remedy for the curse of restricted economy is another curse, another restricted economy. As kindness, love. Responsibility for sacrifice demands its sacrifice. The possibility, the movement, the endlessness of circulation, comes from the good as gifts, always under the curse.

I return from this interruption to Griffin, who perhaps recoils from the curse but presents the strangeness of the curse, nature under the curse, in a strikingly pronominal voice, somewhere between women and nature, woman and animal, women and natural things. Every *and* here gestures to the curse of kinds. And to the remedy, the restitution, still accursed.

We know ourselves to be made from this earth. Whoever *we* are. Griffin's names:

Horses. Cows. Mules.
His animals.
Land. Timber.
His possessions.
Matter. Wind.
What *he* masters.
Her body.
His Power. Vigilance. Knowledge. Control. Certainty. Cataclysm, Secrets.

We are nature seeing nature. We are nature with a concept of nature. Nature weeping. Nature speaking of nature to nature.

In kinds. In the kinds of the earth. Kindredness and kindness in the earth.

We see. *We* know. *We* speak, express, come together and apart.

Nature comes together and apart. In *us*.

Whoever *we* may be. Women. Animals. Forests. Stones. Even, perhaps, men. *Him. Her. Us. Them.*

We are nature. All of *us*, whoever *we* may be, individuals, kinds, collectives, composites. All of *us* and all of *them*. Each and all, separate or together, singular or composite. Beyond gathering.

Nature speaking of nature to nature. Everywhere expressive.

Nature speaking; nature seeing; nature touching. All of *us* and each of *us*, everything expressing, touching, responding, delicately, powerfully.

We are nature with a concept of nature. Perhaps only We, We Humans, desire to know, to possess, a concept of nature, as if nature gathered under a concept instead of flowing, circulating, in *its* or *her* or *their* or *our* abundance. The pronouns insist on gathering nature into *their* identity, as if under a concept. The pronouns resist gathering nature in the abundance of *their* identity, beyond any concept.

Nature weeping; nature desiring. Nature desiring in abundance, from and toward abundance, uncontainable in the abundance of desire, circulating everywhere, each thing, each *we* and *I* striving in its abundance toward *itself* and others among whom *we* are *we*, kin and kind, other *I*s and *they*s, striving toward *them* in the infinite debt that is *our* participation in nature,

nature in nature, filled with endless desire, to touch, inspired in touch, fulfilled in touch in endless debt, yearning, striving, moving. In kind.

We who are nature are always *we*, in debt, called toward some others from *ourselves* toward *them*, toward the others, striving to respond, called to respond, in the responsiveness and debt known to *us* as responsibility. All. Of *us*. And *them*. In nature. As nature. Nature striving, moving, yearning, filled with demands, responsibilities. To be against neutrality. Against the neuter. In the pronouns of nature's desires. In the heterogeneities of kinds. In kindredness and kindness.

Nature weeping. At the violence in nature in infinite desire and responsibility. At evil and the curse.[8] *We* weep at *our* violent and destructive thoughts and deeds, *we men, We Humans*, and others.

> Yes, nature is merciless and insatiable, it is said, red in tooth and claw, it is written.
>
> (That woman is as far from man as man is from the forest monkeys, it is reflected.)
>
> And woman, it is observed, like the Negro, is flat-footed, with a prominent inclination of the pelvis making her appear less erect, and her gait less steady.
>
> That as regards his intellectual faculties, the Negro partakes of the nature of the child or the female or the senile white.
>
> Slavery is said to be a condition of every higher civilization.
>
> A woman should be an enthusiastic slave to the man to whom she has given her heart, it is declared. (Griffin, *WN*, 19–32)

We weep. Nature weeps. At the evil kinds do to each other.

If there is a fanatical love of family and kin that would promote the destruction of other kinds, could we mobilize a fanatical love of kinds that would wreak violence against the violence of kin?[9]

I would speak of kindlness as violence against violence in memory of the abundance of kinds. I would speak of this double violence and the infinite memory as *natura naturans*. After Spinoza. Whose ethics, as I understand it, is given in the question, What is it to participate in a kind among other kinds? Answering in abundance, in the abundance of one's self and kind in the abundance of other kinds. Celebrating kindlness.

After Griffin. Whose ethics, as I understand it, is given in the pronouns composing *us* and *we*, especially *she* and *her*, not forgetting *he* and *his*, resistant to neutrality. Being in the neuter is resisted in the gender of pronouns. Which is not to deny the violence of a gendered language, but to reengender every *we* against a neutral gathering.[10]

Abundance, in kinds, given from the good, interrupts this gathering, the hold of the curse and the inescapability of betrayal, interrupts neutrality in the name of kinds.

Nature natures in the abundance of kinds. In the violence of pronouns, resisting neutrality. Kindlness in the earth.

CHAPTER 2

Ranking Kinds

The art of contradiction making, descended from an insincere kind of conceited mimicry, of the semblance-making breed, derived from image making, distinguished as a portion, not divine but human, of production, that presents a shadow play of words—such are the blood and lineage which can, with perfect truth, be assigned to the authentic Sophist. (Plato, *Sophist*, 268cd)

So Plato's *Sophist* ends, with perfect truth, having seized the essence—the form, idea, or kind, the *eidos*—of the authentic Sophist, who is anything, indeed everything, but authentic and perfect: contradictory, insincere, deceptive, imagistic, a thoroughly shadowy and shifty character, bound to human production rather than divine, all by lineage and blood. This is not the first time in the dialogue that the essence of the sophist-kind has been grasped, brought to hand, if it is the last, or best, or whatever. If it is the last—closing the dialogue—it arrives after several others: the sophist's art is "a great and many-sided art *(technē)*" (223c); the sophist a "many-sided *(poikilos*: many-colored, manifold, diverse, changeable) animal *(thērion)*, and not to be caught with one hand, as they say" (226a), appears in many guises (231c), gathered under a single name (232). The question, perhaps, is "how it is that we call the same thing . . . by several names" (251a); how many different kinds can be one kind: a question of knowing, saying, and naming, of the one and many, and being, for us here the being of kinds: of kin and family, genealogy and propinquity, gender, lineage, and blood. So the stranger—*xenos*: another allusion to kin and kind, lineage and blood—says at the end of the dialogue, and throughout. We might recall that Socrates describes himself at the beginning of the Platonic writings as a stranger to Athens (Plato, *Apology*, 17cd).[1]

The project of the dialogue is to trace the genealogy—the family and kind *(genos, gignomenē)*—to which the sophist belongs, knowing that it is multifarious; hoping to gather under a single name, to take in hand, what

cannot be caught with one hand. I retrace this project keeping in play the
multiple meanings of genealogy, lineage, strangers, and blood drawn from
Nietzsche and Foucault, here from Plato in the name of one who was
condemned for his strangeness to Athenian ways. Keeping descent in play
for a while, we may take this project to be one of kin and kind—of *genos*
and *eidos*, the words that, throughout the dialogue, speak of kin and kinds.
The blood and lineage disclosed at the very end of the dialogue are, with
perfect truth, assigned to the *eidos* of the authentic sophist—however strange
it may be to assign to inauthenticity an authentic *eidos*. However strange
it may be to assign to an *eidos* a genealogy.

At the conclusion of the dialogue, the stranger to Athenian blood claims
to have truly captured the family *(genous)* and descent *(geneas)* of the real
and true sophist, the sophist's ownmost *(ousias)* properties. Kin and kind
are linked with being, philosophy, and ideas, with genealogy, family, lineage, descent, and blood, with strangeness and strangers, with humanity
and the divine. All this comes before us in the name of species and kinds.
Propinquity, inseparable from property and propriety.

Beginning at the end seems *wrong*—if any beginning can be *wrong*—
though perhaps every genealogy knows such a beginning, proceeding back-
ward. Perhaps every reading is a genealogy, descending through the
multifarious kinds of the text to reach its one true being, family and kin,
not to mention gender and blood. Perhaps every such reading remains
enmired in the blood of victory and defeat, the descent of those whose lives
and deaths made genealogy possible—every reading an ethical|political
struggle. Suggesting that if beginning at the end is arbitrary, *wrong*, beginning at the beginning, the origin, is arbitrary, *wrong* as well, in similar
ways and respects. Or others. Beginning with the question, what *kind* of
text, what *kind* of reading, what *kind* of questions do we bring to the text,
do we take away—questions of *mimēsis*; and who are *we*, what *kind* of
reader, community, individual, or aggregate—or something else? In what
genealogy? Are we sure, surrounded by these different kinds, that we possess—own and master—a single, authentic essence, that we (or anything)
belong to a single kind? Multiple families and kinds, descents and bloods;
multiple memories of wounds, losses and disasters.

How can we read about the sophist's kind, any kind, without memories
of disaster? Which is to begin again, this time at the beginning. For one
disaster, endlessly repeated, is that the beginning is lost, disappears, dies away
in the movement to the end. Another is that the end is the end, its own
disaster, as the beginning is the beginning, and nothing else—if there is a
beginning and if it is nothing else. Nor, perhaps, is the other kind as much
as we may hope that it be so. As we are not others, whatever our hopes: other
individuals and kinds, other family, kin, and gender. Or if we are.

To begin at the beginning—if we may suppose that there is a beginning, to Plato or his dialogues, to Greek thought or our own—is to begin with a setting, a frame. We begin with the protagonists from *Theaetetus*—Socrates, Theodorus, and Theaetetus—plus a guest from Elea, a foreigner to the Socratic world. I wonder if the provocative link in *Theaetetus* between Socrates' midwife mother, Phainarete, and knowledge, grasping the bird in hand in the frame of birth and generation, might continue in *Sophist* along the lineage of family and kind. Phainarete disrupts the grasp of the hand upon the bird, of the mind upon the truth.[2] Perhaps the Eleatic Stranger disrupts the hold of the mind, even the truth, upon the sophist's kind, or any kind.

The very beginning, the frame, presents the stranger together with the question presented by every stranger, perhaps every encounter or presentation. Of what kind is this stranger? Human or god? A higher power (Plato, *Sophist*, 216ab)? Perhaps a philosopher. Like god and human, philosopher, statesman, and sophist come before us as a multiplicity of kinds *(genē, genos)* (217a). Are they one or many? I pause to wonder, at the beginning, if this question may be understood here differently from one of being: *Are* they one or many, pure or impure? Could it be instead, or also, an ethical question? Not, *are* they good or bad? And which? But are they *good* or *bad* as kinds?—the ranking that goes along with kinds, with purity and impurity. Can we think of, can there be, kinds, one or many, with neutrality, without neutrality? Without dividing the world by rank, into hierarchies of citizens and strangers? Are philosophers, statesmen, and sophists all one family—perhaps ours? Are humans, animals, and gods all one family—again, perhaps ours? Or theirs, the others, strangers? Families or kinds. Are humans strangers to the gods? A different kind? And what of friends? How can we speak of strangers without thinking of friends and kin?[3] The world divided into kinds divides into kin and strangers. If the world is so divided. By rank.

The first words of the dialogue that speak to the end or question for which the discussion is undertaken are *genē* and *genos*: the family, lineage, genealogy, or blood of the philosopher-statesman-sophist. The stranger turns the discussion directly to the sophist, saving the statesman for a subsequent dialogue. The philosopher will appear *en passant*, throughout. The second word to describe the quest is *phulon*, the tribe or sort to which the sophist belongs. Early in the dialogue, the activity undertaken by the protagonists is described as *hunting*, a theme continued throughout the dialogue. They are hunting, not individual sophists but their kind(s), their *genos, phulon*, and *eidē, eidos* (219a, c). I keep recalling what Plato says about *eidē* elsewhere, the divinity and immortality of kinds. I postpone the hunt for a while.

I interrupt to wonder again at the thought that the highest term of approbation Plato is traditionally said to know—*eidos*—pertains to sophists, conceited illusionists and replicators. Can there be an authentic idea of fraudulence and inauthenticity, of indeterminate plurality? This famous question, taken up in different ways in different dialogues, does not receive close attention here. The sophist owns an *eidos* of dishonesty and misdirection.

I mean to raise a somewhat different question here than that posed in *Parmenides*, whether mud and excrement can have an *eidos*, as if kinds might be neutral in being, bearing no relation to the good. I take Plato's claim quite seriously that the good is the cause or origin of knowledge and truth, perhaps of being, though I understand the good as no idea, without an *eidos*, beyond measure. Measure is possible—good and bad, right and wrong, true and false—in virtue of giving for the sake of the good, boundless generosity calling for endless responses. Measure is such a response. Knowledge, truth, and being are such responses, in responsibility and care. And kinds. I have spoken of these as *cherishment, sacrifice,* and *plenishment*. For the moment I postpone their reconsideration. The question here is one of kinds, of the *eidos* as kindlness, for the sake of the good.

The heart of Plato's thought is the idea, *eidos*, understood as given from the good as family, species, kin, and kind. The difficult, perhaps impossible thought that haunts Plato's writing throughout the dialogues is that of differences, plurality, in kinds, and their ranking, the order of caste that haunts the multiplicity of kinds, the neutrality that crushes some kinds, imposes domination. The question of one and many in relation to kinds has passed in Western thought into a question of being and naming. Is it true that where there is one name for many kinds there is one overarching kind? I read Plato as insisting that ethical questions arise before questions of being and naming. How do kinds come from the good? How do they bear weight and authority? What authority over kinds can we give to human worlds that have crushed Socrates in the name of the gods, which impose disaster? These are all questions of ideas, of *eidē*, linked with *genos* and *phulon*, with kin, family, lineage, and blood. Here in Plato, the being of things as kinds descends along lines of blood and kin. I interpose a brief interruption in the name of genealogy.

Foucault speaks of this descent in memory of Nietzsche. "*Herkunft* is the equivalent of stock or *descent*; it is the ancient affiliation to a group, sustained by the bonds of blood, tradition, or social class" (Foucault, *NGH*, 145).[4] Going on to speak of what I understand in Anaximander's name to be given everywhere from the good, memories of violence, exclusion, and domination: "In a sense, only a single drama is ever staged in this 'non-place,' the endlessly repeated play of dominations" (pp. 150–51). *Herkunft*— lineage, descent, family, stock, nation, group, bonded by blood, tradition, and social class—adds to human kinds the violence that kinds bear within themselves. Humanity does not progress to a neutrality free from domina-tion, but in relation to human and natural kinds, perhaps to every kind—*genos, phulon,* and *eidos*—remains in domination. The division of the world into kinds, in memory of the good, institutes injustice. For which the entire ordinance of time pays restitution. The genealogy of kinds—kind|red|ness and kind|ness—traces the destructions imposed in the name of kinds. I close this interruption, returning to the genealogy of the authentic sophist.

For the moment I leave open whether the terrible words that close the dialogue—at whose beginning we now are—impose violence or pay resti-tution, or both: the blood and lineage that can, with perfect truth, be assigned to the authentic Sophist. Perhaps with perfect justice. For the stranger arrives, like a god, who beholds the deeds of humanity, both vio-lent and just (Plato, *Sophist,* 216b). Does he bring justice to the sophist? Or another violence?

Still at the beginning, in memory of this justice or another violence, Socrates speaks of philosophers—he says genuine not sham—who "appear, owing to the world's blindness, to wear all sorts of shapes" (216c). Certainly not a semblance-making breed. Without a doubt. With perfect truth. Even before the stranger—who, like Socrates, may not fit in among the catego-ries already in place in Athens—insists on finding unity in the plurality of guises worn by the sophist, philosophers appear in a plurality of guises, including that of sophist.

All in the name of kinds—*genos, phulon,* and *eidos*—where the good resides. At least, that is how I propose to read the dialogue, not so much to find the elusive sophist but to pursue the good; perhaps not to find it, not to be able to find, or secure, or measure it, but in pursuit, perhaps in vain, with nothing to seize or own. With the possibility that such a pursuit is for the sake of the good, is given from it, without end or culmination. In many guises. In the name of kinds. For the method the Eleatic stranger describes is not a method of apprehending the neutral being of the sophist, but is anything but neutral. A method of seizing kinds that may, in this movement of violence and injustice, be impossible to grasp in the name of the good. Except that the good, given in its name, calls for restitution against injustice, in the name of kinds.

What in kinds—*genos, phulon,* and *eidos*—is given from the good as ethical responsibility? In this dialogue the name and nature of the sophist are given through a certain method of classification and taxonomy. In *Phaedrus* and *Philebus,* Socrates describes a similar method given over to *technē,* dividing on left and right.[5] Concluding:

> Believe me, Phaedrus, I am myself a lover of these divisions and collections, that I may gain the power to speak and to think, and whenever I deem another man able to discern an objective unity and plurality, I

follow "in his footsteps where he leadeth as a god." Furthermore—whether
I am right or wrong in doing so, God alone knows—it is those that have
this ability whom for the present I call dialecticians. (265d–266c)

I have discussed what God alone knows elsewhere,[6] as well as love's madness. I add to this madness here that love is one of the contested terms, like
goodness and justice, and perhaps philosophy, about which "we diverge,
and dispute not only with one another but with our own selves" (263a). And
in *Philebus*, where Socrates pursues a similar taxonomic division given
from old *(palaios)*, it is in the context of unlimit.

> [W]e are not to apply the character of unlimitedness to our plurality until
> we have discerned the total number of forms the thing in question has
> intermediate between its one and its unlimited number. It is only then,
> when we have done that, that we may let each one of all these interme-
> diate forms pass away into the unlimited and cease bothering about them.
> (Plato, *Philebus*, 16de)

We are to let the intermediate forms pass away into the unlimited, into
profusion and chaos,[7] because love, justice, and the good—*erōs, dikē,* and
agathon—are endlessly disputed terms that cannot be settled in their nature by this technical method. Together with beauty and philosophy, even
perhaps with sophistry. All this Plato speaks of in *Philebus* as the indefinite
dyad. More of that in a moment.

Kinds—together with knowledge and justice, in which they participate
profoundly: Plato knows nothing of neutrality—lend themselves to
classification and division, ranking and ordering from high to low, imposing violence and injustice. And some—if not all—kinds remain contested,
stream and gather in profusion, fling open wide the doors of being.

Here in *Sophist* God reappears, dividing on the left and right. Except
that, like Socrates, he who plays God is a stranger to Athens and, perhaps,
to humanity and the gods. And he is allowed to play God only after allusions
to *Parmenides* where old Parmenides shows young Socrates the folly of
attempting to divide being from nonbeing.[8] As if they were divisible kinds
rather than forever disputed.

Could the philosopher *as such* wear many different guises, including
the guise of sophist, concerned with terms that are forever disputed, ap-
pearing in endless guises, resisting the neutrality of being—love, justice,
goodness, truth? Could these endless guises, endless appearances and kinds,
be the challenge to philosophy, given from the good, including the famous
guise of unity in and over plurality? Could the kinds of the earth insist in
their plurality on an ordering, unjust and violent, and at the same time and
in the same ways resist every ordering?

I am speaking again of general and restricted economy, speaking of kinds as always circulating in both economies. I understand this conjunction as what Plato means by the indefinite dyad, passing from the definite number two to infinity, to inexhaustible profusion. But I have not discussed the dyad deeply enough here. All the divisions of which Plato speaks are binary. This number must not be allowed to pass away too quickly.

I have spoken of it elsewhere as sexual difference, returning us to love, madness, and justice, all echoes of the good.[9] A two, a dyad, that remains indefinite without losing its measure. Men and women. Man and woman. Two genders. In profusion. Recalling lineage and blood, dyads of kinds. Recalling family and kin. And genealogy.

For the moment I stay with the number two, leaving general economy aside. If that is possible in speaking of any number, any measure. Without passing away beyond limit.

For the moment I return to the method the stranger describes as the trap, the snare, in which he will seize the sophist. A restricted economy. Not without echoes of general economy. For they are about to embark upon a "very long discussion" (Plato, *Sophist*, 217e), one perhaps that cannot end except arbitrarily. Perhaps this is because the sophist is a "very troublesome creature to hunt down" (218d); perhaps sophistry and philosophy are disputed terms; perhaps kinds participate in general as well as restricted economy.

The method of the hunt is described at length.[10] And perhaps we may wonder at its denouement: To possess, perhaps to kill, the beast? As philosophy? To sacrifice the sophist to the end of philosophy? Could it be that restricted economy aims to possess, to master, own, and dominate? Failing that, to destroy? And what else will be destroyed in this quest? What is the violence of the pursuit of identity in restricted economy? Of the questions of philosophy?

Again, I find myself passing away too quickly from the dyad. We are told that we must stay close to the method, however briefly, before we let it pass away to unlimit. I understand it as the question, belonging to *technē*, of the propriety of methods for knowing and assembling kinds. Do kinds lend themselves to method, as Plato and Aristotle appear to claim and as Descartes famously insists? Or do they, as Plato appears to suggest in *Philebus*, in the name of the good, interrupt every method with something otherwise, every limit with unlimit? Do general and restricted economy interrupt each other at every place, in every kind?

These questions have all appeared in my brief introduction to *Sophist*, in the name of kin and strangers, humans and gods: *genos, phulon, eidos*; *erōs, mania, dikē, agathon*; all joined by lineage and blood. We must not forget love, madness, justice, blood, and kin, all given from the good, in composing our methods for governing kinds.

The method offered by the stranger is the way to hunt—to own, possess, capture, perhaps to kill—the kind—not the individual but the kind. Perhaps we cannot destroy a kind as we might kill an individual. Socrates the individual man was killed but Socrates' kind can never be destroyed, remains to be remembered forever after his death. And what if we forget? I hold this possibility of disaster in kind in abeyance for a while. I pursue instead figures of hunting and possessing. The method is a method of hunting for the sake of owning and possessing the kind. Not for the sake of the kind, or for the sake of the good, or anything else, or nothing. The Plato who repeatedly describes the shepherd's responsibility as for the sake of the sheep here offers a different responsibility analogous to that offered in *Theaetetus*, where knowledge is described as holding the bird, the object, in a cage, owning, possessing, seizing, imprisoning it.[11] We come to another interruption.

I read *Theaetetus* as showing that knowledge is not something that can be possessed, that possessed knowledge cannot be pursued. Inquiry and error are incompatible with knowledge owned, possessed, or seized; that imprisoning truth destroys it. Truth must remain mobile, otherwise, in the endless debt it bears—the ethicality of truth, given from the good. We bear an infinite debt toward truth, a debt that truth itself cannot give, a responsibility to know, to care, to pursue, to question, beyond any grasp or possession. I understand this responsibility to belong to truth, not to us, not to humans, given from the good.

Our desire to know, joined with this immeasurable responsibility to question, may produce a hostility toward inquiry and knowledge, hostile toward every possibility of truth. Plato speaks against such hostility, affirms life and truth, when he has Socrates insist repeatedly that we must never abandon the search for truth.[12] We must not give up searching for knowledge and truth in the face of the endless responsibility we bear never to be content with any truth, never to think we can possess it.

The two greatest sins are to give up the search for truth and to think that we have found it. To claim to know when one does not know, or what one does not know, is worse than ignorance. "When a person supposes that he knows, and does not know; this appears to be the great source of all the errors of the intellect" (Plato, *Sophist*, 229c). Yet hatred of truth is another crime. Expressed in terms of general and restricted economy, the pursuit of truth is endless, given in the circulation of general economy, instituted in restricted economy. Both possession and hatred of truth halt its circulation, as if truth could be held in place. As if owning truth were not its death.

With this understanding, we may return from this interruption to the hunt, the pursuit, of the skeptic's kind. If we come to own and possess this kind, in words or thought, we halt its circulation: one of the greatest crimes.

If we forgo the hunt itself because the nature of kinds can never be known, we halt the circulation in a different way. Returning to the beginning of the dialogue, where the strange old Socrates still speaks before the discussion is taken over by other strangers, we find the question appearing us in a different form. For the sophist is a member of a triad philosopher, states-man, sophist—perhaps an indefinite triad. The two greatest crimes within this triad may be to think that we can distinguish them finally and own that distinction, or to give up the search. These, and perhaps other kinds, are to be pursued, inquired after, sought but never possessed or owned. Perhaps this is true not only of these and other human kinds—male and female, citizens and strangers, good and bad, right and wrong, love and hate, just and unjust, reason and madness; all endlessly disputed kinds—but of natural and other kinds, all the kinds of nature and the divine. Perhaps all kinds participate in general and restricted economy, endlessly limited to be owned, endlessly exceeding every possession. Perhaps this is what I mean by kind|ness, perhaps what Plato means by the divinity of the idea, the kind, and by participation in it: what cannot be possessed or owned; what exceeds possession in identity and difference; what possesses every possession. Perhaps this is true of property itself, private and public, quality and object. That remains the subject of another book.[13]

We return to the method of hunting, the pursuit of a quarry to possess it, possibly to destroy it—the greatest crime, paralleled by that other crime, that we would forgo the hunt. What can we say of a method—an art, a *techne*—that destroys in its undertaking yet that it would be a crime to renounce? Perhaps something ethical, without neutrality. Philosophy as hunting, possessing, destroying. The stranger's example is angling, hunting for fish. The angler belongs to the class, the kind, that produces by art or *techne* (Plato, *Sophist*, 219a), divided in two, *producing (poiesis)* by bringing into existence or through imitation or *acquisition* including learning and hunting. Learning, possessing, hunting all frame the stranger's pursuit of the sophist. May we fear the possibility that they may frame ours? Do we hope to acquire knowledge as if we were sophists?

The method is the method of God on the Day of Judgment, dividing and judging by twos, entirely definitely. No indefinite dyad for God. No indefinite triad or pentad, or anything otherwise. The infinite falls into finite time in binary pairs. Perhaps the tyranny of grammar, as Nietzsche suggests. Perhaps the tyranny of measure. Or kinds. The general economy of God falls into time as the tyranny of restricted economy, as if it were the death of general economy. Perhaps for God. Perhaps not. The possibility that God might judge with infinite measure what cannot be given any measure appears to be the death of God. The death of God in owning what cannot be owned, hunting what cannot be gathered.

Could God Himself tell with perfect assurance the difference among philosopher, statesman, and sophist? *God Himself.* As if God with equally perfect assurance knew he was not she, not god herself. As if we can be perfectly sure that philosopher, statesman, god, even sophist were man not woman. As if god—he or she or whatever—could always know with perfect assurance the difference between woman and man, animal and man, nature and humanity. As if, always as if: pretending what is true in order to hunt for and acquire some other truth. Always *mimēsis.* Could the method of God on the Day of Judgment be *mimēsis,* or *poiēsis,* a tale told of old *(palaios)* to make us strong, sacrificing indefiniteness to the dyad in fear that humans might worship false idols—or none at all?

I return from this interruption to the method of the definite dyad, setting aside its divine indefiniteness, forgetting the gods and the good. The dialectical method, described above from *Phaedrus* as if it were the method of the gods, dividing with certainty, without hesitation, on left and right. Here in *Sophist* it is described in terms of acquisition, the end Socrates rejects with revulsion in *Phaedrus* as sacrilegious: use and profit. Such a *technē* knows nothing of infinite love and desire, of Eros who endlessly moves between heaven and earth, the messenger who traverses the borders between general and restricted economy. In *Symposium* and *Phaedrus,* use, profit, advantage, acquisition, together with their pursuit—hunting to own, possess, and master—all know nothing of infinite love. Why not suppose something similar in *Sophist?* After all, it is not Socrates but a stranger from Elea who is speaking, someone for whom, in Aristotle's words, "the universe is one" in nature (Aristotle, *Metaphysics,* 986b). The universe is one. Being and truth are one. Even, perhaps, the sophist is one, one in many images, semblances, and words, one among the three—philosopher, statesman, sophist. Perhaps the one is indefinite, the indefinite in the triad, in the multiplicity. Pervaded by infinite desire.

Quickly, now, before another interruption, the method of hunting and seizing the sophist. There are

two kinds *(eidē)* of arts *(technōn)* (219c), productive *(poiētikos)* and acquisitive *(ktētikos);*
two kinds of acquisitive arts, voluntary and coercive;
two kinds of coercive arts, fighting and hunting *(thēraō);*

(I cannot resist another brief interruption. One of the productive arts is tending, care *[therapeia],* of living things, we might say of soul *[psuchē];* in these dividings on right and left, *therapeia* is divided absolutely from *thēraō.* Could this pun in Greek, hidden in English, express once more the indefiniteness of the dyad, the impossibility of dividing hunting, acquisition, possession from care? In the language of *Phaedrus,* is the sacrilege, the injustice, that of thinking of profit without care, of love without *erōs*, of being without exposure?

The good calls for us to answer affirmatively, resisting neutrality. In hunting, owning, possessing is care; in being is the good, interruption against neutrality, interrupting the tyranny of *technē*, of restricted economy without general economy, without infinity and responsibility—to care.

I return from this interruption . . .)

two kinds of hunting arts, pursuing living and nonliving things;

two kinds of arts for hunting living things, land and water;

two kinds of water animals, swimming and winged, giving the arts of fishing and fowling;

two kinds of fishing, by net and by blow;

two kinds of blow, by spear and by line.

Angling is an acquisitive art of hunting water animals, fishing with hook, drawing upward. I must add something of the stranger's words: "One half of all art was acquisitive"; "half of the acquisitive art was conquest or taking by force, half of this was hunting, and half of hunting was hunting animals; half of this was hunting water animals" (Plato, *Sophist*, 221ab): half, half, half. The world of kinds is measured by halves. And this is the method by which to catch the sophist, if he (not she) is an artist, a *technōn*, of an acquisitive sort. "And now, following this pattern, let us endeavor to find out what a Sophist is" (221c).

We may imagine that the world of kinds—nature's kinds and species—divide in twos, measured in halves. We may imagine that the human world of kinds—kinds of arts and practices—divide in twos, measured in halves. And we may wonder if either world, nature or culture—if they are two, if they divide by half—belongs to measure except in the fiction of a method for hunting, seizing, owning truth.[14]

And so the hunting figure emerges again in the name of the sophist. For both the angler and sophist are hunters, the one for wild animals the other for tame. We divide in half again. But perhaps we have forgotten the stranger, who hunts the sophist. And perhaps we have forgotten that learning and inquiry are named by the stranger as hunting and acquisitive arts. I would not forget that Socrates regards the claim to possess knowledge when one does not know among the worst of crimes, that Socrates never claims to know, to possess knowledge, but to be always on the way to it. How can a knowledge toward which we are always on the way be a possession? How can its pursuit be given by hunting or any other acquisitive art? For that matter, how can *anamnēsis* be understood as acquisition or possession when we forget?

All of which is to suggest that we may hunt for the sophist, hope to possess his kind, but that nothing important—that which is mad, erotic, ecstatic, and divine, endlessly contested and disputed, in the general economy of the good—can be owned, possessed, or hunted down as if it were a quarry to be gathered, assembled, held in hand like a fish. If a fish, living and breathing, can be held in hand but in a moment and for us, for the sake of the angler, but never for the sake of the fish, which, like the sheep, may know a good that cannot be gathered.

I am interrupted by the fish, who slaps the water with its tail, who like every living thing, resists the neutrality of gathering. Living things are more than empty vessels to be filled according to human purposes. We are interrupted by the mollusk Molly, who squirts water in our faces, reminding us that shellfish are not to be gathered as if they were stones. We are interrupted again by Arachne, who reminds us of the worlds she weaves. All of us are interrupted by stones, who remember beyond the reach of gathering. Kinds exceed the neutrality of their limits. Anticipating Hegel, kinds are more than what is common, exceed identity and difference.[15] All kinds.

We are surrounded by sea creatures who will swim with us on our journeys in kinds, reminding us of the kinds that cannot be gathered. Including the sophist. Gathering is violation. Even in truth.

Which I would say is always present in Plato, wherever the idea, the *eidos*, is described as eternal and divine. Beyond the limits of identity and difference, despite the claims of reason to divide by identity and difference. What belongs to the gods cannot be hunted and gathered as if it were neutral and dead. Especially in Greek.

The analogy with angling concludes with a formula by division in which the sophist's kind is possessed with no regard whatever for the good of the fish or human, no regard for life or soul or the divine: "his art may be traced as a branch of the appropriative, acquisitive family—which hunts animals, living, land, tame animals—which hunts man, privately, for hire, taking money in exchange, having the semblance of education . . . and is a hunt after young men of wealth and rank—such is the conclusion" (Plato, *Sophist*, 223b). If I were Socrates, entering the discussion, I would question the good we may seek for young men. Perhaps their wealth and rank and gender—their privilege—may get in the way. Perhaps such men deserve to be hunted, if any creature does. Perhaps their hunters deserve to be hunted, again if any creature does. And perhaps no creature does, human, animal, or otherwise, in the name of the good. Even the sophist. Even by strangers.

Even so, we have not claimed the sophist. For he may be pursued along another genealogy, another line of kin and blood. "Let us take another branch of his genealogy, for he is a professor of a great and many-sided art" (223c). I have recalled the disruptive, anarchic role of genealogy in Nietzsche and Foucault, not to trap and seize the quarry, but to express its fluidity and mobility. The sophist's art is indeed fluid, changeable, multifarious, anarchic and disruptive. Perhaps like every kind given blood in genealogy, every descent, every idea and kind, *genos* and *eidos*. What if the identity of the sophist, given here by genealogy, expressed the anarchy present in every identity, every idea, the anarchy in the idea, the *eidos*, of kinds? What of the possibility that this dialogue reflects a hunt to contain and master kinds through genealogy, *genos* and *eidos*, always to find that genealogy cannot contain, that *genos* and *eidos* bear an anarchic side, given as genealogy, as family, kin, and kinds, in blood and descent?

What if history were the discipline, the method, of mastery and containment, to own, possess, perhaps to destroy the living creature in its kind, where genealogy revealed the life and soul in the kind that outstripped every such possession?

It is not a new idea of ideas that they outstrip every finite grasp, outstrip the hunters and their methods. It may be somewhat more provocative to imagine that every kind is defined by an idea, an *eidos*, that outstrips every method and every search, every identity. And still we search. In fluid, changeable, multifarious, even anarchic and disruptive ways. If we must. We philosophers. Who are not so far from the gods, or sophists.

Our first genealogy was framed by the distinction between production and acquisition, dividing acquisition into voluntary and coercive possession. Production and liberty can never on this method belong to sophists.

Our second genealogy accepts the distinction between acquisition and production, still holding at bay the possibility that the sophist may produce nothing whatever. Acquisition is divided differently:

two kinds of acquisitive art: hunting and exchange;
two kinds of exchange: giving and selling;
two kinds of selling: one's own products and those of others;
two kinds of selling: in city, retailing; between cities, merchanting;
two kinds of merchanting: food for body *(sōma)*, food for soul *(psuchē);*
two kinds of food for soul: music *(mousikē)*, arts, knowledge for instruction or amusement;
and so forth.

The sophist never produces but seeks to acquire; never gives but sells the knowledge of virtue: "that part of acquisitive art which exchanges, and of exchange which either sells a man's own productions or retails those of others, as the case may be, and in either way sells the knowledge of virtue, you would again term Sophistry?" (224e). To which Theaetetus replies, "I must, if I am to keep pace with the argument." And what if he chooses not to keep pace, or cannot? What is the relation of this argument to truth?

Always divided neatly into two. Except that every genealogy fails to capture the variegated heterogeneity of the sophist's art. Its general economy.

Hunting.
Possessing.
Coercing.
Selling.

If these are sophistry, what is genealogy? For these two genealogies are followed by a third, following the line of fighting under acquisition, divided earlier from hunting:

two kinds of fighting: competitive and pugnacious;
two kinds of pugnaciousness: violence *(biastikon)* and controversy;
two kinds of controversy: forensic and disputation;
two kinds of disputation: with and without art;

Concluding that the sophist "is the moneymaking species of the eristic, disputatious, controversial, pugnacious, combative, acquisitive family" (226a). Filled with violence. Along the way, however, the sophist passes very close to philosophy: "that which proceeds by rules of art to dispute about justice and injustice in their own nature, and about things in general, we have been accustomed to call argumentation [eristic]?" (225c). The philosopher wastes or loses money; the sophist makes it. As if we could strictly divide those who earn and those who lose money from each other, as if we could strictly divide acquisition from authenticity, taking from giving, as if we could purify the form, as if genealogy were such a purification rather than impurification.

I will not continue these binary genealogies, hunting to own the kind, the *eidos*, of the sophist, to possess an *eidos*, infinite and divine, multifarious and anarchic, by a method of division. In every case, we divide by two as if one half were applicable, excluding the other half as inapplicable, arriving at a measure by halves. Except that the sophist's kind, perhaps every kind, requires many genealogies; for what we have cast away returns along another line of descent, and then another. In every case, something relevant appears, shown to be relevant in a destructive way. It is tempting to think that the ruin is given by the nature of the sophist. Yet—to take one example—he is granted to teach young Greeks virtue and knowledge of virtue, though perhaps pugnaciously and moneygrubbingly. I think it important to consider the social and economic rank presupposed for those who do not need to earn their livelihood. Including Socrates himself.

I will not continue these genealogies. Nor does the stranger, with a single exception. This many-sided animal, not to be caught with one hand

(226a)—even perhaps with two, with pairs of hands divided in two, though that is the alternative suggestion (226b)—now is sought in the domain of "menial occupations which have names among servants"—"sifting, straining, winnowing, threshing"; names of dividing, measuring, including and excluding. In all of these is implied a notion of division (226c); all terms, that is, that can be understood, however menial they may sound, to represent the stranger's method of gathering. Gathering and hunting, like exchanging and disputing, all divide one from the other, excluding, destroying what does not gather. Suggesting, I believe, that the gods may not approve of this destruction, with their eyes upon the sparrow.

The stranger follows with another, stronger figure of destruction in which we may discern the entire history of Western philosophy. "In all the previously named processes either like has been separated from like or the better from the worse" (226d). The former has no name, though perhaps it is closer to a philosophy that keeps in touch with the gods. The latter is *purification (katharmos)*. The history of Western philosophy is firmly named here *purification*, firmly dividing the better from the worse, as if we do no harm in that division, as if the pure were always better than the impure.

We can be sure that such a philosophy knows nothing of neutrality. If philosophy is purification, it has always resisted the neuter, historically at the expense of women and others. Yet we must ask from within the same resistance, what of resisting purification? In relation to kinds, is not *Sophist* to be understood as that moment in Plato where the possibility of knowing and possessing ideas—kinds—in their purity, undivided, is finally laid to rest? So that the impurity of the sophist returns in the impurity of every idea—that is, every kind. The art of dialectic is said to be purification (227c). Could that be the sophist's art? Could this be the impossible distinction demanded of us between sophist and philosopher? The sophist-philosopher divides like God on right and left to purify the world. The philosopher claims to be God. And, when God expires, this image of philosophy, divided into right and left, high and low, superior and inferior, philosopher and sophist, expires with it. Not into neutrality. That belongs to purity. Into the anarchic struggle of kind in kind, kind with kind, along difficult lines of descent and blood, without purity. Genealogy resists neutrality. Genealogy resists purity. The thought of kinds to which we are led in *Sophist* is to kinds without neutrality and without purity, an infinite and anarchic struggle of better and worse without a neutral rule that divides the world on right and left. We are led to kindlness.

Purification is divided into two, and again and again, passing through body and soul (229) and instruction to refutation or cross-questioning *(helegchō lekteon)*, the greatest of purifications (230e). The worst thing is to claim to know what you do not know. The greatest thing is to be disgraced and dishonored *(helegchos)* by cross-examination, to be refuted, to be shown that one does not know, in words rather than in violence and blood. The greatest purification is not to know what is pure and impure, but to be shown that one does not know, to know that the purest knowledge is impure. Refutation is the impurification of every pure knowledge and truth. Here we come as close as possible to a point of division between sophist and philosopher, except that it casts a dark shadow on the method of division. The sophist claims to know, does not seek refutation but authority. The philosopher loves being refuted. That is the passion of philosophy, a purification without purity. For no kind can be pure, neither the sophist nor any other. Kinds and genealogies are expressions of impurity, in kin and kind. In blood and violence.

What follows the recognition that one who claims to know uses that knowledge to deceive others (235a) is an extraordinary interruption of the method that we may have supposed might give us such a knowledge. The interruption is provoked by the famous sophistic question of whether we can speak of nonbeing. Perhaps a famous philosophic question. Can we speak of anything without speaking of what it is not? Can we know anything without knowing what it is not? Can something be—an individual or kind—without being other individuals or kinds? The dialogue opens from purification to the most far-reaching question of purity: can something be and be known to be something—in its identity and kind—without always being other, something else, without being and nonbeing together, without being impure. The greatest purification by far is to know the impurity of kinds. Together with their purity. Given from the good. The kindIness of being and nonbeing.

The stranger has shown the sophist to belong to a kind that appears or seems without being, but we cannot speak of what is not, of nonbeing. "To speak of what is not 'something' is to speak of no thing at all" (237e); "it is unthinkable, not to be spoken of or uttered or expressed" (238c). To say that the sophist, or any one or kind, deceives by semblances, saying or showing what is false, we contradict ourselves by speaking of nonbeing.

We may be forgiven if we think that the stranger is speaking of what is false, what is not. Can we speak or think of what is false, what is not, of nonbeing? Can we speak, with less confusion of what is true, what is, of being (243c)? When philosophers—Parmenides and others—have "tried to determine how many real things there are and what they are like" (242c), they have treated us like children. Perhaps there is no number of real things, no number of kinds, not even pertaining to any kind. When we speak of hot and cold, are we speaking of one or two or three? Are they one as well as hot and cold? Unity and otherness always mingle and participate.

Unity and otherness always mingle and participate in kinds, including our quarry's kind, the sophist. And the philosopher. For the stranger claims to have found the philosopher before the sophist (253c), "Dividing according to kinds, not taking the same form for a different one or a different one for the same" (253d); "knowing how to distinguish, kind by kind, in what ways the several kinds can or cannot combine" (253e). "It is, then, in some such region as this that we shall find the philosopher now or later, if we should look for him. He too may be difficult to see clearly, but the difficulty in his case is not the same as in the Sophist's" (253e–254a). The stranger does not fulfill this promise except within the general economy of kinds that resists distinguishing philosophy from statesman and sophist without treating them as the same.

The question of nonbeing is interpreted here as the question of mingling and impurity of kinds. Some kinds—same and other, motion and being—mingle and multiply. Some do not. Kinds are and are not the same as other kinds. "So, in the case of every one of the forms *(eidōn)* there is much that it is and an indefinite *(apeiron:* infinite) number of things that it is not" (256e); "And, moreover, existence itself must be called different from the rest" (257a); "When we speak of 'that which is not,' it seems that we do not mean something contrary to what exists but only something that is different" (257b). Kinds are the same in kinds and infinitely different; kinds are always same and other, where otherness is not contrariety but heterogeneity in kind. Genealogy is the infinite tracing of this sameness and difference, impurity in purity, pertaining to the sophist, in many-colored and varied hues, and to every kind. Genealogy as kindlness traces general economy in restricted economy, in the giving of the good.

I do not believe it arbitrary that the stranger speaks twice of music *(mousikos)*, first as an art of the soul (224a), then as the art of mingling of sounds, analogous to grammar (253). Who less than a philosopher might imagine that the art of grammar was the art of discourse, that the art of musical combinations was music? Nor do I believe it arbitrary that the understanding that every *eidos* is infinitely same and other is followed by a reference to beauty, where "whenever we use the expression 'not beautiful,' the thing we mean is precisely that which is different from the nature of the beautiful" (257d): different but not contrary. Non-beauty is not contrary to the beauty described in *Symposium* as incompatible with all binary oppositions (Plato, *Symposium*, 210e–211e). Kinds mingle, proliferate, among other kinds, sometimes in hierarchy and domination, sometimes resisting every domination and hierarchy. Restricted and general economy again. "We have shown that the nature of the different has existence and is parceled out over the whole field of existent things with reference to one another, and of every part of it that is set in contrast to 'that which is' we have dared to say that precisely that is really 'that which is not' " (Plato, *Sophist*, 258de). Always species, families, and kinds. Infinite and not contrary. Altogether, it would seem, a kindlness incompatible with hunting by twos.

Yet with this understanding of kinds, we return to the hunt for the sophist's kind, returning to the distinction between production *(poiēsis)* and acquisition: "under the head of the acquisitive we had glimpses of the Sophist in the arts of hunting, contention, trafficking, and other kinds of that sort" (265a). Now under imitation *(mimētikē)*. Productive art, *poiētikes*, divides into divine and human, where

> all mortal animals and also all things that grow—plants that grow above the earth from seeds and roots, and lifeless bodies compacted beneath the earth, whether fusible or not fusible. Must we not attribute the coming-into-being of these things out of not-being to divine craftsmanship and nothing else? Or are we to fall in with the belief that is commonly expressed? (265c)
>
> That nature gives birth to them as a result of some spontaneous cause that generates without intelligence *(dianoias)*. Or shall we say that they come from a cause which, working with reason and art, is divine and proceeds from divinity? (265cd)

All things are divine, from the gods—or perhaps from the good. Leading to an interruption.

We may be reminded of Aristotle's *Physics*, book 2, and Heidegger's reading of the distinction between *phusis* and *technē*, as if the nature that moved from and to itself did so without intelligence, according to a spontaneous cause, distinguished from reason and art, always *technē*, always from without, even perhaps for the gods. Movement from within is not caused by the gods, but pertains to nature. As if it knew nothing infinite, nothing divine, in form or kinds. As if being and its self-movement might be pure.

Heidegger reads Aristotle, speaking of nature and things that exist "by nature, some from other causes" (Aristotle, *Physics*, 2, 192b), that "each of them has within itself a principle of motion and of stationariness (in respect of place, or of growth and decrease, or by way of alteration)" (192b).

> Nature then is what has been stated. Things have a nature which have a principle of this kind. . . .
>
> This then is one account of nature, namely that it is the primary underlying matter of things which have in themselves a principle of motion or change.

> Another account is that nature is the shape *(morphē)* or form *(eidos)* which is specified in the definition of the thing. (192b–193a)

On Heidegger's reading, no space emerges between *phusis*, that which moves from and to itself, and *phusei*, things by nature, which move in and of themselves according to their form, their *eidos*, species, kind. "The originating ordering *(archē)* of [each natural being's] being-moved and standing still (rest)" (Heidegger, *OBCP*, 227) moves without a pause, without a hesitation concerning the privilege of *morphē*, the end for which each thing moves from and in itself. Heidegger's reading moves without interruption down the line of thought to the most hateful and violent ends possible in reading Aristotle, the risks and dangers of the privilege of form without interruption from the good.

> *[P]husis* is *archē kinēseōs*, origin and ordering of change. (p. 230)

> *[M]orphē* is the Being of *phusis* as *archē*, and *archē* is the Being of *phusis* as *morphē*, insofar as the uniqueness of *morphē* consists in the fact that in it the *eidos* of itself and as such brings itself into presence. (pp. 267–68)

What is fundamental to *phusis* as *ousia* is bringing itself to presence as *eidos* and *morphē*, as the end for which it has being, toward which it moves in coming to appearance. Metaphysics brings into presence as form, privileges truth, knows nothing of the infinite debt that demands endless interruption.

In this way, in Heidegger's words, *"Aristotle's PHYSICS is the hidden, and therefore never adequately studied, foundational book of Western philosophy"* (p. 224), explaining how Aristotle under stands form as domination, insists on ranking kinds. I offer a few selected passages.

> Hence we see that is the nature and office of a slave; he who is by nature not his own but another's man, is by nature a slave; and he may be said to be another's man who, being a human being, is also a possession. (Aristotle, *Politics*, 1254a)

> Where then there is such a difference as that between soul and body, or between men and animals . . . the lower sort are by nature slaves, and it is better for them as for all inferiors that they should be under the rule of a master. (1254b)

> In like manner we may infer that, after the birth of animals, plants exist for their sake, and that the other animals exist for the sake of man, the tame for use and food, the wild, if not all, at least the greater part of them, for food, and for the provision of clothing and various instruments. Now

if nature makes nothing incomplete, and nothing in vain, the inference must be that she has made all animals for the sake of man. (1256b)

A question may indeed be raised, whether there is any excellence at all in a slave beyond those of an instrument and of a servant—whether he can have the excellences of temperance, courage, justice, and the like; or whether slaves possess only bodily services. . . . A similar question may be raised about women and children, whether they too have excellences; ought a woman to be temperate and brave and just, and is a child to be called temperate, and intemperate, or not? . . . For the slave has no deliberative faculty at all; the woman has, but it is without authority, and the child has, but it is immature. . . . Clearly, then, excellence of character belongs to all of them; but the temperance of a man and of a woman, or the courage and justice of a man and of a woman, are not, as Socrates maintained, the same; the courage of a man is shown in commanding, of a woman in obeying. . . . [A]s the poet says of women,

Silence is a woman's glory,

but this is not equally the glory of man. (1259b–1260b)

Ousia leads down the road to property and possession, in the privilege of disclosure, the gathering of being in truth. Yet *phusis*, perhaps not so quickly becoming *phusei*, the being of beings as end and form, moves infinitely from and to itself, touching what cannot be measured in form but what must be expressed in kinds. If we imagine that something of the good is given between *phusis* and *phusei*, analogous to general and restricted economy—something infinite in kind, in debt to the gods, and something definite in kind, fulfilled in the being of each natural thing—then something analogous is given in the very nature of species and kinds—something infinite in kind, given in care and nurture from the good, and something finite in kind, ranking things in their kinds from high to low. This interweaving of general and restricted economy haunts Plato's genealogies throughout *Sophist*, in the name of *genos* and *eidos*. Something similar haunts Aristotle's understanding of *phusis*, something that cannot be expressed in terms of nature or being without the good.

Returning from this interruption to the stranger's question, can we imagine natural creatures and things created and produced without intelligence, without soul, without regard, value, care, in their kind? As if they were neutral, dead machines? Or shall we understand *phusei* to participate in kinds filled with soul, *psuchē*, which has care for all things everywhere (Plato, *Phaedrus*, 246c)? What can such a care mean except kindlness, returning us to the call of the good embodied in restricted and general economies of kinds? All things are produced according to a purpose, under *morphē, eidos*, and *technē*, to fulfill an end, ranking the kinds of the world from high to low, in violence and domination; and in such a ranking, in every ranking, in the nature of natural things and kinds, something infinite, beyond the ranked being of kinds, echoes and glows. Interrupting every measure, calling for endless restitution for the injustices in kinds, especially perhaps the neutrality of kinds, as if without ethical responsibility. Things and kinds are measured in relation to something that exceeds every measure. Including the sophist.

For the final trap for the sophist follows the line of descent of judgment-pairs on right and left. Production divides into divine and mortal. Human production divides into productive and acquisitive. Acquisitive art divides into original and imitative. Imitative art divides into art with and without knowledge. Always damned, we might say. Always art, *technē*, restricted economy. Concluding with the passage with which we began.

> The art of contradiction making, descended from an insincere kind of conceited mimicry, of the semblance-making breed, derived from image making, distinguished as a portion, not divine but human, of production, that presents a shadow play of words—such are the blood and lineage which can, with perfect truth, be assigned to the authentic Sophist. (Plato, *Sophist*, 268cd)

A hateful, exclusionary reading of the multifariousness of kinds, all descending onto the head of the sophist, who appears to bear the brunt of every binary division, demonized, damned. In the context of the recognition that every kind is infinite, same and different, impure. All these evils assigned to the sophist are figures of impurity. All are figures of measure of what may be immeasurable, the distinction between purity and impurity in kind.

Unless we understand this blood and violence to return us to the profusion of kinds traced in genealogy, where the quarry—nothing to own or possess—is philosopher not sophist. Where the many guises of the sophist return to haunt the genealogy of the philosopher. Where the damnation of the sophist haunts the divinity of the philosopher. And thereby, perhaps, every kind, the kindlness of kinds, resisting the two greatest crimes: thinking that we have grasped the identity of a kind, halting its circulation; and thinking that we have nothing to seek, no identity in kind, that kinds belong to no economy. The ranking of kinds belongs to them in their nature, given from the good. We may neither accept this or any ranking without question, endless questions, nor refuse to undertake the measure. This impossible task is that of the good, marked in different—or perhaps similar—ways by sophist and philosopher, under the signs of *mimēsis* and *logos*, linked by *eidē*, kinds.

CHAPTER 3

Nature's Kinds

The *monad* of which we shall here speak is merely a simple substance, which enters into composites; *simple*, that is to say, without parts. (Leibniz, *M*, #1)

Take away from the dog its animality, and it becomes impossible to say what it is. All things have a permanent inward nature, as well as an outward existence. They live and die, arise and pass away; but their essential and universal part is the kind; and this means much more than something *common* to them all. (Hegel, *EL*, §24, Zus., 47)

The living individual, which in its first process comports itself as intrinsically subject and notion, through its second assimilates its external objectivity and thus puts the character of reality into itself. It is now therefore implicitly a Kind, with essential universality of nature. The particularising of this Kind is the relation of the living subject to another subject of its Kind: and the judgment is the tie of Kind over these individuals thus appointed for each other. This is the Affinity of the Sexes. (§220)

If a monad is simple, without parts, then it must be singular, pure, independent of any kind. That is how we may think of entelechies, self-organizing and self-moving creatures, especially when they lack windows through which anything can enter or depart (Leibniz, *M*, #3). If there are composites, Leibniz says, there must be simples, "for the composite is only a collection or *aggregatum* of simple substances" (#2). And perhaps the kind is only a collection of singulars, gathered together in space and time or language and thought. For Leibniz, that is, not for Spinoza, who understands nature to be composed of singulars and kinds.

I disown the argument that if there are composites there must be simples. I take everything to be complex according to Anaxagoras's suggestion:

> For of the small there is no smallest, but there is always a smaller, for it is not possible for what is not to be. But of the great there is always a greater also. And it is equal in number to the small, each thing being with respect to itself both great and small. (Anaxagoras, fragment 9.9; Robinson, *EGP*, 178)

I read this passage less to describe the determinate size and number of smaller and greater things than to speak of the impurity and heterogeneity of things. Each is indefinitely complex, composed of parts without number, composing environments without number. Each participates in the abundance of nature: infinite numbers of infinite kinds.

Each determinate thing is an aggregate composed of infinite others and, together with other such things, composes infinite other aggregates. Each is uncontainable, singular and collective, haunted by infinity. Complexity of complexity interrupts the magisterial ordering of the world divided into singulars and kinds. As Hegel claims in the name of kinds.

I began with Leibniz who denies that monads are composite, thereby perhaps also denying that they are infinite in kind. The question I wish to consider for a moment is whether the creative and self-organizing movement of an entelechy can be singular in the absence of kinds, as if individuals were alive and kinds were dead. This is a thought I believe quite alien to Plato. Perhaps also to Leibniz as well as Spinoza. It is suggested by the idea of entelechy, the self-organizing movement of monads, "sources of their own internal activities *(autarkeia)*" (#18). In a world full of life and soul everywhere, why should we suppose that kinds are dead? In a universe without neutrality, where each monad exercises a claim upon the rest, how can anything be neutral? This is the question to which we find ourselves led repeatedly, that of the neutrality of being in kinds, which is anything but neutral.

Were this to be a different kind of exploration of Leibniz, I might explore the principle of the identity of indiscernibles, which says that "the monads, if they had no qualities, would be indistinguishable from one another" (#8); and that "It is necessary, indeed, that each monad be different from every other. For there are never in nature two beings which are exactly alike and in which it is not possible to find an internal difference, . . ." (#9). Every relation, Leibniz is understood to claim, is an internal relation, reinforcing the inward unity and identity of the singular. Such a view collapses the distinction between individual and kind, where two different individuals might arise in different times and places though identical in their qualities, might inhabit different worlds.

More of different worlds a bit later. Leibniz's monads are not composites but they are indeed like kinds, multiple, collective, and infinite. Especially, they are like Anaxagoras's infinite worlds of great and small, infinity, like kinds, in every singular.

> 12. . . . there must be an individuating *detail of changes*, which forms, so to speak, the specifications and variety of the simple substances.
> 13. . . . there must be in the simple substance a plurality of affections and of relations, although it has no parts.

Each monad comprises an uncontainable multiplicity and variety, affections and relations, without complexity or composition. Such a view of individuals collapses the distinction between individuals and kinds as if individuals took priority over the multiplicity that inhabited them. Kinds are the kinds they are—collectives, aggregates, multiplicities—in virtue of other kinds and individuals: collectives of collectives. Individuals are what they are—collectives, aggregates, multiplicities—in virtue of other individuals and kinds.[1] Something of the collapse between individual and kind can be seen in Leibniz, who speaks of kinds when he speaks of the abundance within each monad:

> 64. Thus each organic body of a living being is a kind of divine machine or natural automaton, which infinitely surpasses all artificial automata. . . .
> 65. . . . each portion of matter is not only divisible *ad infinitum*, . . . but also each part is actually endlessly subdivided into parts, . . .
> 66. Whence we see that there is a world of creatures, of living beings, of animals, of entelechies, of souls, in the smallest particle of matter.
> 67. Each portion of matter may be conceived of as a garden full of plants, and as a pond full of fishes.

Like Anaxagoras, Leibniz describes a world of abundance in which every portion of matter is filled with entelechies, living beings. Every thing is composed of countless other living things and kinds. Reaching extreme profusion in the infinite mirrors, representations, of a universe without windows.

> 56. . . . each simple substance has relations which express all the others, and that, consequently, it is a perpetual living mirror of the universe.
> 57. . . . there are as it were so many different universes, which are nevertheless only the perspectives of a single one, according to the different *points of view* of each monad.

Leibniz's universe is infinite: infinite entelechies in infinite kinds composing every particle of matter; infinite perspectives on this infinite abundance.

Perhaps most striking of all, each monad is a perpetual living mirror of the universe, of other living mirrors, infinite mirrors of infinite mirrors. Nature's expressiveness as *mimēsis*.

Infinite mirrors of ponds and fishes. Carp and trout thrash about in joy. Arachne and Molly ask to be remembered in the lives of stones.

Bringing us back to indiscernibles and neutrality. For suppose we understand the principle of the identity of indiscernibles in relation to the good, not whether individuals may differ in their being without differing in quality and kind, but how we may bear responsibility to singulars in virtue of their uniqueness and heterogeneity in qualities and kinds. Responsiveness toward individuals bears two immeasurable excesses of kindlness: singularity over any kinds, and multiplications of kinds in profusion beyond any containment or regulation. Kinds in abundance. Given from the good.

Leibniz addresses the ethical side of nature's abundance, given over to a God that rules. For among the "infinity of possible universes in the ideas of God" (#53), God chooses according to a sufficient reason "which determines him to select one rather than another" (#53).

> 54. And this reason can only be found in the *fitness*, or in the degrees of perfection, which these worlds contain, . . .
>
> 55. And this is the cause of the existence of the Best: namely, that his wisdom makes it known to God, his goodness makes him choose it, and his power makes him produce it.
>
> 90. Finally, under this perfect government, there will be no good action unrewarded, no bad action unpunished; and everything must result in the well-being of the good, . . .

Elsewhere, Leibniz describes this perfection in another way, still under the rule of God as King: "the world is most perfect, not only physically, or, if you prefer, metaphysically, because that series of things is produced in which there is actually the most of reality, but also that it is most perfect morally, because real moral perfection is physical perfection for souls themselves" (Leibniz, *UOT*, 351). Leibniz knows as well as any that "not only innocent brutes but also innocent men are afflicted and even put to death with torture"; even so "all things, and consequently souls, attain to the highest degree of perfection possible" (p. 351). He reduces the abundance of the world, infinite infinites in individual and kind, in infinite debt, to a totality without remainder.

And with neutrality, the neutrality of the world under God, as if God were neutral with eyes upon the sparrow and the child. As if there could be a relation to the good without remainder. As if the good might be measured

finally in a world of immeasurable abundance and disaster. Infinity, in singularity and kind, marks the impossibility of measuring the good, which
appears as interruption. Leibniz leads us to the edge of the abyss in being
marked by the good, and recoils. Yet on the way he speaks in a powerful way
of the non-neutrality of the abundance of creatures and things. And of the
ways in which this non-neutrality shows itself in a plenitude of creatures
and a heterogeneous multiplicity of kinds. The general economy of the
world becomes God's restricted economy, the last thing possible in the
name of the good.

Leibniz comes so close to the explosive possibility of abundance in
relation to God that his recoil seems a profound betrayal. For before he
speaks of God resolving the infinite variety in each monad, in the universe,
in the mirrors within each of the mirrors of the others, and in the infinite
varieties of perceptions, relations, and kinds—each of these multiplying the
others—he asks us to think of the divine creativity that falls from the
infinite profusion into time as the "continual fulgurations of the Divinity"
(Leibniz, *M*, #47), reminding us of the lightning bolts of Zeus, flashes of the
divine that lighten and destroy. Creation is light and dark, where each bears
the infinite mark of the other—infinite in God. Here the fulguration is
another infinite, unlimit and excess, for and within the infinite infinites of
the world, bearing and expressing within itself not good and bad, life and
death, but neither. This is, I believe, Spinoza's view. All these infinites and
unlimits express what is beyond measure as bearing ethical weight in relation to measure. This ethical weight resists the neutrality—here, the
lifelessness and soullessness—of kinds, struggling against the tyranny of
kinds, against the inexpressiveness of being. Nature's *mimēsis*. Infinite
mirrors and representations. Another side of betrayal.

Thus, we may understand God's role as giving beyond measure, not to
make everything whole, but the superabundance of abundance, the wealth
of possibilities and actualities, mirrors and representations, giving and calling from the good not to reduce infinity in individuals and kinds to finiteness,
general to restricted economy, where general economy is not another
economy, not a total economy, but the mobility, excess, expressiveness, and
fluidity of circulation that every restricted economy strives to bring to
rest—in the double sense of death and excess, remains and remainder. For
the sake of the good, let us think of God not as the great builder but as the
great disturber, demanding that we respond to the infinite and immeasurable call of the good. Everywhere in every thing. Which is immensely present
in its expressive abundance in Leibniz.

And Hegel, with whom I return to the fulguration. Expressed in relation to kinds. And perhaps we may read Hegel as addressing the most
fundamental question of kinds, how to resist their neutrality and tyranny.

Which is not to say that Hegel resists the tyranny, but that he speaks explicitly to neutrality.

It is famous if not notorious in Hegel that the ultimate reality is the concrete particular, the individual in kind, the Notion. Nothing in the universe is in this sense dead, moribund, lifeless and spiritless. The task of the dialectic is to make intelligible the truth that everything in nature is alive, filled with spirit. Many understand this march to devour everything in its path, to place the variety of a world that cannot be contained under the tyranny of a Master-Spirit, who subjects the living vitality of individual things to the oppression of the Idea. As if the Idea were dead. Or as if it were King, anything but neutral.

To this powerful image of divine rule, we may bring some of the same concerns we brought to Leibniz, keeping fulguration in mind. For although the individual is empty without the concept, and the concept blind without the individual—Kant's formula cannot be avoided here—Hegel calls attention to something more, perhaps still Kantian.

The subject of §24 in the *Encyclopedia Logic* is Objective Thoughts: "*the science of things set and held in thoughts*" (Hegel, *EL*, 45), where we must not avoid the most violent possibilities in thinking of setting and holding things in thought, to master and control them. Does the kind, the universal, dominate the thing? In the very long *Zusatz*, Hegel addresses this question directly. "To speak of thought or objective thought as the heart and soul of the world may seem to be ascribing consciousness to the things of nature," producing "a certain repugnance against making thought the inward function of things" (p. 46). A certain repugnance against the neutrality of being? A certain repugnance against the dominance of nonhuman things by humanity? Whatever the answer, the issue is the neutrality and lifelessness of the natural world, the objectivity of neutral kinds as if empty of life and soul and thought.

Hegel continues in the name of the concept, speaking of something infinite in kind. "Now, the animal, *qua* animal, cannot be shown; nothing can be pointed out excepting some special animal" (p. 47). Take away the kind from the dog and it becomes impossible to say what it is—where the kind is much more than what is common. Perhaps it becomes impossible for the dog to be what it is, or anything. The individual is an individual in virtue of its infinite kind. At least for animals, including dogs. Perhaps for plants and stones. Perhaps we do not think, after Descartes's inward movement to the self-sufficient rational soul, that the same is true for human beings, at least rational human beings, especially French or German.

To the extent that the kind is what is common, it seems that the individual who contemplates that individuality inwardly knows singularity over and above commonality. I am not just a member of a kind. To which two responses are essential, kindlred responses. One is that perhaps even human beings, however inward and spiritual, may not be just members of a kind—human, spiritual, French or German kinds—but are nothing except in kinds. That is the truth I am exploring at the heart of the good, that the good is given in kinds though not restricted to kinds. The other is Hegel's, that the kind is not just something common but much more, perhaps unlimited, uncontainable.

Hegel follows with words that few might read today except as thought containing the world: "If thought is the constitutive substance of external things, it is also the universal substance of what is spiritual" (p. 47). The universal substance is spiritual; the universal substance is thought. That which is alive, immeasurable, uncontainable, divine, is spirit, thought, consciousness, perhaps soul. Thought contains the life of the world. We might respond with Socrates' words that soul has care of all things. Even so, to name as soul that which cares in place of that which rules and owns might still deny life and care and gifts from the good to natural creatures— mollusks and dogs and other animals—and bodies, including stones and dirt. Leibniz speaks of the profuse life and variety in every scoop of dirt. I would not like to forget that variety, nor forget that every grain of dirt is filled with infinite creatures, each a fulguration of God.

To name the caretaker is to grant it—Him—mastery. And I believe that is what Hegel does. I think that Hegel leans too much toward the tyranny of kinds. That does not take us away from the deeper insight I read in these passages, that kinds are fulgurations of the infinite, that which cannot be contained, that which refuses containment in the very possibility of the containment of thought. The kind is much more than what is common, where we may imagine that that commonality is what thought hopes to grasp.

A major part of Descartes's agenda is that humanity be distinguished from animality absolutely by reason. Animals have no reason at all. Hegel shares that agenda unblinkingly, though he offers a view that might have taken a very different direction. "Man is a thinker and is universal: but he is a thinker only because he feels his own universality. The animal too is by implication universal, but the universal is not consciously felt by it to be universal: it feels only the individual. The animal sees a singular object, for instance, its food, or a man. For the animal all this never goes beyond an individual thing" (p. 47). It is not enough that something divine and infinite participate in animals and dirt, not enough that divinity fulgurates and teems in each helix and grain. God must know His work, must recontain his uncontainability. If we are speaking of freedom, and of course we are, then the uncontainability in kinds resists the neutrality of being in the possibility that every singular thing is free in its kind, uncontainable even by God. Leibniz refuses that possibility, but comes very close. Hegel refuses it more absolutely, giving universality exclusively over to the contemplation of human beings.

Yet even this is close to the possibility of kindlness, taking for granted that to be anything whatever, animal, human, or dirt, is to be uncontainable, demanding infinite care and consideration, in its kind, and kinds of kinds. Kinds are the forms in which thought contains—the animal but perhaps not the human. Kinds are the infinite movements in which thought fails to contain—the human, but perhaps also animals and dirt. As kinds.

Expressed as genealogy, provoking an interruption. For Nietzsche says something of kindlness about man.

> What alone can be our doctrine? That no one gives man his quali-
> ties—neither God, nor society, nor his parents and ancestors, nor he
> himself. . . . No one is responsible for man's being there at all, for his
> being such-and-such, or for his being in these circumstances or in this
> environment. . . . It is absurd to wish to devolve one's essence on some
> end or other. (Nietzsche, *TI*, p. 500)

He frequently says something similar about human greatness, as if not to possess an essence, a kind or end, were humanity's uniqueness. It is absurd to give one's being over to one's kind, to let oneself be contained by one's form or kind.

Yet Nietzsche also frequently speaks of man the animal.

> We no longer derive man from "the spirit" or "the deity"; we have placed
> him back among the animals. We consider him the strongest animal
> because he is the most cunning: his spirituality is a consequence of this.
> On the other hand, we oppose the vanity that would raise its head again
> here too—as if man had been the great hidden purpose of the evolution
> of the animals. Man is by no means the crown of creation: every living
> being stands beside him on the same level of perfection. And even this is
> saying too much: relatively speaking, man is the most bungled of all the
> animals, the sickliest, and not one has strayed more dangerously from its
> instincts. But for all that, he is of course the most *interesting*. (*A*, 580)

Well, maybe he is or isn't. Maybe women and slime molds are interesting in their own ways. And dirt. This is to speak in kindlness against the tyr-anny of kinds, usually and incessantly the tyranny of Man the God whose Kind rules over all other kinds, rather than in care and fulguration.

Nietzsche appears to suggest that essence contains and destroys the vitality and life of "man." Yet he does not deny human beings their quali-ties, only their tyranny. It is absurd to make one's essence dependent on the limits of kinds—on their restricted economies. But no one speaks more of general economy than Nietzsche: the profusion of instincts and bodily forces, uncontainable by spirit. General economy has no name, certainly not the name of spirit. Kinds express both this unnameability and the determinate profusion of names.

Returning to Hegel, who I understand to speak as much as Nietzsche of general economy in terms of kinds, the unlimit and nonneutrality of kinds, everywhere in nature and humanity, the uncontainability of spirit fulgurating in every grain and particle, still uncontainable. Yet contained in and by the humanity of spirit, refused to animals and other creatures.

I might have said this before, but I say it now. If the world is God's world, and God is infinitely good and infinitely creative, then that goodness and creativity, infinitely uncontainable and unmasterable, the infinite mark of the divine, are present in every grain and particle, every creature and thing, which outstrips every tyranny and rule.[2] Western thought has largely denied this picture of things, partly under Aquinas's reinstitution of the tyranny of form, perhaps more insistently under the spread of European trade and world conquest. Everything contains the infinite plenitude of God, including Africans, women, and animals, but European man may rule, under God, as if God. The tyranny of kinds is the attempt to contain the uncontainability of kinds.

Named as such in Hegel, in a circular movement that reinstates the domination of humankind. Always the domination of some kind. As if by the will of God.

I interpose an interruption in the name of the neutrality of kinds, as if we might be and think without kindlness and genealogy, with neutrality. I pause for a moment to undertake a thought of natural kinds as if we may neutrally think of individuals and kinds, without ranking or responsibility, neglecting historical dominations and violence. We might have understood Leibniz's rule of God in neutral ways, God the great neutralizer. Yet the eye that falls upon the sparrow and the child falls with tenderness and love. Even so, the rule of God, never without neutrality, imposes a totality indistinguishable from the neuter, assembling all the precious things of the world under divine governance regardless of their harm.

In a secular universe, after God, it seems that atoms and particles and their kinds impose a different kind of question, not which kinds are better and worse, which high and low, domination and violence, but how do we tell? How can we be sure? Which of the kinds that come to our attention can we trust?—again without neutrality, restricted to truth.

The question of kinds for Quine and Putnam is not what in the nature and being of individuals is universal and more, named as kind, irresistible resistance to neutrality, but what can we know, what confirms an induction, in kind? I use their discussions as examples of a discourse that insists on its own neutrality in a movement against neutrality.

Quine begins his article on "Natural Kinds" with the question: "What confirms an induction?" (Quine, *NK*, 155). He alludes to two "puzzles": Hempel's puzzle of the non-black non-ravens, and Goodman's puzzle of the grue emeralds.

> Hempel's puzzle is that just as each black raven tends to confirm the law that all ravens are black, so each green leaf, being a non-black, non-raven, should tend to confirm the law that all non-black things are non-ravens, . . . What is paradoxical is that a green leaf should count toward the law that all ravens are black. (p. 155)

> Goodman . . . proposes to call anything *grue* that is examined today or earlier and found to be green or is not examined before tomorrow and is blue [not green]. Should we expect the first one examined tomorrow to be green, because all examined up to now were green? But all examined up to now were also grue; so why not expect the first one tomorrow to be grue, and therefore blue? (pp. 155–56)

These have become famous "puzzles" of induction, taken thereby to relate to kinds. Do black ravens compose a kind where non-black non-ravens do not? Do green emeralds compose a kind where grue emeralds do not? What composes a kind?

I have approached these questions in terms of trust. Which of the kinds, or at least the labels purporting to name kinds, can we trust? Which relations are reliable? I suppose it is worth wondering whether that is what kinds are for, to meet our trust, to be reliable. Why might kinds—think for a moment less of ravens and emeralds than of racial and gender kinds—be expected to confirm our inductions, to maintain our trust, rather than to transform our relations to others and ourselves? Whoever we are, in our own kinds.

I have approached these questions in terms of trust because I take for granted that they can be given no neutral answer, that we come to epistemological issues of kinds as we come to every such issue, from the situated concerns in which we as inquirers occupy places in the world. What appears to be at stake is an image of knowledge, most likely scientific knowledge, that provides classifications and taxonomy, achieves confirmation, independent of the desires of social and historical human beings who engage in scientific inquiries—and, where relevant, independent of the human beings who may be so classified and confirmed. Objectivity and neutrality are taken for granted in this view of science regardless of arguments suggesting that such a view has historically come at the expense of women and other kinds of humans, whose classification is never neutral and never objective, and which has been passed off as such at their expense. To which I respond—the purpose of this overarching project—that it may come at the expense as well of ravens and emeralds and other natural things and kinds.

The issue, Quine notes, is one of similarity, and he is famous for his critiques of similarity—synonymy in meaning, for example, related to analytic and synthetic statements. Here he appears to take similarity for granted. "The notion of kind and the notion of similarity seemed to be substantially one notion" (p. 159). If similarity is problematic, fundamentally, then so is the idea of kind. Yet, "A standard of similarity is in some sense innate. This point is not against empiricism; it is a commonplace of behavioral psychology" (p. 162). It might indeed be innate, or perhaps enforced by social codes. The question is not so much whether "we" must think in kinds, but at what expense we pass off their social and ethical neutrality. Ravens and emeralds keep their counsel. Women and minorities are another matter. Molly splashes sand.

"We have seen that a sense of similarity or of kinds is fundamental to learning in the widest sense—to language learning, to induction, to expectation . . . and further irreducible" (p. 168). In other words, kinds express something fundamental and irreducible in human life and thought—regardless of their neutrality. Yet "one's sense of similarity or one's system of kinds develops and changes and even turns multiple as one matures, making perhaps for increasingly dependable prediction. . . . Things are similar in the later or theoretical sense to the degree that they are interchangeable parts of the cosmic machine revealed by science" (p. 171). I cannot imagine a stronger sense of the domination of science here, a stronger resistance to kindlness, especially if we think in terms of social rather than mechanical kinds. Maturity in relation to race, class, and gender is not a product of a world picture of human taxonomy composed of interchangeable parts. Why, then, without at least some reflection on the maturity described, should we assume a world picture of a cosmic machine with interchangeable parts made up of emeralds and ravens? Could it be true that atoms and particles—electrons and neutrons—are not entirely interchangeable, but that we allow our ignorance to blind us to other possibilities? Or, for that matter, our knowledge. What but infinite care for every individual particle and kind would compel us to undertake the kinds of reflections that might give us another view of the cosmic machine?

Leibniz, after all, holds a diametrically opposite position on the uniqueness and singularity of the parts that make up the cosmic machine. More than anyone he reminds us that it is God's machine, precious and infinite. Compared with this, Quine's view is God's without infinity. "In general we can take it as a very special mark of the maturity of a branch of science that it no longer needs an irreducible notion of similarity and kind. It is that final stage where the animal vestige is wholly absorbed into the theory" (p. 174). The maturity of humanity, marked by scientific knowledge, is given by leaving the animal vestige behind, by "the evolution of unreason into science" (p. 175), always at the expense of animals as a kind.

If Leibniz holds a different view of the cosmic machine, filled everywhere with creatures, he is nevertheless the model for all the views of that machine that insist on neutrality. In a secular age God's care becomes no care at all, merely the God's-eye view, lofty and without concern for any that might be harmed in man's maturity. Quine's cosmic machine is reminiscent of Leibniz. Other neutral views of kinds follow Leibniz in other ways.

I am speaking of possible worlds. I take Putnam as my example here though others might prefer Kripke. Putnam's example is *water*, which comes to possess what Quine calls *scientific maturity*. We imagine that we can recognize water by its properties—liquid, colorless, and so on—but do not know that it is H_2O. We imagine another possible world in which it possesses other properties, XYZ. Does it change in its properties from world to world? The answer depends on science, not on the profuse and precarious nature of things: "Suppose, now, that I discover the microstructure of water—that water is H_2O. At this point I will be able to say that the stuff on Twin Earth that I earlier *mistook* for water isn't really water. . . . Once we have discovered that water (in the actual world) is H_2O, *nothing counts as a possible world in which water isn't H_2O*" (p. 130). We may remind ourselves that Freud describes his audience of scientists as sure that they can tell a woman from a man, insisting on doing so. And perhaps some scientists can tell an African American from a Caucasian, an Aryan from a Jew, insisting on doing so. Perhaps wherever we say that "nothing counts" we have passed off neutrality as anything but neutral.

Leibniz speaks of infinite numbers of possible worlds against neutrality. One of the infinite number is best. That is one extreme refusal of neutrality, given by totality. Yet I think that totality and neutrality are inseparable, that God's rule but not God's care takes hold. What if in the infinite multiplicity of possible worlds, filled with infinite creatures and things, never a smallest, never a greatest, and never anything neutral; what if in this infinite infinity, everything was precious, lovely, singular and kind, something to admire, cherish, mourn for its passing? Even where it harmed others. In its imperfections. The wonder of God's machines. What if in this infinite infinity, kinds expressed not what is common, but what we can trust, where *trust* is an ethical and political term to which we bring infinite questions and responsibilities? Kindlness resistant to neutrality and reliability.

I return from this interruption for the sake of neutrality—never I hope to undertake another—to the non-neutrality of kinds, mightily expressed by Hegel. At the expense, as always, of animals, and plants: everything nonhuman. Man alone, not the animals, knows the universal in himself, the universal in the universal, knows himself as "I."

> [I]t is man who first makes himself double so as to be a universal for a universal. This first happens when man knows he is "I." By the term "I" I mean myself, a single and altogether determinate person. And yet I really utter nothing peculiar to myself, for every one else is an "I" or "ego," and when I call myself "I," though I indubitably mean the single person myself, I express a thorough universal. (Hegel, *EL*, 49)

A universality cursed by death, justifying humanity's domination of animals.

> It is in the kind that the individual animal has its notion: and the kind liberates itself from this individuality by death. (p. 52)
>
> Next comes the Curse . . . that turns chiefly on the contrast between man and nature. Man must work in the sweat of his brow: and woman bring forth in sorrow. . . . The beasts have nothing more to do but to pick up the materials required to satisfy their wants: man on the contrary can only satisfy his wants by himself producing and transforming the necessary means.
>
> To such extent as man is and acts like a creature of nature, his whole behaviour is what it ought not to be. For the spirit it is a duty to be free, and to realise itself by its own act. Nature is for man only the starting-point which he has to transform. (p. 56)

Hegel describes the curse of kinds as clearly here as possible. The universality of humanity's kind depends on the exclusion of animals. Human freedom is marked by the contrast with animal necessity, unable to know the universality of its universality. The animal is neither "I" nor animal in the sense that it is not cursed by that knowledge, free in that curse.

I am as certain of the curse as I am of anything—which is to say, not certain at all of what it portends. Nor how we have understood it or lived with it: the curse of humankind—like the wandering Jew—that marks humanity's superiority. Why not understand this entire account of the curse as the curse of mastery, the master's superiority over the slave as a double curse: the curse of the superiority that takes the curse as truth?

Man as spirit is *absolutely not* a creature of nature. Yet the movement of spirit returns to nature. Could we understand this return as expressing a truth that there was nothing to leave, no absolute difference, that the curse marks kinds with the mark of death and with the curse that we take the curse as truth? Hegel speaks directly to this, I believe, later in the *Encyclopedia Logic*, first in a famous passage that appears to me to contradict every narrow reading of the inclusiveness of spirit, including the superiority of humans over animals. "Logic shows that the subjective which is to be subjective only, the finite which would be finite only, the infinite which would be infinite only, and so on, have no truth, but contradict themselves, and pass over into their opposites" (§214, p. 355). Every *only* marks alienation, abstraction, emptiness, including every superiority. Every height, every domination, rests on exclusion. Only men. Only spirit. Not also animals, plants. Inclusiveness is the return from *only*. To which we who are wary of the privilege of the dialectic may respond that we do not know why such an inclusion does not overcome superiority, does not eliminate neutrality. In the name of life rather than spirit. Cursing the curse.

Individuals in their universal nature participate in their kind, leading Hegel to gender. "The living individual, . . . is now therefore implicitly a Kind, with essential universality of nature. The particularising of this Kind is the relation of the living subject to another subject of its Kind: and the judgment is the tie of Kind over these individuals thus appointed for each other. This is the Affinity of the Sexes" (§220, p. 361). Kind is tie and affinity, linking man and woman, male and female, by genealogy, in blood. Why not human and animal, animal and plant, human and stone? The affinity of the sexes is not their commonality but the heterogeneous infinity in kind that presupposes universality in nature, the infinity and abundance of kinds. In ethical terms, the infinite in each kind is that which is more than what is common, and different, whatever, the source of debt and responsibility, in kind. Responsibility is kind|ness, impossible without the kind.

In this way, Hegel speaks of kinds beyond their commonality—especially including the commonality of their name—and beyond their neutrality. Whatever one thinks of the domination of spirit, it is touched by something excessive, beyond measure. Much more than measure. Which is not another, grander measure but something otherwise, in the kind|ness of kinds

I believe that Hegel speaks to the otherwise than being in the name of kinds, and that it behooves us to listen. If the good is otherwise than being, in interruption and exposure, then perhaps we may think of what is otherwise, what is infinite in its call, as *singulars and kinds, saying and said*: language and corporeal expression. Singular things express themselves, are expressed everywhere in and as the kinds in which they participate, which constitute them. The affinity of the sexes, with its fearful risks, is propinquity, profoundly relevant to individual things in their kinds. Genealogy is one expression of this kindlness; geography is another. Kinds inhabit their places, always on the move, nomadic, wandering, in place. Exposure is geography, in place, always elsewhere.

I hold geography in abeyance for a chapter. I turn to the world ordered in kinds, in multitudinous profusion.

CHAPTER 4

Ordering Kinds

The fundamental codes of a culture—those governing its language, its schemas of perception, its exchanges, its techniques, its values, the hierarchy of its practices—establish for every man, from the very first, the empirical orders with which he will be dealing and within which he will be at home. At the other extremity of thought, there are the scientific theories or the philosophical interpretations which explain why order exists in general, what universal laws it obeys, what principle can account for it, and why this particular order has been established and not some other. But between these two regions, so distant from one another, lies a domain which, even though its role is mainly an intermediary one, is nonetheless fundamental: . . .

. . . Thus, in every culture, between the use of what one might call the ordering codes and reflections upon order itself, there is the pure experience of order and of its modes of being. (Foucault, *OT*, xx–xxi)

The epic scope of Foucault's discussions in *The Order of Things* requires that I restrict my focus to a narrow window onto that work, excluding—not without violence—some of its most important themes. Not without violence, I restrict myself here to what he says of order, knowing that *The Order of Things* is the title of the English translation, that the French—*Le mots et les choses*—does not speak of order but of words. Nor do I mean to speak except in passing of the sovereign subject and object of representation.[1]

I would explore the idea of order, including the middle region of order itself, given form in classical representation in taxonomies of kinds. Foucault describes a "Chinese encyclopaedia," found in Borges, as expressing a world ordered in kinds, and how bewildering it may be to think of such an order at its limits.

This passage quotes a "certain Chinese encyclopaedia" in which it is written that "animals are divided into: (a) belonging to the Emperor,

(b) embalmed, (c) tame, (d) suckling pigs, (e) sirens, (f) fabulous, (g) stray dogs, (h), included in the present classification, (i) frenzied, (j) innumerable, (k) drawn with a very fine camelhair brush, (l) *et cetera*, (m) having just broken the water pitcher, (n) that from a long way off look like flies." In the wonderment of this taxonomy, the thing we apprehend in one great leap, the thing that, by means of the fable, is demonstrated as the exotic charm of another system of thought, is the limitation of our own, the stark impossibility of thinking *that*. (Foucault, *OT*, xv)

I take the stark impossibility of thinking *that* to insist on the irresistible necessity of thinking something else, *otherwise*, though that may be an oversimplification. In any case, the impossibility belongs to language. "[W]here could they ever meet, except in the immaterial sound of the voice pronouncing their enumeration, or on the page transcribing it? Where else could they be juxtaposed except in the non-place of language?" (p. xvii). This language, with its non-place, its impossibilities and necessities, marks its separation from the world. And that may be the point. For paralleling the emergence of Man the Subject in modern life is the withdrawal of language from nature to representation: no longer a thing of the world. And paralleling the subsequent disappearance of Man is the return of language to the world from "the imperious unity of Discourse" (p. 386). The crucial phrase is "the non-place of language," as if language uniquely knew or announced its non-place, at least in French, English, and Spanish if not Chinese.

What, indeed, is so strange about the Chinese encyclopaedia? Forgetting language for the moment, perhaps for longer, can we let pass the claim, without question, that it represents something impossible to think? Or say? For us? For a Chinese? "There would appear to be, then, at the other extremity of the earth we inhabit, a culture entirely devoted to the ordering of space, but one that does not distribute the multiplicity of existing things into any of the categories that make it possible for us to name, speak, and think" (p. xix). Is there something European in the nature of intelligibility that is now taken for granted but that once might not have been so, and—marked by the word *Chinese*—may not be so *elsewhere*? Some find in classical Chinese taxonomies orderings unintelligible to a European gaze, perhaps to a contemporary Chinese gaze. If we take such a claim for granted. Thinking *that*—unintelligibility.

The issue is of kinds, doubly expressed as genealogy—at least two kinds of genealogies: the hierarchical trees that capture the movements and identities of families and kinds; and the historical disruption of such movements. Traditional and Nietzschean genealogy. Such a pairing, however liberating, fails to express its own geography. I said that I would recall the geography of kinds, something of Chinese, African, nomadic kinds. I defer geography together with geophilosophy to the next chapter.

Here, however, the Chinese encyclopaedia without geography means something very different. With geography, expressing the possibility that Chinese thought might be very different from European thought, including the most radical European thought, the encyclopaedia speaks to what every taxonomy must fail to express—something of locality and contingency. Without geography, the encyclopaedia speaks to the endless excesses of representation and language—neutrally, without cultural specificity. If they can be spoken. If with neutrality. If we can live without geography.

In *the prose of the world*, named from Merleau-Ponty, Foucault describes a world of kinds and meanings in abundance, a world filled with signs and portents of God, throughout and everywhere. Everything echoes, mirrors, everything else.[2] He understands this infinite profusion as founded on the same—as I would understand it, a same of endless heterogeneity. Sympathy multiplied repeatedly by antipathy. Yet that is not quite what he says. "By means of this interplay, the world remains identical; resemblances continue to be what they are, and to resemble one another. The same remains the same, riveted onto itself" (Foucault, *OT*, 25).

Elsewhere, he describes another yet perhaps a similar same:

> The univocity of being, its singleness of expression, is paradoxically the principal condition which permits difference to escape the domination of identity, which frees it from the law of the Same as a simple opposition within conceptual elements. Being can express itself in the same way, because difference is no longer submitted to the prior deduction of categories; because it is not distributed inside a diversity that can always be perceived; because it is not organized in a conceptual hierarchy of species and genus. Being is that which is always said of difference; it is the *Recurrence* of difference. (Foucault, *TP*, p. 192)

This wonderful passage, within Foucault's reading of Deleuze,[3] expresses and demands resistance to the tyranny of the same, to regarding kinds as no more than what is common, located in another same—the univocity of being, its profusion, multiplicity, and repetition. Its impurity and heterogeneity. The endless repetition of difference—mirrors, signs, images, and echoes—is resistance to the tyranny of identity.[4] The prose of the world is a world of infinite profusion in individuals and kinds, multiplied everywhere by the mirrors that express and mark them. Corporeal expression is God's love of the world, in abundance.[5]

I hold species in abeyance for a while, postponing the possibility that they express excess: more than a tyranny of the same, otherwise than hierarchy and order. The kind|red|ness of species interrupting their taxonomy. As genealogy.

To speak of the same is to speak of kinds, though kinds are much more than what is common. And it is Foucault's understanding of kinds that defines the center of my discussion here. The taxonomy of kinds in classical representation sacrifices the excesses of language to order. In contrast, Foucault describes the prose of the world as unfolding a world of abundance and profusion, everywhere filled with excess and expression. Yet his reading of the prose of the world, understood as the same riveted onto itself, exposes another sacrifice of the excesses of kinds in the gesture in which it explodes in profusion.

> [T]here are the same number of fishes in the water as there are animals, or objects produced by nature or man, on the land. . . . [A]nd lastly, there are the same number of beings in the whole of creation as may be found eminently contained in God himself, "the Sower of Existence, of Power, of Knowledge and of Love." Thus, by this linking of resemblance with space, this "convenience" that brings like things together and makes adjacent things similar, the world is linked together like a chain. (Foucault, *OT*, 18–19)

We can count the fish, the animals, the things contrived by human beings, all the same number as the number contained in God, suggesting perhaps that this number is not a dead, inert, neutral measure, but living, pulsing, power, knowledge, and love, in fish, animals, and artifacts, also in mollusks and stones. (Molly laughs: she is sometimes taken for a stone.)

This picture of the great chain of being leaves out the explosive volatility of an infinite mirror mirrored and mirroring, making adjacent what can have no number but unlimit, nonnumber. Spinoza's God and Nature link the world in a infinitely infinite chain, filled with the abundance of infinitely infinite kinds. If mirroring is the same, then mirrors fastened to themselves, mirroring each other's mirrors, do not rivet the same onto itself but explode it into profusion. The prose of the world is volatile, disruptive, infinitely infinite, and more. Everything everywhere answers endlessly to everything else, heterogeneous and impure. Foucault leaves out God. Yet even the god who governs all the answers, who represents the same to which everything answers everywhere, is infinitely infinite, beyond gathering and number. We see this in Spinoza and Leibniz, though Leibniz insists on a totality within the profusion that sacrifices and destroys without responsibility. God's totality restricts the abundance without debt. Totality sacrifices abundance to neutrality.

Could this be the challenge of the Chinese encyclopaedia, that in some undefined, neutral way, something of the plenitude of kinds, expressed in such a strange and wonderful gathering, is said to be impossible to think without taking responsibility for thinking it? In the prose of the world, where everything answers to everything else, and especially where language, thought, and representation all pertain to that world in its profusion, answering to answering to answering, what could we say or think is impossible to think or say? Could this impossibility be something we must absolutely refuse in the name of a neutrality without responsibility? Or take responsibility for in the name of *mimēsis*?

Foucault speaks both of nature's expressiveness and of the need to restrict its movement, to rivet it in place.

> And yet the system is not closed. One aperture remains: and through it the whole interplay of resemblances would be in danger of escaping from itself, or of remaining hidden in darkness. . . .
>
> *Convenientia, aemulatio, analogy,* and *sympathy* tell us how the world must fold in upon itself, reflect itself, or form a chain with itself so that things can resemble one another. They tell us that the paths of similitude are and the directions they take; but not where it is, how one sees it, or by what mark it may be recognized. (Foucault, *OT*, 26)

The aperture must be closed within the infinite play of openings and resemblances that mark each other in ways beyond the order any system can impose. Foucault describes the prose of the world as a system of marks and expressions, throughout nature in memory of God, that would appear to be too much, too excessive, beyond even the excesses of language. Signatures, resemblances, all forms of the same multiply in profusion, as I would put it, everything citing, coding, expressing everything else. I would return us to nature's expressiveness, *mimēsis*, where endless echoes and mirrors and resemblances mirror and echo anything anywhere, expressing a God without limits, nature unlimited. The same is everywhere different, claims the same in profusion. The prose of the world is the earth's abundance in expression.

We may think of this profusion under the curse, as Foucault asks us to do. Yet it is a curse we have never witnessed before or elsewhere: profusion, abundance, cursed by expression, *mimēsis*.

> Every resemblance receives a signature; but this signature is no more than an intermediate form of the same resemblance. As a result, the totality of these marks, sliding over the great circle of similitudes, forms a second circle which would be an exact duplication of the first, point by point, were it not for that tiny degree of displacement which causes the sign of sympathy to reside in an analogy, that of analogy in emulation, that of emulation in convenience, which in turn requires the mark of sympathy for its recognition. The signature and what it denotes are of exactly the same nature; it is merely that they obey a different law of distribution; the pattern from which they are cut is the same. (p. 29)

We might add, with univocity in mind, that the "same nature" would appear to resist all the restrictions that form and syntax impose. The world together with its signatures explode in volatile profusion, filled with expression. Spinoza may be the only traditional philosopher who allows this infinite its infinity, knowing that in the ways in which things are bound to each other, in infinite profusion, something of God's and nature's ethics resounds. Still cursed.

The role Foucault gives to signs is of closing the circle, though every indication is that signs, expressions, including the movements of language, tear open the fabric of the world, exploding every attempt to contain it. *Mimēsis* again, with its different faces, general and restricted economy. "And what other sign is there that two things are linked to one another unless it is that they have a mutual attraction for each other, . . . that there is an affinity and, as it were, a sympathy between them?" (p. 28). What of the possibility that every thing in every place has affinities for other things in other places? That sympathy and affinity know no bounds? Foucault speaks of the ways in which sympathy can restrict, can curse the plenitude with exclusion, closing down the profusion at its heart. He speaks much less of the ways in which the profusion breaks out of every limit that would contain it. "To search for a meaning is to bring to light a resemblance. To search for the law governing signs is to discover the things that are alike. . . . 'Nature' is trapped in the thin layer that holds semiology and hermeneutics one above the other" (p. 29). Nature is imprisoned under the curse; the endless plethora of multiple marks and mirrors and signs of infinite signs and mirrors and marks is empty.

> First and foremost, the plethoric yet absolutely poverty-stricken character of this knowledge. Plethoric because it is limitless. Resemblance never remains stable within itself; it can be fixed only if it refers back to another similitude, which then, in turn, refers to others; each resemblance, therefore, has value only from the accumulation of all the others, and the whole world must be explored if even the slightest of analogies is to be justified and finally take on the appearance of certainty. . . . And for this reason, from its very foundations, this knowledge will be a thing of sand. (p. 30)

A knowledge that insists on justification cannot stand before the heterogeneity of the world. The infinite collapses knowledge—I would say, a certain purity of knowledge—into nothing. And what of kinds, the profusion of the kinds of things in nature, the kinds of things under God, the kinds that pertain to human beings? The principle that nature is knowable insists that kinds demand taxonomy, order: *mathesis, taxonomy, genesis*. Yet it also expresses the infinite beauties of God's infinite kinds that inhabit and compose infinite orders, all themselves expressive.

Foucault describes the end of the prose of the world as emerging in a double movement of the order and excesses of language. I believe this double movement was restricted to language at a moment in which something more superabundant than language shone on the horizon and marked with the curse the rule of kinds against which Foucault's archaeology and genealogy are deployed. Much of this can be seen in Foucault, narrated as the fortunes of language. "It is rather an opaque, mysterious thing, closed in upon itself, a fragmented mass, its enigma renewed in every interval, which combines here and there with the forms of the world and becomes interwoven with them" (p. 34): infinite, unbounded, profuse truths of marks and marked, mirrors and mirrored, volatile and profuse. Language undergoes a transformation, a curse, in which it closes onto itself at the moment that it is woven among the forms of the world, trapped together with nature in the thin layer that meaning forms on the surface of things. Leaving behind, perhaps, the trace of a moment in history in which God's infinitely infinite marks and revelations pervaded nature and natural things in every place and thing, no matter how small or large. The order of the prose of the world was transformed from the abundance of language and world into something thin and imperious. Language and world were cursed by order. And blessed.

Foucault understands this ordering of language as a peculiarly modern phenomenon. Yet we have seen that form and language joined much earlier in Greece to impose order on things. I am inclined to read the prose of the world, certain medieval moments in relation to the beauties of nature and God, as promising—at least for the moment—another, infinite, sense of order in which the sacrifice of order demanded by the syntax of language is itself sacrificed to God's abundance. An order in which nothing makes impossible the impossibility of the Chinese encyclopedia, but presents us with its enigmatic fascination as something to admire. Such an order would not recognize the poverty of the plethora, would not recognize and participate in the curse. And, indeed, that refusal might be another curse.

Abundance does not abolish restriction, does not substitute destruction for structure. It interrupts its rule. Even in a world of infinite variety, everything resembling, marking, mirroring everything else, one must choose to live as one must live to choose. The question is always, with what necessities and what authorities? The prose of the world, in its abundance of resemblances and signs, promises life and choice without authority, filled with beauty, possibilities close to Nietzsche. Yet God remains just out of sight, everywhere, offering infinite authority. Perhaps that is the curse of a tradition that, at least for a while, exploded the possibility of any authority. Under the Church's authority.

And so we do not escape authority, but transform it. And the form of that transformation is from the authorities that bear the rule of God in a world of volatility to authorities that vest in men rather than women, that subordinate and denigrate bodies, sometimes torture and kill them, frequently women. Even so, they possessed limited authority for their own authority. Moreover, the secularization of this authority paradoxically brought a more authoritarian authority, insisting on the governance of reason and, in Foucault's account, on the rule of language, like God standing apart from the world. "In the seventeenth and eighteenth centuries, the peculiar existence and ancient solidity of language as a thing inscribed in the fabric of the world were dissolved in the functioning of representation; all language had value only as discourse" (Foucault, *OT*, 43). Language was separated from the world, made into truthful discourse, given its own autonomy, sacrificed into literature, as *mimēsis*.

> Through literature, the being of language shines once more on the frontiers of Western culture—and at its centre—for it is what has been most foreign to that culture since the sixteenth century. . . . [H]enceforth, language was to grow with no point of departure, no end, and no promise. It is the traversal of this futile yet fundamental space that the text of literature traces from day to day. (p. 44)

The moment with which I am concerned here is the system of kinds Foucault describes in the great quadrilateral of classical representation. I have spoken elsewhere of this archaeological|genealogical|geographical moment in which language was seized in a grip that bounded its movements, only to break out again and again—especially in literature—in the excesses of its limits.[6] I understand representation as the expression of things that gather into kinds, expressed in language, in exposure and proximity, in propinquity. I understand representation as *mimēsis*, given from the good, in debt, resisting injustice and neutrality, exceeding and multiplying every repetition. Classical representation is a particular episode—a restricted economy—in the life and history of a representation that exceeds every location, an economy defined by two predominant conditions. The first is the separation of representation from nature.

> In the Classical age, nothing is given that is not given to representation; but, by that very fact, no sign ever appears, no word is spoken, no proposition is every directed at any content except by the action of a representation that stands back from itself, that duplicates and reflects itself in another representation that is its equivalent. (p. 78)

Representation is everywhere, doubled and redoubled, except in that which is represented, from which representation withdraws, separating language from things. Order belongs to things everywhere, separate from the things themselves, separating things from kinds.

For the second condition is that the world so represented is ordered by classification under several linked and parallel systems: natural order, wealth, and language. If we think of these as economies, systems of exchange and reproduction, if we extend the notion of economy from wealth and money to natural creatures and things and words, then these are the restricted economies of the modern world under whose reign the totality of the human and natural world is subordinated. The condition that everything is given to representation is a condition of totality and authority, utterly neutral and objective, without location or value. Or so it seems. Classical representation presents itself as the totality of representation, a restricted economy standing in for the general economy of expression and propinquity.

The great systems of order that define classical representation are language, classification, and wealth. The systems of order that emerge from classical representation are history, biology, economics, and linguistics. This classification marks an *episteme*, divided by disciplinary classifications. Knowledge is divided into disciplines around the transcendental—or quasi-transcendental—conditions that define Man. Who will disappear when language returns to its profusion, disrupting the systems of classification. Or when representation returns to the teeming world from its closure under the figure of Man.

I have told the latter story elsewhere. As I have said. The story I am interested in exploring here is that of taxonomy, the classification of kinds. Classical representation is representation by classification; the abundance of things and kinds is submitted in the name of knowledge to classification, the taxonomy of living things presented in their natural history as a history of kinds.

> For natural history to appear, it was not necessary for nature to become denser and more obscure, to multiply its mechanisms to the point of acquiring the opaque weight of a history that can only be retraced and described, without any possibility of measuring it, calculating it, or explaining it; it was necessary—and this was entirely the opposite—for History to become Natural. . . . *birds*; . . . *plants*; . . . *serpents and dragons*; . . . *quadrupeds*. (Foucault, *OT*, 128)

Named as kinds.[7] In exclusion.

> Natural history did not become possible because men looked harder and more closely. One might say, strictly speaking, that the Classical age used its ingenuity, if not to see as little as possible, at least to restrict deliberately the area of its experience. (p. 132)

> In this way, a grid can be laid out over the entire vegetable or animal kingdom. Each group can be given a name. With the result that any species, without having to be described, can be designated with the greatest accuracy by means of the names of the different groups in which it is included. (p. 141)

Such a system, such a structure of classification, bears the weight of two related problems: continuity—"there must be continuity in nature" (Foucault, *OT*, 146)—and monstrosity, expression of the curse. The monster, the catastrophe, that which is excluded from the classification, is absolutely required as its condition. "The monster ensures in time, and for our theoretical knowledge, a continuity that, for our everyday experience, floods, volcanoes, and subsiding continents confine in space" (p. 156). Or release. Explode. The system that would define totality and its limits must include—confine and find impossible to contain—what cannot be included. Hegel's principle again, in a different register. The kind, the many kinds, linked and classified and graded, are much more, demand much more, exceed every commonality they establish. Inclusion and exclusion; the inclusion of exclusion. As curse, impurity, abjection.

I interrupt this eighteenth-century sense of biological order and excess with a more contemporary representation of species diversity, another play of restriction and uncontainability.

> *[A] species is a population whose members are able to interbreed freely under natural conditions. . . .*
> This says that hybrids bred from two kinds of animals in captivity or two kinds of plants cultivated in a garden, are not enough to classify them as a member of a single species. (Wilson, *DL*, 38)

A species constitutes a kind whose members interbreed, where the species is composed of its members but where the individuals are multiply constituted by their species: in their qualities and lives but especially through reproduction. Sexuality and reproduction constitute the being of species. (Molly laughs suggestively.)

Biology tells us that species do not mingle and participate in profusion, do not mix lineage and blood. Animal DNA is pure. Except for strange and difficult mechanisms in cancers and microorganisms that recurrently scramble their genetic materials, making them better predators and less vulnerable prey. Wilson's restrictive qualification—not hybrids bred in captivity, garden plants; perhaps also laboratory hybrids, impurities, and monstrosities—explodes into profusion. The world is composed of an abundance of living species marked by reproductive strategies that maintain purity where advantageous, or impurity where that is advantageous, which utilize biological codes—living, corporeal expressions of repetition and variation—to promote the perpetuation of their kinds. A swirling profusion of living kinds adapting, changing, transforming themselves to endure; but where endurance is mobility and transformation, impurity.

I leave aside, at least for the moment, some of the amazing mechanisms that promote natural selection and are its result. I pursue the possibility that natural selection can select on anything, does so fitfully and frequently incoherently, unpredictably, but more important does so always in relation to family and kind, in lineage and blood—with DNA and RNA the blood. Does so powerfully and effectively, producing new and remarkable kinds. Natural selection is radical genealogy perpetuating, promulgating, and generating novel kinds. Natural selection is *mimēsis*, the expression of things in the world in kinds, repetitive and novel kinds. Kinds are the *mimēsis* of natural things—their kind|red|ness and kind|ness

I would not then link natural selection too closely with biological abundance for fear that it would embody another exclusion, celebrating the organizing and emergent powers of life at the expense of inanimate things, as if inorganic things were dead, or celebrating the kinds there are over the kinds that might be.[8] Perhaps we need to remember that if inanimate things are machines, they are machines with unbounded possibilities, always more than what we may expect from them as what they have in common with other machines. Configurations, twists, many contingent factors multiply the kinds inherent in every kind, mingling kinds together among the inorganic and partly organic materials of natural things and kinds. Every individual thing participates in kinds and kinds of kinds, inhabits environments and environments of environments, habitats of habitats, filled with transformations and possibilities; configurations, structures, classifiable and ordered; exceeding any given order.

The biological world is an ordering of species whose task is to perpetuate themselves by changing themselves; which do so by guarding and transforming the precious biological codes that define them.

> Biological diversity—"biodiversity" in the new parlance—is the key to the maintenance of the world as we know it. Life in a local site struck down by a passing storm springs back quickly because enough diversity still exists. opportunistic species evolved for just such an occasion rush in to fill the spaces. They entrain the succession that circles back to something resembling the original state of the environment. (Wilson, *DL*, 15)

Equilibrium, one might say, strangely incongruous with the emphasis on diversity. Univocity, I might say, where *something resembling* means impurity, multiplication and variation.

Opportunistic species are frequently the most adaptive. Some viruses and other microorganisms adapt with amazing speed to changing circumstances that threaten their survival—the survival, it must be said, of the species rather than the individual, though without their members the species are nothing.

Could one name of the diversity of life be the univocity of being, abundance in the earth? Could it be given other names, countless names in profusion? Wilson speaks of *biophilia* and wilderness, other names, perhaps, for cherishment and abundance in kinds, for kindlness. "Wilderness settles peace on the soul because it needs no help; it is beyond human contrivance. Wilderness is a metaphor of unlimited opportunity, rising from the tribal memory of a time when humanity spread across the world, valley to valley, island to island, godstruck, firm in the belief that virgin land when on forever past the horizon" (Wilson, *DL*, 350–51). An image of colonial expansion not without contamination. Yet let wilderness be abundance, let it reach out across every horizon, across valleys and islands, crossing from person to person, inner and outer boundaries and thresholds, abundance in the earth, here and there, disrupting every border. Including the borders between kinds and species. Under the curse. Paying endless restitution.

Expressed as the abundance and expressivity of kinds, species, of natural and human kinds, all adaptive, mobile, and profuse, each in its own ways struggling to maintain its borders—maintain them by transforming them, itself, and its members. Through life and through death. It is too late to hold any of these boundaries fixed, including the boundary between living and nonliving, inorganic and organic kinds. Living things fill every pore and crevice of the earth, incorporate every kind of inorganic molecule, put them in circulation. Biodiversity is natural diversity. As it has always been. For all these biological species, swirling in adaptive profusion, emerged from the welter of elements and compounds, astronomical and planetary objects. Natural diversity promises biological diversity; and more, beyond the living things we know, unimaginable possibilities of life, and death, and more.

Within devastation and extinction. Abundance is not big or small, is not diminished by the disappearance of species, cultures, or languages. Which is not to deny that the extinction and disappearance are disasters, cause suffering and harm, reduce the wealth of possibilities for life now on earth. General economy is not the totality of all exchanges, the sum of all accumulations. Abundance is not the aggregate of the species and kinds in existence, nor of the kinds that may come into existence, but something else, immeasurable. It is the giving in every place that exceeds its boundaries, given in exposure and proximity, responsiveness and responsibility. Always in kinds. For the sake of the good. Abundance is nothing, or everything without totality, or something otherwise. Always in kinds. Biological species and kinds express the expressiveness of individuals in relations and kinds—exposition, writing, coding, representativity—in the natural world, in being, in the earth, the endless excess of heterogeneity and abundance interrupting the play of identity and difference. As expression and representation. As *mimēsis*.[9]

I return from this extended interruption to the closing grid of classical representation to gather up what was present throughout in the absence of neutrality. To sacrifice and exclusion. Concluding with the crucial moment in which ethics and economics joined forces in the production of value. The word *value* emerged in *The Order of Things* at that moment in the prose of the world at which the world and its knowledge appeared poverty-stricken, a thing of sand. Value insisted on measure. To which I have repeatedly responded that something more fundamental, pervasive and sweeping, is given from the good that allows us to think of measuring the world in value.

The measure of value in classical representation is given by the quadrilateral of articulation, designation, derivation, and attribution that forms around and links language, nature, and wealth.

> The theory of value makes it possible, in fact, to explain (whether by dearth and need or by the superabundance of nature) how certain objects can be introduced into the systems of exchanges, how, by means of the primitive process of barter, one thing can be posited as the equivalent of another, how the estimate of the first can be related to the estimate of the second in accordance with a relation of equality. (Foucault, *OT*, 200–202)

Value belongs to circulation and exchange, brought under measure in the analysis of wealth. Economy here is the circulation of goods, beyond measure, brought under, dominated by, restricted to exchange and equivalence. Money is born in equivalence, emerging in the clusters of measure and restriction that define systems of exchange. Economics was waiting to emerge, but the scene was set in exchange and currency—a system of circulation that entwines itself as value around wealth, inseparable from language and natural things.

The act in which wealth emerges in exchange is based on substitution and restriction. What emerges is value, from something beyond value—beyond exchange, equivalence, and substitution, beyond money and wealth, still value, given from the good, still ethical. Exchange and substitution define money in virtue of its representativity.

> The two functions of money, as a common measure between commodities and as a substitute in the mechanism of exchange, are based upon its material reality. (p. 169)

> For Classical thought in its formative phase, money is that which permits
> wealth to be represented. Without such signs, wealth would remain im-
> mobile, useless, and as it were silent. (p. 177)

The order of representation doubled, tripled, and more. "Just as in the
order of representations the signs that replace and analyse them must also
be representations themselves, so money cannot signify wealth without
itself being wealth. But it becomes wealth because it is a sign; whereas a
representation must first be represented in order subsequently to become
a sign" (p. 177). In relation to goods beyond measure, the question of
wealth, of money, trade, and economy, is how things that circulate beyond
measure become commodities in a system of exchange. "It would be untrue
to say that nature spontaneously produces values; but it is the inexhaustible
source of the goods that exchange transforms into values, though not without expenditure and consumption" (p. 195).[10] Nature's inexhaustible abundance, spontaneity, and generosity are the conditions of value, of goods that
are scarce, restricted, exchanged, expended, and consumed. What makes
value possible is sacrifice under the curse.

> The creation of value is therefore not a means of satisfying a greater
> number of needs; it is the sacrifice of a certain quantity of goods in order
> to exchange others. Values thus form the negative of goods.
>   But how is it that value can be formed in this way? What is the origin
> of this excess that makes it possible for goods to be transformed into
> wealth without being effaced and finally disappearing altogether as a re-
> sult of successive exchanges and continual circulation? (p. 192)

Value is formed by sacrifice, brought under a system of exchanges and
substitutions, regulated by taxonomic systems of order. Value is given order
by sacrifice, and something—perhaps everything, perhaps nothing—is
sacrificed to value. The good, nothing at all, is sacrificed in its abundance—
the abundance of the earth—to value. Perhaps nothing can eliminate this
sacrifice, can escape the curse. But the sacrifice and curse mark the good
in debt and responsibility. Abundance in the earth is expressed in the curse
of kinds. Kindlness insists on memories of sacrifice in kinds.

     I hold the curse in abeyance for a chapter to speak of becoming in
kind.

CHAPTER 5

Becoming Kinds

Why are there so many becomings of man, but no becoming-man? First, because man is majoritarian par excellence, whereas becomings are minoritarian; all becoming is a becoming-minoritarian. When we say majority, we are referring . . . to the determination of a state or standard in relation to which larger quantities, as well as the smallest, can be said to be minoritarian: white-man, adult-male, etc. Majority implies a state of domination, not the reverse. . . . In this sense, women, children, but also animals, plants, and molecules, are minoritarian. . . . It is important not to confuse "minoritarian," as a becoming or process, with a "minority," as an aggregate or a state. Jews, Gypsies, etc., may constitute minorities under certain conditions, but that in itself does not make them becomings. One reterritorializes, or allows oneself to be reterritorialized, on a minority as a state; but in a becoming, one is deterritorialized. (Deleuze and Guattari, *TP*, 291)

All becoming is becoming a kind: becoming-animal, becoming-woman, becoming-child, becoming-Jew, becoming-gypsy, becoming-minoritarian (but not, it seems, becoming-minority); perhaps becoming-rhizomatic and becoming-nomadic; all described as becoming-intense, becoming-imperceptible. I would say, becoming-impure; yet every kind is already impure, perhaps intense and imperceptible even where all too solid. All becoming a kind where the question of *what* becomes is enigmatic. Though not without an answer. All becoming belongs to Man the Subject. "In a way, the subject in a becoming is always 'man,' but only when he enters a becoming-minoritarian that rends him from his major identity" (p. 291). Man exists to become, a Nietzschean thought. All becoming flows back upon singularities in the earth, a body without organs (BwO).

[T]he Earth—the Deterritorialized, the Glacial, the giant Molecule—is a BwO. This BwO is permeated by unformed, unstable matters, by flows in

79

all directions, by free intensities or nomadic singularities, by made or
transitory particles. . . . There simultaneously occurs upon the earth a very
important, inevitable phenomenon, that is beneficial in many respects and
unfortunate in many others: stratification. Strata are Layers, Belts. They
consist of giving form to matters, of imprisoning intensities or locking
singularities into systems of resonance and redundancy, of producing upon
the body of the earth molecules large and small and organizing them into
molar aggregates. (p. 40)

Difficult questions arise for becoming a kind in relation to the earth,
the body without organs, if the subject is always Man, or if what becomes
falls back upon singularities to imprison them in kinds. I postpone these
questions for a moment to consider the becoming of becoming. Perhaps
the question of *what* becomes presupposes too much. The *what* is always
a molar aggregate, a stratum, locking singularities into systems of molecules. What of a becoming, always in kinds, that does not presuppose a
being that becomes, not even a being of singularity? Here the full body of
the earth, free intensities and flows, express excess. *Becoming in kind—*
nomadic, rhizomatic, minoritarian—expresses excess beyond the imprison-
ments of molar aggregates. Not a free excess as if without limits, but the
limits of every limit, becomings of every becoming, porousness of every
layer, remainder in every kind. The general economy of kinds where every
kind belongs to restricted economy.

Becoming that does not take place to become something, that always
takes place in impure and liminal kinds, is a wondrous thought. I wonder
at the possibility that becoming here might be neither the infamous flux in
which all identities dissolve or the impermanence of constancy and identity,
but stranger, linked with the excesses of kinds that we have encountered
throughout our discussions, in Plato especially, marked by Hegel as more
than what is common. Even imprisoned intensities and locked singularities,
bound in molecules, molar aggregates, and belts, are profoundly more than
any molecule or prison can contain. Kinds exceed whatever limits would
contain them, even under domination and oppression. I take for granted
that domination and oppression can be resisted in the countless ways that
resistance is called for and more, including the ways in which resistance
fails, in the shadow of an uncontainable debt. I understand this debt to be
given from the good. I am exploring the ways in which such a debt pertains
to corporeal kinds, each and every kind, interrupting the closing of its
identity around what is common, always what is more than any commonality or identity. Kindlredlness and kindlness, always in debt, bearing responsibility, in memory of the good.

I am exploring how such a debt and responsibility might pertain to
becoming; not becoming-something but becoming in kind, the uncon-

tainability of becoming as the giving of kinds from the good. Every major figure in Deleuze and Guattari—rhizome, becoming-minoritarian, the body without organs—is a figure of uncontainability in a world filled with containment. Becoming in kind expresses an uncontainable circulation of kinds together with their limits and identities. Whereas free intensities and nomadic singularities relate to the full body of the earth and the body without organs as if they might be composed of entirely indeterminate movements, becoming in kind expresses the inescapability of composition, of structure. Becoming in kind expresses deterritorialization, presupposes territory and structure. Kinds compose the world, but composition presupposes decomposition, territoriality presupposes deterritorialization, deconstruction presupposes structure. All expressed in kinds.[1]

I am exploring how becoming in kind relates to the Western history of becoming, the flux on the one hand, everywhere becoming, the transformation of identities and places of individual things on the other. In both cases, I believe, the force of Greek thought and its successors insists that becoming bears the mark of being even for those who take becoming to be all there is. The flux is the endless being of becoming. The mobility and transformation of time in singular things is the inconstancy of their being. Again, perhaps in Spinoza, for whom there is neither flux nor change as such, but endless striving to persevere in being, we may consider the possibility that being is becoming, even for God, endless unfoldings filled with infinite numbers of infinite kinds. Something in God insists on becoming in kind, insists on the succession of finite things, *ad infinitum*, in kinds. Calling forth an interruption.

Perhaps in Nietzsche, the endless play of blind forces may be understood as endless becoming. Or what he says of "man" may be understood to pertain to all qualities and kinds: nothing gives anything its qualities.

> Man is a rope, tied between beast and overman—a rope over an abyss. A dangerous across, a dangerous on-the-way, a dangerous looking-back, a dangerous shuddering and stopping. (Nietzsche, *Z*, p. 126)

> What is great in man is that he is a bridge and not an end: what can be loved in man is that he is an *overture* and a *going under*. (p. 127)[2]

Humanism did not die with Nietzsche, though perhaps it was badly wounded. Yet many choose to read these passages to suggest that if Man is not given his qualities, He alone must choose. Choose to be! Let that be your becoming! Still humanism, insisting on humanity's being. Nor did humanism die with Deleuze and Guattari—if it can die before God—if we understand becoming in kind to be what men must choose. Choose to become an animal, a woman, a Jew. As if man could choose. As if only men can choose. Man the Subject.

I persist in believing that something quite different and remarkable concerning becoming and kinds echoes throughout these passages from Spinoza through Nietzsche to Deleuze and Guattari. It is difficult to understand, to gather. Sometimes it seems familiar, so that we may read free intensities and nomadic singularities, the full body of the earth, the body without organs, to remind us of indeterminateness and flux. All is movement, flow, fluidity, transformation: at bottom, indeterminate. Becoming is without territory. At the same time, perhaps inexplicably, flows and movements are frozen, imprisoned in strata, territorialized. Being is flux, becoming; being is layered, hierarchical, dominating. I have suggested that such a reading subordinates becoming to being, the being of flux, of indeterminateness and perhaps nonbeing. Such a reading would understand becoming in kind as becoming a certain kind of being.

Finite being in Spinoza is driven by infinite desire—to preserve oneself in becoming. And the man (or thing) without qualities is a rope suspended over the abyss: a bridge and not an end, not a being, an overture—a beginning, becoming; a responsibility for becoming, not the end of another's responsibility. The rope, the between, the abyss, all remain to mark becoming, in kinds. I take the becoming here as excess, immeasure, not the indeterminateness of being, as if indeterminateness and nonbeing were another being, but the responsibility of becoming in kind, kindIness as exposure toward kinds. Always excessive, beyond the limits of any beings in kinds.

Spinoza was not the first to express the enigmatic becoming of kinds. Nor are Deleuze and Guattari the most expressive—though at moments they exceed the possibility of containing the uncontainable thoughts they articulate, an excess I understand as crucial to the articulation. The most famous words on the flux have been read in many different ways:

> All things come into being through opposition, and all are in flux like a river. (Heraclitus fragment 5.10 [DK 22 A 1; Robinson, *EGP*, 89])

> It is necessary to understand that war is universal and justice is strife, and that all things take place in accordance with strife and necessity. (5.22 [DK 22 B 80; Robinson, p. 93])

> Nature loves to hide. (5.39 [DK 22 B 123; Robinson, p. 96])

Flux, becoming, is strife and opposition, hides itself, loves to escape measure. This is much more than a neutral, anonymous being in which all identities are dissolved. It is a passionate, contradictory nature that insists on exceeding measure. Even so, the *logos* tells us that all things are one (5.33 [DK 22 B 50; Robinson, p. 95]), compounding the aporia. One in becoming, I suggest, not in being. One rope strung over the abyss, between one kind and another. Becoming in kind exceeds the limits of both the indeterminateness of the flux and any kind. Becoming and kind are always more than what is common, what is identical, and always more than what is different.

Deleuze and Guattari appear at times to speak of *what* becomes, the being of which becoming is predicated: the nomadic singularity. Yet the role of the singular is surely to exceed the limits of the kind, any kind, under which it may be appropriated, ranked, and dominated. I leave aside here my reservations concerning the emptiness of singularities, as if they bear the weight of all excess. I have discussed that elsewhere.[3] My desire here is to pursue excess beyond the singular to the kind, driven by becoming, releasing the authority of the proper name as excess. Even the common name, the kind, exceeds what is identical, common, exceeds the bonds of universality. But I am getting ahead of myself in becoming.

I suggest we pause for an interruption before reading becoming in kind as a singular individual or being changing in its qualities and predications to become an example of a kind. That would entail that something gives the being its qualities: it itself or its causes. It would entail that becoming is subordinate to being; would keep the individual being and subject at the center of a world filled with kinds as if participating in a kind were a violation of singularity. I understand individuals and kinds to compose each other, historically in systems of domination. But the composition, the structure, is excessive on all sides. Beyond the excessive individual are excesses of becoming and kind.

I believe that to understand the excessiveness of all this excess is to understand something fundamental about genealogy and its limits that escapes the genealogical accounts in Nietzsche and Foucault, marked by Deleuze and Guattari in their chapter on "The Geology of Morals"—as I understand it, marking the excessive limits of genealogy itself. I understand this excess in relation to the giving of the good, resisting neutrality, bearing endless responsibility. Becoming in kind is an ethical thought, thrown over the abyss where we and other things find ourselves together in debt, touching each other in endless becoming, all in kinds. I postpone genealogy for a while to further examine becoming in kind. It is not without difficulties in its most provocative forms.

I conclude this interruption in the name of becoming in kind to imagine that Deleuze and Guattari offer in this name a reading of participation *(metaschesis)* in kinds, in the ideas, still an impossible, ethical thought. To participate in the kind is not to be that kind, without remainder, as if no more than what is common; nor is it to be a member of that kind, again without remainder, as if membership exhausted both individual and kind.

The individual exceeds the kind; the proper name exceeds the common. But also, the kind exceeds the individual—an insight traditionally associated with Plato; the common name exceeds the proper—a dangerous line of thought indeed. Here we may understand participation in the kind, the idea, as becoming excessive in kind, becoming the anomalous, proliferating, heterogeneous kind. The divinity of the idea marks the excess of both individual and kind, especially in the remainders of their relations.

I briefly interrupt again with another allusion that crosses this reading of participation in kinds at a different angle. Deleuze distinguishes repetition from generality and difference from conceptual difference. "If repetition exists, it expresses at once a singularity opposed to the general, a universality opposed to the particular, a distinctive opposed to the ordinary, an instantaneity opposed to variation and an eternity opposed to permanence. In every respect, repetition is a transgression. It puts law into question, it denounces its nominal or general character in favour of a more profound and more artistic reality" (Deleuze, *DR*, 2–3). The univocity of being as repetition and difference—as general economy, I would say—always transgression, but never, perhaps, in opposition. Opposition belongs to restricted economy, to generality and law, not repetition. Kinds are repetitions—and more: neither singular nor general—and both; neither eternity nor permanence—and both; always more than any, putting law, intelligibility, and neutrality into question, beyond question, in exposure and proximity. Experience is repetition in difference, difference in repetition, beyond generality and law, as participation, as transgression, as propinquity in kind. I return from this interruption.

The chapter in *A Thousand Plateaus* to which I will give attention here, concerned with becoming in kind, begins with becoming-animal: a rat, a pack of rats. Becoming-animal occupies the mobile and excessive space between the molecular and the molar. "[T]here is a becoming-animal not content to proceed by resemblance and for which resemblance, on the contrary, would represent an obstacle or stoppage: the proliferation of rats, the pack, brings a becoming-molecular that undermines the great molar powers of family, career, and conjugality" (Deleuze and Guattari, *TP*, 233). And of genealogy. More of that later. Ending with the possibility that "the same animal [can] be taken up by two opposing functions and movements, depending on the case" (p. 233). If the molecular and molar are oppositional. If resemblance and commonality can slow the excessive movements of kinds. Deleuze and Guattari speak of stocking up kinds in their identities and differences under the sign of resemblance, molar animals, and of dispersing them into the pack. I persist in the possibility that pack and kind, stockpiled under the sign of resemblance, are always more than identity and difference. Every kind is more than the identities and differences it marks and gathers.

I am interrupted by Molly, who insists that we recall the distinction between molar and molecular, echoing her name. Can we draw a line between molar order and molecular disorder, between pack and rat, rats and mollusks, mollusks and stones? Or is our desire, our need, to count and divide an effort to contain the uncontainable? Put in the following paradoxical form: the uncontainable can be contained, is always contained—and yet. The kind is the identity of the pack—and more. It is men who become-animals, who become rats. Do they become mollusks, or stones? Can women or animals become molecules? Are these further lines of demarcation and domination?

Men become animals in the interests of the men, not the animals, even where the interests are molecular. "Society and the State need animal characteristics to use for classifying people: natural history and science need characteristics in order the classify the animals themselves. . . . But we are not interested in characteristics: what interests us are modes of expansion, propagation, occupation, contagion, peopling" (Deleuze and Guattari, *TP*, 239). Even with deterritorialization in mind. "We think and write for animals themselves. We become animal so that the animal also becomes something else. The agony of a rat or the slaughter of a calf remains present in thought not through pity but as the zone of exchange between man and animal in which something of one passes into the other" (Deleuze and Guattari, *WP*, 109). Perhaps one way only, in The Thinking Man's terms. Invoking several reflections:

Are expansion, propagation, occupation, contagion, and peopling not characteristics? Do we put the qualities, the characteristics, aside in propagation and contagion, expel them from multiplicity? Are diseases and nomadic movements not mobilities of kinds? Kinds themselves, I say, are marked by classification, taxonomy, identities and differences; and in that marking, to the depths of their becoming in kind, they become, propagate, move. To the genealogy of family and kind Deleuze and Guattari add geology. To genealogy and geology I add geography, always exceeding proper places, always exceeding the borders of kinds. Nomadic movements require their geography, the geography of kinds. Kinds are always in place, moving elsewhere. I continue to hold genealogy, geology, and geography in abeyance.

Animals as such will not do. Only certain kinds of animals. Almost certainly not mollusks, Molly grumbles. And why not mollusks or ants?

> We must distinguish three kinds of animals. First, individuated animals, family pets, sentimental, Oedipal animals, each with its own petty history, "my" cat, "my" dog. These animals invite us to regress. . . . *[A]nyone who likes cats or dogs is a fool.*[4] And then there is a second kind: animals with characteristics or attributes; genus, classification, or State animals: . . .

> Finally, there are more demonic animals, pack or affect animals that form a multiplicity, a becoming, a population, a tale . . . Yes any animal is or can be a pack, but to varying degrees of vocation that make it easier or harder to discover the multiplicity, or multiplicity-grade, an animal contains. (pp. 240–41)

And why should it be easier (or for that matter, harder) for us—we men—to discover the multiplicity if there is always multiplicity? Why might it not be a greater burden and responsibility to resist the easier and to pursue the molecular in the firmly entrenched characteristics of the molar—always eluding our grasp? Why should becoming-animal be easy? Why should becoming-animal be for us? Why not for them? Or for the good—nothing at all, filled with endless exposure and proximity?

Deleuze and Guattari speak of lines of flight, but they also interpose lines of demarcation. And perhaps, within my excessive admiration for the excesses of their understanding of both becoming and of kinds, I hesitate to endorse some of the demarcations. "If the anomalous is neither an individual nor a species, then what is it? It is a phenomenon, but a phenomenon of bordering. This is our hypothesis: a multiplicity is defined not by the elements that compose it in extension, not by the characteristics that compose it in comprehension, but by the lines and dimensions it encompasses in 'intension' " (p. 245). Here is my hypothesis: a multiplicity, anomaly (animaly?), heterogeneity, is an individual and a species, composed of elements and characteristics, all pervaded by lines of flight and borderings. All of these, especially species and kinds, can be what they are only in virtue of their mobilities and borders. Nor do I think that this more supplementary view differs from the full body of the earth and the body without organs. I have Spinoza in mind, for whom nature is absolutely infinite in infinite numbers of kinds, made up of infinite becomings of singular things, all participating infinitely in kinds. My concern is with the animal that is become and that becomes, the woman who becomes and who is become, with the kinds and individuals in lines of flight. I am inclined to be a fool, to like cats and dogs, and women and men, and stones and plants and other animals, as the kinds they are and more. Moreover, who cares whether I or you like them, love them, when we find ourselves face to face with them, bearing responsibility toward them? And others.

I am now prepared to undertake a leap, a line of flight, passing over some wonderful moments in Deleuze and Guattari's chapter concerning werewolves and vampires (pp. 249–53), bodies, power, and haecceity in Spinoza (pp. 253–60), approaching geography: "On the plane of consistency, *a body is defined only by a longitude and a latitude*" (p. 260), bewaring of the word "only." Why not supplementarily? In any case, I pass breathlessly over the plane "which knows only longitudes and latitudes, speeds and haecceities, the plane of consistency or composition" (p. 266), where geography knows nothing of the kinds that inhabit its places, to where girls appear, "fugitive beings" (p. 271), the becoming of becoming-woman. As in becoming-animal, do not become an animal.[5] In becoming-woman or becoming-child, do not become a woman or child, do not participate in their kind. "[T]here is a becoming-woman, a becoming-child, that do not resemble the woman or the child as clearly distinct molar entities (although it is possible—only possible—for the woman or child to occupy privileged positions in relation to these becomings)" (p. 275). My discussion in the rest of this chapter will be devoted to this question of privilege in relation to a kind.

Privilege is a word from which I would fall back, away. The far-reaching question on which Deleuze and Guattari take an unqualified stand is whether members of a kind—in their language, a molar kind: child, woman, animal—might bear a unique if not privileged relation to the minoritarian movements possible in virtue of that kind. The relation is between minority identities and minoritarian becomings. Deleuze and Guattari appear to repudiate the relation, so to speak, without qualification. From the passage opening this chapter: "It is important not to confuse 'minoritarian,' as a becoming or process, with a 'minority,' as an aggregate or a state. Jews, Gypsies, etc., may constitute minorities under certain conditions, but that in itself does not make them becomings." It is indeed important to understand that *minority* and *minoritarian* speak to different conditions and relations, the one to identities and states, the other to becomings in kind. But that does not mean that they are not intimately related, that they are not inextricably confused: not *our* confusion, we philosophers, but *their* confusion as kinds. I understand kinds to occupy this space of confusion between minority and minoritarian, the space between. Kinds are always between, as kinds, in kin, represented in genealogy, re-represented as geology or geography. General and restricted economy are inextricably confused, the confusion of impure kinds.

I interrupt this line of flight to pursue two thoughts of woman as kind, closely related to the question of privilege. One is the theme of place that moves throughout much of Irigaray's writing: woman without a place of her own, representing place for man.

> Woman is still the place, the whole of the place in which she cannot take possession of herself as such.
>
> . . . She must continue to hold the places she constitutes for the subject, a place to which no eternal value can be assigned lest the subject remain paralyzed forever by the irreplaceableness of his cathected investments. (Irigaray, *VF*, 227)

> Woman is neither open nor closed. She is indefinite, in-finite, *form is never complete in her*. She is not infinite but neither is she *a* unit(y), such as letter, number, figure in a series, proper noun, unique object (in a) world of the senses. . . . This incompleteness in her form, her morphology, allows her continually to become something else, though this is not to say that she is ever univocally nothing. (p. 229)

Irigaray pursues a multiple movement of place|non-place around the historical place of women. Woman has no place of her own, has always represented place for man. Women are a historically oppressed minority, subjected to domination. As a consequence, in the same relation, woman is neither open nor closed, indefinite, infinite, always incomplete. As a consequence, in the same relation, women are minoritarian as a kind. Irigaray explores the difficult and enigmatic relations between the historical domination of women as a (minority) kind and the possibility that a kind—woman as a (minoritarian) kind—might release the closure of identity under the form of kind. I understand this enigmatic relation to pertain to kinds as such, to every kind, not just women, or men, or animals, or children. Yet that it pertains to kinds as such does not eliminate the historical or geographical possibility that historically oppressed minorities bear a special and unique relation to minoritarian becoming—without privilege. Why can we not grant the uniqueness of lived experience without privilege?

The second interruption may appear quite different, but I understand it as a repetition. Wittig repudiates the categories of man and woman together with all fixed categories of kinds. "But for us there is no such thing as being-woman or being-man. 'Man' and 'woman' are political concepts of opposition, and the copula which dialectically unites them is, at the same time, the one which abolishes them. . . . The concept of difference has nothing ontological about it. It is only the way that the masters interpret a historical situation of domination" (Wittig, *SM*, 29). Against the closure of such categories of domination, she speaks of writing not from a position of subjection but universally, speaks of lesbianization as the exaltation of the subject and of "standing on one's own feet as an escapee, a fugitive slave, a lesbian" (Wittig, *SME*, xiii), all figures of excessive becoming.[6] The category of domination is linked with the dissolution of the category in excess. Minority experience is linked with minoritarian mobility and excess. The kind—lesbian, woman—occupies a double role in which historical subjection and the earth's abundance are inextricably joined. Without privilege.

In a similar way, perhaps, we may think of the dissolution of the subject as the repudiation of the privilege of transcendental experience, of the universality and purity of a subject's experience that give him—not it, Him—authority over his practices. Yet I cannot imagine that we would wish to deny the remarkable relations of human beings, animals, and others to their feelings, perceptions, and responses, including the unique relations of minorities to experiences that lack a history of public representation. I mean to pursue the possibility of experiences and relations that demand to be recognized as such without authority.

I return from this interruption to Deleuze and Guattari, postponing further consideration of Irigaray and Wittig. I would certainly agree that children, women, and dogs may carry no authority in relation to the becomings of their kinds. Indeed, I would hope to resist every claim to authority from within the impossibility of escaping authority. Becoming in kind, opening a line of flight, resists authority. It does not and cannot ignore the qualities and characteristics—molar and determinate—that define the kind that might become, always excessive.

One would think that Deleuze and Guattari mean to say this when they give priority to becoming-woman. "Although all becomings are already molecular, including becoming-woman, it must be said that all becomings begin with and pass through becoming-woman. It is the key to all the other becomings" (Deleuze and Guattari, *TP*, 277). Why should this be so? Not for the kinds of reasons Irigaray and Wittig give, related to women as a minority, but to the warrior's becoming *as a warrior*. "We have seen how the man of war, by virtue of his *furor* and celerity, was swept up in irresistible becomings-animal. These are becomings that have as their necessary condition the becoming-woman of the warrior, or his alliance with the girl, his contagion with her" (p. 278). *His* furor and celerity. The majoritarian becomes minoritarian, again leaving Penelope at home, for whom no special relationship exists with becoming-woman. Sex is still given by men to men. "*Sexuality proceeds by way of the becoming-woman of the man and the becoming-animal of the human:* an emission of particles" (pp. 278–79). Always an emission of particles, never absorption, fluidity, corporeal exposure without incorporation. Dissemination. Insemination. Always masculine. Always majoritarian.

I'm sure that is the point: the becoming-minoritarian—imperceptible, intense, nomadic, rhizomatic—of the majoritarian. Leaving in limbo the difficult links between minority and minoritarian, experienced uniquely by minority kinds of human beings, creatures, and things. Perhaps limbo is where they belong. I would hold on to the possibility that minority experience is vital to minoritarian becomings, always of a kind, different kinds, mixed and impure kinds. Without privilege.

In a becoming, one is deterritorialized (p. 291); becomings are minoritarian (p. 291). Does this suggest that only (white? European?) men, majoritarian par excellence, can become minoritarian? Deterritorialization presupposes territorialization, domination, as reterritorialization presupposes deterritorialization. Yet although women, children, but also animals, plants, and molecules are minoritarian, "even blacks . . . must become black. Even women must become-woman. Even Jews must become Jewish" (p. 291). The subject is always "man," displaced from "his" major identity. And what of diasporic African Americans, women, and Jews, already and woundingly displaced from their major identity—if there be such? What of the possibility that the subject "man" no longer occupies a place, dominant or otherwise, in the full body of the earth?

Indeed, majoritarian, dominating kinds that claim and enforce undue authority must become other kinds, dispersing their authority into minoritarian kinds. Becoming in kind concerns the possibilities in every kind of becoming otherwise, still in kinds. But becoming in kind concerns other possibilities than these, especially for minoritarian, minority kinds that have never known public authority, that need to find a place—without instituting another privilege and authority—to be their kind, in restitution for their wounds as subjected kinds. The subject who is always man is always, I believe, subjected; and even when dominating, gives himself over, throws himself down into abjection under the yoke of authority. Authority always exceeds the rules and laws and identities that define it.

All of this bears upon becoming in kind. For if we understand becoming in kind, many kinds, in relation to authority, then becoming a minoritarian kind resists authority, but authority cannot be resisted or discarded with impunity or without impurity. Becoming in kind takes on responsibility for authority, either in resistance or under rule and law. All of this is to say that becoming in kind bears responsibility, undertakes a movement for the sake of the good. In kinds. Which is to say that territorialization and reterritorialization are not only inescapable but responses in exposure to the good.

I have spoken repeatedly of the universalization and exaltation with which Wittig resists becoming a minority in a way that closes off excess, resisting the call of the good. Something similar appears in Deleuze and Guattari. With perhaps a difference—I am not sure.

> A woman has to become-woman, but in a becoming-woman of all man. A Jew becomes Jewish, but in a becoming-Jewish of the non-Jew. A becoming-minoritarian exists only by virtue of a deterritorialized medium and subject that are like its elements. There is no subject of the becoming except as a deterritorialized variable of the majority. (Deleuze and Guattari, *TP*, 292)

Let us try to say it another way: There is no becoming-man because man is the molar entity par excellence, whereas becomings are molecular. (p. 292)

Man—the dominant, territorial majoritarian—must become minoritarian by becoming woman, gypsy, or Jew. Perhaps "jew," as Lyotard puts it, the figure that occupies the forgotten limits of the dominant European subject. But Jews: Do they have a responsibility to deterritorialize the majority? Or do they bear such responsibility only when they become the majority? Do women bear responsibility to save men—or man—from the disasters of the majority? Wittig and Irigaray deny it. And so do I.

Perhaps that is not what Deleuze and Guattari mean. Yet the dependence of minoritarian becomings on majoritarian dominance, the inescapable reference of becoming in kind to the molar entity Man, reinstates the subordination of becoming in kind even along lines of flight away from domination. If Man is at the center, then that center must be deterritorialized, must be resisted. But people, creatures, natural things live and experience away from the center, have their lives and joys. And if they bear a political responsibility to join in resistance, they do not bear it chiefly to the majority, but to themselves and for the sake of the good.

Becoming in kind occupies the movements of general and restricted economy, where neither becoming nor kind can be classified in either economy. Territorialization, deterritorialization, reterritorialization do not exhaust the geography of becoming in kind because they retain the picture of the world drawn up by majoritarian geographers. Becoming in kind opens onto other possibilities from within the restrictions of domination and oppression on all sides, along lines of flight from majoritarian to minoritarian, but also in the identities of kinds known by minorities. Always under suspicion. Always resisting neutrality and authority.

Deleuze and Guattari close their chapter on becoming in kind with a beautiful Nietzschean thought far exceeding any minoritarian identity. They speak of becoming-music. "Music is a creative, active operation that consists in deterritorializing the refrain. Whereas the refrain is essentially territorial, territorializing, or reterritorializing, music makes it a deterritorialized content for a deterritorializing form of expression" (Deleuze and Guattari, *TP*, p. 300). Music is deterritorialization par excellence, perhaps, general economy, within the territoriality of its refrain: *mimēsis*. I have not considered the relation between becoming in kind and *mimēsis*, marked by music, I believe, because of the resistance music bears to closing the identity of a kind under any dominant identity, even within its refrain.

How might music express becoming in kind? How can music express becoming minoritarian kinds? I believe it is because music, however formal, elite, and dominant in its social spaces, cannot demarcate its kinds, its content, and hold it fast. The reason why the content of music is so difficult to articulate is that no hierarchy analogous to the gaze delimits its boundaries. Works of music may be ranked hierarchically—always, I believe, in contaminated realms. But the ranking of the so-called content—let us say God, immortality, and man—is undercut at every moment by the intensity of the Dionysian passions that crowd in.

How does music express becoming in kind? The answer, I believe, is that it does so by not doing so, that music is filled with kinds, always becoming, always moving, traditional and variable kinds, which are altogether relevant as the kinds they are—majoritarian—and entirely irrelevant at the same time. Music disturbs the categories of kinds that define the worlds in which music takes place, resists the neutrality of kinds in the intensity of its passions. Music is becoming-intense even where it is most familiar. Perhaps.

We might wonder if music is unique in relation to becoming in kind. "Is the situation similar for painting?" (Deleuze and Guattari, *TP*, 300). We might pursue *mimēsis* everywhere as becoming in kind. I would follow a different line from becoming-music to becoming in kind, less along the divide between majoritarian and minoritarian kinds than in relation to the worlds in which kinds become. Becoming music participates in and delimits worlds, opens onto geography. I have postponed geography to this point in suspicion that our dwelling upon kinds might hold us bound to genealogy. I propose now to explore this possibility. To interrupt genealogy with geography in kinds.

Deleuze and Guattari interrupt genealogy with geology: *the geology of morals*. And they repeatedly gesture vigorously toward geography, for example, speaking of the "[p]rinciple of cartography and decalcomania: a rhizome is not amenable to any structural or generative model"; "The rhizome is . . . *a map and not a tracing*" (Deleuze and Guattari, *TP*, 12); and speaking of the plane: "We call this plane, which knows only longitudes and latitudes, speeds and haecceities, the plane of consistency or composition (as opposed to the plan(e) of organization or development). It is necessarily a plane of immanence and univocality. We therefore call it the plane of Nature, although nature has nothing to do with it, since on this plane there is no distinction between the natural and the artificial" (p. 266). I undertake another interruption in the name of kinds, speaking of geophilosophy: the geography of morels. I propose to examine the idea of geography and, especially, of geophilosophy, which Lyotard claims to detest (Lyotard, *HJ*, 5), and which Deleuze and Guattari discuss at length.[7]

Like Lyotard, but without detestation, I mean to understand geophilosophy and the geography of living things as radical, disruptive figures. I mean to explore a geography that does not fix borders in place. With Deleuze and Guattari:

> The principle of reason such as it appears in philosophy is a principle of contingent reason and is put like this: there is no good reason but contingent reason; there is no universal history except of contingency. (Deleuze and Guattari, *WP*, 93)

> Geography wrests history from the cult of necessity in order to stress the irreducibility of contingency. It wrests it from the cult of origins in order to affirm the power of a "milieu." (p. 96)

As I understand them, geography and geophilosophy speak of and in resistance toward a sense of philosophical place that might be mine, ours, owned, occupied, and secured—heard in Kant—against other relevant claims; and toward a sense of no-place: everywhere, nowhere, neutrality. Geophilosophy resists neutrality, philosophy in the neuter, the double neuter of proper place and absence of place.

Returning to Lyotard's detestation of geophilosophy under the name of Heidegger—the Heidegger question as the question of geophilosophy as the question of ethics for our time—for some, never for all. "He wanted to rejoin the Greeks through the Germans, at the worst moment in their history: is there anything worse, said Nietzsche, than to find oneself facing a German when one was expecting a Greek? How could Heidegger's concepts not be intrinsically sullied by an abject reterritorialization? . . . Heidegger lost his way along the paths of the reterritorialization because they are paths without directive signs or barriers" (Deleuze and Guattari, *WP*, 108–9). Heidegger lost his way as perhaps any may in deterritorialization and reterritorialization without directions. Geophilosophy as the locality and contingency of philosophy, without authority, where any may go wrong, including philosophy itself, at any point of truth or goodness. No guarantees, as Lyotard says, against shame and infamy. Certainly not in the neuter. In geography I hope to echo Levinas and Irigaray against the neuter. In geophilosophizing geophilosophy.

Levinas resists the neutral assembling of being in the name of the face: "The face . . . is not the disclosure of an impersonal Neuter *(Neutre)*, but *expression*" (Levinas, *TI*, 51). This ethical movement where expression resists neutrality is the moving spirit of my geography, except for the face. I offer geography to travel from the face without giving up resistance to neutrality. I recall *mimēsis* as expression, the *mimēsis* of bodies in proximity and exposure. Geophilosophy is unabashed about *mimēsis*, its own and others'.

Irigaray speaks against neutrality in terms of sexual difference, against *"the sexual indifference that underlies the truth of any science, the logic of every discourse"* (Irigaray, *IR*, 118), the objectivity that oppresses.[8] A bit more geographically, however, she speaks of woman as place for man but as having no place of her own, no-place, as open, never closed; and she describes intermediary figures, angels:

> who transgress all enclosures in their speed, tell of the passage between the envelope of God and that of the world as micro- or macrocosm. They proclaim that such a journey can be made by the body of man, and above all the body of woman. (Irigaray, *ESD*, 16)

> The angel is that which unceasingly *passes through the envelope(s)* or *container(s)*, goes from one side to the other, reworking every deadline, changing every decision, thwarting all repetition. (p. 15)

With due respect to Aristotle and Freud as well as Lyotard, I take her to embark upon geophilosophy. All *mimēsis*, new or old, miming *mimēsis*. Without attempting to classify the immense and threatening difficulties of denying and ascribing place to woman, I suggest that we understand place and no place to join in geography, resisting neutrality—in this case especially sexual indifference.

I return from this interruption to Deleuze and Guattari with two concluding geographical thoughts, one a repetition the other somewhat newer. The first is that the full body of the earth is filled with machines, desiring and writing machines. Including animals. Yet is it possible for the dog or sparrow, like the woman or child, to occupy a privileged position in relation to becoming-animal? And what of the rhizomatic mushroom? What of becoming-plant or becoming-stone? Another set of regulated borders, still geography, geophilosophy. Perhaps philosophy continues to retain its traditional *humanist* geography—Derrida's term—in restricting citation and iteration to humanity. Iteration, phrasing, and expression fail to halt at the borders of humanity. "These possibilities or necessities, without which there would be no language, *are themselves not only human*" (Derrida, *EW*, 285).[9] They may indeed be moral, or morel. Where does geography end? Where *mimēsis*? In the full body of the earth. Instituting and resisting privilege everywhere.

My second, related thought concerns the possibility expressed in some radical ecological writings of a nonanthropocentric perspective.[10] "We can have only the barest sense of what ethics for a culture truly beyond anthropocentrism would actually look like"; "Indeed, when anthropocentrism is finally cut down to size, there is no reason to think that what we will have or need in its place will be something called *non*anthropocentrism at all" (Weston, *BEE*, 232). Or whatever. Perhaps the full body of the earth. But I would insist on its geography. Or geology. A philosophy, an ethics, without contested borders is no philosophy, no ethics, at all. Philosophy and ethics are geophilosophy and geoethics. Yet geography cannot contain its borders, takes the gift of the earth for granted and the endless responsibilities given from it, to find oneself a place, in place, and to resist every domination of place.

CHAPTER 6

Blood Kinds

Genre is confused with species. Genre becomes the human race *[le genre humain]*, human nature, etc., as defined within patriarchal culture. This genre corresponds to a people of men which rejects, consciously or unconsciously, the possibility of an other genre: the female. There is nothing but *le genre humain*, in which sex only has real value if it pertains to the reproduction of the species. From that point of view, genre would always be subordinate to kinship. . . .

We have to reinterpret the notion of nature that underlies such imperatives. (Irigaray, *NSR*, 201)

The word [*Geschlecht*, then] signifies the human species *(Menschengeschlecht)* in the sense of humanity *(Menschheit)* as well as the species in the sense of tribes, stocks, and families, all that struck again [*dies alles widerum geprägt*: struck in the sense of what receives the imprint, the *typos*, the typical mark] with the generic duality of the sexes *(in das Zwiefache der Geschlechter)*. (Derrida, *G2*, 185)

Herkunft is the equivalent of stock or *descent*; it is the ancient affiliation to a group, sustained by the bonds of blood, tradition, or social class. The analysis of *Herkunft* often involves a consideration of race or social type. But the traits it attempts to identify are not the exclusive generic characteristics of an individual, a sentiment, or an idea, which permit us to qualify them as "greek" or "english"; rather, it seeks the subtle, singular, and subindividual marks that might possibly intersect in them to form a network that is difficult to unravel. (Foucault, *NGH*, 145)

The terms that represent kinds, throughout Western history, have been terms of blood, lineage and blood, accursed. Genealogy, together with its surrogates and representations, runs down, falls back, along lines of kinship and blood. In European history. And elsewhere. Certainly in European readings of Asian and African descent. *Genre, Geschlecht, Herkunft*, French and

German words for genus, species, propinquity, and kind, descend along lines of blood and kin through gender, reproduction, and sexual differ-ence, seizing women as the gender whose blood is spilt in reproduction, in the very possibility of descent, and imposing something obscure on nature, on animate and inanimate things, whether claimed to belong to genealogical kinship or excluded from the family of things that matter, the things related by blood. Lineage, kin, and blood touch sexual differ-ence—gender, men and women, family, and reproduction—and sexual indifference—objectivity, detachment, and neutrality—however obliquely and inarticulately.

The history of blood for women, and for animals, is filled with con-taminated memories of violence, oppression, and destruction—so polluted and ambiguous that the bond between women and animals is fraught with adversity. Yet it cannot be avoided, along two linked lines of thought: that of kinship and reproduction, intimately bound to women and the places assigned them under the social contract; and that of sacrifice and consump-tion, stockpiling, eating, and destroying animals to live well and to placate the gods. These represent the lines of thought I will pursue in these chap-ters, inseparably linked blood relations that constitute the family of Man in its place of mastery over nature. Including animals and women. All in memory of the curse.

I have noted where Griffin speaks of woman and nature linked in flesh and consumption, gathering together under the curse several difficult streams of blood: "She will eat the flesh she appears to love. Her hunger is never satisfied. . . . The color of her blood is the color of calamity, of fire, of evil. . . . She loves blood. . . . She devours even herself" (Griffin, *WN*, 83).[1] Adding the possibility of redemption, women reconstituting their relation-ship to the earth, still in blood. *"Now we will let the blood of our mother sink into this earth. This what we will do with our grieving. We will cover her wounds with mud"* (pp. 217–18). Blood retains the double flows that link women with nature, with animate and inanimate things: memories of oppression and destruction, of sacrifice and consumption, joined with gen-eration and reproduction. Fear and grief in blood together with memories of birth and generation, all in blood. From which we may say men recoil, and toward which we may say that they respond by devouring animal blood. Spilling and devouring blood.

I postpone consuming and devouring to the next chapter, knowing that such a separation is an act of violence, so that I will be interrupted frequently in this chapter by memories of sacrifice and consumption. Here, however, I wish to pursue the intricate complexities of the lines of lineage and blood marked in genealogy, recalling how from the beginning of our discussion of kinds, we have found ourselves in blood. The perfect truth of the utterly inauthentic sophist is given as his lineage and blood. Genealogy as kind|ness, marked in blood.

Words for lineage, intimately linked with genealogy, in French, German, and English, are *genre, Geschlecht, Herkunft*, and kinds, race, kin, and kinds, terms of blood. All terms that touch blood and kin and lineage, explicitly or implicitly. The sexual indifference, the objectivity and neutrality of scientific, rational discourse, of any discourse of humanity or of natural things, is sexual difference, gender, in blood. "Freud brought to light something that had been operative all along though it remained implicit, hidden, unknown: *the sexual indifference that underlies the truth of any science, the logic of every discourse*" (Irigaray, *PDSM*, 69).

Irigaray ascribes this insight to Freud: science is instituted in a sexual indifference that is anything but indifferent, sexed. Derrida explores the sexual indifference of philosophy, for example in Heidegger, where *Dasein* is constituted by a sexual neutrality that is anything but indifferent. "[I]t is as if, in reading Heidegger, there were no sexual difference, nothing of that in man, or put otherwise in woman, to interrogate or suspect, nothing worthy of questioning, *fragwürdig*. It is as if, one might continue, sexual difference did not rise to the height of ontological difference, on the whole as negligible, in regard to the question of the sense of being, as any other difference. . . . [I]nsofar as it is opened up to the question of being, insofar as it has a relation to being, in that very reference, *Dasein* would not be sexed" (Derrida, *G1*, 65–66). The denial, Derrida insists, opens onto questions of sexual difference, gender and desire, at the very point of denial. The denial raises questions of the denial. "What if 'sexuality' already marked the most originary *Selbstheit*? If it were an ontological structure ipseity? If the *Da* of *Dasein* were already 'sexual'? What if sexual difference were already marked in the opening up of the question of the sense of Being and of the ontological difference? And what if, though not self-evident, neutralisation were already a violent operation?" (p. 74). Carried from the question to the violence, bringing neutrality and neutralization to the fore. "*Dasein* in general hides, shelters in itself the internal possibility of a factual dispersion or dissemination *(faktische Zerstreuunt)* in its own body *(Leiblichkeit)* and 'thereby in sexuality' *(und damit in die Geschlechtlichkeit)*. Every proper body of one's own *[corps propre]* is sexed and there is no *Dasein* without its own body" (p. 75). The issue is one of blood, understood as sexual difference and violence. But the issue is also, perhaps the same issue, one of neutrality, neutralization, the operations that deny kin and blood and sexuality to the primordial relations of humanity to the world—*Dasein*—perhaps of world to world, natural things—animate and inanimate—to each other, insofar as that world is gendered—for example, through language. Derrida tells this story of the operations of neutrality that reinstate the oppression of women and the exclusion of animals from ethical care in the name of Heidegger. He repeatedly insists that any rigorous philosophy of our time must pursue an intimate relation with Heidegger. Perhaps so. But the violent operations of neutralization neither begin nor end with Heidegger; and the consequences of neutralization remain the exclusion and domination of women and animals along lines of blood. Even—or especially—Levinas, for whom the possibility of ethical life and philosophy turns on resistance to neutrality, constitutes that resistance in terms that place women in the home, providing hospitality for men, and, we have seen, that exclude animals from consideration, without the slightest intake of air.[2] I postpone Heidegger's rigor to a later interruption.

It is surely strange that the terms that define the issue of neutrality for us here are anything but neutral: *genre, Geschlecht, Herkunft,* kin and kind. Lineage and blood relate, as the Eleatic Stranger says, to every ordering by kinds, where every stranger, every strange thing, marks the absence of neutrality. The kinds of the world—*eidos, genos*—are relations of family and blood. Though we moderns appear to have forgotten. We institute our hierarchies of blood in a forgetting that pretends to neutrality without responsibility. This may be the crux of lineage and blood together with the genealogical terms that mark their kinship without neutralization. Genealogy bears a certain responsibility that objectivity and neutrality deny and reinstitute in the gesture of denial. The force of my project here, recalling gifts from the good, is to insist that the giving is without neutrality, that every neutralization—a violent operation—fails to accomplish neutrality, fails to nullify responsibility, fails to resist the injustices of every production.

The bloody side of these genealogical terms—recalling that I hope to resist the hegemony even of genealogy, of kindlness—is not the truth of kin and kind they gather, but the heterogeneities and impurities they mark, the mingling and mixing of kinds. Kinds in lineage and blood come forth in ambiguous profusion, overlaying, overlapping, intermingling beyond any system of classification. That is the burden of terms like *genre, Geschlecht, Herkunft,* and kinds: they exceed every limit that would demarcate a kinship without impurity. They exceed the authority of blood. Not without violence and domination. Indeed, in violence and domination, exceeding their own authority, challenging the very possibility of authority.

I have alluded to Foucault's account of genealogy in "Nietzsche, Genealogy, History," rich one might say in terms of lineage and blood. That is the line of thought before us here, begun with the Eleatic Stranger: genealogy descends along lines of kin and blood, expressed in terms of utmost impurity—blood again. Indeed, the point of this discussion may well be, more than any other, that the history of genealogy—its genealogy—expresses a movement of purification—again, the Eleatic Stranger's word, *katharmos*—whose predominant ethical burden is to resist purity. For the stranger is a stranger, *xenos*, and the greatest purification by far is refutation, destroying the kinship structure taken for granted. In this sense, genealogy is the construction of the family tree, the lines of descent along blood and kin, building the boundaries between those who belong by blood and those who do not, kin and strangers; and at the same time and inseparably, perhaps, the deconstruction, the impurification, of that family tree as the refutation of every attempt to purify by blood, to purify the state in kind. This would place nation, family, and kind, represented by genealogy, as governed by the task to purify what cannot be purified, what cannot be made pure. Genealogy is impurity ordered by blood. Closely allied with it, kindlness is impurity ordered by kinds.

This is how I understand Foucault's account of genealogy, though he begins with a strange and contrary figure, apparently at odds with what he says elsewhere of genealogy, linked with *"an insurrection of subjugated knowledges"* (Foucault, *2L*, 81):

> Genealogy is gray, meticulous, and patiently documentary. It operates on a field of entangled and confused parchments, on documents that have been scratched over and copied many times. (Foucault, *NGH*, 139)
>
> Genealogy, consequently, requires patience and a knowledge of details and it depends on vast accumulation of source material. . . . In short, genealogy demands relentless erudition. (p. 140)
>
> Genealogies are therefore not positivistic returns to a more careful or exact form of science. They are precisely anti-sciences. (Foucault, *2L*, 83)

I am concerned about the return of terms that mark "the institution and functioning of powers which are linked to the institution and functioning of an organised scientific discourse within a society such as ours" (p. 84): rigor, precision, meticulousness, order, patience. Nietzsche's genealogies seem to me to be Dionysian, volatile, explosive, imaginative, impatient. Insurrections, interruptions, defying—perhaps in the most "rigorous" way—every canon of rigor. Resisting the authority of rational, proper discourse—its authority, not its truthfulness.

This is a subject for discussion elsewhere.[3] Except for rigor, toward which I would express some caution, together with objectivity and erudition—terms that, in the West, define the better philosophy, the superior thinking, under whose authority many have been silenced, neutralized. I postpone rigor for a while, returning to it later in Heidegger's name. I return to descent and blood, one might think anything but gray and meticulous—perhaps volatile and red.

Birth, origin, descent: histories of blood, blood in birth, blood of violence and domination, all linked as *Abkunft, Herkunft, Geburt*. Pursuit of the origin, we may say, allows for two inseparable undertakings: genealogy as the "attempt to capture the exact essence of things, their purest possibilities, and their carefully protected identities" (Foucault, *NGH*, 142); and "the secret that they have no essence or that their essence was fabricated in a piecemeal fashion from alien forms" (p. 142). Both appeared in our reading of *Sophist*, as purification. The purity of lineage and blood, blood and kind; the purification in recognizing that no blood lineage can be pure, a purification in kind that profoundly resists purity. Purification against purity, refuting, confounding, repelling purity. "What is found at the historical beginning of things is not the inviolable identity of their origin; it is the dissension of other things. It is disparity" (p. 142). In lineage and blood.

Expressed "more exactly" (p. 145) through *Entstehung* and *Herkunft*, where "*Entstehung* designates *emergence*, the moment of arising" (p. 148): *parousia*. Speaking of what I understand in Anaximander's name to be given everywhere from the good, memories of violence, exclusion, and domination: "humanity installs each of its violences in a system of rules and thus proceeds from domination to domination" (p. 151).[4] *Herkunft*, descent, family, stock, nation, group, propinquity, bonded by blood, tradition, and social class, add to human kinds the violence that kinds always bear within themselves, obscured and forgotten, especially in relation to natural kinds. Humanity does not progress to a neutrality free from domination, but remains in domination in relation to human kinds, and natural kinds, perhaps every kind—*genos, phulon*, and *eidos*. The division of the world into kinds, in memory of the good, institutes domination and injustice. For which the entire ordinance of time pays restitution. The genealogy of kinds traces the destructions imposed in the name of kinds. Without which there could be no abundance.

Herkunft and *Entstehung* express the impurity of purity, the mingling of kinds that every genealogy traces in the double and triple meanings of blood—and more; the blood of birth, linked with reproduction and domestic roles assigned to women; the blood of violence and domination, linked with the production of every identity and kind; the blood of lineage, along whose lines purity emerges—the fabrication of purity in lines of descent, demanding purification, purification against purity, purification of every bloody thought of purity. Genealogy as *Herkunft* links family, stock, nation, group, descent, kin, kind, gender, women, humans and animals, humanity and the world of natural kinds, links them in their impurity, *Entstehung*, within the movement of the blood identities genealogy hopes to define.

A bloodless description followed by flesh and blood:

to follow the complex course of descent . . . is to identify the accidents, the minute deviations—or conversely, the complete reversals—the errors, the false appraisals, the faulty calculations that gave birth to those things that continue to exist and have value for us; it is to discover that truth or being do not lie at the root of what we know and what we are, but the exteriority of accidents. (Foucault, *NGH*, 146)

> Finally, descent attaches itself to the body. It inscribes itself in the nervous system, in temperament, in the digestive apparatus; it appears in faulty respiration, in improper diets, in the debilitated and prostrate body of those whose ancestors committed errors. . . . because the body maintains, in life as in death, through its strength or weakness, the sanction of every truth and error, as it sustains, in an inverse manner, the origin—descent. (p. 147)

Truth and error marked by flesh and blood. This is Foucault reading Nietzsche, but it may be Foucault's genius to insist on the body's genealogy. "The body is the inscribed surface of events. . . . Genealogy, as an analysis of descent, is thus situated within the articulation of the body and history. its task is to expose a body totally imprinted by history and the process of history's destruction of the body" (p. 148). A fourth meaning of blood, then: *the body*—endless bodies—filled with impurities and ambiguities, is present as the site and object of every genealogy, pure and impure. The endlessly repeated play of dominations, the history that proceeds from domination to domination, are enacted in the blood of bodies: man and woman, animal and vegetable bodies. Perhaps material bodies. Kinds of bodies. The order of the world requires endless purification of the neutrality and universality claimed in the name of kinds that inflicts violence and domination upon human and other bodies. Purity and neutrality remain in the endless impurity of lineage and blood, perpetrating destruction on some rather than other kinds of bodies.

I allude repeatedly to blood even where some may say there is no blood, no blood spilt, no blood flowing through veins and arteries, no family and kin. Yet the classification of natural kinds, even those devoid of arteries and veins, wallows in blood. The neutralization of gender, race, and class differences commits a violent operation; neutralization takes place in memory of human blood, diminished, abject human kinds; nonhuman blood and violation, where only human kinds and their blood matter, only certain human kinds, certain human families and their blood. I will pursue this line of thought further in German, preceded by an interruption in French.

Genre, the word for gender in French, is also the word for genus and kind, a word that can never be neutral in a gendered language. "*Genre* is not in fact merely something to do with physiology, biology or private life, with the mores of animals or the fertility of plants. It constitutes the irreducible differentiation *internal to the 'human race' ['genre humain']*. *Genre* represents the site of the nonsubstitutable positioning of the *I* and the *you* of their modalities of expression. Should the difference between the *I* and the *you* disappear, so do demand, thanks, appeals, questions" (Irigaray, *TG*, 140–41). This is a powerful argument against the neutralization of natural kinds, animate and inanimate *genres*. *Genre*, the word for gender and kind, always turns back upon the human race *[genre humain]*. Echoing in the neutral discourse of the kinds of nature are the genders and kinds of human history, anything but neutral. *Genre* and neutrality are intimately linked. Irigaray hopes to invert and to interrogate their relation. At stake is nature's non-neutrality.

> When I question discourse . . . I observe, first of all, that the neuter is apparently something to do with *nature*. *Il pleut, il neige, il vente, il tonne* . . . express forces *[puissances]* that resist human power *[pouvoir]*, its formalization. This is not an inert matter which imposes itself upon or is distinct from man, this is an *animate* nature whose language *[langage]* is spoken more or less capriciously and is now expressed *in the neuter*: in its movements, its manifestations, its rhythms, but also when we grasp it through our sense-perceptions: . . . The sense which could invert things is basically *touch*, our body as *tactile tool* for apprehending and manipulating the world, ourselves, the other. (p. 141)

I have elsewhere discussed how Irigaray understands touch as the sense that can transform, invert, the relation in discourse between animate and inanimate natural things, that can bear the intimate corporeality of a world without neutrality.[5] Touch touching touch. Here I am more concerned with the link between neutrality and inanimate nature—if anything in nature is inanimate or neutral—born in genders and kinds, linked with the categories of language. *Genre* falls back and down upon itself, upon the exclusions it institutes. Kinds touch each other without neutrality.

> Three *"il,"* three so-called "neuters" which are worth questioning, especially in their intervention between the two human *genres*: the language of nature, the word(s) of exclusively male god(s), the cultural order and its discourse through things. (p. 142)

> The sexuation of discourse does not in fact correspond to a few words more or a few words less. . . . Nor does *the mark of gender* in language *(langue)* (masculine, feminine, neuter) exhaust the meaning of a sexuate generation of messages. It is often revelatory of social and historical phenomena. It shows how one sex has subordinated the other or the world. Thus, in French at least, the masculine gender always takes syntactic

precedence: a crowd of 1000 people made up of 999 women and one man will be described as *ils étaient*; . . . What is more, the neuter is expressed by the same pronoun as the masculine: *il tonne, il faut*. . . . These syntactic laws reveal the dominance of one sex over the other. (p. 144)

The language with which we speak of nature, animate and inanimate, is gendered, sexed, anything but neutral. "What becomes apparent when we analyse the expressions of the subject in language, representations, art, legends and myths is that *sex [sexe] is a primal and irreducible dimension of subjective structure*. We are sexuate and we produce sexuate forms" (p. 146).[6]

I understand these arguments to present a thought of nature and nature's kinds intimately linked with human genders, races, classes, and other kinds, so intimately that the purification demanded by thinking harder of nature and kinds leads away from purity toward impurity. To the argument that nature is always given in gendered terms because nature is given in language to Us, I respond that nature is given somehow and somewhere among natural things and kinds, always impurely. The giving is expression, impurity, responsiveness, responsibility, anything but neutrality. The gendering of nature does not make everything in nature animate, bringing the dead to life, but expressive and responsive, given from the good. The impurity and complexity of *genre* in French, of *gender, race*, and *kind* in English, presuppose the complexity and impurity of every natural thing and kind.

Returning to the language of this chapter, nothing in nature is free from descent in lineage and blood, on two sides: the production of anything as a something, in language or discourse, bears the social history of its production, a history steeped in human blood; and what is produced bears an immeasurable mark of impurity and violence under whose seal some kinds—human and otherwise—have been excluded from privilege and authority in the workings of allegedly neutral languages. Nature and natural kinds fall down under the excesses of authority. Human and otherwise. Without authority for that abjection.

I return from this interruption in French to gender in German, interrupted in English. *Geschlecht*, the word for gender in German, is also the word for genus and kind, a word that can never be neutral in a gendered language. A word in German that cannot be imagined to be neutral because of its relation to *Schlag*, to slaughter and death, the deadly act or blow that marks, stamps, dissension—including sexual, erotic dissension, the *polemos* between man and woman, man and animal, humanity and nature: all *Geschlecht*, always Ours, We Humans. Always the human kind, marked in German by *Geschlecht*, in French by *genre*: *Menschengeschlecht, le genre humain. Genre, Geschlecht*, kin, kind, and race.[7]

Derrida's *Geschlecht* writings address the construction of the neutrality of *Dasein* as anything but neutral. The sexual neutrality of *Dasein* evokes the suspicion that the most primordial possibilities for *Dasein*, in its proper body, include sexual difference. There can be no human body that is not sexed. And what, I ask, of other bodies, proper or not: apes, cats, and slime; grass and trees; stones and brooks? In a gendered language, all are gendered, sexed. What of a neutral, objective, scientific language of animate and inanimate bodies? *Genre, Geschlecht,* kin, and kind all resist neutrality in a double memory: of the disasters carried out in the name of neutrality, and in the responsibility, the call, to which the construction of neutrality, objectivity, and science respond. I understand this call and answer as the gathering of being and language in truth for the sake of the good—always nothing. I have explored this gathering elsewhere.[8] Here I am pursuing the giving of kinds, given without neutrality from the good.

Dasein would be sexually neutral, constructs itself as neutral, thereby opening the possibility that it was anything but neutral from the first (if there might have been a beginning). What if the *Da* of *Dasein* were already sexual? How far might this recognition go: Perhaps beyond *Dasein* to Being itself, nature herself? As we have seen recurrently in Griffin. Derrida explores Heidegger's insistence in a Marburg course in 1928 that "*Dasein* is neither of the two sexes" (Derrida, *G1*, 69), provoking a reading that the denial might mark the possibility itself. Leading Derrida to conclude, on the way we might say to "*Geschlecht* II," that "[i]n the Course, for the above given reasons, *Geschlecht* always names sexuality as it is typed by *opposition* or by duality" (p. 83), by *Schlag*. If the question of the neutrality of *Dasein* haunts the first examination of *Geschlecht*, all the later readings take for granted the violent lack of neutrality in *Geschlecht* itself, at least in German if not in other, related languages, French or English; if not, perhaps, in all cultures and languages that understand nature in terms of gender and kind—or that claim not to do so.

Geschlecht—gender and kind—is linked on one hand with *Schlag*, including the stamp, the blow, the violence, that strikes a kind with identity, with acts of humans, gods, and angels, the most primordial, defining, identifying blows; linked on the other hand to genus, stock, ancestry, gender, race, nation, and kind. Kin and kind, family and nation, gender and descent, all are intimately linked in German, under *Geschlecht* and *Herkunft*, to lineage and blood, to belonging and alienation, to political boundaries and exclusions, wherever kinds are struck the blow that names them, defines them, institutes them—the blow, we may say, that falls upon them in history and language, but that takes for granted an infinitely prior blow—of kind, blood and descent—in the name of The Human. All of which is to say that kinds in nature cannot be neutral, at least for humans who relate to nature and natural kinds, but perhaps in the heart of kinds themselves, in the families, the kin, the kindlness that haunts every kind with lineage and blood, with genealogy.

All this pertains to the term *Geschlecht* in German, gathered by Heidegger in his own ways to claim the gendered neutrality of *Dasein* where *Dasein* is anything but neutral from the standpoint of nonhuman creatures and things. I stay with Derrida's reading, postponing the question of Heidegger to an interruption. I follow this line of thought briefly here because I have discussed it in detail elsewhere.[9]

> Here in effect occurs a sentence that at bottom seems to me Heidegger's most significant, symptomatic, and seriously dogmatic. (Derrida, *G2*, 173)

> Apes, too, have organs that can grasp, but they do not have hands. The hand is infinitely different from all the grasping organs—paws, claws, or fangs—different by an abyss of essence. Only a being who can speak, that is, think, can have hands and can handily achieve works of handicraft. (Heidegger, *WCT*, 357)

> Man's hand then will be a thing apart not as separable organ but because it is different, dissimilar from all prehensive organs (paws, claws, talons); man's hand is far from these in an infinite way through the abyss of its being. This abyss is speech and thought. (Derrida, *G2*, 174)

The *Geschlecht* of Man is rooted for Heidegger in the hand—*the* hand, Derrida notes, the single hand of language, never two, never two bodily organs. The hand marks the Human *Geschlecht* by an abyss of essence, an infinite, immeasurable difference by whose measure animals are profoundly inferior. The Kind of Man is marked by the gift of language without the slightest responsibility.

Continuing, Derrida notes, from the handlessness and wordlessness of animals to their voicelessness and friendlessness, longstanding denigrations of animals compared with elevated Man. From the enigmatic and difficult words in *Being and Time*, "as in hearing the voice of the friend whom every Dasein carries with it" (Heidegger, *BT*, sect. 34, p. 206),[10]

> The friend has no face, no figure. No sex. No name. The friend is not a man, nor a woman: it is not I, nor a "self," not a subject, nor a person. It is another Dasein that each Dasein *carries*, through the voice it hears, with itself. (Derrida, *G4*, 165)

> The animal has no friend, man has no friendship properly so called for the animal. The animal that is "world poor," that has neither language nor experience of death, etc., the animal that has no hand, the animal that has no friend, has no ear either, the ear capable of hearing and of carrying the

friend that is also the ear that opens Dasein to its own potentiality-for-
being and that . . . is the ear of being, the ear for being. (p. 172)

Molly demands an interruption in the name of rigor.

All these separations and exclusions of animals from proper *Dasein*
take place in Heidegger's name. And Derrida understands this name to
represent a fateful juncture of thought in our time. The question for us, for
me, is how? I believe that something important can be found in Heidegger,
said to be inescapable, crucial to rigor and philosophical reflection. With
what authority, and what insistence, for whom and for how long?

Beyond the question of the excessive authority with which one claims
philosophic necessity for a proper name, including Plato and Aristotle no
doubt as well as Heidegger, is the nature of the demand. Heidegger's words,
exactly? Heidegger's life, perhaps? Heidegger's readings of Nietzsche and
Aristotle, perhaps of Plato? Whose reading of those readings? Must all
philosophy—European, American, other—from this time forth read
Heidegger again and again with rigor, with loving care? With too much
love, and care, and authority?

On the hither side, shall we think of reading Heidegger under the
mark of Derrida's reading of the play of neutrality and nonneutrality in
relation to *Dasein* and animals, humanity and nature, as repetitions of
humanism in texts that are cited repeatedly against humanism?[11] Shall we
read Heidegger as an example of this betrayal of antihumanism, or of something else, anything else? Perhaps the betrayal in rigor, another insistence
on human authority. Again, with what authority, and whose? Haunted by
which specters and ghosts?[12] Which examples? Of which kinds?

The example brings us back to kinds. If Heidegger is an example, the
question is always, of what kind? Do we, shall we, *can we*, read Heidegger
as an example of one or more kinds? If so, how shall we decide which kinds?
If not—and *can we not?*—do we read Heidegger, and other philosophers,
writers, as singular without repetition or kind? The strange answer, keeping
Derrida in mind, is that in the very process of reading Heidegger, reading
a text of Heidegger, reading any texts or writing, following any trace of
mimēsis, however prominent or slight, we trace an immensely subtle and
convoluted line between the ways in which the singular author, text, inscription exceeds every repetition and kind, refuses to be an example of a
kind, and the iterability of all inscription and writing in which every author
and text repeats, reinscribes, retraces other ghostly inscriptions, in kinds.
Writing, thinking, reading are all citational, iterable, originations and repetitions of kinds, where origins and repetitions are inseparable, perhaps
indistinguishable: violent, responsible, promising a future, anything but
neutral. Genealogy again.

> It belongs to the structure of fundamental violence [including writing, practice, positioning, controlling the limit] that it calls for the repetition of itself and founds what ought to be conserved, conservable, promised to heritage and tradition, to be shared. A foundation is a promise. (Derrida, *FL*, 38)

> Iterability requires the origin to repeat itself originarily, to alter itself so as to have the value of origin, that is, to conserve itself. (p. 43)

> Iterability requires the origin to repeat itself originarily, to alter itself so as to have the value of origin, that is, to conserve itself. Right away there are police and the police legislate, not content to enforce a law that would have had no force before the police. This iterability inscribes conservation in the essential structure of foundation. (p. 43)

Iterability insists on singularity and repetition, inseparably, where each exceeds the other. Deconstruction is the tracing, in reading and writing, of the excessive traces in every inscription. Touch touches individuals and kinds touching each other and themselves beyond the limits of any boundaries. Genealogy is the tracing, in descent, of the iterability—the expressiveness, inscribed in blood—of kin and kinds. The *mimēsis* of kindІness.[13]

Mimēsis insists on singularity and kind, inseparably, each exceeding the other and itself, as itself. To read an author or text—Heidegger's *Sein und Zeit* or Derrida's *Geschlecht* articles, for example—is always to read a singular, original, founding work, no matter how trite or repetitious, and a repetitious, citational work coded in relation to countless others, prior and successive. Every work is both single and participates in multiple kinds. Every author is both single and a member of multiple kinds. Every author and work and person and thing is both singular and a member of countless kinds, each of which exceeds the others, singular and kind. The kind exceeds both the singular and other kinds. Exceeds itself, I would say, the lesson of genealogy and iterability. The example of Heidegger does not conflict with Heidegger the singular but expresses the iterability of every trace of the singular—multiply excessive. Including the example of Heidegger the National Socialist. The example exceeds every kind of which it is an index. As the kind exceeds the example.

No matter how uniquely we relate to text and history, we make of them examples. No matter how concretely we propose an example, we find that it and the kinds to which it points exceed every limit in their repetitions. And finally, among the excesses of every citation, specification, founding, or repetition are excesses of authority. In this sense, every reading and writing and trace and inscription is ethical, given from the good, answering to something for which it is responsible, for the sake of something immeasurable, toward which it cannot be sufficient, in relation to which nothing can be sufficient because there is no measure. And still we answer. And still we measure.

Allowing me to conclude this chapter with Derrida's acknowledgment of this impossibility in measure, in the name of a specific, embodied, bloody kind, opening onto every kind. For the moment I refer to cats, perhaps mine, perhaps Derrida's, the cat who lives with me, or him, or you, that I feed every day though I do not feed many other cats, countless hungry cats, or other people, millions and more starving people, toward whom we owe responsibilities, fulfilled for most of us—Sister Theresa an exception, and even she had her limits—by feeding our own and perhaps our neighbors' cats. Derrida speaks in the name of his cat, my cat, some individual cats, of the absolute imperative duty binding us to every other. An absolute responsibility without justification. And still we act with justification in everything we do. At every moment, whatever we do, we encounter this absolute responsibility and the justifications that surround it.

> How would you ever justify the fact that you sacrifice all the cats in the world to the cat that you feed at home every morning for years, whereas other cats die of hunger at every instant? Not to mention other people? How would you justify your presence here speaking one particular language, rather than there speaking to others in another language? And yet we also do our duty by behaving thus. There is no language, no reason, no generality or mediation to justify this ultimate responsibility which leads me to absolute sacrifice; absolute sacrifice that is not the sacrifice of irresponsibility on the altar of responsibility, but the sacrifice of the most imperative duty (that which binds me to the other as a singularity in general) in favor of another absolutely imperative duty binding me to every other. (Derrida, *GD*, 70)

> By preferring my work, simply by giving it my time and attention, by preferring my activity as a citizen or as a professorial and professional philosopher, writing and speaking here in a public language, French in my case, I am perhaps fulfilling my duty. But I am sacrificing and betraying at every moment all my other obligations: my obligations to the other others whom I know or don't know, the billions of my fellows (with out mentioning the animals that are even more other others than my fellows), my fellows who are dying of starvation or sickness. (p. 69)

There's a little too much singularity and individuality for my taste in this remarkable account of duty and betrayal. *I-I-I* sacrifice and betray my own, my son, the other, every other singular other. But also my family. And all the cats. The singular cat I feed—I live with and feed several—is a cat, neither a dog nor mollusk. Molly squirts water in my face. Cats, of course, eat chicken, beef, fish, and seafood when I feed them, eat mice and rabbits on their own. I eat none of these animals though some people eat cats. Yet still, I feed my cat or cats, care for and tend to the need of my cats, and friends, a family. I hope to do so. I think it may be ethically wonderful to do so. To care, to cherish, is to be within an infinite and impossible responsibility. Met where we are, in exposure and proximity. Face to face and skin to skin.

Of course, I might feed Molly or other mollusks, or worms: but at most some, never all. And I might eat mollusks—perhaps excluding Molly—or leaves, seeds, or nuts. We answer to an immeasurable and infinite responsibility by performing finite responsibilities. We answer to immeasurable calls from the good by measured responses. Incapable of avoiding harm. Celebrating the abundance of things by actions in our proximity. I am speaking of cherishment, sacrifice, and plenishment, where the immeasurable exposure toward all things, any things, individuals and kinds, is cherishment; where the impossibility of accomplishing our responsibilities is sacrifice; and where plenishment is the life, the finite and restricted economy of *bearing responsibility for sacrifice within the impossible demands of cherishment*. I take it this is what it means to avoid giving sacrifice the privilege and authority it has had throughout most of world history. The history of sacrifice is filled with claims to its goodness. I believe that nothing can make violence good, nothing can measure sacrifice's value. The history of sacrifice is a history of domination, violence, and oppression. Plenishment resists the goodness of sacrifice, including the goodness of humans eating animals and of cats eating mice. However unavoidable. Plenishment resists the ethical innocence of meat, of food, of sacrifice, of life. In the name of kinds.

CHAPTER 7

Consuming Kinds

Through butchering, animals become absent referents. Animals in name and body are made absent *as animals* for meat to exist. Animals' lives precede and enable the existence of meat. If animals are alive they cannot be meat. Thus a dead body replaces the live animal. Without animals there would be no meat eating, yet they are absent from the act of eating meat because they have been transformed into food. (Adams, *SPM*, 40)

For everything that happens at the edge of the orifices (of orality, but also of the ear, the eye—and all the "senses" in general) the metonymy of "eating well" *[bien manger]* would always be the rule. The question is no longer one of knowing if it is "good" to eat the other or if the other is "good" to eat, nor of knowing which other. One eats him regardless and lets oneself be eaten by him. (Derrida, *EW*, 281)

The sublime refinement involved in this respect for the other is also a way of "eating well," in the sense of "good eating" but also "eating the Good" *[le Bien manger]*. The Good can also be eaten. And it, the good, must be eaten and eaten well. (p. 283)

Discourses as original as those of Heidegger and Levinas disrupt, of course, a certain traditional humanism. In spite of the differences separating them, they nonetheless remain profound humanisms *to the extent that they do not sacrifice sacrifice*. (p. 279)

It is necessary, Derrida says, to eat, to eat well. *Il faut bien manger*. At least for Judeo-Christian-Greeks. And others. It is necessary, required, demanded in the name of the good to devour the flesh and blood of others, victims and gods. To devour the Good *(le Bien)*. To devour in blood the kinds of the earth.

It is also necessary, I say required under the law, that goods be stockpiled, stored up, held in reserve to be available on call. It will require some effort to insist on this point, but consuming and stockpiling both impede the circulation of goods, do so in blood, in the destruction and misery of some kinds thrown down under the authority of others—who, I insist, throw themselves down abjectly under the authorities they institute. We know that among the things humans do with food—too much food, perhaps, or too much authority and greed—is to stockpile it rather than consume it. Following Derrida's extreme provocation a bit further, what large numbers of humans appear to do for the sake of the good is to own it or consume it. With few exceptions. As if without alternatives. Always written in blood on the skins of bodies, families and kinds of goods.

These topics—consumption, stockpiling, storing, owning, devouring the good, the goods that flow in its giving, the blood and lineage of the families and kinds of the earth—compose the crux of the central chapters here. Yet it may be said that the entire project, not just this volume but all the volumes, concerns the links between the violence of blood, visited on some kinds of bodies rather than others, justified in the name of some kinds and others, and the lineage and blood that fill the earth's abundance of kinds. In this chapter, I will pursue Derrida's thought of the requirement of eating well: requirement itself, if anything can be said to be required, under or beyond the law, and the consumption said to be required, demanded, of the good as if something—nothing—immeasurable might be devoured. Let us say, with responsibility. Or perhaps, consuming responsibility as we insist on devouring the good. We humans devouring others in the name of sacrifice. Devouring others and their kinds from within an immeasurable obligation to respect and care for them. A circulation beyond humanity, as responsibility.

> Responsibility carries within it, and must do so, an essential excessiveness. It regulates itself neither on the principle of reason nor on any sort of accountancy. (Derrida, *EW*, 272)

> I have spoken of the "yes, yes," of the "[to?] come" or of the affirmation that is not addressed first of all to a subject. . . . Such a vigil leads us to recognize the processes of differance, trace, iterability, ex-appropriation, and so on. These are at work everywhere, which is to say, well beyond humanity. (p. 274)

> [I]f one re-inscribes language in a network of possibilities that do not merely encompass it but mark it irreducibly from the inside, everything changes. I am thinking in particular of the mark in general, of the trace, of iterability, of differance. These possibilities or necessities, without which there would be no language, *are themselves not only human.* (p. 284)[1]

Responsibility as expression, *mimēsis*, representation, iterability. Devouring and stockpiling as resistance to the general circulation, abdicating responsibility.

I begin with some interruptions, setting the stage more intricately than I have so far. First, I recall Griffin's link of blood and consumption with death, thinking of women and the curse they bear. Echoing words we have heard before.

> That the infant girl wishes to be eaten, devoured by her father, . . .
> That women have a lust for pain. (Griffin, *WN*, 45)
>
> She will eat the flesh she appears to love. Her hunger is never satisfied. . . .
> She devours even herself. (pp. 83–84)

Consumption here is linked with abjection in the names of woman and nature. *She*—woman and nature—would consume *herself*. Eating falls down into abjection; *he or she* who eats, who insists on eating, who lives to eat—well or good—consumes *him- or herself*. Consumption and blood remain bound to the curse. We might expect women's blood to celebrate the generation and productivity of nature. *Poiēsis* and *mimēsis*.

I interrupt this interruption with three others, intimately related to consumption, blood, and *mimēsis*. Adams speaks of animals and women as absent referents, where butchering transforms living, responding, suffering creatures into dead bodies, meat, and where women's oppression is transfigured by silence.

> This chapter posits that a structure of overlapping but absent referents links violence against women and animals. . . . Just as dead bodies are absent from our language about meat, in descriptions of cultural violence women are also often the absent referent. . . . Women, upon whose bodies actual rape is most often committed, become the absent referent when the language of sexual violence is used metaphorically. These terms recall women's experiences but not women. (Adams, *SPM*, 42–43)

Dead bodies—I would say, living creatures and their bodies—are erased from our language and practices toward meat; violence toward women is dissolved into pervasive metaphors of violence silent concerning women.

The absent referent obscures the living, breathing, caring, suffering beings whose sacrifice is demanded so that human beings shall eat well, so that men—humanity in general, Man—shall reproduce well, be fed well, cared for well. Sacrifice imposes a double wound, a double absence—and more. Here, in Adams, animals are—it is claimed *justly*—sacrificed to the well-being of human beings, disappearing—another sacrifice—into the absence of reference to animals. Meat imposes a second sacrifice on the sacrifice of animals and other natural creatures and things to humanity. The question Adams asks, then, the challenge she brings to sacrifice, is Derrida's question and mine: Can we, will we, how might we *sacrifice sacrifice*? Sacrifice multiplies repeatedly, excessively, as humanism, in consumption, without the least vestige of this question. I hope to question if not overthrow a certain humanism, if that were possible or desirable.

I interrupt this double interruption to think of the *mimēsis* of the absent referent in a different way, hoping to undo some of the violence I imposed in my earlier reading of Foucault. For he speaks of violated, disciplined, inscribed bodies, bodies regulated and made available under norms of law and practice in ways closely related to consumption and stockpiling under modes of disciplinary inscription.

> [T]he body is also directly involved in a political field; power relations have an immediate hold upon it; they invest it, mark it, train it, torture it, force it to carry out tasks, to perform ceremonies, to emit signs. This political investment of the body is bound up, in accordance with complex reciprocal relations, with its economic use; it is largely as a force of production that the body is invested with relations of power and domination. (Foucault, *DP*, 25–26)

The body—whose body or bodies, which kind of bodies, who are the absent referents?—is marked, trained, tortured, invested with relations of power and domination. Animal bodies as meat, women's bodies as reproductive vessels. Absent referents.

Foucault speaks of absent referents in terms of lateral effects, opening up a different absence and a different referent:[2] "the penalty must have its most intense effects on those who have not committed the crime; to carry the argument to its limit, if one could be sure that the criminal could not repeat the crime, it would be enough to make others believe that he had been punished" (Foucault, *DP*, 95). I would extend the force and range of lateral effects to absent kinds always abjectly present, relevant, wherever force, violence, and law are present. Their greatest effects always fall back on others than those who represent their explicit objects. Animals and women are absent referents where the lateral effects fall back upon the men—the human subjects, however anonymous and absent—who benefit from them, if anyone or anything does. Sacrifice multiplies among the lateral effects falling back down and upon the constitutive abjection of those who impose it and insist on it. The striking feature of humanism, strongly emphasized by Foucault, is that the human subject whose agency is at stake in sacrifice is always among its greatest victims, silently, absently, laterally, abjectly. Which is in no way to deny the harm that sacrifice does to others.

I interrupt this multiple interruption with another in the name of sacrifice. Bataille speaks repeatedly of sacrifice—consuming, expending, devouring, squandering rather than possessing, owning, stockpiling.

> The living organism, in a situation determined by the play of energy on the surface of the globe, ordinarily receives more energy that is necessary for maintaining life; the excess energy (wealth) can be used for the growth of a system (e.g., an organism); if the system can no longer grow, or if the excess cannot be completely absorbed in its growth, it must necessarily be lost without profit; it must be spent, willingly or not, gloriously or catastrophically. (Bataille, *AS*, I, 21)

The earth is excessive—general economy—filled with things that must be spent, squandered, gloriously or catastrophically. I wonder at the binary structure of Bataille's understanding of excess as expenditure. I hold this concern in abeyance.

Bataille links expenditure and consumption with two ideas crucial to the discussion here. One is sovereignty as *nothing*. Extravagance and consumption produce nothing, represent excess and abundance beyond restricted economy, beyond property and law. "The main thing is always the same: sovereignty is NOTHING" (Bataille, *AS*, III, 430). Extravagance and consumption express the wild abundance of things. "The history of life on earth is mainly the effect of a wild exuberance; the dominant event is the development of luxury, the production of increasingly burdensome forms of life" (Bataille, *AS*, I, 33). The second idea here is that extravagance is intimately linked with sacrifice, on two sides: against *servile use* and the production of *victims*.

> Sacrifice restores to the sacred world that which servile use has degraded, rendered profane. (pp. 55–56)

> The victim is a surplus taken from the mass of *useful* wealth. And he can only be withdrawn from it in order to be consumed profitlessly, and therefore utterly destroyed. (p. 59)[3]

Nature, for humanity, is "nature transfigured by the *curse*" (p. 78). Including eating. To death. The victim is a surplus, human or animal, accursed, destined for violent consumption. By whom, we must ask? And with what responsibility? The curse tears the victim, human or animal or something else—away from the order of things, radiating profundity.

> The animal or plant that man *uses* (as if they only had value *for him* and none for themselves) is restored to the truth of the intimate world; he receives a sacred communication from it, which restores him in turn to interior freedom.

> The meaning of this profound freedom is given in destruction, whose essence is to consume *profitlessly* whatever might remain on the progression of useful works. Sacrifice destroys that which it consecrates. (pp. 57–58)

Sacrifice here—eating, consuming, devouring, destroying—is the glorious curse, human glory, always at the expense of animals, and women. First animals.

> It is *man*, in a word, being that which alone matters to me and which the animal cannot be. (p. 133)

> What marks us so severely is the *knowledge* of death, which animals fear but do not *know*. (Bataille, *AS*, II, 82)

Endless denials of animality to humans *as the curse*, endless lateral effects on men.

> I submit that man is an animal who does not simply accept the natural given, who negates it. In this way, he changes the natural external world; he derives from it tools and manufactured objects that form a new world, the *human* world. Concurrently, man negates himself; he trains himself; he refuses, for example, to give to the satisfaction of his animal needs that *free* course on which the animal places no restraint. It must still be granted that the two negations by man—of the given world and of his own animality—are linked. (pp. 52–53)

> Man essentially denies his animal needs, and this is the point on which his basic prohibitions were brought to bear, some of which are so universal and seemingly so self-evident that there is never any question of them. (p. 53)

Abjection, the curse, falls back upon those who sacrifice others. This abjection|subjection curses humanity as the abject subject; curses humanity's victims—women, animals, children, everything whose domination and destruction institutes the figure of the human subject; and curses nature. Returning us abjectly to blood. "It is clear that we are sorry we came from life, from meat, from a whole bloody mess. We might think, if need be, that living matter *on the very level at which we separate ourselves from it* is the privileged object of our disgust" (p. 63). And the gift, still under the curse. Of women. "Thus, women are essentially pledged to *communication*, which is to say, they must be an object of generosity of those who have them at their immediate disposal. The latter must give them away, but in a world where every generous act contributes to the circuit of general generosity" (pp. 42–43). Women are gifts pledged to the social bonds of men, to family and kin, not themselves giving and givers. Women and animals as kinds bear the brunt of sacrifice.

With this understanding, I return from these multiple interruptions, understanding eating, consuming, devouring *and* stockpiling, reserving, owning, possessing all as falling under the curse, nature under the curse, emphasizing two crucial insights. First, the principle of lateral effects, that those who consume, squander, expend, as well as those who "servilely" stockpile, own, and use, all bear the weight of the curse in instituting their own abjection. The abject subordination of those who sacrifice to the authority of the institutions they have themselves constructed, or have found themselves within as subjects bearing the marks of that construction, the weight of the edifices of expenditure and sacrifice that fall down upon the subject-agents through lateral effects, all demand deconstruction and more deconstruction, sacrificing sacrifice. The second insight, returning to Griffin and Adams, is that the victims of sacrifice are never isolated individuals but are members of kinds in lineage and blood, demanding genealogy as deconstruction and the deconstruction of genealogy, again sacrificing sacrifice as kindlness

Ending all these interruptions in the name of sacrifice and the curse, I return to eating well, the good, *le bien manger*, to the relation between stockpiling and consuming, perhaps for the moment understood as meat. Eating well, eating meat. Eating the good—if that is possible—as meat and blood. Meat everywhere linked with authority, political and other authority—for example, religious, Church authority, eating the body and drinking the blood. Derrida has two—for me, preliminary—thoughts on this link worth noting before deepening the questioning:

> I would ask you: in our countries, who would stand any chance of becoming a *chef d'État* (a head of State), . . . by publicly, and therefore exemplarily, declaring him- or herself to be a vegetarian? The *chef* must be an eater of flesh (with a view, moreover, to being "symbolically" eaten himself—see above). (Derrida, *EW*, 281)

> Does [Hinduist culture] not, precisely, set in opposition the political hierarchy—or the exercise of power—and the religious hierarchy, the latter prohibiting, the former allowing itself, indeed imposing upon itself the eating of meat? Very summarily, one might think of the hierarchy of the *varna*, if not of the castes, and of the distinction between the Brahman priests, who became vegetarians, and the Kshatriya warriors, who are not. (p. 284)

Derrida says, with modest resistance to universality, that he speaks of *chefs* in our countries, *chefs* who head the family-state. The head of the family-state must eat meat, in our Greek-Judeo-Christian countries. "Heidegger was a Judeo-Christian thinker" (p. 284) (elsewhere Greek-Judeo-Christian).

And Levinas.

> The "Thou shalt not kill" . . . has never been understood within the Judeo-Christian tradition, nor apparently by Levinas, as a "Thou shalt not put to death the living in general." It has become meaningful in religious cultures for which carnivorous sacrifice is essential, as being-flesh. (p. 279)

In other countries, some openly vegetarian countries, the link between eating meat and political power remains.[4] What shall we make of this link between eating dead bodies and hierarchical power?

Adams offers a sweeping historical vision that I believe neglects all kinds of possibilities.

> What is it about meat that makes it a symbol and celebration of male dominance? In many ways, gender inequality is built into the species inequality that meat eating proclaims, because for most cultures obtaining meat was performed by men. Meat was a valuable economic commodity; those who controlled this commodity achieved power. If men were the hunters, then the control of this economic resources was in their hands. (Adams, *SPM*, 34)

I find this both too sweeping and too indecisive on the question before us, the link between male dominance and meat. Perhaps it is time to take more seriously the possibility Adams raises that it is dead animals, not meat—not always eaten—that celebrate and institute the dominance. For dead animals, or living animals on the way to sacrifice and death, are frequently celebrated as marks of power to be consumed by fire, to be burned, buried, displayed, glorified, tortured, in resistance to nature's abundance.[5] Human power over the natural world, natural kinds, is displayed as the glorification and mutilation of animal corpses. Sacrifice is animal sacrifice more than any other. Derrida says something close to Adams's words, with a shift of emphasis.

> The virile strength of the adult male, the father, husband, or brother (the canon of friendship, as I have shown elsewhere, privileges the fraternal schema), belongs to the schema that dominates the concept of subject. The subject does not want just to master and possess nature actively. In our cultures, he accepts sacrifice and eats flesh. (Derrida, *EW*, 281)

Here the strong, virile male accepts and performs animal sacrifice as well as eating flesh. I think of storing and owning flesh beyond its consumption.

If I hesitate at the reasons Adams and Derrida give for the mark of meat as a symbol of domination, I do not hesitate at her recognition of the complex and entwining marks and referents that link meat with power and the domination of women and animals together—inseparable from slavery and other dominations. She speaks of parallel trajectories; I would speak of complex flows and folds, foldings back, lines of flight, links doubled, tripled, and more.

> What we require is a theory that traces parallel trajectories: the common oppressions of women and animals, and the problems of metaphor and the absent referent. I propose a cycle of objectification, fragmentation, and consumption, which links butchering and sexual violence in our culture. Objectification permits an oppressor to view another being as an object. The oppressor then violates this being by object-like treatment: e.g., the rape of women that denies women freedom to say no, or the butchering of animals that converts animals from living breathing beings into dead objects. (Adams, *SPM*, 47)

All in terms of consumption reiterating forgotten referents and marks. I recall *mimēsis* as resistance to stockpiling and consumption, endlessly struggling to trace the marks of forgetting.

Derrida suggests that political power is openly linked to the consumption of animal flesh—and perhaps to the domination of women—not absent, obscure, or hidden at all. Hunters, chiefs, corporate executives have a stake in openly consuming bloody corpses, identifying individual animals as marks of their power. Power over men is marked by power to consume animals and to subordinate women, frequently as openly as possible. For some. Absent referents and false mass terms—expressions and marks of reticence and obscurity—may serve to mask the reality of power for most—the principle of lateral effects—in a context in which domination is explicit for many, the open torture and killing of animals and consumption of flesh. The referent of meat is both absent and present, doubled and tripled and more. Meat as referent expresses the stockpiling of matter for consumption, power over flesh, and the victories of hunters and chiefs over natural resources. Meat joins together consumption and stockpiling.

This is perhaps the central theme of the remaining chapters of my discussion here of human and natural kinds. I understand the social contract, the production and implementation of social power, as the stockpiling and consumption of kinds, animal, human, and other natural kinds, perhaps as Derrida suggests, the consumption—but also the reservation—of everything, including the powerful, perhaps including nature itself, all and every natural kind, perhaps including the Good (but not the good), to be eaten, consumed, owned, stockpiled, held in reserve. As sacrifice.

Again, then, I hesitate at the separation of consumption and storing, stockpiling, holding in reserve. Bataille separates consumption from use, profit, utility, and growth. Derrida speaks of eating everything, eating everywhere, consuming and letting oneself be consumed. The question of whether it is "good" to eat or be eaten vanishes in the consumption that is the remaining mark of goodness.

> The moral question is thus not, nor has it ever been: should one eat or not eat, eat this and not that, the living or the nonliving, man or animal, but since *one must* eat in any case and since it is and tastes good to eat, and since there's no other definition of the good *[du bien]*, *how* for goodness' sake should one *eat well [bien manger]*? And what does this imply? What is eating? how is the metonymy of introjection to be regulated? (Derrida, *EW*, 282)

The only criterion left of goodness is that one must eat and one must eat well. The entire tapestry of life is organized around eating, consuming, taking in well, the social organization of sacrifice.

> "One must eat well *[il faut bien manger]*" does not mean above all taking in and grasping in itself, but *learning* and *giving* to eat, learning-to-give-the-other-to-eat. One never eats entirely on one's own: this constitutes the rule underlying the statement, "One must eat well." It is a rule offering infinite hospitality.... This evokes a law of need *or* desire ... one must begin to identify with the other, who is to be assimilated, interiorized, understood ideally ... speak to him or her in words that also pass through the mouth, the ear, and sight, and respect the law that is at once a voice and a court. (pp. 282–83)

Yet something of meat, within the absence of its reference, something of the stockpiling in the larder where one holds onto, freezes meat and other consumables, stores them to possess them, perhaps never to consume them, seems to me crucial to this sacrificial relation to the other. One consumes the other through the orifices of mouth, ear, and eye, and other orifices; one consumes and one holds, possesses, owns a body, holds it in reserve for a consumption that may never arrive. Meat is both consumable and stored, massified, objectified, turned into a commodity, possessed, held in reserve. In the name of sacrifice.

This multiple pairing—absent and present reference; consuming and reserving, pure and impure—speaks to the proliferation of kinds in nature and humanity that expresses the complex relations I speak of as kind|ness: domination linked with generosity as *mimēsis*. Before passing from meat and flesh to this multiple pairing in other contexts, I would return to something of utmost importance for the good as I understand it here, giving and calling for responses in its name, for its sake. I speak in particular of sacrifice, and of what Derrida says of sacrificing sacrifice. Some of the most compelling critiques, thoughts that we may not wish to abandon in any ethical relation to individuals and kinds, remain humanisms to the extent that they do not sacrifice sacrifice. Some of the most ethical thoughts we may know, worldwide. They justify sacrifice to oneself of the other, or sacrifice of oneself to the other, or of others to still others, all with authority.

The utmost question of sacrifice is whether it can be just, whether it can or should be justified, whether justification pertains to it. What if it did not? What if we could not escape sacrifice—as we cannot escape violence—but sacrifice and violence were never just, never justifiable, never redeemed under law? What if law were another violence, another violation, another sacrifice without redemption? What if we lived in the immeasurable responsibility Derrida describes to care for all individuals and kinds in infinite ways under the impossibility of avoiding sacrifice? Without justification or redemption. No beautiful or glorious sacrifice.[6] Yet with joy as well as sorrow in the inescapability of sacrifice. Joy without redemption. *Mimēsis* without domination. Plenishment in the earth, sacrificing sacrifice, for the sake of the good.

The work of the good is done, must be done, in sacrifice as well as cherishment, in infinite care for the destructions of sacrifice. This work is plenishment in the earth, in relation to the earth's abundance of kinds.

This work is what remains before us in relation to kinds. For a while I pursue this double relation of consuming and storing kinds in relation to other corpses than animal corpses, inscribed on human flesh, in blood.

CHAPTER 8

Stockpiling Kinds

I Am Because We Are. (Hord and Lee, *IABWA*)

[I]n our calmer moments we must acknowledge that human beings are divided into races; that in this country the two most extreme types of the world's races have met, and the resulting problems . . . form an epoch in the history of mankind. (Du Bois, *CR*, 19)

> Slaves and domesticated animals exist in relationships of domination, requiring a master as much as a servant. . . .
> The drive for control is so essential—and so similar, whether the object of control is a slave or a domestic animal—as to overwhelm most distinctions between humans and animals. (Jacoby, *SN*, 92)

Consider the irony: precisely when those "others" gain the complex wherewithal to gain a countervailing subjectivity in the republic of Western culture, our theoretic colleagues declare the subject to be mere mystification. It is hard not to see this as the critical version of the grandfather clause, the double privileging of categories that happen to be, as it were, preconstituted, a position that seems to leave us nowhere, invisible and voiceless. (Gates, *CR*, 323–24)

Without a doubt, at least in European cultures and their posterity, kinds are to be consumed, in blood. So Derrida tells us. Tightly linked to sacrifice. Responding that these views, and others, including writings critical of humanism, remain profoundly humanistic *to the extent that they do not sacrifice sacrifice*, do not sacrifice the justice and right of sacrifice. My project is directed toward sacrificing sacrifice, for the sake of the good, given in immeasurable responsibility; toward sacrificing the honor, glory, and goodness of sacrifice to a giving without return, resisting neutrality. Where plenishment bears the inescapable burden of sacrifice without restitution and where nothing can make sacrifice good.

These are words of anticipation, putting me ahead of myself. I remain within the cultures that dominate, oppress, and consume some kinds in the name of the sacrifices that construct the human subject—whoever that subject might be and in whatever cultures. As to the consumption of human and other earthly kinds—human, animal, vegetal, artifactual, corporeal—I recall that consumption is not all that humans do with these kinds. Bataille opposes consumption to use and profit. Kinds are stored, stocked up, for use and profit, accumulated, held, and exchanged. The possibility of economic development and trade depends on the construction of means for accumulation as well as circulation: storehouses, borders, categories, representations. Perhaps not to consume kinds as much as to hold on to them, grasp them, seize them in the grip of mastery. As if the master were not in the grip of other kinds. "Everywhere everything is ordered to stand by, to be immediately on hand, indeed to stand there just so that it may be on call for a further ordering. We call it the standing-reserve *[Bestand]*" (Heidegger, *QT*, p. 298; *QTOE*, p. 17). Kinds are accumulated, as if by nature, stockpiled ready to hand, hoarded behind closed doors, stored and distributed as property—especially those kinds excluded from ethical consideration: ordinary things, implements, animals, women, and slaves. Stored, seized, classified as kinds to be held in reserve. As possessions.

From the beginning of human society—agricultural, sedentary, building, and dwelling societies—animals, plants, and humans have been stored, held, controlled, and mastered, in the grip of carefully worked out technologies of domestication and domination. Whipping, chaining, branding, castration, cropping are among the techniques regularly applied to human slaves and domestic animals: "virtually all of the practices cited [toward domestic animals] . . . were ones that humans also applied regularly to human slaves" (Jacoby, *SN*, 92). To certain kinds of human beings, by nature; to certain kinds of creatures, also by nature. Barbarians, dark-skinned people, Africans, poor women, by nature are available to be enslaved. Cows, mules, horses, sheep—animals bred to work; steers, pigs, calves, chickens, lambs—animals bred for slaughter: kinds made available for human use. Stocked up, stored, held in reserve for use as the kinds they are, available for our use *in any way whatever.*

Shall we, in memories of kinds stockpiled for use and domination, ranked under threat of destruction to be mastered, continue to employ classifications of kinds as if neutrality were a possibility? Neutrality belongs to this history as a prevailing condition of domination. That is what genealogy tells us, among other things, that the sorting of human and other kinds by knowledge, as if we might neutrally know the truth of kinds, is written in blood. Sorting by disciplinary knowledge takes place to rule, for use and mastery. Sorting in the name of knowledge and truth is written in the blood of victims who are mastered, held in reserve, treated as property, possessed and owned, stocked up—frequently in chains, behind fences; mutilated by castration and branding—for the purposes of those who claim to own them, who possess them as property under law, where law defines the right to reserve other people, creatures, and things for the use of the master. Said to be by nature, in the nature of the kinds themselves.

Shall we imagine that kinds by nature might be redeemed from this history of domination into a neutral neutrality that does not write its laws in blood? My entire project is directed against this possibility, in resistance to domination and to neutrality, a resistance based on kindlness, celebrating the profusion of heterogeneous kinds in the earth.

I am because we are. *We* are african americans—or women, jews, gypsies. All minorities, minoritarian, celebrating the transformation of a kind from oppression and domination to something richer, more interesting, *becoming*-kinds: *becoming* a *we* as if, perhaps, never able to *be* a *we*. *I* am because *we* become, because *we* celebrate and resist and mobilize our collective forces, exalting the infinite possibilities of *our* kind. Always on the edge of contamination, of injustice, where a kind might institute another domination in kind by nature, might hold other kinds in reserve for itself.

> [T]he history of the world is the history, not of individuals, but of groups, not of nations, but of races, and he who ignores or seeks to override the race idea in human history ignores and overrides the central thought of all history. What, then, is a race? It is a vast family of human beings, generally of common blood and language, always of common history, traditions and impulses, who are both voluntarily and involuntarily striving together for the accomplishment of certain more or less vividly conceived ideals of life. (Du Bois, *CR*, 21)

I'm sure the history of the world is a history of kinds, the creatures of the earth struggling as members of kinds to live and perpetuate themselves as collectives, families, and kins as well as individuals. The purpose of this book is to explore this ethical truth that the earth is composed of kinds— *and* individuals, *and* social groups, *and* habitats *and* landscapes, *and* so forth. The division of human kinds into any particular kinds—by gender, race, class, nationality, kin, or ethnicity—exists, I believe, to rank, ultimately to dominate—even where, as in Du Bois, the classification is celebrative.

This is not to claim, as I think some do, that celebration is always oppressive; that every celebration of kind legislates the domination of that kind. *We are* might be *and you and they are too*. All becoming. Nor is it to claim, as I think many "Westerners" do—almost the definition of European thought—that every kind, every *we*, is finally individual, as if there were only individuals, only singulars. *I am because we become and are* is true, always true, for every I. Every I participates in kinds. In many kinds, impurely and heterogeneously, not to a single kind. What I find difficult to accept in Du Bois is not the existence of kinds composed of common blood, language, and history, but his attenuation of the complexities, impurities, and hybridities of every family and kind, every genealogy. "We find upon the world's stage today eight distinctly differentiated races, in the sense in which History tells us the word must be used" (Du Bois, *CR*, 22). If women are a kind with a common history, lineage, and blood, they differ by nationality, ethnicity, class, and race—if there are such kinds, wherever there are such kinds—perhaps by family and blood. If there are 8—or 88, or 888—races or other human kinds, they differ in complex, subtle, and nuanced ways, differ by the countless other kinds among which they mingle and in which they participate. "But while race differences have followed mainly physical race lines, yet no mere physical distinctions would really define or explain the deeper differences—the cohesiveness and continuity of these groups. The deeper differences are spiritual, psychical, differences—undoubtedly based on the physical, but infinitely transcending them" (p. 23). I forebear pursuing a line of thought that would hold Du Bois hostage to the recognition that all such ideas of deeper differences between groups of people have supported ranking by nature for the sake of domination. Black is beautiful. Or femininity. This line of thought is contaminated even for those who would celebrate blacks or women. Celebrate how? For what? Recalling that the conjunction African American/American African speaks of diaspora, hybridity, crossing, impurity. The recurrent truth of kinds, revealed in the genealogies that would trace their lineage in blood, is that they mingle and participate impurely within the limits and boundaries of the institutions, regulations, and forces that would define their purity. Human beings mingle and participate as kinds among other kinds, have always done so, as quickly as they could. Impurity has been the recurrent condition of the division of human beings into families and kinds that insist on the purity of their lineage. Typically paid for in blood. Shakespeare tells us of it repeatedly: *Romeo and Juliet, Othello, The Merchant of Venice*. Purity expresses the possibility of stockpiling and storing kinds for use, permeated by impurity, as *mimēsis*. I interrupt this discussion in the name of *mimēsis* and impurity.

Kinds mingle and participate as kinds, exceeding the boundaries of every kind and individual: always more than what is common in the multiplicity, profusion, and heterogeneity of kinds. Perhaps the central theme of this book is that heterogeneity is of kinds, not individuals, not the difference between two individuals face to face, abstract, empty, singular individuals, but individuals clothed in the profusion of different kinds. Heterogeneity is impurity, always therefore more than what is common. Yet without kinds, heterogeneity is nothing. And the reverse. In this sense, all kinds—human kinds especially—express something of *mimēsis* in the heterogeneity of kinds, mingling and participating in kinds. Kinds are expressive, corporeal expression. Heterogeneity and kinship are expressive, express iterability, citation, *mimēsis*, impurity in kinds. Genealogy expresses the expressiveness of kinds in blood, purely|impurely. In kind|ness.

Storing, stockpiling, owning, holding in reserve all presuppose abundance: an abundance of individuals and their properties, an abundance of kinds, perhaps Spinoza's infinite numbers of infinite kinds, all expressive. Perhaps something beyond even that immeasure. Eating, consuming, devouring kinds also presuppose abundance: an abundance of individuals and kinds available for consumption, filled with endless remainders. This abundance is not the generosity of a nature that gives large quantities of foods, materials, and possessions to human beings for their use—though it may indeed do so. Value—stocking, reserving, exchanging, consuming—is the sacrifice of a wealth of individuals and kinds.[1] The abundance of nature, giving in the name of the good, exceeds this generosity beyond the limits of measure, exceeds it in the unlimits of expression, as *mimēsis*.

Kinds of the earth are possessed and stored as values, stockpiled, owned, and sacrificed. Some kinds of goods are sacrificed so that there might be values, that is, other kinds exchanged, circulated under the curse. Possession, exchange, circulation, and consumption are all given from the good under the curse. In sacrifice. But perhaps not all circulation, not the circulation of general economy, circulation itself, the immeasurable, incalculable giving of abundance, again in kinds, always more than what is in common or singular. Kind|ness expresses the doubling of this giving and its sacrifice in the expressive abundance of kinds.

I return from this interruption to the chains and whips whereby animals and human beings have been stocked up as values for possession, consumption, and exchange. Stocked up and circulated as values in kinds. I mean to consider the tools of mastery over domestic animals and human beings—animals and people who are possessed by others, regarded as owned, dominated by chains and whips and mutilation, exchanged, circulated, and consumed by others, treated as things—indeed, less than many things. For some kinds of things—diamonds, works of art, prophetic and poetic writings—are regarded as irreplaceable, precious beyond exchange, possession, and use. As are some kinds of human beings, who deserve the best we can give them, my children if not yours, famous celebrities, aristocrats, leaders of the state. And still they circulate beyond measure and calculation. Circulate in memory and imagination, the doubled gifts of value: circulating in possession and exchange under sacrifice; circulating beyond possession and exchange, beyond measure, in a giving that evokes the possibility of sacrificing sacrifice. Value is an intermediary figure, falls between general and restricted economy, abundance and sacrifice. Plenishment is where value falls between, intermediarily, always moving against the limits of sacrifice.

In kinds. The subject of this chapter is the stockpiling, storing, accumulation of kinds under the curse, as sacrifice, in memory of consumption and blood. In the abundance of kinds. Linked here with the domestication of animals and the enslavement of human beings—certain kinds of practices, certain kinds of mastery, certain kinds of animals and human beings. Always kinds. Falling between general and restricted economy. The abundance of kinds and the sacrifice of kinds in possession, consumption, and blood of kinds.

Can we understand racism, sexism, classism, speciesism—every *ism* of kinds—in terms of possession, consumption, and blood? In terms of general and restricted economy? In terms of abundance and the curse? I would see how far we can take this understanding, explore this possibility. Under a few guidelines to begin, contingent and non-legislative guidelines. Under the generic guideline that no choice can be made between general and restricted economy, they are not alternatives between which to choose. For two reasons. One is that general economy, abundance, is not something to choose instead of restricted economy, nor do we choose restricted economy under the curse. We are in abundance together with the inescapability of sacrifice, of exclusion. The second is that choice belongs to restricted economy under the curse. General economy, abundance, knows nothing of choice. We cannot live without choices, decisions, judgments, but every choice falls under the curse of sacrifice, promotes injustice and disaster. And every such choice is made in the giving of abundance in the earth from the good.

Giving us four guidelines toward the stockpiling of kinds:

1. The kinds of the earth circulate in abundance beyond measure, cursed by sacrifice. The curse of sacrifice does not diminish abundance though it is defined by mastery, by the restriction of individuals and kinds.
2. Restriction is possession, accumulation, domination, mastery, exchange, substitution, consumption, following lines of descent, lineage and blood.
3. Restriction is choosing good over bad, superior over inferior, better over worse, useful over useless, liberation over tyranny. All choice of goods depends on sacrifice, takes place under restriction.
4. Abundance marks every restriction, every limit, at least twice: with disaster beyond measure, and with responsibility beyond every limit to resist disaster, to sacrifice sacrifice.[2]

What might one say of gender, race, and animality in relation to consumption, possession, and blood, if these define social contracts, restricted economies, that human beings cannot avoid but that do not exhaust the abundance of kinds, which are always more than what is common, more than any restriction, always more in abundance? My project is based on the endless links of domination and mastery among human and other kinds. Yet I would stay for the moment with racism, with domination by blood, postponing further discussion of the mingling and impurity of kinds and dominations. I return to Du Bois and the celebration of race, keeping its abundance in mind.[3]

Can one celebrate race—let us say, the Negroes of Africa, the temperament of black folk—in a history of slavery and discrimination based on race? Another example.

> Negritude is nothing more or less than what some English-speaking Africans have called the *African personality*. It is no different from the "black personality" discovered and proclaimed by the American New Negro movement. . . .
> . . . It is obvious that peoples differ in their ideas and their languages, in their philosophies and their religions, in their customs and their institutions, in their literature and their art. Who would deny that Africans too have a certain way of conceiving life and of living it? (Senghor, *N*, 45–46)

Who would deny that Africans—or any other people, creatures, and things— have a certain way of living and being? It cannot be denied, but it can be questioned endlessly, surrounded by incessant mirrors of representation and desire, of *mimēsis*. Perhaps negritude and the Negro race are entirely too visible here. Celebration makes them visible, perhaps too pure. I would not forget invisibility and impurity. Perhaps humanism fails to perceive invisibility. Or struggles with it, the invisibility of black and white people, of kinds of people, of kinds of creatures and things, where they are entirely too visible to be seen. Yet strange and enigmatic. Missing persons mark the colonized world. The world.

> One day I learnt,
> a secret art,
> Invisible-Ness, it was called.
> I think it worked
> as even now you look but never see me . . .
> (Meiling, *SHL*; quoted in Bhabha, *II*, 208)

With this interruptive gesture I postpone postcoloniality to the next chapter. Invisibility cannot be postponed. "A black feminist ideology, first and foremost, thus declares the visibility of black women" (King, *MJMC*, 312);[4]

"negritude . . . is essentially relations with others, an opening out to the world, contact and participation with others. . . . [I]t is a humanism of the twentieth century" (Senghor, *N*, 46). A humanism that sacrifices sacrifice? A visibility without invisibility? Memory without forgetting? Difficult questions for kinds that continue to experience domination. Kinds in confusion.

We seem to take for granted that there are races, visible clusters of physical and temperamental qualities of human beings, clusters of qualities defining human kinds. And we seem to take for granted that these clusters are something to celebrate after a history of denigration and hate. As, perhaps, Jews—Jewish people—claim to celebrate the history of their people, reflecting intelligence, curiosity, and spiritual enlightenment, within a history filled with hatred and destruction toward Jews, no end to anti-Semitism in sight, rendering Jewish people invisible, forgotten, one way or another. Descendants of slaves.

To many members of other kinds, including dominant kinds, such celebrations belong to "identity politics" in which groups and kinds of people mobilize their energies in their kind. Why is this not minority fascism, fascism in reverse? Whites claimed to be better than blacks, justifying their enslavement; Germans claimed to be better than Jews and threatened by them, justifying their destruction. Can we think of celebrating a kind without justifying the possession, consumption, and destruction of other kinds?

That is, of course, what Du Bois hopes to do, granting a multiplicity of races, identities based on history and blood, together with a multiplicity of ideals of life. If human beings can grant the possibility of a multiplicity of ideals and dreams, why not grant the possibility that different peoples, cultures, races, nations, kinds—perhaps every individual and kind—differ in their dreams and ideals? Such a granting of multiplicity and heterogeneity may promise a very different politics, a very different world, in which no kind or culture insists on dominance over other kinds, the privilege of its ideals over the ideals of others. Perhaps no human kind or culture might then insist on its dominance over other kinds, human or nonhuman. We hope to escape the curse.

The central thesis of this picture of the multiplicity of kinds—not quite abundance—is that for each human individual, that individual belongs to a particular kind—race or culture. I am because we are. And indeed, I would say, have been arguing throughout, that individuals participate in an abundance of kinds. Each individual. The idea of race appears to insist that each black individual must acknowledge being black, each Jewish individual must be a practicing Jew—suggests, I fear, a certain tyranny.

Such a tyranny is described by Deborah Jowett, speaking of the suggestion by a "community activist" that one way of practising "respect for the environment" while fostering "community responsibility" would be to form a committee or group to inspect neighbourhood garbage. . . . Committing a garbage crime, e.g., throwing out too much garbage, or the wrong garbage, or not composing, etc., would result in some sort of censure or possibly even a fine being levied by the garbage surveillance unity. The speaker thought that the risk of social ostracism would do a lot to promote "environmentalism" while at the same time it would strengthen "community ties." (Jowett, *OOPN*, 26)

Strengthen the *we*, the community, a bit tyrannically perhaps. Clearly stockpiling, storing, consuming, a kind of community imposing sacrifice, written in blood. This possibility is present in every *we*, every community, every kind, that insists that belonging to a kind sets a standard against which members of that kind are to be measured—even where they belong to other kinds as well. Jowett's ethics follows a beautiful and persuasive line of thought, with Levinas in mind, related to individual proximity. I postpone this proximity to the next chapter as an interruption. Here I would pursue the idea of race in kind along the edges of tyranny.

Can we speak of race without racism, without a hierarchy ranking kinds of people from better to worse? Every *ism* is such a ranking, contaminating every relation to kinds. This is the curse, always a curse in kind, in blood, possessing and consuming kinds by right, under law, with objective, neutral justification. Neutrality establishes a hierarchy without neutrality, named as sexism, classism, racism—I might call it *kindism*, another name for the tyranny of kinds. An ugly name for an ugly practice. The kinds of the earth, the earth's abundance, are classified and ranked as if by neutrality, creating a hierarchy imposing domination, anything but neutral.

Leading more generically to the ethical question of this book. Can we speak of, live among, kinds without tyranny, without stockpiling or consuming kinds, without a hierarchy ranking human beings, animals, plants, and things from better to worse? Without preparing them for the feast? Without ordering them for use? Without bringing them under the curse? Can we name a kind without insisting on its genealogy in blood? Can we live in kindlness?

Du Bois thinks we can, multiplying races and kinds in plurality. Though he names a small number of major human families linked by language, history, and blood. And perhaps we should beware of every suggestion that this triad serves to order these and other families and kinds without ambiguity and disaster. As if this triad defined what was common and different among the vast families of human beings—also, perhaps, dividing humans from animals and plants. As if race were nothing more than what was common. As if what was more than common was not always cursed.

I look to other inquiries into the curse of kinds. For example, Appiah finds three doctrines that may be equated with racism:

1. *Racialism*: a sort of racial essence—hereditable characteristics divided by kinds of human beings;
2. *Extrinsic racism*: that racial essences are empirically linked with certain morally relevant qualities;
3. *Intrinsic racism*: that racial essences are inseparable from certain morally relevant qualities. (Appiah, *R*, 4–6)

He disagrees with racialism but thinks it may not be pernicious as a cognitive doctrine. "Provided moral qualities are distributed across the races, each can be respected" (p. 5). This is, perhaps, Du Bois's view. One can hold racialism and some kinds of kindism in a non-invidious way. As strongly as I favor the plurality of kinds, and would advocate it for others, I do not believe it is respected by human beings who have to struggle to hold firm the boundaries of their institutions and laws. Democracies struggle endlessly with moral conflicts among members of different groups—typically cultural and religious. As soon as race echoes culture and religion, moral ranking is imposed.

Appiah imagines that extrinsic racism can be settled by empirical information—another belief, perhaps, in the superior powers of a neutral rationality. Those who believe in the inferiority of certain kinds of human beings can be shown the evidence, and they will or should be convinced. "Evidence that there are no such differences . . . should thus lead people out of their racism if it is purely extrinsic. As we know, such evidence often fails to change a extrinsic racist's attitudes substantially. . . . [W]hat we have is no longer a false doctrine but a cognitive incapacity" (p. 5). What we have is intrinsic racism. Yet the question is whether racism, or racialism—any *ism*—permits of neutrality, or whether the grouping into a kind, however plural and celebrative of kindred differences, is from the first resistant to neutrality. Intrinsically. Whether, indeed, the claim to neutrality is already not neutral, as Irigaray says. Whether, indeed, cognitive capacities are not intimately entwined with moral capacities far beyond neutrality, always more than what can be known in common. Whether, more generally, the reserving and holding kinds by classification is not always for consumption and use, inscribed in blood. Ethics under law is the stocking up of kinds for classification and use, written and released by genealogy in blood. Insisting on something ethical, given and giving from the good, beyond and more than owning, consuming, and blood. Beyond measure.

Beyond measure, however, is not beyond kinds, because kinds are more than what is common, more than measure, more than what can be owned, consumed, and used. If it is true that to speak of kinds is always on the one hand to come too close to tyranny, it is true as well that kinds exceed every tyranny, every ranking, possession, consumption, and use. This is the truth of kind|ness—however enigmatic—crucial to understanding the social and historical construction of race, largely absent from Appiah's discussion, a construction that does not disappear into neutrality.

Turning elsewhere, anticipating something of the discussion of different social worlds in the next chapter, members and strangers: "The house of 'critical theory' has thus been divided on the issue of 'race,' sometimes against itself: . . . 'race' is without scientific basis as an explanatory notion (Frankfurt School); 'race,' while real, is a factor of conflict secondary to the primary contradiction of class struggle ('classical,' 'official' Marxism); 'race is the basis of a nation—a group whose members share common history and culture ('official' Marxism of 1928–57)" (Outlaw, *TCTR*, 75). Outlaw reminds us of the intractability of race within the political movements that would obliterate its harmfulness. Critical theory remains divided, each school taking an authoritative stand on race and its reality. To which Outlaw asks— the question it appears no critical movement or theory can quite ask— "what is that reality? And 'real' for whom?" (p. 76); "We must not err yet again in thinking that 'race thinking' must be completely eliminated on the way to emancipated society" (p. 78). We must not imagine that kinds will be abolished in the liberation of individuals, even the most heinous and destructive of kinds. We must not imagine that we can escape the curse.

Even so, it is crucial—for Outlaw as well as for my discussion here— to emphasize that every kind—perhaps especially including races together with other kinds around which hierarchical *isms* have formed historically— is always more than what is common, always more than any essence, more than any neutral being or gathering. Race, gender, and nationality mark the descent of human history and the natural world in blood, the groups of kin and kinds, the families whose kindredness defines what it is to be human or otherwise, never in the neuter.[5] Always impure. Which is anything but to admire the hierarchies of rank that have been inscribed throughout history in blood. The marks of kin and kind have stocked up the earth's abundance for the use and consumption of some kinds, linking use, consumption, and authority. The question continues to remain, how we can enjoy identities of kin and kind in the name of the good without reserve, resisting use, possession, and consumption? Which is to ask, how can we sacrifice sacrifice, dominate domination, curse the curse of restricted economy, always given in kind? I hold this question in abeyance, though it has emerged repeatedly as kindness.

For the moment, I remain within the curse of kinds to consider other understandings of its necessity. One is Delacampagne's thesis that "racist discourse, as we have known it in Europe since the nineteenth century, did not appear ex nihilo. It is the fruit—or the inheritor—of other, older discourses, whose first elements can be located in the philosophers of antiquity. . . . [I]t developed in the midst of a system of thought that strove to be rational; it progressed hand in hand with the very foundations of Western rationalism" (Delacampagne, *RW*, 83). The intimate link Delacampagne explores between the development of reason's authority and the history of racism is essential to my understanding of neutrality—philosophy, science, reason in the neuter, which turn out to be anything but neutral. Reason's claim to authority is linked with political authorities thoroughly invested in hierarchical privilege. The question is whether this intimate and reciprocal link is peculiarly Western, suggested both by Delacampagne's title "Racism and the West" and his examples of the Greek view of barbarians, the historical massacres of Jews, and the recurrence of slavery. Without the right to speak of other cultures with authority, I understand the link between epistemological and political authority to be intrinsic and pervasive, at least demanding vigilance, resistance, and responsibility. Racism is linked with ethnicity and nationality, with slavery by nationality and kind, in the service of hierarchical authority. This hierarchical authority is itself linked with racism and with colonialism and war. I am by no means as sure as others are that there is a fundamental difference between the institutional slavery of the African slave trade in Europe and the Middle East and the enslavement of individuals defeated in battle, where those individuals belong to certain groups and kinds: barbarians, strangers, aliens, those who in kind are not like us. Where *we* capture, enslave, or eat *others* who are exactly like us—not another tribe or family or kin or gender, but *us*—except for defeat in war, or some other mark of possession, perhaps there is no mark of inferiority in kind. Perhaps. Possession remains a crucial thought to think. Postponed to another volume. Here I acknowledge the powerful force of institutionalization.

Here, another thought appears in Delacampagne: "the ideological struggle against racism . . . should not have the 'perverse effect' of leading us to deny the real diversity, biological *and* cultural, existing within the human species" (p. 88). The real diversity of kinds of which institutional racism is a perverse effect, an infamous recognition that heterogeneity is not between individuals but kinds. The thought that Du Bois attempts to articulate, with countless difficulties. The reason, I persist in saying, is that kinds are always more than what is in common, more than that in endless and incalculable ways. Racism calculates and stores up the inexhaustible heterogeneity of kinds in hierarchies of authority, possession, and institutionalization. Singularities of individuals without kinds know nothing of diversity and heterogeneity.

I conclude this discussion of racism and slavery as acknowledging—with far too many perverse effects—this excess of kinds over what is common. I conclude with two expressions of this excess, two acknowledgments of what is more than common in kinds. I will resume this discussion of the perversion of heterogeneity in kinds in the next chapter, written in the blood of strangers.

I refer here to two readings of a critical view of race that in the utmost force of their critique claim a certain universality. I speak of *a certain* universality in memory of that very different universality—in terms of exaltation and excess—found in Wittig's resistance to minority writing and subjectivity.[6] For there is, perhaps always, an irresistible insistence on a certain universality in the most critical perspectives taken toward it. A claim that always exercises another authority, constitutes another hierarchy. Perhaps in other kinds of universality, another liberation.

Gates notes the irony whereby members of minority kinds who are finally empowered to insist with authority on their own subjectivity find that the subject and subjectivity are now denied authority: "a position that seems to leave us nowhere, invisible and voiceless" (Gates, *CR*, 324). He speaks of "[t]he universalism that undergirds poststructural antiuniversalism" (p. 324). Antiuniversalism asserts itself with universality, a universality that can only be understood in terms of reserving, possessing, and consuming. The subject is abandoned, universally, as if that act were neutral, critical in the neuter, without concrete political implications for some kinds of people—the same kinds who traditionally have been crushed at the bottom of the hierarchy.[7]

Balibar describes this inescapable universalism in terms that closely parallel my understanding of excess. "[W]e see that racism figures on both sides, the universal and the particular. The excess that racism represents with respect to nationalism, and therefore what it adds to nationalism, tends at one and the same time to universalize it, correcting in sum its lack of universality, and to particularize it, correcting its lack of specificity" (Balibar, *PU*, 283). Racism expresses excess on both sides, universal and particular. Race and, I would say, racism, every kind. Race ties up with universality, corrects universality, links with nationality. All the properties of race exceed nationality, presuppose universality. "[T]there well and truly exists an 'internationalism,' a racist 'supranationalism,' that ends to idealize certain timeless, or pseudo temporal, communities such as 'the Indo-Europeans,' 'The West,' 'civilized man' " (Balibar, *PU*, 286).

He speaks specifically of racism rather than race, understanding racism as paralleling nationalism: advocating a hierarchical as well as essentialist view of race and nationality. Racism is filled with excess, ethical, political, and ontological. I would speak of race and kinds, recalling the words I have pursued throughout this discussion, that the kind is always more than what is common. This *more than* opens in every direction: toward rank and hierarchy, slavery and domination; toward heterogeneity and diversity; toward mobility and variability; toward a critical vigilance in which every critical perspective turns back upon itself, vigilant toward its own contaminations. Sacrificing sacrifice.

I interpose a stunning interruption in relation to the excesses of race as directed toward other kinds.

> In all these universals we find the *same question* repeated: *the difference between humanity and animality*. . . . [W]e thus find the paradoxical figure of an evolution that must *extract* humanity properly so called . . . from animality, but *by means* that typify animality . . . , in other words by an animal competition *between* degrees of humanity. . . . The animality of man, in man and against man . . . is the particular method that theoretical racism adopts in thinking about human historicity.
>
> . . . The "secret" whose exposure it continually replays is that of a humanity forever emerging from animality, and of a humanity eternally menaced by the grip of animality. (p. 291)

A humanity eternally menaced by animality is one forever cursed by the curse. Racism names the animality of humanity as borne particularly by some races, some kinds, rather than others. And animals. We have seen the same movement at work in relation to women. It is time to confront the curse of animality as the possibility that humanism remains in every figure that replays the curse.[8] The curse Balibar describes is notable because in the universality it claims for humanity—in the name of race—it denies universality and excess in animals, plants, and stones. Only humanity, and humanity's universality, is at stake in animality. Not animals or their animality. As Europe's universality was at stake in aboriginality. Universality here is never universal, exceeds the limits of universality by insisting on some ranked authority.

Allowing us to occupy this link of humanity and animality in a different way, with another, crucial interruption. For if we can allow ourselves to think of this relation in a multiple way, accepting its intimacy, excess, and even universality, then at least a double responsibility is demanded of us. One is expressed by Jacoby, acknowledging that within the history of domination, domestic animals and slaves have been treated similarly, and that the tools developed for the mastery of animals have been models for the mastery of humans. This supplements our ongoing recognition that the domination of women and of nature are linked. The domination of human beings, the tools of the trade for enslavement and oppression—including reason itself—are linked profoundly with the domination of nature and natural things, including animals. I would add plants and natural things, habitats and rocks. Holding them in abeyance.

For the moment, I remain within this link of humanity and animality, human slavery and animal domestication. Jacoby insists that within this crucial and essential link, we can know that the enslavement of animals is entirely different from the domestication of animals.

> [B]y conflating slaves with domestic animals, those who justified slavery in this manner were overlooking a key distinction: through neoteny domestic animals had evolved over generations to that the "natural" state was one of co-existence with humans. (Jacoby, *SN*, 95)
>
> There is certainly much to criticize about the contemporary treatment of domestic animals, but those environmentalists who suggest the "liberation" of domestic animals ignore the long evolutionary history that humans and animals share, making them dependent on each other for their mutual survival. (p. 97)

I am sure that if I were the descendant of slaves, and as a Jew I am, I would not care to understand slavery as analogous *in all relevant ways* with animal husbandry. Even so, I would insist that this distinction is not based on better information about domestic animals. Information concerning slavery, racism, and domestication—including women in the home—is never neutral. The domination of human beings is not the same as the domination of animals in all ethical respects. Nor is slavery the same as the oppression of women. Despite intimate and terrible links.

Spiegel claims the opposite, insisting on the dreadful nature of the comparison. "Comparing the suffering of animals to that of blacks (or any other oppressed group) is offensive only to the speciesist: one who has embraced the false notions of what animals are like" (Spiegel, *DC*, 30). Comparing how? Comparing what? The pain? I'm sure that there has been more animal suffering throughout history than all the suffering of slaves and their descendants. Animals suffer. And there have been far more of them, treated in terrible ways. Even worse than inmates of the worst concentration camps. But must one be a speciesist—whatever that is—to insist that Nazi concentration camps were especially horrible because they were directed at human beings? Must we collapse all distinctions of kinds in ethical consideration? Can we insist on maintaining distinctions of kinds in ethical consideration?

Finally, is the ethical thought and life of kinds without kindism—kindness as an ecology of kinds—always more than that what is in common, more than, other than, neutrality? Always written in blood, even by the victims, and toward their liberation? Which is to speak of sacrifice and sacrificing sacrifice. Thoughts I continue to hold in abeyance.

CHAPTER 9

Strange Kinds

Foreigner: a choked up rage deep down in my throat, a black angel clouding transparency, opaque, unfathomable spur. The image of hatred and of the other, a foreigner is neither the romantic victim of our clannish indolence nor the intruder responsible for all the ills of the polis. . . . Strangely, the foreigner lives within us: he is the hidden face of our identity, the space that wrecks our abode, the time in which understanding and affinity founder. . . .

Can the "foreigner," who was the "enemy" in primitive societies, disappear from modern societies? (Kristeva, *SO*, 1)

Homer tells us that gods attend upon the goings of men of mercy and justice, and not least among them the god of strangers comes to mark the orderly or lawless doings of mankind. (Plato, *Sophist*, 216a)

La realité comporte le différend.[1] (Lyotard, *D*, 90)

To read Fanon is to experience the sense of division that prefigures—and fissures—the emergence of a truly radical thought that never dawns without casting an uncertain dark. . . . *"The Negro is not. Any more than the white man."* (Bhabha, *II*, 183)

Have aliens, strangers, "foreigners," always been "enemies," especially in "primitive" societies? Could they be descended from the gods? Can modern, perhaps civilized societies come to regard strangers less as enemies than ourselves? Questions reminiscent perhaps of coloniality. Some primitive societies and not others. Different ways in which societies bring strangers into themselves. Exogamous cultures in which women are strangers, sometimes seized by force. Not to deny the history of slavery, strangers enslaved for being strangers. Nor to deny the history of European wars and European colonization, of others, strangers, made enemies by force. Sacrificed to European civilization.

141

Throughout these reservations, I understand Kristeva to mark something of utmost ethical|political concern. The social contract rests on the distinction between Our Kind and Other Kinds, dividing citizens from strangers, our kin from others, by descent and blood. In the name of The Human. Geophilosophy reasserts geopolitics in denying its legitimacy.

> "What is my relation to the other?" "What are the limits and the rights of a group?" "Why should not every man have the rights of a citizen?" In France, pragmatic matters immediately become ethical. The "completely political" aspires to become the "completely human" with that spirit of lay universalism that was necessarily to confront the Nation, which is universal because it is proud of having invented the "rights of man," with the *very legitimacy of "foreigner"*. (Kristeva, *SO*, 39–40)

In France, the foreigner defines the idea of the rights of man, in general, a thought, an experience, of universality—at least, of universalism, cosmopolitanism, legitimation. The universal rights of men in general memorialize the institution of foreignness, the thought of other kinds. Humans and animals, men and women, French and Arab, all pairs defining the other as stranger, defining the stranger within the institution of universality. What if we question the ideas, the institution, of legitimacy and universality in the name of kinds and their descent?

We have followed descent down genealogical lines, through *Herkunft, Entstehung, Geschlecht*, and *genre*, to race, kin, and kind. It is time to pursue these ties by blood as they separate kin from strangers. Keeping in mind that kin and kind are always more than what is common, that blood exceeds in violence and abjection every kinship tie. Excesses of state, institutional, and customary authority that inscribe the alienness of strangers upon their bodies—and ours—in blood. Whoever *we* and *they* may be.

Right from the start, however, let us refuse something of the image that *primitive* societies regard strangers as enemies, always and everywhere, whatever societies may be primitive. For if some tribal societies kill every member of another tribe they may encounter, sometimes eat them, sometimes enslave them, others develop elaborate rituals and ceremonies to welcome strangers into their midst. Throughout Africa, we are told, before colonization and after, people traveled with great mobility, nomads, emigrants, participating in societies other than their own, frequently remaining outsiders. Many traditional African societies developed *threshold rituals*, ceremonies whereby such outsiders might cross the line between inside and outside. Such outsiders have been described as *liminaries*, intermediary figures in intermediary movement, outsiders of other kinds crossing thresholds, much closer to Homer's description of strangers who reveal the inner truths of the social contract (Trumbull, *TC*; Turner, *RC*).[2] In Simmel's classic words, referring to both "primitive" and "civilized" societies, the stranger understands something of the host society that its members do not know, because of threshold, intermediary movements, because of continuing liminal strangeness. Filled with danger. "This freedom, which permits the stranger to experience and treat even his close relationships as though from a bird's-eye view, contains many dangerous possibilities. From earliest times, in uprisings of all sorts the attacked party has claimed that there has been incitement from the outside, by foreign emissaries and agitators" (Simmel, *S*, 146). Strange in kind:

> As such, the stranger is near and far *at the same time*, as in any relationship based on merely universal human similarities. Between these two factors of nearness and distance, however, a peculiar tension arises, since the consciousness of having only the absolutely general in common has exactly the effect of putting a special emphasis on that which is not common. For a stranger to the country, the city, the race, and so on, what is stressed is again nothing individual, but alien origin, a quality which he has, or could have, in common with many other strangers. For this reason strangers are not really perceived as individuals, but as strangers of a certain type. Their remoteness is no less general than their nearness. (p. 148)

Strangers are perceived as of a certain type, a kind, where the kinds that mark the social group are taken for granted, Strangers mark kinship in blood as no kin ties can. Intermediary movements and threshold figures mark kinds in blood.

Calling for an interruption in the name of strangeness in kinds. A marked interruption. For to the repeated traces and boundaries of the social contract whereby members of a human social group encounter members of other social groups as strangers, we may bring memories that human beings encounter strangenesses everywhere, in every social world, surrounded by multiple habitats and environments. The strangeness of animals, plants, and inanimate things, strange in their ways of life, the look in their eyes—those with eyes—the paws, fangs, talons, or claws that grasp, multiple senses far more acute than any human sense, and finally, the extrusions, protrusions, exposure of things to each other, evoking responses of such nuance and complexity that the most sophisticated sciences, in all the splendor of what they know, know more every day about what they do not know.[3]

Reality is composed of *le différend*.[4] Not just human reality. Composed of what we do not know, may never know. Not because of the limits of knowledge, or culture, or language. But because of the abundance of kinds and the thresholds that pervade them, what is immeasurable and incalculable in their abundance.

Reality is composed of *différends*, heterogeneity and diversity, anarchic intermediary movements. Framed by Lyotard as language, discourse. "By its rule, a genre of discourse supplies a set of possible phrases, each arising from some phrase regimen. Another genre of discourse supplies another set of possible phrases. there is a differend between these two sets . . . because they are heterogeneous" (Lyotard, *DPD*, xii). Reality is made up of *différends* between genres of discourse. This seems a bit strange—not to its discredit— and a bit authoritative, as if at the same time, reality were composed of language: phrases, genres of discourse, and *différends* between. *Only* language? That presupposes that language and reality can be divided neutrally, the assumption of classical representation that all the discourses mentioned and this entire project resist. Perhaps language *and* reality, where language participates in the world and reality is constructed, coded, cited, iterable—that is, expressive. Reality as *mimēsis*, heterogeneous corporeal expression. Not only language. Not only human. Well beyond humanity and language. Beyond itself.

Leading back to the difficult and complex word *genre*.[5] Gender, sexual difference, race, stock, kind; intimately linked with *Geschlecht, Herkunft, Entstehung*, and kind. Leading to the radical suggestion that resistance to neutrality is resistance to the autonomy of reality from language and culture—from *genre, Geschlecht, Herkunft, Entstehung*, kin, and kinds: that is, from blood; to the autonomy of language and discourse from nature and the earth. In particular, *genre* in discourse is intimately linked with kin and kinds, in violence and blood, in kinship, generation, and love, still blood. With kindness.

Suppose we understood the *différends* between genres of discourse to be the *différends* that make up nature and reality. *Genres* are indisputably kinds. In discourse, they institute roles for linking phrases, defining, delimiting, and ranking kinds, establishing the rules whereby kinds are dominating and dominated. Among and within and around the instituted genres, rules for instituting family ties, kinship, descent by blood, rules for delimiting the kinds of the earth, are *différends*, heterogeneities, circulations of individuals and kinds and events, all expressive: phrases—which are not governed by the rules of instituted genres and which express and reveal the heterogeneities that pervade them. Between and among the rules of identity and intelligibility that prescribe to the social contract are other contracts and no contracts at all, other circulations.

This is a picture of general and restricted economy as kindredness, *genre*, in strangeness and kinds. Heterogeneity is strangeness, circulating in the form of individuals and the kinds in which they do or do not participate that unseat the rules of social contracts among human beings to the limits of identities among other kinds.

"The title of this book suggests (through the generic value of the definite article) that a universal rule of judgment between heterogeneous genres is lacking in general" (Lyotard, *DPD*, xi). Reality is made up of *différends* without a general rule to eliminate them. Or to sacrifice them. Every rule belongs to some kind, some *genre*, cultural or natural. Every kind is local and contingent. Resistance to totality, to the neutral gathering of being, can be expressed in terms of the contingency and locality of *genres*, including kin and kinds, and discourse. The limits of kinship are written in blood.

Bringing us back to strangers and strangeness. I pursue the possibility that we may interpret what Lyotard says of *différends* and *genres* in terms of strangers, identifying strangeness with heterogeneity and *différends*.[6] Reality—human worlds under the social contract, but also natural habitats and environments—is made up of citizens and strangers. Social worlds are constituted by rules; and between and around every system of rules, every social contract, every institution under law—every *genre, Geschlecht, Herkunft*, kin and kinds—are conflicts of intelligibility and obligation that cannot be settled in between, or in any institution except by force. Strangers, nomads, minoritarians, travel between one system and another—including women, who move at the thresholds of *genre*, in and out of families and kinship defined by blood.

Can the stranger cease to be an enemy in modern society? In any society? Can the stranger cease to threaten the stability of society, family, kin, and kind? Simmel offers a famous answer: the stranger who hovers at the margins, on the threshold, opens up visions and truths that permeate a society, always forgotten; and in doing so, strangers are always at risk. Recalling Socrates' suggestion that the god of strangers comes to mark the *polis*. As does philosophy, which may always travel in strangeness, appear as a stranger—thereby always at risk. One risk is Socrates', to be destroyed as a stranger. The other, perhaps greater, is to cease to be a stranger, to be welcomed without strangeness.

This latter risk is the central one of which Lyotard speaks, and one toward which I find Kristeva strangely silent. If the stranger ceases to be an enemy, could it be in virtue of ceasing to be heterogeneous, because all strangeness has been gathered into homogeneity? Let us wage a war on kinds without strangers; let us be witnesses to what is always more than any kind can contain, more than can be stored or possessed or owned; let us activate heterogeneities; let us save the strangeness of kin and kind!

Bringing us to another interruption in the name of heterogeneity and strangeness, before returning to issues of nationality. I have noted Jowett's resistance to the idea of community, to ethics defined by community, insisting on what is common. Against this, with Levinas in mind, she pursues an ethical relation of proximity, exposure to others in our vicinity. Exposure to others in the face, in debt and responsibility, defined by proximity and exposure.

> There are two women, sisters in their nineties, who live across the street
> from me. . . . They ask for nothing, but their vulnerability and need accuse
> all of us who regard them, we who are farther away from death than they
> are. . . . The accusation born out of what both separates and connects us
> is more near and more devastating than justice or "the community"; it is
> given through proximity not of my choosing. If there is the possibility for
> goodness here—which would still not be justice, cannot be justice—it is
> because of the haunting and relentless claim of my neighbours on my life,
> my place in the sun, my occupation of space. (Jowett, *OOPN*, 27–28)

Jowett interprets proximity in terms of the lived experience of spatiality, temporality, and specificity of kin and kind. The sisters who are neighbors impose a debt in their proximity, asking for nothing. Asking for nothing, in proximity, in touch, they call for everything. As sisters. As vulnerable and frail. As the individuals and the kinds they are. As the neighbors and strangers they are.

Jowett transforms insistence on commonality in practices and obligations into a debt, an obligation, always more than what is common in exposure and proximity. She and the sisters are neighbors, exposed to each other, responsible as others, without commonality, in the kindredness of their kinds. The ethical relation is not the abstract relation of the one (subject) toward the Other (subject), rooted in subjectivity, but the concrete relation of individual and kind in proximity, exposed to other individuals in their kinds. Not in the mutual commonality of the one and the other, as if they together made up a kind, but in the heterogeneous differences of their kinds. Young and old; strong and weak; quick and slow. Responsibility is borne by individuals in the strangeness, the differences, of kinship and kind. That is what I take to be witness to *différends*: exposure as responsibility; infinite and immeasurable heterogeneity, in kinds, surrounding and falling between and back down upon the *genres* of every kind.

Including nationality. Allowing us to return to Kristeva's question, insisting on Lyotard's view of politics, thereby of nationality—not *nationalism*, which is another kind of kindism, classifying and ranking kinds of people as if their kinds might be seized and owned. For politics is no genre, bears responsibility toward—Lyotard speaks of the threat of—*the différend*, where the definite article denies the possibility of linking heterogeneous *genres*, kinds, in general, insists on diversity and multiplicity. Politics here is witness to heterogeneity, in the abundance of kinds, understanding infinity as excess, beyond totality and domination, always in kinds.

Including nationality. For the link between nationality and politics is so intense, so intimate, that it bears detailed examination. Of course, everything I have considered in this book, and everything that will follow, is political—but perhaps not national: resistance to a kind that can govern all other kinds.

> Politics ... is the threat of the differend. It is not a genre, it is the multiplicity of genres, the diversity of ends, and par excellence the question of linkage. (Lyotard, *DPD*, 138)

> Politics always gives rise to misunderstandings because it takes place as a genre.... At the same time, though, politics is not at all a genre, it bears witness to the nothingness which opens up with each occurring phrase and on the occasion of which the differend between genres of discourse is born. (p. 141)

It may be misleading to say that something with the name of a kind—politics—is no kind. Politics may not be a kind that governs all kinds, but a kind that interrupts kinds, inhabits their interruptions, a kind exceeding kinds. "Everything is political if politics is the threat of the differend on the occasion of the slightest linkage. Politics is not everything, though, if by that one believes it to be the genre that contains all the genres. It is not *a* genre" (p. 139). Perhaps what Lyotard calls politics is closer to what I think of as the good: giving forth the heterogeneous identities and excesses of kinds. In the pressing sense of life under government authority, politics, governance, and nationhood have been linked throughout the world, if only as vestiges of colonization. Perhaps something—nothing: the good—interrupts the authority of such a politics.

Leading perhaps to the question, what kind of politics—governance, state, tribal, and institutional authority—can be understood as no genre, threatened by strangers and heterogeneity? What politics of nationality and authority, what rule of strangers, can be said to follow from the rule that politics is no genre? If it is or could be a rule.

Following one line of thought in Lyotard, politics (as we know it) defines the rights and duties of citizens among themselves, under government or law. Something different, perhaps nothing at all—no genre—defines the relations of that society or government to other societies, other systems of law, other genres, other kinds. In between, intermediary movements. This is a view reminiscent of Hobbes: a system of force that produces law; a system of law that produces ethics, defines the relations of members of the society to each other and the state. Between and among states there exists no system of law, no force forceful enough to institute an overarching social contract. There exists no law or politics between politics as the genre of institution and law, defined by force, and another politics without a genre, outside institutions and law, occupying the space of *le différend*: no space at all, nowhere. In this nonexistent space, there can be seen and felt the arbitrariness of every social contract. Hobbes would overcome this arbitrariness by force. Lyotard insists that it cannot be overcome but remains in endless intermediary movements, struggling against excessive authority.

Strangers, here, in flesh and body, represent, reproduce, and enforce in vivid terms, in corporeal proximity, this absence of a rule of politics, this arbitrariness of power. Not to deny power or its effects, but to resist the excessiveness of its authority. It is enough that societies should institute conformity by force. It is another matter to claim the authority of that force by right, as if something—reason, politics, some genre rather than another, something beyond the limits of any genre—might authorize an arbitrary code of law. Strangers occupy the dangerous place where the arbitrary limits of a culture or genre, of a kind, under rule or law, claim excessive authority. Strangers are the *différends* of power.

To which I would add, after Foucault, that in this sense the most obedient citizens are strangers.

> —Power is . . . exercised from innumerable points . . .
> —Relations of power . . . have an immediately productive role, wherever they come into play.
> —Power comes from below; . . .
> —Where there is power, there is resistance, and yet, or rather consequently, this resistance is never in a position of exteriority in relation to power. (Foucault, *HS*, 1, 94–95)

Resistances, *différends*, strangers are uncontainable in any system of power, law, or genre, excesses of kinds, and marks or signs of uncontainability—following Simmel. Strangers and strangeness are everywhere within the force of law, within the claims of the state, within insistence on the rationality of institutions, within any system of authority and intelligibility, within every kind.

This uncontainable resistance to power—politics without a genre—may be what delimits the stakes for the genre of politics—for states, governments, and institutions that insist on their right to govern, if only by force, to claim legitimacy or rationality or divinity, or something else, something deeper and more fundamental underlying authority. Authority is always excessive in the double sense that wherever it exists it claims too much, too much right, too much force, exercises too much terror, harms some kinds more than any institution can justify with authority; and that within all these excesses, the limits of authority are always in question, always threatened by resistances, however obscure, however subordinated and terrorized. Resistance can come from anywhere. Any authority can be overthrown. Socrates was a stranger to Athens. Destroying him did not save Athens from destruction. I leave aside whether these destructions were connected. It does not matter.

What does matter is the relation between strangers and authority, bringing us back to nations, tribes, and kin, the blood that is shed to protect the proper boundaries of the *polis*: blood of strangers, blood of kin. The threat to the *polis* from within and without, impossible finally to resist. Insistence on purity, threatened always by impurity, from within as well as from without. All these themes of strangers, nationality, and kinship relate to authority and force on the one side, to purity and impurity on the other. The impossible demand for purity, a theme of power, plays itself out in the blood of strangers, insisting on the purification of blood,[7] always somehow coalescing upon the bodies of women who traditionally are strangers in every exogamous society, in every domicile.

This is the link that I would take back to Kristeva, who concerns herself with the possibility of a nationality without nationalism, a global, political world without strangers—at least, harm to strangers—from within the possibility that we recognize our strangeness to ourselves. To which I would add that, historically, strangeness has been present in every domicile, at every border of the self, is represented in the psychoanalytic frameworks with which she works, suggesting that perhaps it is this very strangeness, the strangeness in and of proximity, the strangeness of the neighbor—my mother, brother, sister, kin; the person next door or who sits at my side at social ceremonies—that marks the hatefulness and abjection of the stranger. Rage at the abject stranger, the outsider who has arrived, mirrors the abjection of the subject, always thrown down under the yoke of authority.

Kristeva concludes her meditation on national strangeness with a double gesture, looking toward community and the strangeness of individual subjects, divided as I have mentioned repeatedly, by authority and rank: subjection and abjection; abject-subject-object.

> A paradoxical community is emerging, made up of foreigners who are reconciled with themselves to the extent that they recognize themselves as foreigners. The multinational society would thus be the consequence of an extreme individualism, but conscious of its discontents and limits, knowing only indomitable people ready-to-help-themselves in their weakness, a weakness whose other name is our radical strangeness. (Kristeva, *SO*, 195)

In the name of Jowett, I would resist this insistence on community, however paradoxical, resist indomitability and individuality, people whose primary relation is to themselves, among others. People are not individuals first, or individuals-in-relation-to-other-individuals first, or second. The primacy of individuality or community gives rise not to the paradoxicality of radical strangeness but to its abjection. Jowett explores the thought that responsibility pertains to being-in-proximity, for whatever being—individual or collective; human or otherwise. Being-in-proximity is not being-together, not even *Zuzammengehörigkeit*, not a gathering or belonging, but vulnerability and exposure. Proximity is exposure to the other, to others whatever and whoever they may be, singular, collective, or otherwise. Exposure as expression. *Exposition*. In kind.

Exposition—exposure and expression—resists the sameness of community and kind with responsibility, toward what is common and what is more than common, what exceeds the bond of kin and kind. This may be paradoxical only for those who insist on kin and kind as nothing but what is common, nothing but the bond, without strangeness. I hope to emphasize the remainders of every kin and kind, every bond of propinquity, written in blood by violence and domination. Calling for a vigilance that may not always be present in Kristeva. In words that immediately precede the above: "we are, for the first time in history, confronted with the following situation: we must live with different people while relying on our personal moral codes, without the assistance of a set that would include our particularities while transcending them" (p. 195). Individuals and community, moral and religious ties and particularities. Whereas, I would say, the most rigid codes and powerful bonds are filled with strangeness marking both their authority and the inescapability of resistance. Strangers from within and without are resistances to authority; some of the most loyal subjects implement State or Church authority through practices that undermine it, if only by reshaping the territories that delimit the scope of that authority. Stretching its range too far. Enclosing too many heterogeneous genres.

I find Kristeva's approach fruitful in her focus on political authority, not in terms of citizens, who represent what is common, but of foreigners, who express what is more than common, perhaps what cannot be contained in what is common. And she does so from within as well as from without, albeit in narrower terms than I would prefer—the strangeness of the (psychoanalytic) subject, rather than of any (abject) subject thrown down under authority, even the subject's own. The theme I wish to pursue for just a bit longer is that of nationality—perhaps quite different from the refrain of community. Diverse kin and kinds linked and divided by blood, gathered together into a single nation, united under a common authority. Memory and blood; memory of democratic blood. "What might be involved, in the final analysis, is extending to the notion of *foreigner* the right of respecting our own foreignness and, in short, of the 'privacy' that insures freedom in democracies" (p. 195).

Perhaps democracy resists every final analysis of state, religious, institutional, or other authority; perhaps the suggestion must be resisted that authorities should *extend* respect to others as if they owned the right to do so rather than the force; perhaps nothing ensures freedom or anything else in democracy; perhaps *privacy* is within the scope of public, institutional authority: and still there is (some kind of) democracy and freedom, some resistance to authority, public and private. All pervaded by, linked with strangeness. Foreigners—hated as the other—and foreignness—the otherness within and around us—are inextricably linked in the policing of every border, inside and outside, every bordering that produces inside and outside. The border of every kind is defined by strangers and constituted by strangeness—always more than what is other.

The consequence of this discussion is that politics is always claimed as a genre, with a territory—claimed in the institution of authority. Yet politics is no genre, lacks every territory. For it bears responsibility for resisting this insistence and its claims to own authority. The borders under which any authority can be held are always under assault, sites of strangers who have been driven to the borders by an insistence on policing strangeness. I understand this in terms of every kind, including nature's kinds. Politics is both the genre that insists on authority, constituting itself and its others in relations of kin and strangers, and the non-genre, the nothing, that resists every such constitution in the name of authority. Restricted and general economy. The borders of every genre, every kind, are given over to the doubled role of politics as domination and insurrection. Kin and kind bear the mark of a responsibility to resist the policing of their borders at every border post that can be defined.

We have seen this insurrection written along lines of blood in *Geschlecht and Herkunft*, the terms of genealogy and propinquity. Here it is written in the practice of politics itself, carried from the natural world of species and kinds to those who would govern by claiming authority. Let us insist on democracy. For the moment. However minoritarian. Bringing us back to the politics of strangers. In interruption.

It is time to confront the corporeal presence of strangers, first in the United States then elsewhere, in that multiple sense of elsewhere that haunts our exploration of kinds. Including other kinds, Molly insists. I hold some kinds in abeyance.

The United States was founded by immigrants—but not just any immigrants.

> The first U.S. naturalization law (passed during the second session of the first Congress in March 1790) reserved naturalization for those "aliens being free white persons." (Cose, *NS*, 11)
>
> By limiting naturalization to whites, the first Congress of the United States made generations of judges into arbiters of racial purity. Time and

again would-be Americans of various hues—Mexicans, Japanese, Armenians, East Indians—were forced to be certified as "white" or as exceptions
to the rule. As recently as the 1940s, trials of whiteness were still being
held. (p. 209)

The 1952 McCarran-Walter Act, by eliminating all racial restrictions
to naturalization, brought such judicial race reckoning to an end. (p. 210)

At the moment that I write, the United States has embarked on practices
claimed to be driven by fiscal considerations—"welfare reform"—that have
two overt consequences. First, inner-city recipients of welfare—predomi-
nantly African American, mostly mothers with dependent children—will be
forced off welfare; and second, legal immigrants—many African and Asian—
will be ineligible for welfare benefits. The social costs of such policies are
enormous; it may cost far more in the long run to address the consequences of such policies than to adjust current benefits. At the same time,
support is growing for making English the official language of the United
States. It is not enough that English is the language in which institutional,
corporate, and technological transactions take place, worldwide. At the same
time that English is becoming the second language of choice, throughout
the world, spoken and taught by more people than any other language,
legislation is being introduced to make it officially the first language of the
United States.

The question I would ask, in such cases, is whether these current
policies are driven by the same considerations as the earliest naturalization
policies in the United States: white-only; fear of strangers, judged by "means
of sight, hearing, smell" (Kristeva, *SO*, 187). This is the presence of the
stranger to another. Returning to the stranger's presence to self. "He bleeds
body and soul, humiliated in a position where, even with the better couples,
he or she assumes the part of a domestic, of the one who is a bother when
he or she becomes ill, who embodies the enemy, the traitor, the victim. . . . Is
this the dialectic of master and slave?" (p. 6). I think we should resist the
return of the dialectic of master and slave, as if it represented a stage of the
journey the soul must bear within itself whenever it considers other ethical
possibilities. I would begin elsewhere, with the relation Levinas describes as
exposure and proximity, in vulnerability and responsibility toward others.
Yet it seems essential to grant, withholding all dialectical necessity, that
throughout history—Eastern, Western, Northern, and Southern: everywhere
if not universally—ethical exposure and proximity have frequently been
withheld from strangers, from those who differ in kin and kind, in blood
and descent, in look and smell and sound; including women and children,
without whom there could be no human kin and kind; including animals
and other living things, toward whom we are exposed in vulnerability;
including all the kinds of natural creatures and things we claim to own,

framing their strangeness so that we owe them no debt, denying them the slightest proximity. Animals have no reason at all. And plants. Stones are dead, inanimate, neither speak nor show. Atoms and molecules are all exactly the same, we say we know. Yet upon closer scrutiny they are all exceedingly strange. As Descartes knew, knew how remarkable the qualities of animals are, with or without reason. As all living organisms are, in their endless struggles to perpetuate their kind. As the tracks of geology and geography are, traced in stone. Who knows what bodies can do, living or nonliving, in the endless strangeness of the earth's abundance?[8]

We are exposed everywhere, in proximity, in our vulnerability toward the vulnerability of others, to heterogeneity and abundance, to the multiplicity and diversity of kinds. The mark of such exposure toward others in kin and kind is strangeness, the look, smell, and sound of the other kind— or other marks, or none at all except the historical record written in blood: having an alien mother, or father, or coming from another tribe. Without visible or audible marks. Blood is inscribed in kin and kinds, marking strangeness, presenting us with strangers next door or inside our homes, within our families. Purity of kin and kind is filled with impurity, inside and out, marked by strangers. Nation, state, institutions, families hold borders firmly against those excluded, who surround our social worlds, inside and out, with marks of strangeness. Including ourselves, as Kristeva says. Propinquity in strangeness.

As I would say, the curse of humanity—perhaps everywhere, perhaps restricted to the European-Greek-Judeo-Christian subject—is abjection: exclusion of others, animals, strangers as unworthy, unlike us; abjection as the condition whereby the subject throws himself down under authority. *Him*self! The authority that establishes the boundaries whereby some are excluded establishes conditions for the subjection of those included. Lateral effects. We are strangers to ourselves, I believe, in the lateral effects of the exclusion of others. Captive to the insistence on purity within, we confront our endless heterogeneity as impurity within and without.

If law is given from the good, giving in the abundance of kinds, then it resists as well as enforces the curse. The promulgation of law challenges the authority of every state and legal authority. That, at least, is how I understand democracy: the inexhaustible task of resisting democratic authority—no authority at all—in the production of that authority. Democratic authority is endless, unlimited, nothing at all. In the abundance of the earth, endless, unlimited, nothing at all. Given everywhere in kinds.

Returning to the United States and its history of white male democracy, where despite every attempt to contain multiplicity and diversity, to restrict abundance, democracy has struggled openly and effectively with its own impossibility. Under slavery and after abolition. In the restriction of citizenship to whites and the denial of the vote to women. In the melting pot of different languages and cultures. Fostering multiculturalism or opposing it.

The greatest threat to this struggle inherent in democracy over the borders that define and delimit every kind is resistance to the struggle itself to the point where some authority—the state, the law, philosophy, science—claims the right to police the struggle, instituting democracy's authority. As the regulation of strangers: defining and delimiting their strangeness in kind, human and otherwise; defining and delimiting as well, by lateral effects, kinship and familiarity.

Calling for another interruption in a postcolonial place, marked by a profound and moving strangeness in the legacy of histories of domination and sacrifice. I find the following words miraculous and revelatory. First from Jussawalla's *Missing Person—*

> No Satan
> warmed in the electric coils of his creatures
> or Gunga Din
> will make him come before you.
> To see an invisible man or a missing person,
> trust no Eng. Lit. That
> puffs him up, narrows his eyes,
> scratches him fangs. Caliban
> is still not IT.
> (Jussawalla, *MP*; quoted in Bhabha, *II*, 188)

Bhabha reads Fanon as addressing the invisibility of the (postcolonial) black man: " '*The Negro is not. Any more than the white man*' " (Bhabha, *II*, 183). Very much the black *man*, for "[w]ith a question that echoes Freud's '*What does a woman want?*' Fanon turns to confront the colonized world. 'What does a man want?' he asks, in the introduction to *Black Skin, White Masks*: 'What does the black man want?' " (p. 185).

The emergence of the human subject as socially and psychically authenticated depends on the *negation* of an originary narrative of fulfillment or an imaginary coincidence between individual interest or instinct and the General Will. (p. 194)

The representative figure of such a perversion, I want to suggest, is the image of post-Enlightenment man tethered to, *not* confronted by, his dark reflection, the shadow of colonized man, that splits his presence, distorts his outline, breaches his boundaries, repeats his action at a distance, disturbs and divides the very time of his being. This ambivalent identification of the racist world . . . turns on the idea of man as his alien-

ated image, not Self and Other but the Otherness of the Self inscribed in
the perverse palimpsest of colonial identity. (p. 187)

Two "missing persons" speak, tethered to the colonial subject as that
subject is tethered to them: one above, "the postcolonial bourgeoisie"
(Bhabha, *II*, 188); then, "listen to its echo in the verse of a black woman,
descendant of slaves" (p. 189):

> One day I learnt,
> a secret art,
> Invisible-Ness, it was called.
> I think it worked
> as even now you look
> but never see me (Meiling, *SHL*; quoted in Bhabha, *II*, 189)

Invisibility is the mark of the postcolonial, post-something subject, post-
anything woman. In a different way, perhaps, than the disappearance marked
by Gates, the irony that the subject disappears when those denied historically the right to subjectivity gain the authority to insist on their own.
Tethered and bound by abjection. Perhaps this invisibility together with
this insistence can be understood in terms of strangeness. Not a countervailing subjectivity in the republic of Western culture but a powerful subjectivity that insists on yet is haunted by its strangeness. Marked by a
terrible invisibility. Yet more than terrible, and more than invisible. Liminal, ambiguous, diasporic.

Jussawalla offers another, stranger strangeness in this postcolonial
landscape, something that touches the secret heart of language in a way I
have never heard before, infinitely distant I believe from the contemporary
European and American insistence on language. Perhaps because the languages of that insistence remain European. The missing person remains
missing in another voice, another *mimēsis*.

> A-'s a giggle now
> but on it Osiris, Ra.
> An 𑀑's an er... a cough,
> once spoking your valley's with light.
> But the a's here to stay.
> . . . .
> You're polluting our sounds. You're so rude.
> "Get back to your language," they say. (Jussawalla, *MP*; quoted in
>   Bhabha, *II*, 201)

This requires extensive commentary from Bhabha, without which I and
most readers, I suspect, would be lost in strangeness. Another invisibility.

Another empty meaning. Or anything but. Bhabha's meditation on invisibility passes into other invisibilities. Some are audible. Some are inaudible no matter how loudly they ring. The voice of *mimēsis*.

> There is something supplementary about *a* that makes it the initial letter of the Roman alphabet and, at the same time, the indefinite article. What is dramatized in this postcolonial circulation of the *a* is a double scene on a double stage, to borrow a phrase from Derrida. The A—with which the verse begins—is the sign of a linguistic objectivity, inscribed in the Indo-European language tree, institutionalized in the cultural disciplines of empire; and yet as the Hindi vowel अ, which is the first letter of the Hindi alphabet and is pronounced as "er," testifies, the object of linguistic science is always already in an enunciatory process of cultural translation, showing up the hybridity of any genealogical or systematic filiation.
>
> Listen: "*An अ's an er . . . a cough*": in the same time, we hear the *a* repeated in translation, not as an object of linguistics, but in the *act* of the colonial enunciation of cultural contestation. (Bhabha, *II*, 201)

To be understood, finally, in terms of strangers, kin and kinds, always more than what is common among individual agents. Returning us to politics as no genre, endlessly struggling with instituted *genres*.

> What remains to be thought is the *repetitious* desire to recognize ourselves doubly, as, at once, decentered in the solidary processes of the political group, and yet, ourselves as a consciously committed, even individuated, agent of change—the bearer of belief. . . . We may have to force the limits of the social as we know it to rediscover a sense of political and personal agency through the unthought of the civic and the psychic. (Bhabha, *II*, 207–8)

The political, the ethical, the civic lie betwixt and between, at the margins, across the thresholds, here between the individual, individuated agent and the group, the kind. The postcolonial condition, on Bhabha's reading, lies in the strangeness of individuals and kinds. The civic and the psychic, given in the supplement of the *a*, the cough. In postcoloniality something profoundly ethical, ethicality itself, appears as invisibility, disappearance, otherwise in abundance, in *mimēsis*.

Strangers do not speak our language. They do not look like us. They look, smell, and sound strange and different. And yet, they are us. And we are they. But the force of the *are*, the *we* and *us* and *they*, is always more than what is common. Always strange. And more than strange. More in heaven and earth than any category or kind. Always in kind.

Echoing Bhabha's words again and again, and later again,[9] repeating, citing, doubly, multiply, always in kind, ethical representations, perhaps the representation of ethicality, the giving of the good, in the abundance of kinds. The repetitious, endless, immeasurable desire to recognize ourselves and others doubly, triply, and more, to recognize, represent, express, to know in truth. In our exposure touching others, touching ourselves, in the exposure of others to us, in exposure and proximity, always in kind, in propinquity. In the kind we are as agents, as ethical; in the kinds we are as bearers of representation and belief. If we think of this complex profusion of mirrors of *mimēsis* and representation beyond the limits beyond which Bhabha takes us as given from the good, as giving in abundance, general economy, the unbounded circulation of *mimēsis*—expression, exposure, representation—then each expression is of a kind, in a kind. Immeasurably given from the good. in kindness.

CHAPTER 10

Ecological Kinds

A shallow, but presently rather powerful, movement, and a deep, but less influential, movement, compete for our attention. (Naess, *ECL*, 27–28)

5 A platform of the deep ecology movement

(1) The flourishing of human and nonhuman life on Earth has intrinsic value. The value of non-human life forms is independent of the usefulness these may have for narrow human purposes.

(2) Richness and diversity of life forms are values in themselves and contribute to the flourishing of human and non-human life on Earth.

(3) Humans have no right to reduce this richness and diversity except to satisfy vital needs.

(4) Present human interference with the non-human world is excessive, and the situation is rapidly worsening.

(5) The flourishing of human life and cultures is compatible with a substantial decrease of the human population. The flourishing of non-human life requires such a decrease.

(6) Significant change of life conditions for the better requires change in policies. These affect basic economic, technological, and ideological structures.

(7) The ideological change is mainly that of appreciating *life quality* (dwelling in situations of intrinsic value) rather than adhering to a high standard of living. There will be a profound awareness of the difference between big and great.

(8) Those who subscribe to the foregoing points have an obligation directly or indirectly to participate in the attempt to implement the necessary changes. (p. 29)

Be deep; avoid the shallows; police the borders of the best!
Cherish the earth!—and yet . . .
The distinction between deep and shallow brings me wonder at the ethics of the deep ecological movement, not because something else is

better—nothing is better than cherishing the earth—but in the sacrifices it insists on imposing. Without *mimēsis*. Without sacrificing sacrifice. Compared, for example, with Foucault's words on resistance, quoted briefly in the previous chapter to note the strangeness within. Here I note Foucault's refusal to name the better in resistance, to mark the superior in strangeness.

> These points of resistance are present everywhere in the power network. Hence there is no single locus of great Refusal, no soul of revolt, source of all rebellions, or pure law of the revolutionary. Instead there is a plurality of resistances, each of them a special case: resistances that are possible, necessary, improbable; others that are spontaneous, savage, solitary, concerted, rampant, or violent; still others that are quick to compromise, interested, or sacrificial; by definition, they can only exist in the strategic field of power relations. . . . They are the odd term in relations of power; they are inscribed in the latter as an irreducible opposite. Hence they too are distributed in irregular fashion: the points, knots, or focuses of resistance are spread over time and space at varying densities, at times mobilizing groups or individuals in a definitive way, inflaming certain points of the body, certain moments in life, certain types of behavior. (Foucault, *HS*, 95–96)

Power *and* resistance are distributed in an irregular fashion, impurely, mimetically. I have read this understanding *as political*, concerned with power, force, domination, and authority, together with the resistances, incalculabilities, and excesses that pervade every kind of event, institution, and practice. Resistance as power divided against itself. Violence against violence. Sacrificing sacrifice. This reading marks the omnipresence of strangers and strangenesses, understood as the resistances, the *différends*, the excesses, inside and out, of systems of authority. Here I read this understanding *as ethical*, understood as expressing the impossibility of calculation in general, wherever responsibility is in question, wherever injustice calls for liberation—again, in general, universally, in principle. With certainty and security. In endless debt.

Power and resistance, strangeness and difference, are mobile, transitory, fractured, local, and contingent. Including ecological movements. At a particular time and in a particular place, "shallow" practices may provide powerful and effective resistances; "deep" practices may reinforce institutional powers. The distinction between shallow and deep occupies sites of institutional authority. Foucault's view of power together with resistance, as I understand it, bears profound implications for material practices. Refusing binary oppositions in ethics and politics marks two pervasive contingencies in such practices, inherent in ethical responsibility. One is the insecurity of every ethical|political judgment, where ethics cannot take place without judgment. This is nothing new. Philosophers from Plato through Hume, Marx, Kierkegaard, and Nietzsche to Dewey and Levinas in different ways have emphasized the contingency and locality of practice. One reading of excessive and impossible responsibility speaks to such contingency.

The second is something different, perhaps more relevant to environmental issues. It is expressed in part by Derrida that within immeasurable responsibility, demanding finite practice and calculation, "the incalculable and giving idea of justice is always very close to the bad, even to the worst for it can always be reappropriated by the most perverse calculation. It's always possible" (Derrida, *FL*, 28). In the extreme—I regard it as inescapable—the good *is* very bad. Feeding my cat, or other cats, caring as much as possible for some goods, is always to deny others, not to feed some cats or undertake some tasks. And worse: the very best institutional practices become bad in time. Dewey insists on this point repeatedly—the key to a pragmatist ethics.[1] The very best practices cause great harm. The very best resistances impose violences and dominations. Still best yet unjust. Demanding restitution. Ethics requires sacrifice and its sacrifice.

On the other side, however—as I read Foucault—the worst practices may promote effective resistances. Goods and bads are dispersed and mobile in complex and difficult ways. This does not preclude judgment, only absolute and universal judgment as if without contingency and *mimēsis*. Goods and bads are odd terms throughout experience and the world. Nothing is inside ethics, secure in its goodness, without fear of compromise. Nothing is outside ethics, secure in its evil. Even compromise, even domination, can serve the mobilizations of resistance. Moments of power and resistance are dispersed and incalculable. So are goods and bads, dominations and liberations. On one side, this is a dark and difficult truth. How can we be sure that we pursue and undertake the better? It is a terrible struggle, yet we cannot be secure. On the other side—if there are sides at all—this is a glorious and wonderful truth. Everything, everyone, everywhere, participates in the good and—this is quite different—may contribute in incalculable ways to the better. And the worse. Cherishment is the passionate experience of this irregularity and incalculability of goodness. Sacrifice is the intense experience of the irregularity and inescapability of badness. Plenishment bears the experienced, expressive weight of both, sacrificing sacrifice in the name of cherishment: sorrow at responsibilities we cannot meet, sometimes disastrously; joy at responsibilities we fulfill, the tasks we and others are able to accomplish. Even shallow practice does its work, sometimes more of the work required in the ecological movement than the deep.

A single example. The shallow movement, in Naess's words, engages in a "Fight against pollution and resource depletion. Central objective: the

162 *The Gift of Kinds*

health and affluence of people in the developed countries" (Naess, *ECL*, 28). The deep movement rejects "the man-in-environment image in favour of *the relational, total-field image*" (p. 28). One question is, which of these is right, better, more truthful? I have difficulties with the total-field image, which seems to me to conflict with locality and contingency.[2] I lean to an extreme sense of ethical ecology that presupposes neither relationality nor totality. An ecology of kinds without tyranny, an ethic of heterogeneity. Perhaps resistant to the name *ecology*. Another question is, which will do more good? Suppose the deep theory is right or true, but does not give rise to a political movement, does not gather an audience? Suppose the shallow movement saves more human, animal, and vegetal lives in assembling more visible support for nurturing practices? One implication of locality and contingency in ethics, of irregularity and dispersion, is that one must not choose principles over care, that the very best principles and practices may do untold harm and, in reverse, some of the worst practices may do great good.

This brings me to what everyone who reads Naess sympathetically recognizes to be his invaluable contribution to the environmental and eco-logical movement and the ethics and politics that go together with them. For the deep movement blunts its militant contrast with shallow theory and practice in giving rise to a platform. It is as a platform that the green movement has gained support. It is as a platform that I mean to understand the ethics and politics that underlie it. A platform that encourages alli-ances. A platform expressive of impurity.

We may understand what is at stake in such a practice in terms of the police activated by it, the borders and boundaries to be held by force, the exclusions and punishments mobilized against those who are not loyal to ecological principles: Jowett's garbage police. How does such a platform do its work in practical terms? We may think of political party platforms in a democracy that express commitments at a time of election. Perhaps the most prominent, multiple truth of such a platform is that it may represent sincere and powerful commitments joined with multiple contingencies. For no one believes that a party in a democracy has the power to enforce all its commitments. No one believes that a platform plank entails that if the party wins the election, it will institute whatever the plank demands. The party may not control enough votes. Even more, another contingency, it will have to enter upon another political process to institute its measures, and the political landscape may change. The electorate may not support a given plank though they support the party strongly. Support of a plank is variable and contingent, by party officials, elected representatives, and loyal (and disloyal) members of the electorate. Finally, democracy itself is not one thing, and platforms vary with the different role of parties under different systems of representation and governance. The party platform is where democracy meets *mimēsis*, for good or ill.

I have some reservations about the deep ecology platform. I will mention a few. But I would back the platform enthusiastically because it is better than any other likely to gain support, because it is a step in the right direction, because I share deep values with it despite the differences, because of all sorts of considerations I might not be able to articulate, though I can articulate serious reservations. What if we took this as a model for ethics and politics, understanding the latter to express the variability and contingency that surround any platform, understanding the former to express the responsibilities, loyalties, and commitments articulated in the platform? Why not understand such a model to express the very best we can do in ethical|political practice, especially an ecological and environmental ethics|politics, where profound conflicts of values are inescapable? What if this "platform" represented a model for plenishment?

Some reservations and qualifications. Others may be found in the final chapter. I support the platform but I do not support the ethics—another way of expressing inclusion.

(1) The flourishing of human and non-human life on Earth has intrinsic value. The value of non-human life forms is independent of the usefulness these may have for narrow human purposes.

I believe that everything, living or not, every individual and kind, is to be cherished, participates in abundance. I would not restrict cherishment to life. I have no idea whether this is an intrinsic value or what such a value might be. It might be extrinsic or no value at all, something inherent in the propinquity of things to one another: responsibility instead of value. Value insists on sacrifice, belongs to restricted economy.

Exposure and proximity are incompatible with independence and do not exclude usefulness for human beings. Human purposes are among the goods I would cherish, among others, in abundance.

(2) Richness and diversity of life forms are values in themselves and contribute to the flourishing of human and non-human life on Earth.

Richness and diversity, also simplicity and attenuation, pertain to the abundance of the earth. As in works of art, in *mimēsis*, where richness and diversity are wonderful values yet simplicity and attenuation contribute to abundance. Finally, abundance is present in the most purified worlds. Impurity and heterogeneity pervade every kind, and kind of kinds.

The platform speaks of life forms—of kinds. Richness, diversity, and heterogeneity pertain to kinds. Living and otherwise.

(3) Humans have no right to reduce this richness and diversity except to satisfy vital needs.

Humans may have whatever rights there are. But rights are always in conflict—among themselves, with nurture and care, with what is precious in things, and with other values. Any need can be said to be vital. Other needs than human needs may be vital. And something more elusive. The platform approaches an overriding principle here, neglecting locality and contingency. This does not diminish my support for the platform, with its overriding authority, knowing that it will never be implemented without contingency.

(4) Present human interference with the non-human world is excessive, and the situation is rapidly worsening.

Probably human life will always interfere excessively in the lives of other kinds. As may too many rabbits in Australia and too many mosquitoes in Africa. Too many is always too many for whom, for what? Here, perhaps, for human beings. Perhaps for some human beings more than others. Also, perhaps, for other life forms. Human beings are the most influential life forms on the planet, sometimes with devastating consequences. But there are other disasters: earthquakes, comets, floods, overpopulation. All have disastrous effects on living and nonliving things. Are some better than others? For what and for whom?

I would not rule out increased human interference as a local and continent response to some technological problems. If technology will not always provide a solution, it may sometimes make things better.

I would also hope to distinguish, if proximately and contingently, interference from domination. I would hope to refuse the human domination of the earth, together with other dominations. Interference may be unavoidable. Resistance without interference may be impossible.

(5) The flourishing of human life and cultures is compatible with a substantial decrease of the human population. The flourishing of non-human life requires such a decrease.

All industrial countries are currently experiencing a decline in the rate of population growth, some to an extreme, suggesting that they will soon experience a decline in population. The major population expansions world wide are taking place in undeveloped and developing countries; their rate of growth is also mostly diminishing. Moreover, industrial countries utilize a highly disproportionate share of resources, living and nonliving. I would pursue this struggle with resources more than with population. I worry about ecological practices that benefit rich countries more than poor.

If affluence does not diminish population growth, if having many children is an economic benefit, even necessity, in certain economies, what practice to limit population growth can be defended?

The single change most likely to affect population growth is female literacy. It matches female life expectancy. In the flourishing of women lies any recognizable possibility of the flourishing of other kinds.

(6) Significant change of life conditions for the better requires change in policies. These affect basic economic, technological, and ideological structures.

Yes. And perhaps the transformation of human life and the world. A transformation of culture, language, economy, technology, ideology, perhaps of reason, truth, and law; of ethics and politics; perhaps of humanity itself and of those regions of nature that are touched by human beings—almost everywhere on the surface of the earth.

Ecology as resistance to the domination of nature joins other resistances—to the domination of women, other races, cultures, and classes—in opening the possibility of reexamining and transforming every facet of life and being on earth—if that be possible.

It may not be possible. It may not be desirable. It may not be for the better. For among the transformations is how humanity thinks of what is better, including the possibility that every thought of the better, including Naess's, calls for endless resistances to its authority.

(7) The ideological change is mainly that of appreciating life quality (dwelling in situations of intrinsic value) rather than adhering to a high standard of living. There will be a profound awareness of the difference between big and great.

Naess quotes Father Zossima in *The Brothers Karamazov*: "Love all God's creation, the whole and every grain of sand in it. Love every leaf, every ray of God's light. Love the animals, love the plants, love everything" (Dostoevsky, *BK*, 382–83). Love everything, big and small, little and great. Resist exclusion.[3]

(8) Those who subscribe to the foregoing points have an obligation directly or indirectly to participate in the attempt to implement the necessary changes.

An obligation beyond accountability? Before the arrival of the police? These are questions that pertain to both the obligations and the accountability. Naess's words return from the words of the platform to its praxis. "There is ample room for different opinions about priorities. What should be done first, what next? What is most urgent? What is necessary as opposed to highly desirable? Different opinions in these matters should not exclude vigorous cooperation" (Naess, *ECL*, 31). Perhaps some—perhaps I in a different voice—would protest that if we do not agree precisely on what is to be done we may differ on anything. I say so too, not to undermine this platform with its fluidities and uncertainties, certainly not to obstruct the possibility of vigorous cooperation. I return to Foucault's understanding of resistance, that it may take any form. Similarly, vigorous cooperation—together with some not so vigorous efforts and even obstructions—may take many forms, too many to count, to know, some surprisingly effective when we least expect it. Including shallow ecologies and hostile endeavors.

Hope to share the widest, most beautiful values; love everything, big and small. Hope to implement the most caring, nurturing practices toward everyone and everything, including those who do not share those values and those who would obstruct every caring implementation. Resist every domination including the domination of domination; resist every authority including authority for every resistance. Would this lead to paralysis, amount to nothing at all? Would it be a practice that resembled current practices, in their destructiveness and confusion? Or would it be profoundly different amid the uncertainties, contingencies, multiplicities, and confusions?

I believe the latter. I believe that passionate and vigorous efforts toward cooperation (but perhaps not community) in ethical and political practices based on cherishment toward every thing and every body, every kin and kind, entail resistance to every authority. Cherishment is love without authority. As Zossima says. Without God the Father. Without insistence that one's authority be right, better than and imposed on others. Yet every practice insists on authority and imposes violence on others. Every practice does so, and practices achieve wonderful things doing so. Plenishment insists that we supplement this recognition with another, that such wonderful achievements go hand in hand with destructions, that the authority imposed is always excessive, greater than the practice demands. Demanding endless resistance within the urgency of the very best practices. Cherishment, sacrifice, and plenishment: exposure in abundance.

Ecology becomes ecosophy, the shallow becomes deep, based on "a way of formulating the essential traits of a total view" (Naess, *ECL*, 35). A total view with perhaps too little *mimēsis*, too much authority. Plenishment is neither totality nor fragmentation, but always more, excess and its excess: excessive desire together with excessive resistance to excessive authority, every authority that would divide the better from the worse, the big from the great, knowing that every practice must undertake such divisions. Ecosophy would be, in terms of plenishment, an ethics|politics based on an excessive responsibility inherent in every undertaking, including philosophy itself and its branches. All look to a responsibility that joins them in exposure and proximity. Ecosophy—if there be such—would be philosophy carried on in exposure and proximity: things together with other things, in propinquity, touching other things everywhere, responsive, responding, with responsibility; expressive in every proximity, in *mimēsis*.

If this is a total view, it exceeds totality—neither a view with total authority nor a view that surveys everything. I hope to resist the authority of any claim to institute an authoritative knowledge of nature and value. As does Naess: "an ecosophy becomes *a philosophical worldview or system inspired by the conditions of life in the ecosphere*" (p. 38); but ecology "should never be considered a universal science" (p. 39). Perhaps, like ecophilosophy, it may be "a descriptive study, appropriate, say, to a university milieu" (p. 36). Not to life. What then of life?

"Etymologically, the word 'ecosophy' combines *oikos* and *sophia*, 'household' and 'wisdom' " (p. 37). Returning us to other dominations linked with the domination of the earth. For the household, the *oikos*, is the place where women have been dominated, kept out of public view; the place where slaves were threatened by intimacy and torture; where animals were domesticated. Naess speaks of wisdom in the home, reminding us of Aristotle, for whom wise management in the home subordinates women, slaves, and children. Perhaps wisdom in the home knows no authority, denies its wisdom. As Socrates does repeatedly. Wisdom without authority; the home, the family, the neighborhood as proximity, exposure, vulnerability. Home and family and kind as sites of greatest vulnerability and danger, together with wonderful possibilities of intimacy and joy. The smallest and most intimate places present the greatest risks and dangers. Something to worry about, always. In propinquity. In exposure.

Calling for tremendous changes beyond the idea of change: "Changes have to be from the inside *and* from the outside, all in one" (p. 89); and perhaps from other places, otherwise. Not changes in human beings—as if they were malleable; not changes in human environments and cultural practices—as if there were not huge obstructions: but in the responsibilities we bear to undertake and participate in change. Responsibility is change itself: endless, excessive, and glorious. Endless in its demands; excessive in its implementations; glorious in its achievements. As Naess says in a minimalist voice: "If we can clean up a little internally as well as externally, we can hope that *the ecological movement will be more of a renewing and joy-creating movement*" (p. 91). The hope and practice of plenishment, perhaps far beyond any cleaning up. Transformation! Where we have always found ourselves, on the way toward renewal and joy, guided by endless responsibility.

Ecosophy as excessive responsibility. Plenishment. Renewal and joy. And suffering. Endless vigilance toward injustice. An ethic of kinds without tyranny. *Mimēsis*.

Naess speaks of rights human beings have of "access to free nature" (p. 124); "The parcel of nature in question is part of his or her Self!" (p. 125). I am inclined to think that if human beings have rights, natural things have rights as well, to flourish and prosper, to be. Living and not. Yet I do not think of the good in terms of rights, but in terms of cherishment and responsibility, responsiveness and exposure. I would prefer to experiment with a free economic policy in which the goodness of every thing was incorporated into it, including more than what human beings were willing to pay for, resistant to every restricted sense of possession. We have economic policies that pertain to those who do not choose, who do not buy and sell, who are not consumers. What if these were extended throughout nature and the earth?

One way to understand the discipline of economics is that it is based on a profound refusal to let anyone decide for others what is worthwhile. Only the market can decide. Allowing us to consider extending that notion beyond its present limits to include a critique of the market. No one, no kind, has a right to decide for others, for everyone, for other kinds, what is precious, worth dying for, worth spending for. Economic circulation is without authority. Here general and restricted economy go hand in hand, together with *mimēsis*. The critique is that all economies are restricted economies—quite unavoidable—carried out as if they possessed total authority over goods and prices, over property and value. Recalling Foucault's suggestion that trade depends on the sacrifice of goods to exchange. General economy is abundance in the earth, excessive circulation and exposure, whose recognition—cherishment—resists the authority of every restricted economy. Every restricted economy answers to a responsibility beyond containment, exceeding every restriction.

Perhaps ecosophy can be understood in relation to both economics and politics as the critique, the *mimēsis*, and the sacrifice of the sacrifices inherent in politics and economics, in life and being, resisting the institution of any authority over sacrifice. Sacrificing sacrifice.

I believe that the discipline of economics understands sacrifice in economic terms with little sense of sacrificing sacrifice—not to something higher, but in the earth. Nothing is to be sacrificed to economic development, not animals, landscapes, or human beings; but economic practice is sacrifice. Nothing is to be sacrificed in the name of property; but human life gathers itself around possessions.

I hope to pursue the most persuasive aspect of Naess's ecosophy, the creation of a platform designed to transform human life and its surroundings. Perhaps without loyalty oaths and police. Perhaps so widely and profoundly that nothing in the world would remain untouched—including the sense that humanity might come to love everything to the point that some (wild) things would be left alone. Yet part of this understanding is that it is already too late, that nothing is alone, everything touches other things, and human works pervade the planet. Nothing is wild, untouched by human works. Possibly some habitats may be made "wild"; human footprints may be held in reserve; yet only by a withdrawal within the presence everywhere of human beings and their works. Parks instead of wilderness. It is too late to escape from the touch of humanity, as if there had never been a human influence. It was always too late to escape from the touch of other beings, strange and wonderful things touching other kinds, as if there might be a wilderness untouched by something else. Abundance in the earth is diversity of other kinds and other influences, things touching other things everywhere.

In this sense of always being too late, everything is ethical|political. Naess speaks of another sense of politics. *"All is politically relevant, but not all is politics"* (p. 130). Not all is any single kind, including politics. Yet politics may be no kind, no genre, but the struggle to resist the domination of kinds. Here, as throughout, I wish to admire Naess's norms while expressing reservations about their domination. "But to say that every action and every thought is politically relevant is not the same as to say that 'all is politics.' Nothing is only political, and nothing is not at all political. Ecopolitics is concerned not only with specifically ecological activity, but with every aspect of life" (Naess, *ECL*, p. 130). I prefer to read this not as instituting something which is not politics—life, for example, or wisdom in the home, filled with domination—but as the excess of every aspect of life whose recognition is resistance to neutrality. Everything is ethics|politics as exposure, resistance to neutrality. As exposure and proximity. Something close to Naess's view of ecosophy, perhaps lacking just a bit of vigilance, lacking the intensity of self-critique and deconstruction demanded by endless responsibility to resist neutrality.

Consider an abbreviated version of Naess's account of Gandhian nonviolence:

First-level norm:
     N1 Act in group struggle . . . in a way conducive to long-term universal, maximal reduction of violence!
Second-level hypotheses:
     H1 The character of the means used in a group struggle determines the character of the results.
     . . .
Second-level norms:
     N2 Make a constructive programme part of your campaign!
     N3 Never resort to violence against your opponent.
     N4a Choose that personal action or attitude which most probably reduces the tendency towards violence of all parties in a struggle!
     N4b . . . act . . . always as an autonomous, *fully responsible* person!
Third-level hypotheses:
     H4 . . . give a struggle a constructive character only if you conceive of it and carry it out as a struggle *in favour of living beings* and certain values, thus eventually fighting antagonisms, *not* antagonists.
     . . .

H7 All human (and non-human?) beings have long-term interests in common. (pp. 148–49)

Act together in common; be an autonomous person; avoid and resist violence; favor living beings and what they have in common. All norms I would be happy to pursue in daily life. Except that effective resistance may not always be served by collective movements, commonality frequently insists on too much authority, many people worldwide do not share Western ideals of autonomy, and finally, it may not be possible to avoid violence, though it may be possible to avoid certain overt forms. Perhaps. I have offered somewhat different guidelines, without normativity, resistant to excessive authority. I repeat an abbreviated version here to express something of my difference with Naess—perhaps no difference at all, perhaps an infinite difference.

a. We find ourselves belonging to many different kinds, mixed kinds, kinds belonging to other kinds, by birth, by history, by choice, and by the activities and representations of others. This is our ethical condition. We find ourselves surrounded by many different kinds, which we constitute by our activities and representations, and by which we and they constitute who we are, as human and as individual. To be is to be individual among kinds, individual in virtue of complex and mobile kindred relations. . . .

b. Everything matters, everything is precious, infinitely, inexhaustibly, heterogeneously, every individual thing and every kind. Everything in the earth is precious, in its ways, known and unknown, in the kinds in which it participates. . . . To cherish, love, revere the goodness of things is to let them pursue their own good, with three qualifications:

c. (1) They may not know their own good, though no one else can know it better. (2) Such a good, one's own proper good, is multiple, heterogeneous, impure, bound to others face to face, constituted by memberships, practices, representations, and mobilities. (3) The kinds of the earth, human and other kinds, with their goods, belong everywhere in nature in fourfold relations: constituted by their members, constituting their members' identities, in virtue of their mobilities and circulations, and related heterogeneously. . . .

It follows that:

d. Cherishment in time gives rise to the impossibility of fulfilling the good of heterogeneous things together, and to the impossibility of a measure of fulfillment. This impossibility, sacrifice, knows no rules, demands judgment without criteria, is wounded by endless responsibilities toward the good. This responsibility and judgment bring with themselves a certain joy enriched by sorrow.

e. Among creatures who can choose their good, they must choose and cultivate that good for themselves. None can know the joy and suffering of another, especially another kind, no one can foster the good for another, certainly not the heterogeneous good of other kinds. . . .

f. Nothing can justify the sacrifice of any kind to the good, of any kind, women, children, animals, Jews, not even the AIDS or smallpox virus. Cherishment demands sacrifice, but can never impose in the name of kindness the destruction, death, of a kind, reducing heterogeneity. Such a destruction is profoundly unjust, bears with it responsibility for endless restitution. The sacrifice of an individual, of many individuals, is terrible. But sacrifice is inescapable. Nothing can justify the destruction of a kind in the march of history. Yet history is the recurrence of such catastrophes. (Ross, *PE*, 318–22)

Perhaps everything normative in plenishment can be summarized in the principles—no principles at all—that everything matters and that no one knows another's good, perhaps not even that other. Yet still we struggle for the sake of the good, together with and exposed to others. Perhaps everything fundamental in plenishment is that there is no total view. Yet, "[t]he main goal [of ecosophy T] . . . is to emphasize the responsibility of any integrated person to work out his or her reaction to contemporary environmental problems *on the basis of a total view*" (p. 163). Are you integrated or responsible enough? Do you share my total view? What of those who differ from us by an abyss of essence, or responsibility, or point of view?

Endless questions of responsibility.

(a) Ecosophy ties together all life and all nature (p. 164). And what of the heterogeneity, diversity, and abundance of a nature that cannot be tied together, resisting neutrality, totality, and destruction?

Molly asks to be left alone.

(b) The unfolding of potentialities is a right (p. 164). If rights profoundly and pervasively conflict, can they be possessed as rights? Every right has historically been held against others who do not possess it. Everything and everyone bears an immeasurable responsibility toward others, their actualities and potentialities, and more.

(c) Life as a vast historical process. And other things. The abundance of the earth.

"[T]he development of life on earth is *an integrated process*, despite the steadily increasing diversity and complexity" (pp. 165–66); "Life is fundamentally one" (p. 166). And what if it were fragmentary, unintegrated, variable, heterogeneous? Would that make it less valuable, less precious? What if life were two, or many, or uncountable, or more?

(d) The universal right to live and blossom (p. 166). No right at all, endless responsibilities and exposure. In kinds. Some individuals are prey

for others, individuals cut off from growing and blossoming. As Naess says, resisting the language of rights: "The right of all the forms to live is a universal right which cannot be quantified. No single species of living being has more of this particular right to live and unfold than any other species. Perhaps it is *not* the best way of expressing this to say that there is a right—the *equal* right for all life forms—to unfold its specific capacities. 'Equality' suggests a sort of quantification that is misleading" (Naess, *ECL*, 166). All the forms, not the individuals; potentialities for living their own lives, pursuing their own being, living or not; perhaps not equal—beyond measure; perhaps not a right that can be possessed, if possession of ourselves and others is the foundation of the human claim to own and master other individuals and kinds.

Yet Naess insists on rights, at least insofar as "it is the best expression I have so far found of an intuition which I am unable to reject in all seriousness" (p. 167). I understand rights as a concept under whose ethical|political authority natural creatures and things have been historically dominated. Rights are possessed by some rather than others, are held by some over others, institute binary oppositions that divide those who possess powerful, perhaps unbreakable rights from those who do not, and lead to sacrifice. The right to sacrifice is the crucial right claimed by ethics, by human beings: who has the right (and obligation) to sacrifice whom? Even if the right claimed is the obligation to sacrifice oneself.

Cherishment knows nothing of rights, nothing of its claims and exclusions. Even in Naess, it sometimes appears that only living things can possess a right—to live. Other things—rocks, clouds, landscapes, earth, atoms and molecules—can possess and exercise no rights. Are they not precious, lovely, wonderful in their kinds? May they be used, harmed, destroyed with impunity, without the least care, concern, or responsibility? Love everything! But destroy anything except that which possesses rights.

Love everything! And bear responsibility for that which is or might be good for that thing. Bear responsibility—cherishment—without a possibility of fulfillment. Impossibility of fulfillment does not entail the impossibility of pursuing and accomplishing ethical tasks, bringing goods to pass and avoiding evils. That is always possible, contingently, locally, and incompletely. It is always possible and repeatedly accomplished. Together with sacrifices and disasters, joys and sorrows.

Consider an inclusive ethics of abundance in the earth as the greatest ethical work that any being might pursue, also filled with endless disasters: the greatest joys together with the greatest sorrows. What could be a more wonderful ethical responsibility? In Spinoza's words, *laetitiam* and *tristitiam*: unbounded gladness; endless gloom. In nature's abundance, with or without God. Unbounded abundance gives rise to immeasurable responsibility, an unpayable debt whose restitution is unbounded gladness joined with memories of endless disasters.

What could be a more truthful sense of abundance? What could be more ethical? Or Norwegian?

(d) Friluftsliv: exuberance in nature.

> [I]n Norwegian, there is a clearer, more value-laden word that refers to the type of outdoor recreation that seeks to come to nature on its own terms: to *touch the Earth lightly*. . . . In the following, we retain the original term to indicate a positive kind of state of mind and body in nature, one that brings us closer to some of the many aspects of identification and Self-realisation with nature that we have lost. (Naess, *ECL*, 178)

"[G]uidelines for ethically and ecologically responsible *friluftsliv*" (p. 179):

> (1) Respect for all life. Respect for landscape. . . .
> (2) Outdoor education in the signs of identification. . . .
> (3) Minimal strain upon the natural combined with maximal self-reliance. . . .
> (4) Natural lifestyle. . . .
> (5) Time for adjustment. . . . It is quite normal that several weeks must pass before the *sensitivity* for nature is so developed that it fills the mind. (p. 179)

Perhaps a bit shallow rather than deep. Perhaps an ethics of exuberance, sensitivity, and responsiveness to the abundance of the earth. All immeasurable. Impure.

Concluding with a model that reinvokes the passion and commitment of the platform, a model of "a moving, ever-changing phenomenon" (p. 196) that might be ecosophy and its praxis. An ethics of exuberance, sensitivity, and responsiveness. All immeasurable. Mobile and contingent. Exuberant! With exclamation marks! *Mimēsis*!!

The model, abbreviated but perhaps not attenuated, with exclamation marks of exuberance:

> N1: Self-realisation!
> H1: The higher the Self-realisation attained by anyone, the broader and deeper the identification with others.
> N2: Self-realisation for all living beings!
> N3: Diversity of life!
> N4: Complexity!
> N5: Symbiosis!
> N6: Local self-sufficiency and cooperation!
> N7: Local autonomy!

N8: No centralisation!
N9: No exploitation!
N10: No subjection!
N11: All have equal rights to Self-realisation!
H14: Class societies deny equal rights to Self-realisation!
N12: No class societies!
N13: Self-determination! (pp. 197–207)

The realization of every individual and every kind, impossibly together. With exuberance! Impurity! Sensitivity! Responsiveness! Responsibility! !!!![4]

CHAPTER 11

Weaving Kinds

Reweaving the World: The Emergence of Ecofeminism.

It is my contention that the systematic denigration of working-class people and people of color, women, and animals is connected to the basic dualism that lies at the root of Western civilization. But the mind-set of hierarchy originates within human society. It has its material roots in the domination of human by human, particularly of women by men. (King, *HW*, 106–7)

Part of the work of feminism has been asserting that the activities of women, believed to be more natural than those of men, are in fact absolutely social.

It is as if women were entrusted with and have kept the dirty little secret that humanity emerges from nonhuman nature into society in the life of the species and the person. The process of nurturing an unsocialized, undifferentiated human infant into an adult person—the socialization of the organic—is the bridge between nature and culture. (p. 116)

Men hunt, women weave. Men travel, women weave. Waiting.

In the recesses of time, women shared the world with men. Try to remember. Demeter and Persephone. The goddesses. Remember Mother Earth.

I have been painfully aware of the connection between the demise of the Goddess, the rise of patriarchy, and the rape of the environment. (Abbott, *OGBL*, 35)

The myth of Demeter and Persephone illuminated the experiences of life that through all times remain the most mysterious—birth, sexuality, death—and the greatest mystery of all, enduring love. (Keller, *EM*, p. 41)

175

Mother of us all, oldest of all, of the earth,
    the sacred ground,
nourishing all out of her treasures—children,
    fields, cattle, beauty . . .
Mistress, from you come our fine children and
    bountiful harvests;
Yours is the power to give mortals life and to
    take it away . . .
Hail to you, mother of Gods. (Keller, p. 42)[1]

I remember women in the home, together with slaves, marked by silence. Women who by their nature are fit for silence, in the home, weaving and cooking, most of all fit for children. Women are nature's human reproductive technology, to be employed for human ends. Weaving to serve men, or children, or mankind, or humanity. Waiting to serve.

Women are said to differ by nature in kind from men, serving humanity and nature in the ways they have been designed to serve. Men serve humanity and nature in other ways, by another natural design. Or are served. Penelope waits to serve, spinning and weaving to keep other men at bay. Or something else.

Weaving offers a complex image of ethical ecology—multifarious, mobile, sinuous relations and heterogeneities—with which to resist teleology and totality. Not without a terrible history. Not without risks. Risks and terrors woven into any ecological ethics, too easily forgotten. The greatest danger and most wonderful possibility in linking women with weaving is of marking women's historical experiences, the felt sense of women working together, sharing lives, risking repetition of the hateful side of those lives, the domination of human beings by other human beings, especially women by men. Leading in the extreme—vividly experienced—of the domination of nature by humanity: a domination claimed by right, if never a mastery accomplished.

Do we—do you, do I, do women—remember when the goddesses—Demeter, Persephone, Gaia—touched the earth, Mothers of us all? Without domination? I do not think so. At least, I do not remember. I remember systems of domination of what is natural and female throughout the world, linked with other systems of domination, of people of other classes and colors, of animals and plants. The tyranny of kinds! Have there been exceptions? I am wary of exceptions that set a different standard. I would insist on seeking exceptions to celebrate lives and experiences that have been denigrated, despoiled, frequently destroyed. Kindness without tyranny, if that is possible.

Women weave, not because that is what they are fit to do by nature, but because weaving has been despised in Western societies—weaving together with all "women's work"—treated as inferior because more natural.

Nature transformed is nature envalued; transformed by labor, work, rationality. Nature built. The conversion of vegetable matter into clothing and shelter does not last, does not stock up value. Women do transitory things; men build what lasts: edifices, towers, cleared and fenced-in property. Women invisibly create labor value.

It comes down, I believe, to property. The rape of the environment, of the earth, of human lives, is always a matter of property, of what is owned, claimed by right, what is good and proper. Another book.[2]

This book is concerned with kinds, women and natural kinds. Nature *and* woman. Women *with* nature. Words we have heard before. Always more than words. *Mimēsis. We are women. We rise from the wave. We know ourselves to be made from this earth.* We, we, we. We women. We humans? We creatures? Organic, inorganic? She loves blood. She asks for slaughter. She asks for sacrifice. She, she, she. Mother, daughter, woman nature. Nature without neutrality. But perhaps not female alone, daughter without brother, mother without father and son. As if there might be women without men—for long. Or without technological assistance. Technological feasibility and use are among the concerns that bear upon women and nature today, reproduction and any future, human or otherwise. "[I]n a world where everything 'should' be manipulated to better serve human happiness, rights become the mechanism for eradicating all barriers to the technologically feasible" (Diamond, *BHEPE*, 204).

The dangerous magic of technology. The exalting magic of language, Griffin's pronouns linking nature and women in domination and celebration; linking as exposure, *mimēsis* and proximity. All who live in the earth, where every creature and thing speaks, knows, touches other creatures and things in proximity, endlessly exposed to others. All individuals and kinds, individuals in kinds, constituted by and constituting kinds, kinds constituting each other. The abundance of the earth.

The earth's abundance cannot be expressed today, in Western, European history—by force and development becoming the only history of the earth—without memories of domination, of working people and people of color, women, and animals; the domination of human by human, of women by men. That which links woman and nature evokes inseparable memories of abundance and domination.

Returning to the goddesses who express abundance, remembering their role in dominations. God the Father; the earth the mother, sister, daughter.

Reminding us that resistance to domination endlessly repeats it, in relation to women and nature and other peoples. That ethics after the depredation of the earth would have us accept the disaster rather than resist it. "It is a sad irony that the destruction of the natural world appears to be proceeding apace with the construction of moral theories for how we should behave in light of this fact" (Kheel, *EDE*, 128). Reminding us that at the moment at which disempowered human beings claim empowerment within a different subjectivity, some of those highly critical of Europe's history of domination suggest it is time to dismantle the subject. In histories and institutions of domination, women get it coming and going, together with other marginalized peoples who lack standing within established institutions. If they work within established institutions, in resistance, they accept the structures of their domination. If they would avoid institutional domination, they disempower themselves. Domination remains the structure of all relations of marginalized kinds of human beings, in cooperation or resistance, in celebration or woe.

As may be said of nature and the earth, of natural kinds, organic and inorganic. To refuse the disciplinary, epistemological, economic, technological, ethical, and political structures that have depredated the planet, torn down forests, ripped open mountains, denuded prairies, destroyed beaches, slaughtered and tortured millions of animals, all in the name of what benefits some human beings over others, is to abandon every intelligible, practical, and effective relation between humanity and nature. Effective and powerful instrumental relations are powerful and effective. Scientific truths are truthful and dependable. Yet the ethical work of effective and dependable practices and truths does not stop with this effectiveness and dependability, but is always linked on one side with institutional structures and histories of domination, with state power, and on the other side with excesses and resistances, with endless responsibilities and debts.

These responsibilities and debts answer to the endless production of boundaries and borders in which all work is done—restricted economies— by resisting the measures that police every border. This falling back and down, this resistance to the policing of borders by instituting other resistances—for example, to garbage police—may be understood as answering to something excessive in every border. It may also be understood as expressing the impurity of every kind, including institutions, police, and resistance: general economy, the abundance of kinds. Kindredness and kindness fall back and down excessively upon histories of hierarchy and domination, celebrating the abundance of the earth.

Resistance to the autonomy of the subject is resistance to its purity, the authority of its borders. The authoritative subject—who excludes countless kinds of people from authority—is impure; all kinds are impure, centered or marginal. The empowerment of marginalized kinds of people takes place not in the reinstitution of another centered kind, but in the multiplicity, hybridity, and impurity of kinds, human and otherwise, falling back upon authority and purity. Always in kinds, always empowering kinds, not just individuals, kinds exceeding every purification, every authorized border. An ecology of the abundance of kinds, resisting domination, always abjectly falling down into domination. An ecology of kindness, exposure in kinds.

Not just human kinds, or living kinds, but all natural kinds. For the institution of boundaries between kinds, and kinds of kinds, is never neutral, however scientific or disciplinary, but is linked throughout time and space with histories of domination and mastery. Historically marginalized kinds get it coming and going where purity is demanded, where either they retain the borders they always had, within an institutional reversal, still authoritative, still policed; or where their boundaries are dissolved, denying them standing and efficacy. Yet we may understand coming and going as impurity, doubled against repetition even where falling back and down upon itself. Women get it coming and going in part because all forms of resistance are impotent against entrenched cultural forces, but also in part because they do not collectively pursue equal authority, always seek something more. Similarly, within some hateful claims and disastrous practices, marginalized people's demands for recognition open toward other possibilities than equal authority within the institutions of their domination.

It is possible to discern in the multiplicity of environmental and ecological movements both a preservation of those structures of thought and practice that have instituted depredation and violation of natural creatures, things, and habitats in the name of human possession and use, and something more excessive, immeasurable, celebrative, a responsibility beyond such use and possession, to which those movements answer even when they are silent concerning the values and authorities they would foster.

But perhaps not altogether silent in such figures as weaving and reweaving. For weaving recalls women relegated to the home, women's work, histories of subordination; yet also recalls complex and profuse entanglements, woofs and warps, resists a linear and controlled sense of mastery; even so, weaving does not give up mastery, over thread and yarn, may not relinquish its own authority far enough, especially in a world where weaving is performed by large mechanical installations or by children's forced labor. Every kind of figure remains impure in the insistence of every authority over its identity. Every border remains permeable within the authority that would police its boundaries.

The most truthful truths and beneficial benefits are impure, and their impurities are impure. Expressed perhaps as *re*weaving, iteration, repetition, *mimēsis*, always more than what is common. Such an understanding accommodates the sense that what we gain from disciplinary and taxonomic practices and structures is indeed something true and important; that what we achieve through democratic institutions and practices is worth preserving, valuable, and important, to be repeated, yet not in the ways authorized by those institutions and practices. If that were possible.

Marginalized peoples get it coming and going, and in this history of dominations, in the inescapability of hierarchy and oppression inherent in the profusion of human kinds, something profoundly different emerges in the mobilizations of marginalization. Technology will provide solutions to technological problems; government will provide solutions to political problems; economic development will restore human and natural habitats to worthwhile spheres of life and beauty. But never just in the ways designed by history and by institutional planning, never as designed, never entirely oblivious to the harm such institutional practices and structures have produced, or to the systems of domination and state power with which they are linked. All of these are impure, where impurity carries a triple force: (1) resistance to those forms of purity—natural, human, disciplinary, epistemological—whose claims to authority result from policing borders, excluding some kinds from regard and worth; (2) responsibility against the obliviousness and disaster inherent in this resistance, and within this responsibility still another, toward impurities in oneself and one's kinds: (3) institution of practices of empowerment inherent in the impurity, profusion, and cherishment of kinds.

This returns us to the subject of this chapter, expressed by Griffin as *Woman and Nature* within the enigmas and responsibilities of the *and*: elsewhere known as ecological feminism. For the moment, I insist on the strength of *feminism* within the relation to nature and natural kinds I hope to articulate. Perhaps women's lived experiences offer the possibility of articulating and instituting another relation to the natural world. Perhaps the dualism at the heart of human domination of nature emerges from the domination of human by human, particularly of women by men. Perhaps something within women's experiences—nurturing and mothering—is a bridge between nature and culture. Perhaps in virtue of women's historical links with nature, within hierarchy, domination, but also celebration. Perhaps in women's unique, felt sense of connection to the natural world. "It is out of women's unique, felt sense of connection to the natural world that an ecofeminist philosophy must be forged. Identification may, in fact, enter into this philosophy but only to the extent that it flows from an *existing* connection with individual lives" (Kheel, *EDE*, 137). Perhaps more than women.

I pursue the claim by many feminists, including Kheel, that something vital for humanity's ethical, political, and lived future can be found in women's lived experiences. Not just for women, though that is crucial. Lived experience has been denigrated, truncated, women's without a doubt, and men's; marginalized people's lived experiences, women's and men's; and, perhaps, the experiences of other living creatures, dogs and cats, wolves and ants; perhaps, as well, the proximity and exposure of other things to each other, stones and clouds, atoms and quarks.

I stay somewhat longer with women's lived experiences. Described by Kheel as a felt sense of connection in individual lives to the natural world. Described by King as the experience of mothers nurturing their children. Described by Catharine MacKinnon in quite different terms, tightly linked with domination:

> In male supremacist societies, the male standpoint dominates civil society in the form of the objective standard—that standpoint which, because it dominates in the world, does not appear to function as a standpoint at all. Under its aegis, men dominate women and children, three-quarters of the world. Family and kinship rules and sexual mores guarantee reproductive ownership and sexual access and control to men as a group. . . . The state incorporates these facts of social power in and as law. (MacKinnon, *TFJ*, 237)

This sounds to many ears as a reduction of all marginalizations to heterosexuality, the domination of women and children by men, regardless of color, class, sexual preference, language, cultural background, leaving no room for lesbians and women of color. I read it differently, as expressing room for all such women and men within cultures that frame the world in heterosexual terms, insisting on institutional authority over reproduction. Such a system, matrix, or standpoint dominates all forms of life and thought that fall under it—under, back, and down. Women's concrete, lived experiences testify to this from within the matrix that dominates them. "What do women live, hence know, that can confront male dominance? What female ontology can confront male epistemology; that is, what female epistemology can confront male ontology?" (MacKinnon, *TFJ*, 241). She answers: "The answer is simple, concrete, specific, and real: women's social inequality with men on the basis of sex, hence the point of view of women's subordination to men. Women . . . know inequality because they have lived it, so they know what removing barriers to equality would be" (p. 241). And again, "The first step is to claim women's concrete reality" (MacKinnon, *TFJ*, 244).

Many find this harsh and unyielding, both for women whose lived reality is social inequality and for men and women of marginalized groups whose lived reality is social inequality but not always primarily as women. Such a conclusion follows from reading women's concrete lived reality and social inequality in pure terms, where they are to be understood in impure, excessive terms, retaining and perhaps expanding the force of the social inequalities they address. For MacKinnon surely knows that the social inequalities women experience are experienced by them both as women and as women of certain kinds—classes, colors, ethnic groups, nationalities, histories. It is a matter of how to express this. I read her insistence on the heterosexual structure of social life not as excluding other structures but as emphasizing how a dominant frame such as heterosexuality affects everything. Other such frames, I believe, emerge from state power, economic development, epistemological and disciplinary practices, and relations with the natural world. Each of these permeates the others, as if none of the borders could be closed. Always impurely.

The contribution of ecological feminism as I understand it, paralleling MacKinnon's view, is to insist that the domination of women pervades all social and natural worlds. Ecological feminism is a liminal philosophy resistant to the fixity of every border, including its own, reaching out from women's experiences in developed countries to women's experiences elsewhere, but also to men's, and throughout nature. Paying attention to women's experiences leads to insights that might otherwise remain invisible.

> Developmental projects have destroyed women's productivity both by removing land, water, and forests from their management and control, as well as by the ecological destruction of soil, water, and vegetation systems so that nature's productivity and renewability have been impaired. While gender subordination and patriarchy are the oldest of oppressions, through development they have taken on new and more violent forms. (Shiva, *DNPWP*, 191)

> The old assumption that with the development process the availability of goods and services would automatically increase and poverty would decrease is now under serious challenge from women's ecology movements in the Third World even while it continues to guide development-thinking in centers of patriarchal power. . . . The recovery of the feminine principle would allow a transcendence and transformation of the patriarchal foundations of maldevelopment. It would redefine growth and productivity as categories linked to the production—not the destruction—of life. (p. 200)

The feminine principle here—still forceful in Asia—is not, I believe, alien to men, or Europeans, or animals, or vegetables, or whatever, but emphasizes multiplicity, profusion, liminality, and impurity, including its own. The feminine principle is uncontainable within histories of the subordination of women. I would add that other social dominations, by race, blood, and kind, are also pervasive, uncontainable. And other dominations, other practices toward kinds. Including animals and plants. Wherever human beings can be found, including Asia, other living creatures are also present and dead creatures serve human use. Modern technology, whatever else it may be, is a technology of the use of living creatures. Increased all the more in biological technologies manipulating genetic materials. Human beings have technologically manipulated animals for use for thousands of years, through breeding and cropping. And slavery. Ecological feminism allows us to understand the domination of nature through the prism of the domination of women, a prism vital for any critical understanding of human and natural kinds. Together with other prisms, emerging from other dominations, especially slavery and colonialism, that promise other deep social critiques and ethical benefits.

A striking example is given by King. The activities of women, said to be natural, are absolutely social; indeed, everything natural is absolutely social, but social and natural are inseparable, impure: neither's borders can be held firm. Moreover, women appear to have been entrusted with the dirty little secret of this impurity—the curse—that humanity emerges from nonhuman nature into society, historically and in every human life. Perhaps every life, everything, everywhere on earth, is such an emergence, understanding human society and technology as reshaping the planet. For again, the borders cannot be held firm.

The curse is to be understood in relation to exclusion, insisting on holding the borders of kinds against encroachment. The curse curses nature as nonhuman, polices its borders within against other human kinds— Africans, primitives, gays and lesbians, whatever; polices its borders without against nonhuman kinds—animals, plants, inorganic things—made available for human use in any way whatever. The dirty little secret is that humanity is cursed by nature, is nature abject under the curse. *Under* the curse, not free from it. Impure. The secret is the permeability of every border that would hold some kind of humanity, some part of nature, pure against the encroachments of other kinds. We are cursed by always being other kinds.

I credit feminism in general, and ecological feminism in particular, with having done more work elucidating the details of this secret of the curse than any other school of thought—if either of these can be held firm against the encroachments of other schools. I doubt they can. Even so, the sociality of nature, described by many, emerges in women's lived experiences, their concrete reality. Entrusted with a special, hateful relation to sacrifice: "culture's sacrifice to nature" (King, *HW*, 115). Entrusted, cursed, with the secret of emergence, impurity. Under domination. And in others' lived experiences within domination. Whichever side of authority one finds oneself on, lived experience, however mute, speaks in social terms of nature, speaks impurely however loudly we may scream for purity. The secret is the abundance of kinds.

Allowing us to take up the question posed by King in a different register. "There are two basic differences within the radical feminist movement: whether the woman/nature connection is potentially emancipatory or whether it provides a rationale for the continued subordination of women" (King, *HW*, 110). Whether either may be pure, separated from the other.

The first "implies a separate feminist culture" and celebrates "the woman/ nature connection" (p. 110). King calls those who hold this position *radical culture feminists*, celebrating "the experience of the 'female ghetto,' which they see as a source of female freedom rather than subordination" (p. 111), though "they have inadequately addressed the real diversity of women's lives and histories across race, class, and national boundaries" (p. 111). The second group, *radical rationalist feminists*, repudiate the woman/nature connection. "Anything that reinforces gender differences, or makes any kind of special claim for women, is problematic" (p. 110).

According to a logic of opposition, these are antagonistic positions. In this mood, King asks "How do women who call themselves radical feminists come to such divergent positions?" (p. 110). As if the two positions might not be compatible despite the structure of their opposition. As if women's, and others', emancipatory position could find a pure, unambiguous theoretical expression. The alternative is multiple impurity pertaining to all kinds as kinds, including women, and men, subordinate and dominant—if working-class men and men of color are ever dominant—and to kinds with histories of oppression, marked by impurity: slave-holding women and women slaves; wealthy women and women from ghettos, white, heterosexual women and women of color; men and women, together with landscapes and habitats, with histories of colonial oppression; all impure. If impurity marks the condition of women twice, then emancipation would be marked by impurity many times over, acknowledging histories of oppression as women, women linked with nature, women separated from nature by countless layers of clothing and ornamentation, abused women, ornamented women who serve as expressions of the status of men; and so on. Every emancipatory position would be impure many times over, reflecting the oppression of women in relation to nature—together with people of color, men and women, working-class people, people who cannot find work, and others. All bearing upon heterogeneous kinds, kinds of women, kinds of human beings, kinds throughout nature, all impure, policing their borders on every side, resisting oppression. The names, identities, boundaries of kinds bear ethical|political weight—oppression and emancipation—in their abundance, in the impurities that surround and permeate them. In, for example, Griffin's voice.

Much of which King says in her own voice, reminiscent of what Outlaw says of race.[3]

> Each major contemporary feminist theory, liberal, social, and cultural, has taken up the issue of the relationship between women and nature. And each in its own way has capitulated to dualistic thinking. . . . An ecological feminism calls for a dynamic, developmental theory of the per-

son—male and female—who emerges out of nonhuman nature, where differences is neither reified nor ignored and the dialectical relationship between human and nonhuman nature is understood. (King, *HW*, 116–17)

She is speaking explicitly to those who would understand ecological feminism as "essentialist"—if there be such a thing as essentialism—in claiming that women and nature are linked in their kinds and essences. To which she replies that this link is historical and dialectical. And to which I reply that the link is not the restrictiveness and purity of the kinds associated with women and nature, but their abundance and heterogeneity. Women and nature are linked by ecological feminism in the multiplicity and profusion of the kinds with which they are joined in the impurities of their relationships, including historical oppression and domination. Impurity is the condition of kinds, of lived experiences, and of the practices and reflections that respond to them ethically and politically. In multiple, impure, heterogeneous ways.

> [W]e will fuse a new way of being human on this planet with a sense of the sacred, informed by all ways of knowing—intuitive *and* scientific, mystical *and* rational. . . .
>
> At this point in history, the domination of nature is inextricably bound up with the domination of persons, and both must be addressed—without arguments over "the primary contradiction" in the search for a single Archimedes point for revolution. There is no such thing. And there is no point in liberating people if the planet cannot sustain their liberated lives or in saving the planet by disregarding the preciousness of human existence not only to ourselves but to the rest of life on Earth. (pp. 120–21)

We will overcome dualisms, reenchant reason, join intuition and science. Or hope to do so. We women. As women. Together with women. We will remember as we do so that the domination of nature is bound with the domination of women and other human beings, another linking, crossing, impurity; and there is no Archimedean point, no pure point of liberation. The preciousness of human existence is linked with the preciousness of the rest of the earth—impurely, heterogeneously, liminally.

Such an understanding of the abundance and heterogeneity of kinds bears profoundly on the critical and emancipatory discourses and practices that would respond in depth to the circumstances of the earth at this and perhaps any other time. Every theory, every proposed practice, individual or institutional, is impure, where impurity has less to do with complexity and multiplicity, and more to do with the permeability of borders and the authority with which boundaries of kinds are held in place. The abundance of kinds knows no pure expression, cannot be given a proper name, not deconstruction, ecological feminism, ecological kindism, deep ecology, capitalism, socialism, or liberal democracy. Not even the name of an emancipatory ethics|politics. Not even abundance or kindness.

I conclude this chapter with some questions that arise in the midst of abundance and impurity. What if we understood reweaving the world as alluding to women's historical roles, histories of inequality and histories of celebration, of women by women, women together; also to impurity, mixing, weaving, entangling strands of different colors, different kinds, different materials; beginning without a beginning, ending without an ending; a figure of heterogeneity, abundance, and impurity? Doing the work of the world, human work, without coercive authority: borders without police; permeable, multifarious, mobile yet traditional boundaries. Epistemological, ethical, philosophical, disciplinary.

What if we were critical of interdisciplinary and international ventures in principle, wary of borders and crossings? Because disciplines, knowledges, lives, species, and kinds are always heterogeneous, liminal, impurely woven together in subtle, complex, and multifarious ways. Because nations are impurely woven together with other nations and kinds. Because men and women are present everywhere in human life as men and women multiplied by inexhaustible complexities and complications, crossings and weavings, endless impurities: social, cultural, natural, whatever. Because males and females of every species are essential as males and females to the perpetuation and identity of their species while undergoing endless transformations and transportations—the nature of natural and other kinds of selection. Resulting not in the blurring and vanishing of kinds together— including natural species, tantamount to death—but in the contingency of their local habitats and the abundance of other kinds among whom they find themselves in relation. Crossings presuppose borders of nations, cultures, knowledges, and kinds firmly held in place. What if every such border were liminal, thresholds undergoing endless intermediary movements? Purities and impurities.

Finally, what if this heterogeneity of kinds were nature? Not nature rather than culture, society, or humanity, but the limins, thresholds, intermediary movements of kinds in endless abundance. Against which humanity insists repeatedly on reinstituting the curse that plagues nature and humanity with sacrifice and death, transformed into authority, domination and oppression. The endless abundance of life and death, exposure and proximity, becomes exclusion and abjection under the curse. What if we could think of humanity's ethics as the responsibility humans bear to resist the curse within the abundance of the earth and the inescapability of disaster: cherishment and sacrifice given as plenishment, in kindness? All liminal; everywhere impure; kinds woven and rewoven in their abundance together. As they compose nature with heterogeneity, impurity, *différends*.

CHAPTER 12

Modern Kinds

Now in just these two ways we can also know the difference between man and beast. For it is quite remarkable that there are no men so dull-witted or stupid—and this includes even madmen—that they are incapable of arranging various words together and forming an utterance from them in order to make their thoughts understood; whereas there is no other animal, however perfect and well-endowed it may be, that can do the like.... This shows not merely that the beasts have less reason than men, but that they have no reason at all. (Descartes, *DM*, p. 140)

Until the existence of proof to the contrary, animals have no culture, but only customs and modes of life, and the surest sign of this absence is that they transmit no new legacy from generation to generation. (Ferry, *NEO*, 41)

The modern world, Ferry tells us, rests on *separation*—above all, the separation of humanity from nature as ethical, political, juridical, and rational subjects. Especially, the separation of human beings from animals, who according to Descartes have no reason at all; according to Ferry have no culture at all, act according to their natures, leave no legacies in time.

For unlike an animal, which is subject to the natural code of instinct particular to its species more than to its individuality, human beings have the possibility of emancipating themselves, even of revolting against their own nature. (Ferry, *NEO*, 115)

[A]ll valorization, including that of nature, is the deed of man and..., *consequently, all normative ethic is in some sense humanist and anthropocentrist.* (p. 131)

As if every culture bore the mark of European sensibilities toward mortality, toward history and the curse; as if those that lived without attempting to control their history and destiny were culturally deficient. As Kant and Hegel claim. As if the sacrifices Foucault insists are imposed by values, by restricted economies, always demand the destruction of animals. Molly digs the sand in rage.

I interrupt to recall something of Foucault's rendering of the prose of the world, expressed by Ferry in a striking example.

> 1587: The inhabitants of the village of Saint-Julien took legal action against a colony of weevils. . . .
>
> Forty or so years earlier, in 1545, an identical trial had taken place against the same creepers (or at least their ancestors). The affair ended in victory for the insects, who, were defended by . . . the episcopal judge. The latter had refused to excommunicate them, arguing that as creatures of God the animals possessed the same rights as men to consume plant life. (Ferry, *NEO*, ix)
>
> What kind of breach must have opened within humankind for the ritual performed in all seriousness in one era to turn to high comedy in another? (p. xvi)

A breach Foucault describes as the plethoric yet absolutely poverty-stricken character of an abundance in which "[t]he whole volume of the world, all the adjacencies of 'convenience,' all the echoes of emulation, all the linkages of analogy, are supported, maintained, and doubled by this space governed by sympathy and antipathy, which are ceaselessly drawing things together and holding them apart" (Foucault, *OT*, 25). Foucault relates modernity in the breach to the sacrifice of goods to exchange.[1] Values arise within the curse, cursing humans with loss, cursing animals and other natural things with domination. High comedy indeed! I return from this interruption.

All these absolute denials, of reason, culture, and freedom, in the nature of animals, or nature in general, express the modern world, Ferry claims, and more, the condition of modern democracy.

> For the affirmation of the rights of nature, when it takes the form of the latter's being instated as a legal subject, implies the rejection of a certain type of democracy—a democracy inherited from the Declaration of Rights. . . . The idea that one could "add" a "natural contract" to the Declaration of Rights is not very valid philosophically. . . . [W]ithin the framework of legal humanism, nature can occupy only the status of *object*, not of *subject*. (Ferry, *NEO*, 129)

Yet perhaps this kind of democracy has been oppressive, calling for critique in the name of democracy itself. As many ecologists insist. The high comedy of a democracy cursed by rule. Modernity's curse. I leave this democracy aside for a while to pursue Ferry's insistence on the highest spiritual achievements of secular modernity, at the absolute expense of animals and other natural things—under the curse. Everything Ferry says is under the curse—he claims it as that of modernity. Bataille understands it as belonging to humanity itself.

I interrupt to say something of my reading of Ferry. I read him with fascination though I disagree with virtually everything he says about nature and ethics. I would say that he knows nothing whatever about the good— its immeasurable responsibility and vigilance; nothing of sacrificing sacrifice. He speaks normatively of transcendence, as if giving a measure, where the good knows no measure. Yet if I disagree with him on every detail, every value, every ecological responsibility, I respect his understanding of the urgency and importance for our time of ecological thinking, the attempt to redefine humanity's relation to nature in ethical and political terms—his understanding without his repugnance. I spend this space and time here in critique—a practice I abhor—to express my admiration of his view of modernity and Western civilization. For in my opinion he gets everything right in his account of contemporary movements—everything right and everything wrong; as if he were a visitor from another planet who understood the language but not the customs, not the passions and concerns in deep ecology and ecological feminism, translating the most intensely democratic passions into fascist ideology. He treats all these ethical movements as slightly mad. I find him also mad—mad for humanism without the slightest inkling of the disasters performed in its name; mad for France; mad for the *Declaration of the Rights of Man*—instead of *The Declaration of Independence*, for example, which does not so rigidly restrict itself to Man. Which is not to deny—indeed to passionately affirm—that madness frequently speaks in truth. As he knows of ecological movements in his resistance. And as I mean to express of his own account of the issues they present and his exclusions. That is, I hope to let him define the issues to be examined in this chapter, though I will resist every one of his resistances. I hope to do so without exclusion. I end this interruption.

Ferry says that freedom is the absolute condition of ethics, both for those who would be ethical, who recognize responsibilities, and for those who possess ethical values, bearers of rights. The circle closes tightly— perhaps too tightly for many human beings as well as animals and other natural creatures and things. For not all human beings are free—young children and, perhaps, mad people—yet certainly they possess rights though they may be unable to accept responsibilities. Or the full range of responsibilities we expect from adult human beings. For that matter, many adult human beings in extreme conditions of hardship—prisoners and citizens of oppressive, violent regimes—may be unable to undertake many such responsibilities, a consequence of the harm done to them by their conditions. And many animals, adult and young, respond with sympathy and care toward other animals, if not with the full range of human behavior. And toward humans.

What if we resisted the absolute distinction imposed between human beings and animals—not the distinction but its absoluteness? What if we extended Ferry's reading of Beauvoir's words concerning women to include animals, even plants? "If we fate women to immanency, if we refuse the possibility of transcending nature, their own nature included, and hold them as tied for all eternity to the domestic life to which biology seems to destine them, we reduce them to an animal state" (Ferry, *NEO*, 116).[2] What if we understood all things, natural and human, to be given in abundance and excess, surpassing the grip of fixed boundaries and identities? Including biology. Resisting all attempts to police the borders of the human at the expense of the complexities of nature. The key is to resist glorifying some at the expense of others, to sacrifice sacrifice.

What if we insisted on freedom as the condition of ethics, but loosened the circle, so that freedom imposed responsibility but bestowed no rights or privileges; where freedom was neither the absolute and unqualified ground of ethics—acknowledging creatures and things toward whom we bear responsibility who are themselves unfree, or for the moment unfree, or not free as we would hope to be, or free in the ways they are free; free as we ourselves may never be; a condition but not the sole condition of responsibilities and values; always qualified by situations and determinations beyond the choice of individual agents? What if responsibility exceeded the grasp of freedom as freedom exceeds the grasp of every border, resisting its authority? What if freedom and responsibility were inseparable conditions of ethics, each exceeding the determinants of identity and agency, natural and social: each exceeding the other? What if the excessiveness marked by each, by culture in relation to nature, and nature in relation to culture, could not be contained under any mark of excess: all excessive in relation to the others? Humanity, naturality, responsibility, and freedom; together with language, culture, and history—*mimēsis*; with natural selection, with mobile individuals and kinds: the abundance of the earth in heterogeneous kinds, all expressive, excessive. Kindness in the earth.

Do we know what this might mean for ethics toward human and other creatures and things; what kinds of creatures bear responsibilities, bear values, what may be cherished, cared for, what kinds care for others and under what conditions, with what qualifications? I do not think so. I do not think we have taken the death of God,[3] resistance to abjection and authority, far enough. It was a wonderful achievement to recognize human rights against historical claims—political, religious, economic, and other—to the dominance of some over others. Yet although that recognition came with claims to universality, it has never come close to achieving it. Human rights were implemented by means of war, slavery, colonization; linked with countless *isms*—antisemitism, racism, sexism, classism—marking the limits of human rights qualified by custom and law. *Universality* has never meant universality, in part because of political and economic domination, the persistence of overarching authority; in part because the abstraction of such universality is empty in relation to the division of human and other worlds into kinds; in part because the individuality at the heart of such universality is empty in relation to differences of families, groups, and kinds.

All these groupings into kinds are hierarchical, exclusive. They serve— in Ferry's explicit reading—to mark the ethical superiority of humanity over the world, the superiority of culture over nature under the curse. The separation is an ethical superiority—I say *ethical*, but it is inseparable from politics and economics, from property and law. *Only* humans are free. *Only* humans have culture. *Only* humans are agents. *Only* humans bear responsibility. For themselves! Nature exists *for the benefit of human beings!!!* The low comedy of modernity under the curse.

> The two major problems encountered by deep ecology in its plan to instate nature as a legal subject, capable of being party to a "natural contract," can be further summarized as follows: the first, which is shockingly obvious, is that nature is not an *agent*, a being able to *act* with the *reciprocity* one would expect of a legal *alter ego*. *Law is always for men*, and it is for men that trees or whales can become *objects* of a form of respect tied to legislation—not the reverse. The second problem is less obvious: if we accept that it is possible to speak metaphorically of "nature" as a "contractual party," it will still be necessary to specify what it is, *in nature*, that is supposed to possess intrinsic value. . . . Can one seriously claim that HIV is a subject of law, equal to man? (Ferry, *NEO*, 139–40)

The circle institutes and perpetuates hierarchy and domination. All value belongs to human beings—perhaps not so certain or unqualified a claim as Ferry alleges. Perhaps not an insurmountable logical error, as if logic might impose itself on ethics without qualification. For animals care for their young. And social animals sacrifice themselves for their tribe.[4] Ferry asserts as authoritatively that animals do not choose as Descartes says that animals do not speak. Yet they feel; Ferry knows they feel. Which does not grant them ethical standing. I hold their feelings in abeyance.

Humanity has eliminated smallpox from the diseases that attack human beings. No doubt we hope to do the same for the HIV virus. That is not quite the same as whether we should destroy the last vestiges of either virus. For the world might be impoverished profoundly if something so remarkable were to be altogether destroyed. Can we not admire the resilience and effectiveness of that which causes us harm—admire in an ethical way, as we admire certain criminals? Which is not to say that we should treat them lightly. Do we not bear complex and difficult responsibilities on every side?

Though Ferry criticizes what he calls the insurmountable logical error of neglecting the fact that *only* human beings judge, he can be said to commit another—I would not say "insurmountable"—logical error that takes for granted that because only human beings value, all value is given in human terms, by and for human beings. All valorization is done for human beings—by no means fully accepted by Ferry, yet almost unavoidable. For if animals and other natural things do not possess intrinsic value, then they possess value *for* humanity, *in the light of* human life and judgment. Perhaps these are not the same, but the difference evaporates where it does not become intrinsic.

> It is true that animals *in and of themselves*, because they are sensitive beings and not simple machines, must inspire a certain compassion in us. But the most serious consequences of the cruelty and bad treatment inflicted on them *is that man degrades himself and loses his humanity.* (Ferry, *NEO*, 24–25)

Only the quality of human life is relevant, not animal or vegetal life. Ferry rejects every possibility of values in nature. "[S]hould we merely be safeguarding the sites where *we* live because their deterioration might affect *us*, or, on the contrary, should we be protecting nature in and of itself, because we are discovering that it is not simply a collection of raw materials, endlessly pliable and exploitable, but a harmonious and fragile system, in itself more important and wondrous than the ultimately tiny segment that constitutes human life?" (p. 60). Between these two positions one must choose absolutely. Humanism insists that we choose, sacrificing nature to humanity under the curse. No room exists to explore Serres's provocative suggestion, presented by Ferry, that we turn the protection of law to nature, that we rewrite the social contract, with its history of destructions of women and minorities, in relation to subordinated natural kinds.

> Back to nature then! That means that we must add to the exclusively social contract a natural contract of symbiosis and reciprocity in which our relationship to things would set aside mastery and possession in favor of admiring attention, reciprocity, contemplation, and respect; where knowledge would no longer imply property, nor action mastery, nor would property and mastery imply their excremental results and origins. (Serres, *NC*, 38)

Everything in Serres turns on resisting mastery and possession, toward human beings, animals, and natural things, transfiguring the historical relation of humanity to the world: that of owner and master. Ferry thinks that law is based on the rights of human beings; Serres and I think that law is based on property.

Serres's personal history is beyond reproach. Ferry dismisses his position as "a metaphorical fable more than a rigorous argument ... ('Hello Mother Nature, let's be friends')" (Ferry, *NEO*, 72).[5] Against Jonas, who offers a similar approach to nature, Ferry reminds us of his "professions of faith in favor of Communist regimes" (p. 80). What Ferry cannot stand is "the idea that nature possesses an *intrinsic value* and that it is, as such, worthy of respect" (p. 73):

> it is at least not senseless anymore to ask whether the condition of extrahuman nature, the biosphere as a whole and in its parts, now subject to our power, has become a human trust and has something of a moral claim on us not only for our ulterior sake but for its own and in its own right. If this were the case it would require quite some rethinking in basic principles of ethics. It would mean to seek not only the human good but also the good of things extrahuman, that is, to extend the recognition of "ends in themselves" beyond the sphere of man and make the human good include the care for them. (Jonas, *GPR*, p. 15; quoted in Ferry, *NEO*, 72–73)

Not senseless anymore speaks to the possibility of a transformation of the relation between humanity and nature. And why not, except for the curse?

Ferry presents a fascinating chapter on Nazi law linking radical ecology with totalitarianism. Concluding that "deep ecology presents an unsavory face to the democrat. It also poses just as serious challenges to the humanist ethics it claims to surpass" (Ferry, *NEO*, 127). Indeed there is ecological fascism. I have noted Jowett's version of it and her ethical resistance to it. And humanistic fascism, perhaps more fully documented, by deep ecologists among other critics. Every system claims authority, imposes authority, exceeds the bounds of responsible authority. To which we are called to respond with a responsibility beyond the limits of any authority. Why should it not reach beyond the authority of human law to nature's abundance? Which supports neither German nationalism nor Aryan racialism. Always falling back and down.

In Kantian terms, quite as ambiguously, Ferry denies finality to nature, though we prize it there. "Aside from freedom, traces of which we perceive in the suffering of living beings insofar as it is evidence of a nonmechanical nature, there are two ideas we value and which, therefore, also valorize nature when nature, by chance, happens to 'present' or 'illustrate' them: those of beauty and finality" (Ferry, *NEO*, 142). The circle of finality and freedom tightens into a noose around the necks of animals and other creatures who know no finality insofar as they know no culture—not even domestic animals entirely produced by culture, in a culture built on domestication—but who are prized by humans as if they possessed finality. Even if finality and freedom are valued only by humans, even if human beings are the only beings who know values and responsibility, they are ascribed to nature and natural beings with properties other than those humanity gives them. That is what many people would say who are not wilderness fanatics. Ferry's reading of modernity moves from the exaggerated claim that freedom and culture are owned by human beings to the wilder implication that values and responsibilities are similarly owned—rather than bestowed or received, for example, recognized and given as gifts without return—to the extreme conclusion that all values are *ours*: we recognize them, give them, and they remain with and for *us*. We Humans. We do not prize them because we find them in nature, neither beauty nor finality. We give them to possess them, not to give them away without return.[6]

Leading to the central question of this chapter, stated explicitly by Ferry, though he recoils from the most plausible conclusion. "Must we conclude that the love of man necessarily implies the hatred of nature? Must one give in, because 'ecologists can be fascists,' to the polemical construction that makes the proof of one's humanity depend on one's degree of disdain toward plants and animals? I don't think so." (Ferry, *NEO*, 52). Is political modernity, in which cosmopolitanism and freedom from abuse are the highest political ideals in human life, defined and articulated in terms of a hatred, an aversion, toward nature at the expense of animals and other living creatures? Is human ethics, based on freedom and culture, one that rests finally on the destruction and abuse of anything nonhuman? Does humanism rest on hatred of nature under the curse? It would certainly seem so, in structure and principle, though we might find reasons *in ourselves* to prevent abuse to animals, perhaps for the benefit of human sensibility. Yet if it would benefit human beings to torture animals, if violence toward animals would diminish violence toward humans, that would be entirely justified ethically. Ferry spells out this widespread practice in detail, without approval but also without resources to resist its most heinous implications.

He describes torturing animals in public, ceremonial enjoyment of an animal's pain. I quote in part:

> [A]t four in the morning, a bull is set loose on the streets, where he is riddled with darts, first in the eyes and most sensitive parts. Four hours later, the animal is beaten until he dies of his wounds. . . . he looks like a pin cushion. . . .
>
> . . . It is simply an enactment, solely for entertainment, of the reality of animal suffering. And people find this suffering captivating. The proof

being that this type of entertainment, in which crowds gather to see the intensity of the pain preceding the killing, has its equivalent in every, or almost every, country and at every period. (p. 43)

This is nature profoundly transfigured by the curse, as Bataille says, though he keeps his eye on humanity's curse more than nature's, perhaps neglecting the harm human beings do to animals. But they do harm to themselves under the curse. The abjection of nature always falls back down upon humanity. In negating nature, humanity negates itself. Humanity tortures and destroys natural things, especially animals, to establish the profundity of being human, thereby instituting itself under the curse, destined for violent consumption. Ferry cannot let himself acknowledge this deep connection between violence toward animals and violence toward humans, though he poses the question. He knows that causing harm to animals may cause harm to human beings and their moral sensibilities; and he resists such harm for that reason. Yet he poses the counterargument in almost irresistible form: human beings fulfill themselves by torturing animals, fulfill profound emotional needs.

Why so much hatred if animals are only things? (Ferry, *NEO*, 44)

By acting in this fashion, we do more than legitimize the [sadistic] impulses: we eliminate them, since there is no such thing as sadism toward inanimate objects. But since we are more or less covertly aware that in truth animals are not entirely things that as luck would have it they suffer, the tortures we inflict remain interesting. (p. 47)

Beneficial if they help us release violent impulses that would otherwise be directed at human beings. Or make human beings unhappy. Or, by overpowering the forces of nature, make themselves willing executioners facing blind forces.

Heard within the chilling account he gives of what is interesting in torturing animals.

[B]ullfighting symbolizes man's combat with nature—a nature that is constantly threatening to engulf him from without and from within, while he attempts to break away from it by countering violence and aggressivity with reason and calculation. (Alain Renaut, "L'esprit de la corrida," *La Règle du Jeu*, 6 [Spring 1992]; quoted in Ferry, p. 51)

In barely twenty minutes, a savage force is subjected to the will of man, who manages to slow, channel, and direct its attacks. The submission of brute nature (which is to say violence) to man's free will, the victory of freedom over nature, elicits an aesthetic emotion in the spectator . . . connected to the submission of unreasoning matter to a will that gives it form. (Renaut; quoted in Ferry, p. 51)

One might make a similar case for torturing human beings, especially infants and women, submitting unreasoning and powerless creatures to a greater force, all in the name of art. Some have made it. These are difficult positions to refute once one accepts the premise that nature is there to serve humanity. Perhaps we should torture animals; perhaps we should not. Exclusively in the interests of human beings. Instrumentally. Most likely, some who need to control their violences should impose them on animals rather than on themselves or other human beings; others might not do so.

The issue cannot be allowed the least ethical standing. Animals bear no ethical worth that is not human worth.

> Kant suggests a path for reflection when he writes the following: "Because animals are an *analogon* of humanity, we observe duties toward humanity when we regard them as analogous to humanity, and thus we satisfy our obligations toward it." (Ferry, *NEO*, 54)

> What we need is a synthesis between the Heideggerian *Gelassenheit*, or "letting be," and the imperious "civilizing" activity of the Cartesians. For perhaps the circumscribed respect we owe animals, far from being inscribed in nature or a burden placed upon us by civilization, is in this way a matter of *politeness* and *civility*. (p. 56)

One can hear civilized and cultured Europeans responding similarly to antisemitism: Jews possess no ethical worth, but a good Christian must treat them politely and civilly.[7]

Kant's words can be read more strongly: that although only human beings are free, can belong to a kingdom of ends, animals and other natural creatures are enough like human beings that we are obligated to treat them as ends insofar as we are obligated to treat human beings as ends. Insofar as and by analogy, but not to the extent that we treat human beings as ends. Not because and insofar as they are different—preserving difference rather than similarity. Risking the obvious hierarchy that those who are most like us—civilized, rational, and cultured—are the highest ends, bearing the highest ethical worth, and those who are different are lower.[8]

Leading again to the question as to whether humanism—regarding humans as bearing unique ethical worth—carries within itself a hatred toward animals—the curse, without cursing the curse.

> Is there not, from this perspective, radical antinomy between respect for nature and concern for culture. . . . In this case humanism *in all its forms* would have to be deconstructed and surpassed in order to create the possibility for taking ecological concerns into account.
>
> But this first question depends on the fate of the second, that of the relationship to culture. . . . What concrete form will this freedom take if

not the destruction—the perpetual uprooting—it seems to invite? (Ferry, *NEO*, 17–18)

Ferry believes, after Kant, that human beings can love animals as they love human beings, just not so much or in the same ways. He does not consider the structural implications of the curse, the abjections at its heart, does not think of sacrificing it. He asks the question but does not give it standing. "If we raise our sights from the phenomenology of feelings to philosophy, should humanism itself not be incriminated? . . . Is it not humanism that dictates that compassion toward animals must be ridiculed at any price and qualified as infantile 'sentimentality' "? (p. 47). He understands the question to be whether we can find in humanism something that can sustain respect for animals. Perhaps by analogy with respect for women, people of darker skin, poor people, and Jews. Of course we can. Of course, it has not happened frequently or reliably enough. Perhaps because the issue is structural, not reflective. Perhaps because once borders have been defined, the role of reflection is to police them, with immense ethical implications toward those who fall outside, and with immense ethical implications for those inside.

Leading to the question whether democracy and humanism—as Ferry understands them—might be in fundamental conflict around the borders of the human, instituted in the name of universality. Ferry puts the question from one side; I raise it from the other:

> Is it necessary to ensure the protection of our environment, that we grant it equal, even superior, rights to those granted human beings? To what extent and how can we speak of the "rights of nature"? Does the fact that we recognize nature's dignity imply the radical deconstruction of humanism *in all its forms*? Would an internal critique of this anthropocentrist tradition enable us to do justice to the concerns of radical ecology without renouncing democratic principles? And conversely: How can political liberalism, the liberalism of the rights of man, integrate the preoccupations of environmental ethics? (Ferry, *NEO*, 129)

How can political democracy, responsive to ethical claims that cross every border, stop short of the preoccupations of environmental ethics? And more. In Ferry's words, "the question of the meaning of existence has receded from religious politics and moved into other spheres: those of ethics and culture, *understood as the blossoming of the individual*" (p. 137). Perhaps the blossoming of every individual, human and otherwise, together with the blossoming of the kinds in which those individuals participate, filled with excesses crossing every border.

The issue is the curse, the separation of humanity from nature—or civilization from primitivism, higher from lower culture. The structure of the opposition calls the resources of universalism down upon an absolute distinction, not to dismantle but to enforce it, at the cost, it would seem, of torture, destruction, and death. Under the mark of the curse, humanity claims an absolute rule over nature, animals and other creatures and things it does not own and can impose only by force, including the force of reason and reflection. Reason is the absolute norm of value, owned exclusively and absolutely by human beings.

Why is reason not instead the absolute condition of a responsibility beyond any measure, any value? Why do human beings not bear an ethical responsibility to care for themselves and other creatures and things beyond any accountability? Why is the mark of humanity's freedom not *politesse (humanitas)* but exposure and responsibility? Wherever we are in our exposure, we are ethically responsible beyond any capacities of fulfillment. What of a humanism of exposure beyond the bounds of humanity? A Promethean humanism that remembers Prometheus's gift with its attendant responsibilities, not one that claims "rightfully, that the faculty to separate oneself from the order of naturality is the sign of the properly human" (Ferry, *NEO*, 16)? What of a diasporic understanding of separation, related to strangeness and blood, to impurity, where every separation is joined with impurity, insisting on purity? The purity of humanity and human freedom over animals and animal instinct. And other purities.

What of democracy based on responsibility toward others, not on the rights or interests of any group in conflict with others, or on any individual interests against others, but on individuals and groups in proximity, struggling in the midst of endless impurities and responsibilities, toward others and oneself? A democratic passion to achieve a quality of life and being together, resisting the curse. With the crucial proviso that *together* affirms not sameness or universality or separation but propinquity, the endless process of enacting responsibilities within countless multiplicities and differences. Responsibility, exposure, proximity, and abundance are the elements of democracy. In their conflicts and heterogeneities.

Leading to a very different view of nature and ecology. After humanism. After Ferry. Still radical democracy. Another interruption. I conclude with some brief passages and commentary offered in response to the limits of modernity, marked as ecology.[9] For if we understand modernity as coming to know its own constructions of humanity and nature, then even where we may wish to maintain the edifice fabricated in the name of democracy, we are obliged to consider other possibilities in democracy's name.

If we understand modernity to have constructed both humanity and nature, we may direct a critical eye toward the assumption that Ferry takes to define modernity, that freedom and meaning belong exclusively to human beings.

> The language we speak today, the idiom of Renaissance and Enlightenment humanism, veils the processes of nature with its own cultural obsessions, directionalities, and motifs that have no analogues in the natural world. . . . It is as if we had compressed the entire buzzing, howling, gurgling biosphere into the narrow vocabulary of epistemology, to the point that someone like Georg Lukács could say, "nature is a societal category"—and actually be understood. (Manes, *NS*, 43)

I agree with Lukács that nature is a societal category,[10] understood to mean that the buzzing, howling, gurgling biosphere—and more, throughout nature, living, nonliving, and more—is expanded and transfigured by societal and cultural processes, inseparable from them. Meaning, expression, representation, and *mimēsis* are not only human, restricted to social worlds, or to the biosphere, but are everywhere, doubling, reversing, multiplying. The crucial insight, buried under the curse, is the expressiveness of nature—I would say, everywhere. Nature, bodies, are expressive. That is Spinoza's ethical truth, not exactly absent from modernity. Yet it is silenced under the curse of humanism—nature under the curse of humanity's uniqueness. Postmodernity allows itself to curse the curse, to sacrifice sacrifice, listening to alternative voices, never quite turning its back on modernity.

> In contrast, for animistic cultures, those that see the natural world as inspirited, not just people, but also animals, plants, and even "inert" entities such as stones and rivers are perceived as being articulate and at times intelligible subjects, able to communicate and interact with humans for good or ill. In addition to human language, there is also the language of birds, the wind, earthworms, wolves, and waterfalls—a world of autonomous speakers whose intents (especially for hunter-gatherer peoples) one ignores at one's peril. (p. 43)[11]

At stake are both humanity and ethical responsibility. "[W]e must contemplate not only learning a new ethics, but a new language free from the directionalities of humanism, a language that incorporates a decentered, postmodern, post-humanist perspective. In short, we require the language of ecological humility that deep ecology, however gropingly, is attempting to express" (Manes, *NS*, 45). Perhaps not humility but sonance,[12] cherishment, and glory—Levinas's word—in a world of such expressiveness and abundance. Why not be proud in the abundance of the earth? Why set absolute limits on pride? I think the issue is more of ownership and possession, owning to exclude. Man the owner, master, employer, and sovereign or a humanity endlessly responsive to the echoes of meaning in the abundance of things everywhere. Meanings that always echo in kinds.

Ferry dismisses the possibility of a wider understanding of democracy responsive to the needs and possibilities of agents who do not vote, who cannot stand up for their interests. Yet democracy is not just majority or collective will—though the French version comes close to that—but includes a collective responsiveness to minority concerns, endlessly responsible for overcoming majoritarian silences. With cautions toward possibilities of coercion on all sides—ecological, majoritarian, communitarian, individualistic—we may think of democracy in a wider and more responsible way. "Before us lies a task comparable to that faced by the framers of the American Constitution: just as they created the political grammar of modernism, our task is the creation of a political framework expressing a new understanding of community appropriate to an age of ecological limit and technological prowess. . . . Our sense of community must widen to include the natural world" (Frodeman, *REPRP*, 130). Our sense of democracy and polity, I would say, not community. Perhaps a sense of democratic polity in which we do not insist on community for all, but respect the spaces in which others are other. Let us call them *wilderness* spaces, spaces of wildness.

> Let us begin by emphasizing that the essence of otherness is wildness. If any other is to preserve its (his, her) identity as other, as other in relation to another person, society, species, or whatever, then it must at bottom resist accepting any *final* identity altogether. . . . The maintenance of otherness requires the maintenance of a radical openness, or the maintenance of the sort of unconditioned freedom that permits sheer spontaneity and continuous participation in the emergence of novelty. (Birch, *IW*, 143)

Nature's abundance is given in the wilderness where all ethical values originate: the anarchy of wildness as the possibility of freedom. "No matter how the imperium deals with wild nature, whether by extermination or incarceration and the logically impossible fiction of total management, wild otherness will continue to show up the belief in our culture's most formative myth of law bringing for the bad faith it is" (p. 154). Transforming the idea of ethics itself. Leading from the tightly policed borders of the modern social world, always instituting hierarchy and domination, the tyranny of kinds, to an inclusive ethics, in exposure and proximity. In love. In kindness. In wildness. A love beyond humanism and humanity. Wherever we find ourselves. "[I]n a different world, truly beyond anthropocentrism, we might hope for a much less abstract way of speaking of and for wild experience—for enough sharing of at least the glimmers of wild experience that we can speak of it directly, even perhaps invoking a kind of love" (Weston, *BEE*, 226). Not in a different world, beyond anthropocentrism, but in it and everywhere else in the earth. As repetition and expression. In kindness.

Falling back upon itself. As love, responsibility, and heterogeneity. Resistant to totality, including the totality of wilderness and plurality.

An ethic of inclusion that insists on interrupting every rule, on sacrificing every sacrifice.

CHAPTER 13

Abundant Kinds

> Central to this effort are two basic beliefs. First, that a full apprecia-
> tion of what it means to be human requires that we take proper note of
> human groupings, the definitive characteristics of which (combining his-
> torically mediated physical, psychological, and cultural factors) are consti-
> tutive, in varying degrees, of the persons in the group. Second, that the
> principles on which we would base both the organization of sociopolitical
> life and those intellectual enterprises whose objects are living human
> beings take explicit account of these constitutive differences. (Outlaw, *PER*,
> 306–7)

These final chapters address the abundance of kinds in two inseparable
ways, one expanding the wealth and diversity of reflections on the kinds and
species of the earth, as different kinds of people have experienced them, the
other exploring the abundance as abundance, always beyond what we have
experienced, beyond the boundaries of human life, as we have experienced
the limits of those boundaries. Immeasurable responsibilities beyond any
instituted responsibilities, beyond any instituted limits, beyond the limits of
experience. Always more, expressed as *mimēsis*. The possibility of ethics rests
on an experience, a demand, a call beyond and otherwise, a responsibility
beyond any responsibility, the experience of what is expressive beyond experience, the immeasurability and abundance of nature always otherwise to
itself. Nature and experience are always beyond and otherwise to themselves—
in and as their abundance, the abundance of human and other kinds, everywhere expressive. Abundance is the limit of every limit, the impossibility that
any limit can be absolute, unlimited. With the consequence that the world is
filled with kinds, with their limits, limited by and in kinds; while every kind
is otherwise, multifarious, impure: multiplied by endless other kinds. All
demanding care, attention, responsibility, kindness.

What remains to be thought—repeating Bhabha's extraordinary suggestion of the doubling of *mimēsis*, responsibility, and desire[1]—is the

repetitiveness of *mimēsis* and desire, doubled, multiplied, and more; between the group, the kind, the individual agent, and more, as ethical responsibility, in abundance. I add difference to repetition, endless deferral, interrupting every authority; add the boundlessness of desire, doubled beyond any border that would contain it; add to the individual and kind other kinds, and other individuals, the circulation of strange and unknown kinds; falling back and down upon each other in debt, bearing responsibility. With the extreme addition that this responsibility remains endlessly to be thought and lived, endlessly falls back and down upon itself, given as a call: endless repetition, endless deferral, endless expression, giving in abundance from the good.

Falling back is abundance in the earth. As supplementation, repetition, representation, *mimēsis*. As interruption, always otherwise. Always in debt. The beyond of giving is not somewhere else—though it is always elsewhere in relation to any place—but here and there in every response, at every border, in exposure everywhere, as proximity and expression. I postpone exposure, proximity, and expression in the earth to the final chapter. Here I remain on the side of restricted economy and human kinds reaching beyond themselves toward nature, as human beings sometimes have done. Repeatedly throughout history and the earth. In the impurity and propinquity of kinds.

The purpose of this chapter and the next is to resist every suggestion that an ethic of nature is possible as something that can be thought or practiced, rather than as endless remains. In this chapter, by examining some of the profusion of what has been said of such a thought and practice. A chapter of heterogeneities. In the next chapter, by exploring abundance in general, abundance itself, if there be such.

What, then, shall we make of the profusion and heterogeneity of ways of speaking, reflecting, and pursuing an ethic of inclusion? Shall we speak of *heterogeneities*?

> The title *Heterogeneities* codes the basic argument that reasonably extensive human groups always show deep internal complexities and variations, so that the labels of prejudice, "women," "black," "japanese," and so on, always cover over internally complex and vibrant contradictions within their populations that explode the uniform differences proposed by labels of essentialist prejudice. (Ackerman, *H*, 4)

Every label that marks a kind—not just labels of prejudice—covers over complex and vibrant contradictions: heterogeneities, internal and external differences, *impurities*. "Therefore *any* claims that begin by asserting 'blacks . . . ,' or 'women . . . ,' or 'japanese . . . ,' or 'americans . . . ,' supposedly charting absolute differences between absolutely disjoint human populations, *are already false*" (p. 4). As if heterogeneity were true. As if every truth of labels and kinds—every truth—were false—a Nietzschean claim—and yet, perhaps, still true. The extreme possibility of heterogeneities is that reality is composed of *différends* and that truth is always false—still true. And why not, in the abundance of things? Provided that we understand these claims as expressing a certain responsibility within themselves—endless and immeasurable responsibility—to seek truth within its untruth. Nietzschean and Heideggerian thoughts, with the qualification that truth and untruth are both in debt, given from the good. The Law, in Lyotard's words, is endlessly forgotten. Heterogeneity and abundance are endlessly forgotten. A truth in debt.

Allowing us to read Ackerman perhaps a bit more truthfully. For example—a truth I understand as almost certainly true: "American society is everywhere interwoven with racisms, and native soil provides all americans with an early and extensive internal knowledge of racial insult and behavior" (p. 10). Yet perhaps also false in the sense that society everywhere is divided by blood, riven by differences in kinds. Every society. Yet not every society bears the concrete history of American slavery. Suggesting a paraphrase in Bhabha's terms: the *repetitious* desire to recognize ourselves doubly, as, at once, decentered in memories of our kinds—slaveowners, slaves, and others who have profited and been harmed by slavery's legacy—and responsible for working toward change, both as individuals and as members of multiple kinds. Endless repetitions of repetitions, in kinds, bearing responsibility. Heterogeneous heterogeneities. In debt.

Resisting slavery multiply, profusely, including resistance to every kind of resistance that does not multiply its responsibilities, does not fall back upon itself in critical reflection and practice. Falling back and down upon itself into the world and abundance.

> What is now forming is a global system in which the core and periphery are not distinct, but are layers that can be found within the boundaries of every traditional nation-state. The various bourgeoisies are linked in a fashion that permits currency flows from the bourgeoisies in place at the old periphery to the bourgeoisies at the old core, flows that nonetheless permit great relative wealth to accumulate with the lower-ranking old periphery bourgeoisies. (Ackerman, *H*, 171)

Yet, "The capitalist world system will not stand forever, even it if lasts to the end of humankind" (p. 164).

On Bhabha's reading, we can, perhaps must, accept such a picture from within a far-reaching responsibility to resist such exploitation. Together with a supplement that does not weaken the commitment, given from a falling back and down upon ourselves, our kinds, that resists the labeling of every kind, including *capitalism, elites,* and *bourgeoisies.* None of these is pure, nor is the global system. Capitalism will not stand forever, in part because it is not anything to stand nor does it stand anywhere in particular. As Deleuze and Guattari suggest, capitalism is excessive in every way, like schizophrenia, increasing its dominance at the same time that it divides it by supplementarity and heterogeneity.

Throwing Ackerman's words back upon themselves in supplementation:

> Repudiating *culture* as a theoretical construct is not to deny that one doesn't experience differences when living in different nation-states. It is only to deny that homogeneous *cultures* are the *cause* of the differences. Culture is the result, rather than the cause, of a myriad of individual endeavors undertaken within existing social structures, given the available linguistic and material resources. (p. 186)

Culture, capitalism, the world system, all are results of myriad individual and collective endeavors, heterogeneities of kinds. Opening the possibility of a practice organized around kinds.

> Recognizing heterogeneity and interfusions is the key to breaking out. There is always heterogeneity inside the local game: people who already speak our language but whom we can't understand. There is always heterogeneity inside the other game: people we can understand but whose language we do not yet speak. There is always already criticism inside our game and the other game, points of view that are not complicit with majority forms of discourse and that constitute the informed seeds of strategies for change. (pp. 192–93)

> Theory must be broken from practice in order to free a practice that is knowingly partially blind. (p. 204)

Resistance to the domination of kinds from within a doubly immeasurable responsibility: toward the heterogeneity of kinds, and toward our own inescapable blindness. Our blindness in the heterogeneity of our kinds. And others.

This picture of an ethic of inclusion, drawn around and from heterogeneity, is profoundly European American, framed by a history of domination by colonization and by ownership of the mechanisms of truth: cosmopolitanism and universalism. I include Bhabha and other postcolonial and postslavery writings in which the *post-* remains sutured to its violent history. Gates and Bhabha express in glowing terms something of the ethics and politics I would bring (back) to nature and natural kinds, memories of disasters bound together with immeasurable responsibilities, resistances to injustice. This may be European American, but also, perhaps, post-European American, or post-American European, in the repetitious multiplications in which the *post-* remains tethered to what it would overthrow, both in representation and in development, the movement of history. Perhaps, in today's and any future's world, a worldwide emergence of counter-European American voices retains European American echoes, driven by history and by global economic development. Even where the worst cases of pollution are Southern—on a North South axis—they are not less Northern for that. All this is one way to speak of the ethical|political responsibilities in which ecological issues are located today, human relations to nature refracted through histories of influence and domination.

Yet we may consider some other voices from afar, listening to their different cadences more than their repetitions. For there are other, different histories. And if we—any contemporary or future *we*—cannot escape a history of colonization and universalism, we also cannot escape the local— sometimes profound—histories written and remembered in a different language, memories of other human and natural relations. Other repetitious doublings, multiplyings, of humanity and nature, that open the spaces of responsibility in abundance, the endless giving of the good. Resistant to neutrality, to the gathering of being, to a tyranny of kinds, to a metaphysics without *mimēsis*.

Some wonderful examples, all qualified by the explicit acknowledgment that I speak of them from afar, still European American, or American European, hoping to learn:

> "the Chinese, among all peoples ancient and recent, primitive and modern, are apparently unique in having no creation myth; that is, they have regarded the world and man as uncreated, as constituting the central features of a spontaneously self-generating cosmos having no creator, god, ultimate cause, or will external to itself."
>
> The real issue is not the presence or absence of creation myths, but the underlying assumption of the cosmos: whether it is continuous or discontinuous with its creator. (Tu, *CN*, 67; quotation from Mote, *IFC*, 17–18)

Or whether nature is continuous or discontinuous with humanity.

> Forming one body with the universe can literally mean that since all modalities of being are made of *ch'i*, human life is part of a continuous flow of the blood and breath that constitutes the cosmic process. Human beings are thus organically connected with rocks, trees, and animals. (Tu, *CH*, 74)
>
> This idea of forming one body with the universe is predicated on the assumption that since all modalities of being are made of *ch'i*, all things

> cosmologically share the same consanguinity with us and are thus our
> companions. (p. 76)

One body with the universe may mean that all things are organically connected, bound by rules of identity, made of *ch'i*. All assembled together in
the one body of the world. Yet *consanguinity* may have another meaning,
much closer to impurity and heterogeneity, evoking proximity. Things are
together in one universe as a proximity of strangers in kinds, a multiplicity
of heterogeneous kinds in propinquity, exposed to each other, connected
not by identity or by difference, but by strangeness and alterity. Not a
heterogeneity or strangeness constituted by rigid borders—identity and
difference again—but by impurities and permeable borders: tethers and
sutures repeatedly crossing lines of identification, repetitions, interruptions,
expressions.

Suggesting, perhaps, with *mimēsis* in mind—insisting that it is not
only human, not closed in lifeless neutrality, but that nature is everywhere
expressive—that what we may learn from coming to the limits of European-American philosophy—post–European-American, still European American or American European—may be that every account of nature or culture,
European American, post–European American, or other—is a repetitious
multiplication of expressive desire. Every account of nature. Humanity and
nature are inexhaustibly tethered together in representation and expression. As *mimēsis*. The same is endless heterogeneity, resistant to the neutrality of identity and difference. Even in Chinese. "In the metaphorical
sense, then, forming one body with the universe requires continuous effort
to grow and to refine oneself. We can embody the whole universe in our
sensitivity because we have enlarged and deepened our feeling and care to
the fullest extent" (p. 76). With wariness toward a unity between humanity
and nature filled with growth, depth, and care—all wonderful qualities of
any inclusive ethics—that does not question its own repetitious desires.
That offers itself without interruption. A metaphorically embodied universe,
filled with *mimēsis*.

Another Chinese European American voice:

> "*Tao* is the opening out and arraying of *te*: the process of living and
> growing *(sheng)* is the radiating of *te*."
>   This passage characterizes the "making/becoming" of the particular
> as both "inevitable" and "entirely self-expressive." (Ames, *PTBT*, 126; quoted
> from the *Chuang Tzu*)

> Under this conceptual framework *[tao-te]*, personal cultivation and the
> cultivation of one's environment are coextensive. To reduce nature to a
> "means" is not only to compromise the creative possibilities of nature, but
> also to impoverish one's own. (p. 142)

The expressiveness of every natural creature and thing, opening out, radiating, and growing, marks something largely lost within a certain European-American scientific rationality, yet one fully recognizable, I believe, throughout contemporary life, even by those who would resist it. Put another way, perhaps, it seems to me that to deny feeling and expression to natural creatures and things is a professional, academic denial. Ordinary people know that animals feel, though some scientists tell them otherwise. Some of those ordinary people do not mind animals' pain, think that animals exist to be used by human beings. Many human beings suffer, why not animals? The sense of a buzzing, howling, gurgling biosphere is familiar. It is alive, there to be owned, human property. With or without responsibility. Again, I postpone consideration of owning and possessing to another place.[2]

Here I mean to emphasize certain images of wholeness ascribed to Chinese thought that promote an appealing view of ethics toward nature: integrity, relations to others, treating natural creatures and things as ends, not means, even anarchy, freedom from origins, first principles, and regulation, intrinsic relatedness, and humility. All wonderful components of an integrated, relational life beyond duality and instrumentality. Still lacking, I believe, immeasurability. Still lacking endless repetitions of desire, multiplications of expression. Still containable. Indeed, despite the anarchy, I take the ethics—every ethics, I would say—to express containment and totality in rich and integrated ways. And why not? Except for the insistent demands, the inescapable questions, of whether the richest and most integrated ethics is just, of how it may resist its own injustices, questions of the expressions and desires that constitute any ethics. Questions from general economy, abundance and heterogeneity, for and within every restricted economy. When restricted economy reaches toward totality—perhaps the goal of every philosophical ethics—it can do so hatefully or caringly, meanly or gloriously. But I do not think it can do so responsibly. I keep endless multiplications of desire and representation in mind in resistance to every neutrality. In the giving for the sake of the good.

I turn from a Chinese world view to Buddhism to find lovely images of heterogeneous humanity and nature: for example, the jewel net of Indra.

Far away in the heavenly abode of the great god Indra, there is a wonderful net which has been hung by some cunning artificer in such a manner that it stretches out infinitely in all directions. . . . If we arbitrarily select one of these jewels . . . each of the jewels reflected in this one jewel is also reflecting all the other jewels, so that there is an infinite reflecting process occurring. (Cook, *JNI*, 214)

The cosmos is, in short, a self-creating, self-maintaining, and self-defining organism. Hua-yen calls such a universe the *dharma-dhātu*, which we

> may translate as "cosmos" or "universe" if we wish, with the proviso that
> it is not the universe as commonly imagined, but rather the Hua-yen
> universe of identity and interdependence. (p. 215)

Everything mirrors everything else, in identity and interdependence. Creating, I believe, a certain difficulty, though I would honor Buddhist teachings of how we should treat things everywhere to which we are tethered. The jewel net binds all things everywhere to each other without total identity, as mirrors, repetitions of each other. In a truly ethical practice—some would call it religious. "The Hua-yen vision was first of all meant to tantalize the reader and lure him to *realize* (i.e., to *make real* in his everyday experience) what had been only theory. To realize the Hua-yen universe means to go beyond an intellectual grasp of the system to a *lived experience* of things existing in this manner, for the Hua-yen world view is nothing if not a lived reality" (p. 228). Why not live this kind of life in respect and care for all things bound to each other in interdependence? Except for Derrida's question concerning the institutional structures supported by such an ethics. What system of political, social, and epistemic authority is constituted by this way of life—for all? for some? What hierarchy? Except for Bhabha's question concerning the repetitious desires that constitute this ethics. Except for the giving of the good as endless interruption of every authority, including the authority of interdependence. Three interrelated, interdependent questions and interruptions that open onto immeasurable responsibility. For such a glorious vision of an infinite universe, I wonder if Buddhism knows too contained a responsibility, too tightly bound a heterogeneity, if it knows abundance. "It is not just that 'we are all in it' together. We all *are* it, rising or falling as one living body" (p. 229). As I understand Buddhism.

Another place linked with Buddhism, with Heidegger in mind: "Are we really at home with the world? Or, turning inward, are we at home with our own existence? Do we really know the real nature of the human condition, the involvement of man with his surroundings, and, were we to know some measure of it, can we properly and successfully relate ourselves to the world at large?" (Inada, *EP*, 231). Filled with striking images of dwelling but perhaps not responsibility: *at home; our own existence; really know; real nature; the human condition; properly, successfully*. All terms that collapse the repetitions, that may seek to contain desire. Within an image of the world with which I quite agree, about which I have written frequently, have perhaps never ceased to write about even where I write in interruption more than resistance.[3]

> Buddhist doctrines . . . embody a most unique idea . . .
>   . . . I shall refer to it awkwardly as "the principle of parity of existence" or "the parity principle of existence" or even "the ontological parity of reality" (p. 234)[4]

The principle of ontological parity is that nothing is more real—an unqualified rejection of metaphysical and epistemological hierarchy. Perhaps because reality is always qualified, impure: doublings and multiplications. "[U]ltimately, the true experiential reality . . . is realized by the complete incorporation of all elements of being in a nondiscriminative insight" (p. 237). Perhaps a bit too neutrally. Ontological parity may resist hierarchy but not, perhaps, neutrality. Yet it promotes perfection of individuality and practice.

> The Bodhisattva, of course is a philosophic myth that depicts the perfected individual who "delays" his entrance into *nirvāna* because he is cognizant of the fact that he and others are related or involved in such a way that there is openness on the one hand and extensiveness on the other. It is the perfect model of social concern and action, somewhat akin to what Western religionists allude to as the spirit of ultimate concern. It is at once the perfect model of environmental concern, whereby the social and environmental natures of things are treated together, not in terms of contiguity but in terms of the continuity of reality. (p. 241)

I wonder if such perfection may express resistance to neutrality without attention to its own impurities.

Buddhism knows an ethics toward the earth without exclusion.

> Two of the most important qualities to be developed by Buddhism are loving-kindness and compassion. Loving-kindness is understood as the wish for others to be happy, and compassion as the wish to alleviate suffering. Both start with ourselves, by recognizing the fact of our own suffering and seeking to uproot its causes. Before turning to the plight of others, it is necessary to understand deeply the origins of suffering within ourselves. . . . Ultimately loving-kindness and compassion extend to all living things: people, animals, plants, the earth itself. (p. 4)[5]

With a certain wariness toward the boundary between the living and non-living, given as similarity. Why not dispel the misery of others, at least help them enjoy their lives, their being, their pleasure, whatever they enjoy, or whatever, because they are different from me? Why not begin with the others? Without return. In immeasurable compassion and responsibility? In exposure and proximity.

How can there be an ethics that does not take up this immeasurable responsibility, carrying it with grace and suffering even where it leads to harm? How can we choose to deny some if we do not accept a responsibility toward all? A responsibility we will never fulfill. Yet Buddhism knows it in joy. Loving-kindness as joy. Ethical responsibility. In kinds. In the alterity that marks everything ethical: resistance to neutrality and identity; ethics toward the other as other, in whose otherness is endless injustice.[6] Known in Buddhism as sacrifice. On the way, perhaps, to sacrificing sacrifice. "In this sacrifice, Brahmin, no bulls were slain, no goats or sheep, no cocks and pigs, nor were various living beings subjected to slaughter, nor were trees cut down for sacrificial posts, nor were grasses mown for the sacrificial grass. . . . The sacrifice was carried out with ghee, butter, curds, honey, molasses" (Batchelor, *ESS*, 13; quoted from Kutadanta Sutra).[7] Within a figure I would extend from sacrifice.

> According to the Sigalovada Sutta a householder should accumulate wealth as a bee collects nectar from a flower. The bee harms neither the fragrance nor the beauty of the flower, but gathers nectar to turn it into sweet honey. Just as our own life is precious to us, so is the life of another precious to it. Therefore reverence must be cultivated towards all forms of life. (de Silva, *HWMSD*, 22–23)

As the bee, perhaps even the tiger. Is it not strange—and terrible—that so many human beings would have us imitate the worst behavior of animals, not the best, multiplying the worst exponentially through the use of technology? The hyena, not the bee, churning out blood and gore as quickly as possible. Even as we may care for the hyena.

In compassion and reverence toward all living beings, we repeatedly come to limits defined by similarity. All living things. In the extreme, all beings together. I insist on forgetting and strangeness, things that are not the same together but alien in proximity. Reverence, compassion, and sympathy—cherishment—toward all things in the strangeness of their proximity. Inseparable from sacrifice, knowing that all cannot be together without harm, but resistant to any glorification of sacrifice. Insisting on sacrificing sacrifice in care and love. I add the endless repetitions of desire that mark the contamination of every sacrifice in love and care. The endless heterogeneity and impurity of kinds. So close to Buddhism. In another register. Mindful of another oppression.

Returning to endless questions in the register of the bee, collecting honey, known to Molly in the movement of waves, to Buddhists in the shade of the Bodhi tree.

> Shakyamuni Buddha, in attaining enlightenment, is seated under a tree. It is called the Bodhi tree or the tree of enlightenment. . . . The Bodhi tree posed a question of critical importance: Just how and where does enlightenment take place? Is the tree merely an inert setting, something under which a man sat until one day something profound spread through his mind, the ganglia of his consciousness and to the ends of his body? Or was it, rather, human's companion in Bodhi, that without which he could have no perfection? (LaFleur, *S*, 136)

Stretching toward infinity.

> In the great Assembly of the Lotus all are present—without divisions. Grass, trees, the soil on which these grow—all have the same kinds of atoms. Some are barely in motion while others make haste along the Path, but they will all in time reach the precious land of Nirvana. . . . Who can really maintain that things inanimate lack buddhahood? (LaFleur, *S*, 137; quotation from Feng, *HCP*, vol. 2, 386, describing Chan-jan)[8]

Given as ethical from the good. "By definition *bodhi* would have to be shared by all *sattva*: every kind of being and phenomenon there is" (LaFleur, *S*, 138). Not perhaps as common, shared, but as heterogeneous, impure. "Underneath all the kingdoms, the phyla, the families, the genera, and the species—or their more ancient equivalents—lies their commonality, the embracing rubric called *sattva*" (p. 139). The univocity of being, without neutrality, as heterogeneity and impurity, the commonality of what is uncommon, strange, in endless desire and repetition. In endless *mimēsis*. Echoing in Buddhism.

I do not mean to imply that Asian thought embraces heterogeneity and impurity, or that Buddhism does not police borders of rank as well as political and epistemological authority, demanding greater critical vigilance toward its own oppressions. How does openness toward the buddhahood of stones and dirt work in relation to social hierarchies of privilege and domination? I hope to open critical examination onto discourses and practices less committed to humanity as transfigured by the curse. Insisting on endless multiplications of *mimēsis* and desire. Leading through Bhabha's provocative suggestions to a very different collaboration, perhaps, between Asian and European thought: a post-colonial collaboration, perhaps no collaboration at all, no commonality, but a tethering, a binding: the endless multiplication of desire, practice, and expression that has become humanity's relation to itself and its surroundings. Ethical and political.

Turning to something in Buddhist thought that I would link with Bhabha's thought of invisibility in postcolonial provocation. I am speaking of *emptiness, śūnyatā*. Understood as interdependence, also as something otherwise: interruption. "The point to the doctrine of interdependence is that things exist *only* in interdependence, for things do not exist in their own right. In Buddhism, this manner of existence is called 'emptiness.' Buddhism says that things are empty in the sense that they are absolutely lacking in a self-essence by virtue of which things would have an independent existence" (Cook, *JNI*, 225). Lacking in self-essence resembles social and historical constitution, understands individual things as constituted by their relations to other things and especially to groups, families, species, and kinds. Emptiness resists the autonomy of the individual, perhaps by too total an interdependence, leaving too little room for individual agency and social resistance, for the consciously committed, even individuated, agent of change. Against the history of Buddhism, such commitment and individuation seem uniquely European American.

> The most representative Buddhist doctrines are all familiar to us, namely, suffering *(duḥkha)*, impermanence *(anitya)*, nonself *(anātman)*, saṃsāra, nirvāṇa, the middle way *(madhyamā pratipad)*, emptiness *(śūnyatā), karman*, relational origination *(pratītya-samutpāda)*, wisdom *(prajñā)*, and compassion *karuṇā*. A quick glance at these doctrines will reveal that all focus on the nature of experiential reality. (Inada, *EP*, 233)

Emptiness here is inseparable from nonself. Yet perhaps we may insist on linking the experiential reality and the middle way, interpreting the former in ecofeminist terms, the latter in Bhabha's terms. Not the calculated center or freedom from extremes, but mirroring, doubling, multiplying, intermediary figures, mimetic images of Indra's net. Emptiness as not nothing but too much multiplication, reality, being—giving beyond the given: abundance as interruption. All experienced as shared by some, always more than what is common.

Many ecological writings speak of the interdependence of all things, calling us to a practice of compassion and care. Buddhism shares this language, suggests a vision of the undivided relational nature of things, but offers a certain resistance, expressed as emptiness. If emptiness is not lack but abundance, if nonself is multiplication, if experiential reality remains the touchstone beyond reflection, then we may interpret these ideas in Bhabha's terms and mine. Emptiness and nonself pertain to abundance and kinds, given as responsibility, inherent in experiential reality, which endlessly multiplies itself in *mimēsis* and desire. Endless multiplication of heterogeneous individuals and kinds is an image of Buddhist universes, multiplied by histories of practice and representation.[9]

Leading to a different understanding of abundance and the ethics it calls forth.

CHAPTER 14

Earthly Kinds

The origin of the call that comes from nowhere, an origin in any case that is not yet a divine or human "subject," institutes a responsibility that is to be found at the root of all ulterior responsibilities (moral, juridical, political), and of every categorical imperative. To say of this responsibility, and even of this friendship, that it is not "human," no more than it is "divine," does not come down to saying that it is simply inhuman. . . . Something of this call of the other must remain nonreappropriable, nonsubjectivable, and in a certain way nonidentifiable, a sheer supposition, so as to remain *other*, a *singular* call to response or to responsibility. . . . This obligation to protect the other's otherness is not merely a theoretical imperative. (Derrida, *EW*, 276)

An ethic of the earth:

Responsibility as a call from nowhere, exceeding every place, given from the good. *As interruption.* Interrupting interruption. *Interrupting authority.*

Abundance in the earth as giving, from the good, instituting responsibility. In *kindness.*

Giving, hospitality, generosity, kindness as not only human, and not only inhuman, exceeding every limit.

Limits, boundaries, borders as *heterogeneity*, the abundance and profusion of kinds. Resisting neutrality. Interrupting the tyranny of kinds. In kindness.

The other, the other's otherness, heterogeneity, as *the abundance of kinds*, the endless multiplication of responsibilities toward others and the strangeness of oneself. In *proximity.*

The good given in *exposure.* Abundance in the earth as the endless multiplicity of heterogeneous individuals and kinds exposed to each other in profusion. In propinquity.

Exposure as *expression* in proximity, instituting responsibility. As sensibility, touch. Things touching, responding to each other as kinds. As *mimēsis*. Expression in abundance.

Abundance as *mimēsis*, throughout nature and humanity, expression everywhere without neutrality. In responsibility.

Responsibility as responsiveness, to a *debt*, a *call*. Exposure as *mimēsis*.

The responsibility to all things and kinds in the earth surrounding human life, making it possible and framing its projects; an earth abundant in the things and kinds that compose it in proximity, all things exposed to each other, touching each other, in propinquity, in kind, where exposure is proximity and expression; an earth abundant in expression, in *mimēsis*, things and kinds endlessly falling back upon themselves, in debt, as immeasurable responsibility, in interruption; the good giving everywhere in the earth in abundance endless calls to respond, to care, in kindness, in immeasurable responsibility and debt, inherent in exposure and proximity: all excessive. Resisting neutrality and *the curse*. Within endless reversions; endless abjections.

Cherishment is kindness toward all things and kinds in abundance, responsibility beyond measure, endless giving, boundless generosity. Exposure. For the sake of the good.

Sacrifice is the inescapability of measure, limits, borders in the economies of life, working toward cherishment's responsibility under the curse, the impossibility of giving without taking.

Plenishment is the lived experience of bearing this immeasurable responsibility, borne under the curse of sacrifice in sorrow and joy, everywhere throughout the earth, beyond every border, in every restricted economy, resisting every justification of the curse, every glorification of sacrifice, endlessly sacrificing sacrifice, cursing the curse in love and care.

An *ethic of inclusion*; an ethic that includes; giving all things from the good in the abundance of kinds, in endless responsibility. In kindness.

Instituting responsibility in the abundance of the earth where institution expresses restricted economy, bound by limits, boundaries, borders, and where abundance and responsibility express general economy, immeasurable intermediary movements, crossing borders and thresholds, interrupting institution. Instituting responsibility as the founding and unfounding of borders, liminality itself, resisting neutrality. Exposure as proximity, propinquity, expression, interruption.

Resisting the neutrality of every kind and of every limin circumscribing a kind. With Western history in mind, resisting the authority of humanity, under science or God—*humanism*; resisting the inertness and silence of nature—*mechanism*; resisting the totality of infinity—*universalism*; resisting Cartesianism, utilitarianism, legalism, authoritarianism, kindism, every *ism*; resisting the tyranny of kinds; resisting the hegemony of reason, language, humanity, and nature; the neutrality of reason, language, nature, and humanity. Resisting the authority of European history, life, and thought; knowing the immense influence of European history on global politics and economic development. Knowing the wonderful work that these have done in the name of the good, and their destructions. Demanding resistance and interruption.

Instituting responsibility in resistance to every authority and neutrality, including one's own—without abolishing that resistance. In interruption.

All in the abundance of the earth, in the giving, from the good. Where abundance is beyond, without measure, filled with individuals and kinds defined by measures; where abundance knows no size, is neither big nor small, but is imbued with large and small individuals and kinds; where abundance is not totality or progress or eternal life or being, founds no authority, but is pervaded by individuals and kinds that suffer harm and destruction, that die, under instituted authority. Abundance is neither disaster nor fulfillment, but is filled with, joined by, endless disasters and achievements. All general economy, the endless circulation of restricted economies; all restricted economies, the endless circulations of general economy. All responsibility, resisting neutrality, resisting totality, resisting the assembling of a neutral being without responsibility. Interrupting every *All*. In kinds.

Resistance to neutrality entails the expressiveness of every being and thing. Every thing, every body, touches other bodies in proximity, interrupts them in their skin, calls them to respond, expressing something of infinite responsibility, a responsibility that cannot be fulfilled or measured or restricted—to human beings—but crosses thresholds and boundaries. *Mimēsis*. Abundance and responsibility are liminal; liminality is abundance; abundance is expression; all bearing responsibility to institute and to resist borders.

Borders delimit and define individuals and kinds, imposing an immeasurable burden to delimit and unlimit—the expressiveness of things known as *mimēsis*. Borders delimit agents, communities, ethnic and other kinds, the multiple kinds of human cultures, always falling back upon themselves in profusion, falling back onto other heterogeneous species and kinds, animals, plants, landscapes, earth, stones, and more. In propinquity. No limit exists to abundance and responsibility in exposure. Reality is composed of liminality and impurity, of abundance and responsibility, exposure and proximity. Abundance is exposure in proximity beyond the hold of any border, including the borders of totality and universality. Abundance is geoethics, geopolitics, and geophilosophy, together with their endless interruption.

In this volume, I have been concerned to understand abundance and responsibility in relation to heterogeneous kinds: responsibility as the

propinquity of families, species, and kinds, in society and in nature; heterogeneity and abundance as the purity and impurity of kinds. Heterogeneity
is impurity, which can neither be thought nor experienced nor instituted
except in kinds, in blood. Propinquity in disaster and blood. *Geschlecht,
Herkunft, Entstehen, genre*, kinds: impurities of genealogy and descent. As
ethical responsibility.

Leading to a program, more effectively perhaps, with Naess in mind,
to a platform. Repeating the platform of deep ecology from within abundance, endless desire and responsibility, multiplying in profusion, interrupting and exercising its authority. Enjoying the idea of a platform as a
place from which to begin another ethics, a practice demanding loyalty
without insistence on undivided authority. A practice devoted to the abundance of kinds, heterogeneity, throughout the earth, without extreme regu-
lative authority. I explicate the platform in terms of plenishment to express
inclusion.

*(1) The flourishing of human and non-human life on Earth has intrin-
sic value. The value of non-human life forms is independent of the usefulness these may have for narrow human purposes.*

The proximity of human and nonhuman life, and all other things and
kinds, whatever they may be, touches every thing and kind in the earth in
propinquity, in exposure. Everything speaks, expresses, in exposure and
proximity. Instituting immeasurable responsibility, beyond fulfillment, toward every thing and kind, within every thing and kind. Endlessly resisting
the domination of either individual or kind.

Individuals, species, families, and kinds live and die, flourish and decline: feast and famine. Abundance is not flourishing as increase, always at
the expense of others. Natural kinds support each other's growth even as they
compete for space and as their mutual support leads to the decline of others.
Flourishing may be too close to mastery and domination, neglecting the
harm that kinds impose. Flourishing may be another noble value on the edge
of fascism, where every system of values resides. Sacrificing to higher causes.

Understood as distinct from mastery, flourishing throughout nature
and human life pertains to species, families, genders, kins, and kinds: to
heterogeneity in abundance, in propinquity; to the abundance of individuals within a family, including crossings and impurities; to the abundance of
debt within a people that maintains itself across generations and eons; to
the abundance of species with identities and borders, crossed impurely with
mobilities and variations in profusion. To kindness.

I do not know if every thing and kind has intrinsic value, in itself or
for human beings—if either value would be intrinsic. I would disrupt every
border between what has value and what has not, resisting neutrality and

the curse. Within such an interruption and resistance, we may interrupt the thought that human identities and uses are not relevant. I would emphasize exposure and propinquity.

But not just human exposure to other humans and natural things, not just human propinquities. All things are exposed to others in proximity, in kindness, touching, responding to each other. All things are expressive in proximity. Exposure, proximity, propinquity, expression, responsiveness are not only human. Yet these may be difficult if not impossible for human beings to know, to experience, toward other creatures and things. Perhaps immoral, wicked. We may hope to share the lives and feelings of other human beings very different from ourselves, but it may be unjust to insist on doing so. Respect for others, individuals and kinds, entails respecting the possibility that they may remain alien to us, heterogeneous, still demanding our respect and care in propinquity. Respect for natural things and kinds begins from a kindness we bear toward them in the absence of any possibility that we share the earth together except in the proximity of heterogeneities and interruptions.

Keeping Bhabha's thought in mind that responsibility and heterogeneity are located in repetitious multiplications of desire and *mimēsis* in which we—humans, Europeans, postcolonials, whatever—are at stake as both individual and kind. Within a certain invisibility.

Responsibility as interruption in proximity, toward all things beyond measure, given measure in propinquity: in exposure and relation; in the abundance of the earth. Hark to the singing of all things in the abundance of the earth, heterogeneous kinds, beyond ownership and mastery! Resist neutrality and totality! Sacrifice sacrifice! Be kind and seek to multiply kindness!

(2) Richness and diversity of life forms are values in themselves and contribute to the flourishing of human and nonhuman life on Earth.

Richness and diversity of kinds of living and nonliving creatures and things express abundance in the earth. This abundance is the immeasurable condition of responsibility, giving from the good in responsiveness and debt. Without it, there could be no ethics or responsibility. Or life. It is the condition of the flourishing of life, or love or care. It knows no border between living and nonliving, but respects the importance of every border, instituting kinds. Calling for endless interruption.

Yet richness and diversity do not always contribute to flourishing. Individuals die, kinds vanish from the earth. Abundance includes this death and extinction—in part because some must die that others may flourish—without equanimity, as if death were something other than death, other than sacrifice. Sacrifice is disaster. Abundance multiplies disasters, catastrophes, as it multiples achievements and fulfillments. The abundance of the earth is filled with injustice, against which plenishment mobilizes resistance. Including its own injustices.

Abundance contributes to richness and diversity, but is not itself a good. Perhaps richness and diversity are not goods, not always, not everywhere, not for everyone or everything. But without abundance, there would be no goods, no values—and no bads, no evils. Evil names the disasters of an earthly abundance without totality and neutrality: local and contingent disasters, inseparable from joys, from goods. Goods in local circulation always produce disasters.

Resist injustice in the abundance of the earth, against the authority of every border, in the heterogeneity of kinds.

(3) Humans have no right to reduce this richness and diversity except to satisfy vital needs.

Human beings have all kinds of rights—and nonrights—as do other creatures and things. If any creature or thing has rights; if rights are something that can be owned, possessed, employed; if rights are without impeccable authority. Whatever rights may be taken to be, they are local, contingent, without absolute authority. They mark a form in which human beings have instituted and claimed authority—for themselves, for some, over others.

We might hope to give up all thought of rights, for human beings and others, if we could otherwise institute the relation between authority and responsibility. The rights that pertain to human beings within a legal community mark their own authority within the authority of the state, express a shared and divergent but immeasurable responsibility that breaches the borders of every instituted authority. Authority is excessive, for individuals, groups, and the state—as domination and resistance. Responsibility is excessive, for individuals, kinds, and institutions, interrupting every authority.

Rights are either instituted, legitimated, authority without responsibility or excess; or they are, by those who defend their theoretical history, tied to freedom, excessive in both authority and responsibility. Rights can either be instituted without interruption, under law, or marks of endless interruptions and responsibilities. *Mimēsis.*

Suggesting that we think of rights together with abundance as multiplying representations of authority and resistance, linked with needs. Understood as responsibility, human and otherwise: repetitious desires to flourish amid endless interruptions of every border. Especially including humanism's borders, sometimes named as human rights.

The Declaration of the Rights of Man becomes the legal institution of resistance to every authority in the name of freedom. Let us call it *abjection.*

I insist on adding abjection to the platform: expulsion of authority within and without. Every right claimed by Man institutes abjection for

Man, the Human Subject, Bearer of Rights, and for others, human and otherwise. Under the curse.

(4) Present human interference with the non-human world is excessive, and the situation is rapidly worsening.

The influence of human life and economic development upon the surface of the earth is immense and growing. Yet it occupies but a tiny corner of the universe, over a tiny segment of its history. Is this excessive? My understanding of excess is different, addressing what is uncontainable and immeasurable, neither small nor large. Both human and nonhuman worlds are excessive, beyond containment, beyond good and bad, better and worse. Abundance and heterogeneity are beyond better and worse.

Two examples:

(i) Against the suggestion that indigenous life and culture are better left pristine, many native peoples insist that they have the right to determine their own development, including industrialization and world markets. The issue is not of decreasing influence but of increasing local authority. Otherwise lack of interference is another form of colonialism. Analogously:

(ii) Against the suggestion that we should eliminate land and water management, leaving them to develop freely, many argue that it is too late, that the entire planet has been influenced by economic and industrial development, that it is impossible to avoid human interference; the alternative is to pursue more responsive relations between humanity and nature, smaller and more sustainable technologies responsive to human and well as nonhuman needs; large-scale technologies and economies in which all costs are taken into account, including long-term and widespread costs to other species and kinds.

Human impact upon the earth is huge and growing, and will not go away. It may not be reducible in scale or scope. It can and must become more responsive and self-critical, especially against uncritical ownership and instrumentality. The situation needs to be improved for nonhuman species, for many disappearing cultures, and for many human beings living in poverty and disease.

(5) The flourishing of human life and cultures is compatible with a substantial decrease of the human population. The flourishing of nonhuman life requires such a decrease.

Some observations:

(a) Virtually all living species, animal or plant, increase in population to the limits of available resources. Why should human populations be different?

(b) Virtually all living species expand and contract successively, decreasing in population where resources are limited, sometimes cataclysmically.

(c) Human peoples expand in population to the limit of available resources, apparently limited by three things, disease, affluence, and literacy. Human cultures have voluntarily decreased their populations as they have become literate and industrialized. Especially female literacy.

(d) All decreases promote authoritarianism, illiteracy, or poverty. Any other possibilities are as yet unknown, and may be part of the indefensible optimism that has driven industrial society since Descartes. Together with colonialism.

(e) All programs to decrease population without authoritarianism presuppose the kind of economic and industrial development that is most harmful to the flourishing of other life on earth. Save one: increasing female literacy, perhaps the one worldwide program with a chance of saving the earth.

I fear the sacrifice of human beings and their needs to anything higher, human or otherwise; fear it as ecological fascism. Every institutionalized system of value and authority runs the risk of fascism. Including ecology.

Human life takes place in exposure, among different human beings, in different cultures, families, and kinds, among different natural creatures and things, in different species and kinds. In propinquity. In this exposure resides an immeasurable debt to cherish every individual and kind, including those whose existence we think threatens our own. Perhaps it does not do so, or not as greatly, or in the ways we think. And even if it does, we are called upon to care, to resist disaster, to criticize every measure, even the best, wherever it institutes sacrifice, ourselves or others.

Promote female literacy and women's control over their lives! Plenish the earth!

(6) Significant change of life conditions for the better requires change in policies. These affect basic economic, technological, and ideological structures.

Yes. But beware of every better, even the best.

Beware the purity of the better; hope that significant change of life conditions may emerge from pollution and impurity, not as cleanliness and purification, but retaining heterogeneity. Challenge every authority; resist every border.

(7) The ideological change is mainly that of appreciating life quality (dwelling in situations of intrinsic value) rather than adhering to a high standard of living. There will be a profound awareness of the difference between big and great.

Dwell at the borders; cross every threshold. Avoid another line between big and great, or between a high and low standard of living for human beings. Another line to be challenged and resisted. Perhaps in the name of the nonliving.

The ethical change is that of cherishment, bearing responsibility toward every thing in exposure and proximity, listening to the voices, the expressions, of every thing and kind in propinquity and touch. In the light of such exposure, seek to better yourself, your kind, those in your proximity, and others, resisting hierarchy. Care for the consequences of what you and other humans do without boundaries and borders; struggle to achieve what is best amid endless conflicts of life and being; resist every attempt to justify sacrifice. Resist neutrality; accept responsibility for sacrifice; sacrifice sacrifice.

(8) Those who subscribe to the foregoing points have an obligation directly or indirectly to participate in the attempt to implement the necessary changes.

Yes. Without qualification. Always in exposure and proximity.

Undertake responsibility within exposure and proximity to all things in the abundance of the earth, a responsibility to live and think differently, responsively, without end. In sorrow and joy. And kindness.

Plenishment in the earth.

Returning to the guidelines in chapter 10 toward living for the sake of the good, reframed in the context of this platform. Perhaps another platform, more abundant, liminal, intermediary, impure, more responsive to exposure. Perhaps linked more with responsivity than normativity. Joining abundance with exuberance. Summarized in the overarching principles— no principles at all—that everything matters and that no one knows another's good, not perhaps even that other, individual or kind. Yet still we struggle to achieve our ideals, together with others, liminally and impurely, exposed to others in propinquity and kindness. Abundance in proximity; endless liminal responsibility: impurity, complexity, *mimēsis*.

Everything in the earth touches other things, responds to them in proximity; and every response is exposure, *mimēsis*, liminal, boundless, resistant to borders, multiplying meanings, linkings, crossings, impurities, impurifications. *Mimēsis* is exposure, impurifications and multiplications, intermediary movements; corporeal, expressive, responsive, responsible. The liminal, intermediary crossing of being and the good as expression, *mimēsis*. The abundance of the earth as joy and sorrow, celebration and pain, growth and disaster, tragedy and comedy, and much, much more.

I would like to build on Naess's platform, not to assemble another in competition or opposition, but to supplement the platform with a certain responsibility that I do not find articulated there. A Buddhist tone, perhaps, or something more abundant, more exuberant. As Naess says, *Friluftsliv: exuberance in nature. Cherishment.* But where he thinks of touching the earth lightly, I think of endless exposure, of sacrifice and harm—a darker image—and of sacrificing sacrifice within the exuberance of *mimēsis*. *Sacrifice!* But hate it, avoid it wherever possible, understand it as disastrous, undertake it without celebration. Sacrifice becomes plenishment in the infinite responsibility to sacrifice sacrifice in the name of the good.

Allowing a return to Naess's normative ecosophical model with another ecosophy—not T, perhaps, but CSP for cherishment, sacrifice, and plenishment; P for short. With exclamation marks! *Mimēsis!*

N1: Self-realization!
Cherishment!
For oneself, one's kind; for others and their kinds; without fulfillment; each thing or kind responsible for its own good beyond the care of others.
Kindness!
Interruption!
H1: The higher the Self-realization attained by anyone, the broader and deeper the identification with others.
No measure of cherishment, of self, of realization; no privilege of identification; cherishment is kindness toward others as other, not as the same.
Mimēsis as nonidentification!
Resist neutrality!!
N2: Self-realization for all living beings!
Kindness toward all things!!
N3: Diversity of life!
Abundance in the earth!!
N4: Complexity!
Abundance! Kindness! Profusion! Mimēsis!
N5: Symbiosis!
Exposure! Proximity! Propinquity!
N6: Local self-sufficiency and cooperation!
Locality, contingency, exuberance, interruption!
N7: Local autonomy!
Local determination!!
N8: No centralization!
Interruption!!
N9: No exploitation!
Resist domination, oppression, exploitation!!
Resist the authority of resistance!!
Intermediary movements!!
N10: No subjection!
Resist subjection, abjection, authority!

N11: All have equal rights to Self-realization!
Exposure everywhere! Proximity! Propinquity! Kindness!
H14: Class societies deny equal rights to Self-realization!
N12: No class societies!
Dominate domination!!
N13: Self-determination!
Resist neutrality!!

Abundance!
Heterogeneity!
Kinds!
Responsibility!
Cherishment!
Sacrifice sacrifice!!
Plenishment!!
Intermediary movements!
Liminality!
Impurity!
Exuberance!
Interruption!
Mimēsis
Kindness!
!!!

What ethic, what measures of good and bad, right and wrong, are given in the abundance in the earth, immeasurable giving from the good in kindness, as endless responsibility? I return to Bhabha, doubled and more, who speaks directly to this question from a postcolonial perspective.

> Despite its firm commitments, the political must always pose as a problem, or a question, the *priority of the place from which it begins*, if its authority is not to become autocratic. (Bhabha, *II*, 207)
>
> What must be left an open question, *post*-poststructuralism, is how we are to rethink ourselves once we have undermined the immediacy and autonomy of self-consciousness. . . . *[B]etwixt and besides* the lofty dreams of political thinking, there exists an acknowledgment, somewhere between fact and fantasy, that the techniques and technologies of politics need not be *humanizing* at all, in no way endorsing of what we understand to be the human—humanist?—predicament. (pp. 207–8)

An ethic that arises in the question of the place or kind from which it begins within immeasurable exposure to others and a responsibility to resist oppression and to remember disaster. Interrupting and decentering several endless movements: the repetitious desire that impels the project of resistance; insistence on totality and universality; the mobility and excesses of authority; identification and participation in groups and kinds; the centering of agency, individual, social, and otherwise; the crossing of borders instituted in projects of representation; the paranoia of belonging to a history where every project is too late, interruption and more interruption.

Evoking an immeasurable ecology—neither shallow nor deep—linked in an untold relation to the good, given as endless responsibility to do work, demanding measure, calculation, boundaries, institutions—all capable of, certain, to do harm, assured of injustice. Every individual unjustly takes the place of another; every kind delimits and inhibits other kinds while fostering others. These individuals and kinds, abundance in the earth, are injustice joined together with the only possibility of justice, its work. All the work of institutions, all the tasks of ethics, promote and institute injustice. But on the other side—if it is a side, or other, perhaps a flank or hand or paw, perhaps something otherwise—institutions accomplish whatever goods can be accomplished, answering to the call from the good.

An ethic that keeps its borders open but hopes to work without borders; that interrupts every rule, including the rule of interruption.

An ecological ethic. Ecology as inclusion. As interruption. As love and care. In kindness.

Leading to the possibility that an inclusive ethic, understood as plenishment, is neither shallow nor deep but more radical, beyond ethics, in whose giving lies the possibility of ethics.

Cherishment: the kindness that every ethics demands, emerging in every place, resisting every demarcation, filled with marks and borders. *Mimēsis*. Interruption. Love.

Sacrifice: the demarcations and borders that work demands, always in memory of cherishment. Interrupting interruption. Sacrificing sacrifice.

Plenishment: experiencing the abundance of the earth as cherishment in memory of sacrifice, sacrificing every sacrifice, every boundary, crossing every threshold with responsibility.

Which is to say that plenishment is liberation without a guarantee of accomplishment, the only fulfillment possible in the work of ethics and politics. Liberation without plenishment is authoritarianism.

Which is to say that ethics and politics are no genre. We have heard that before. Ethics and politics take place among the kinds of the earth, but compose no kinds themselves, no kind of project, no kind of institution, provide no safety, demand no kind of agency.

Which is to say that an ecological ethic is ethics itself, responsibility, in the abundance of the earth, radical beyond all radicality, resistant beyond all resistance to injustice, everywhere and in every place, kindness exceeding every kind. How far, we may ask, will an ethical responsibility beyond measure take us? And how long? Perhaps neither of these has a measure. Perhaps this radicality is so radical that it cannot be measured. Perhaps we cannot expect more of a transformation in the earth through such an ethic than we have gathered from more traditional policies of development and property. They are too drastic to bear. And perhaps we cannot expect to know how long before an ethic of responsibility is shared everywhere because it has always been shared and known, will never arrive on the scene as if beginning something entirely new. Perhaps an ecological ethic is already here, already late, more of the same, and different.

Allowing me to conclude with some examples, crossing difficult thresholds, human and otherwise, interrupting every movement.

1. Perhaps the most intractable yet inescapable set of entwined issues for an inclusive ethic concerns the encroachment of human life upon the habitats of animals and wilderness regions—if any habitats can still be considered wild or belonging to animals more than human beings. At every boundary between human settlements and outlying regions, animals and human beings come into conflict, usually leading to the destruction of the animals, especially larger, glorious animals like lions, tigers, wolves, and elephants. Some of this is due to human resistance to predation, real or imagined, though the greater issue concerns the destruction of habitat for animals that need to roam over great distances for food or social activities.

Regions set aside for animals meet one set of concerns, seldom effectively, though they exacerbate conflicts at their boundaries, especially where animals cross. And they are very costly. Economic development of farmland, political development of regional enclaves, all work against holding territory for animals against human encroachment. This puts immense destructive pressure on larger animals. But it puts destructive pressures on tribal life, especially on traditional forms of human life that do not undertake economic and political development. If animal species are vanishing at a disastrous and growing rate, human cultures and languages are vanishing even faster.

With respect to human cultures, policies can be defined consistent with the guidelines and principles specified above within the complex difficulties facing the world. Local self-determination for the individuals and groups under pressure. No one knows the good for others better than those others, even where they do not know it themselves. Economic, political, and cultural development takes place between local determination and global influences, calling for intermediary movements that prevent global developments from freezing into patterns destructive of local cultures, central policies that implement local empowerment, policies whose primary purpose is to foster and sustain local economies and authorities, policies and practices that maxi-mize local interruptions.

The issue for human ways of life and language under pressure is how to pursue political and economic developments responsive to changing circumstances and local variations, resistant to neutrality and totality, there-fore resistant to majority rule and centralized institutions except as they promote local responsiveness and responsibility. Centralized authorities are responsible for practices promoting economic and political stability and freedom from corruption and crime, consistent with as much responsive-ness to local, minority variations as possible.

It may be worth noting, parenthetically, that the structure of this pattern loosely corresponds to the United States system, a shared and fre-quently conflicted authority between federal and state institutions. With the qualification that states may not represent local structures responsive to minority differences. I include not only named minorities—African Americans, Native Americans, Hispanics, women, lesbians, gays—but local religious and social groups. In every group and institution, corresponding pressures exist between collective uniformities across the entire group and subgroup variations.

All this is the structure of kinds, purity and impurity, uniformity and heterogeneity. It is the struggle in human social, cultural, and political life with heterogeneity. It is the struggle for local authority where some local institutions are harmful to their members and dominate minorities (some-times majorities). It is the struggle against the tendency of global develop-ment toward uniformity and central authority within the division of the world into local economic regions. It is the struggle against the dominance of local cultural practices imposed as global truths and values, a struggle against neutrality.

One might say that the tendency of both political authority and eco-nomic development is toward global centralization and uniformity. The van-ishing of local cultures and economies supports that conclusion. The growth of large-scale institutions does so also. The spread of industrialization and market economies promotes a global world system rather than local self-determination. Yet perhaps the tendency is not altogether one-sided, espe-cially given the possibility that so many local cultures have descended into a poverty and a political instability that makes it impossible for them to con-tinue successfully. Certain features of global economic development appear to be essential against both poverty and authoritarianism.

At the same time, many local regions have insisted on local em-powerments, promoting local sustainable practices, local economic and political empowerment, resistances to uniformity and collectivity. This is a worldwide phenomenon, notable particularly in the most developed countries as resistance to achieved centralization. Less developed regions frequently struggle against divisions that foster poverty.

Why not take this political and economic struggle as the world condition, closely related to the development of global systems, tempered and interrupted by insistence on impurity and heterogeneity? These will remain within the most uniform of societies and practices, within the most uniform of perceptions and emotions: individual and group variations, by family, gender, kin, and kind. Why not take kin, kind, gender, class, and so on to represent the struggle that defines democracy, seeking to implement democratic practices resistant to the tyranny of kinds, to endless struggles over heterogeneity? Local self-determination, responsive to local variations of groups and individuals, joined with the need for economic and political stability! A democracy whose institutions promote interruption and heterogeneity! Including the interruption of every institution to foster and regulate heterogeneity! Including disciplinary institutions, practices of truth! *Mimēsis!*

Democracy *is* heterogeneity. Capitalist economy *is* locally competitive economies. With the qualifications that democratic institutions institute homogeneity; that capitalist economies widen disparities between rich and poor to a point destructive to local groups, destroying their identities; that capitalist economies promote uniformities of labor and distribution, working against heterogeneity; that no economy is perfect, so that every market economy neglects major economic and social costs. One of the tasks of democracy becomes how to foster economic development responsive to the range of costs embedded in its institutions, especially hidden and unknown costs. One way of thinking of democracy is as an insistence that all costs, all exchanges and substitutions, be discounted by unknown costs, incalculable goods. Becoming-minoritarian to an extreme. Democracy would be the discounting of every authority in the name of heterogeneity, open to an indefinite future: general as well as restricted economy. Discounting here is the inclusion of unknown, uninstituted, incalculable goods as interruptions, implementing this impossibility, expressing and representing the cost of their representation—my reading of *se rabattre sur* and *mimēsis*: falling back and down upon every authority and economy. Bearing the costs of every economic institution, including the costs of bearing the costs, understood in relation to representation and expression. Economic and political representation as circulation and interruption. As *mimēsis*.

Leading to inclusive practices and perceptions in nature. For the concerns of an inclusive ethic remain the same in relation to natural creatures and things, issues of heterogeneity and interruption in relation to political authority and economic development. Perhaps the guidelines that responded to human cultures under pressure may respond to analogous pressures on natural species. The principal guideline is local determination: no one can know the good of another better than that other—individual and kind—even where that other does not know or cannot articulate it. Local determination as letting-be. As interruption.

Except that it is too late for many animals, plants, and their habitats. As it is too late for many human cultures. Many animals are adapting, especially smaller animals that can live effectively at human borders—coyotes, skunks, squirrels, and weasels; various microorganisms and quasi-organisms, which have shown themselves to be amazingly adaptive, beyond human technological capabilities. Molly reminds us of mollusks and barnacles. Kindness includes respect for kinds that have evolved in seas and forests over millions of years, and also for kinds that have adapted to flourish remarkably well in human environments. All are abundance in the earth.

I believe the responsibilities human beings bear to their environment are analogous to the responsibilities central governments and institutions bear to local heterogeneity. To implement policies that foster local determination where it is always too late for the localities, which must adapt or die, *on their own terms*. The responsibility is to wildlife and natural habitats, where no habitats are wild and animals undergo adaptations. The most voracious of all natural kinds, humanity, is imposing tremendous adaptive pressures on other species. a pressure that we cannot imagine will go away. I do not envisage significant diminution of human populations, or withdrawal from productive territories, or the retreat of economic development. But in every case, counterpressures exist within the ongoing movements, pressures toward local variations, toward practices and representations of interruption.

Should we let species die out—precious, magnificent animal species, tigers, elephants, pandas? Or should we keep them alive in zoos at best? For the while, keeping them alive seems better than letting them die out, if we have the power to do something about it. Their loss would be disastrous—to them, to the environing world, to us. Yet keeping them alive means nothing without their local determination, without having lives of their own to live, where they may flourish—or not—on their own terms, even if that means death, to themselves and others. All that central authorities can do is to insist on heterogeneity—kinds and their impurities—within democracy, resisting majoritarian domination and global economic uniformity. In both cases, minorities and local cultures have shown great resilience, if not as great as we might wish, interrupting the institutions of common practices. Analogously, many forms of life and wildernesses have shown great resilience against the encroachments of human and natural cataclysms. Why not take advantage in every social policy of this magnificent adaptability?

Resist the most destructive and oblivious of social and economic practices by fostering local determination! Human and otherwise. Bear the costs of institutional and representational practices. Foster wilderness and anarchy as interruptions.

2. Such practices and understandings may not promote the abolition of hunting or meat-producing industries. Nor the use of animals for experimentation. In every case, however, local determination for animals, plants, landscapes, and objects—including artifacts—entails that multiple considerations are always in play.

Large-scale industries and institutions promote competing accomplishments reminiscent of the struggles around heterogeneity discussed previously. They deliver products in large numbers, distributed over large populations, frequently at low per-unit costs. I use economic language to speak of political products: army, police, criminal procedures. Yet the word *low* is misleading, for the social costs are frequently immense, especially to heterogeneity and self-determination. Industrial and political development provide the means whereby local cultures now are possible and sustainable, at the cost of virtually destroying their uniqueness. This is true for all the examples above, distinguishing an entirely local practice of hunting from the regulation and administration of hunting practiced by most governments worldwide. Hunting, experimentation, slaughterhouses, and mechanized agriculture all take place as industries with enormous consequences for human, animal, and vegetal life, as well as the environment. Why should they not be asked to bear responsibility for heterogeneity commensurate with the scale of their consequences?

To take the easiest and hardest cases first, experimentation on animals is said to save human lives, to promote medical practices of great benefit to human beings. And other animals, I might say, cared for in veterinary practices. But the documented abuses are terrible.

Not very long ago, and still today, human beings were used as experimental animals. I include German concentration camps, experiments on prisoners and inmates of asylums, military experiments, and the Tuskegee study on African Americans. One might conclude that experimentation itself knows no ethicality, that it takes neutrality for granted, frequently disgracefully. An ethical society must insist that scientific and medical experiments take responsibility for resisting a neutrality they are designed to institute.

Some of that has been accomplished. Certainly we could go further. But it might be sufficient to insist that experimentation on human beings bear full ethical, political, and economic costs. Perhaps survival is at stake as if humanity were at war with disease. But war is anything but neutral. And so perhaps are science's practices and experiments. Which on the understanding I am offering does not mean abolishing either, but insisting on the open, critical examination of the practices, especially the representational practices, that compose their institutional authority.

Why not think of animal experimentation as analogous, critical perhaps of the extreme view that all such practices should be abolished, but much more knowingly critical than present law provides, with memories of countless historical abuses, of experimentations on human beings, linked with slavery, imprisonment, and war—the most abusive of human practices? Critical of the institutions that have been created to impose experimentation on human beings and animals within authoritarian systems of regulation that are structurally hostile to heterogeneity. Critical of systems of knowledge that deny their own responsibility in the name of neutrality.

Ferry criticizes the easy transition from democratization for human beings to rights for animals and the natural environment. And perhaps we should not conclude that stones have rights. Perhaps we should not conclude that human beings have rights, have ever had effective rights within the discursive practices that insist upon them, given widespread practices of imprisonment, slavery, experimentation, and war. But a more difficult and more productive transition may be defensible, from the institutional treatment of human beings in slavery, prisons, and militaries to the institutional treatment of animals, plants, and natural things. Perhaps we need to be critical beyond measure, excessively so, of every institution that treats any thing, living or other, as if it may be treated as a possession with impunity, without qualification or responsibility. By individuals but much more in relation to powerful institutions. Resisting domination and neutrality.

Such an ethical vigilance, insisting on responsibility and cherishment, does not entail the abolition of experimentation, not even on human beings. Perhaps it should be voluntary for human beings. Perhaps some experiments on human beings suffering from diseases that make them incapable of voluntary choice may save others tremendous suffering. Perhaps animals should be experimented on only on similar terms, where clear and devastating consequences are at stake. I would say that our practices are not ethical unless we consider these possibilities as deeply as we can. Unless we interrupt every institution that insists on regulating our practices, perceptions, and understandings, every institution that imposes authority.

Similarly, perhaps we can undertake public examination of meat-producing industries and practices, considering costs to the environment, to human beings, and to animals—let us say, equally. Not that we equate human beings and animals in all respects, but that we consider animal suffering as suffering indeed, consider destruction of habitats as destruction, not just human deprivation, ask for justifications based not on arbitrary lines of demarcation between kinds but on the devastating impact on human and animal life of continuing or discontinuing the production of meat. I would say that without a doubt, nothing can justify large-scale meat-producing industries. Vegetable-producing industries may require major modifications, though countless human lives would be at stake. If we are to experiment on vegetables for human consumption, can we consider the possibility of experimenting on them to determine the practices which are better for plants? And their predators?

Similarly again, management of wilderness regions and landscapes—it is too late to imagine that they may exist without management of some human kind—may require that we let some regions follow their own destinies while we intensely manage others. History has shown that much of the intensive management of landscapes—beaches for example—has been destructive to the natural conditions the management was designed to promote. There are countless lessons in large-scale human practices that have straightforward implications for economic development, where development is required to pay full social and environmental costs. I insist that it is possible to take full costs to the environment into account, however inexactly, as it is possible to take indirect costs to urban environments into account. If central policies mean anything, they bear responsibility for insisting on heterogeneity against local irresponsibility—keeping in mind that heterogeneity resides finally in such local practices and understandings.

Some conclusions, all qualified by excessive responsibilities:

Should we be vegetarians? Or vegans? Of course. But . . . Perhaps it is not so bad to eat cheese or drink milk, especially for infants or children who need extra calcium. Eggs are especially to be avoided where mass-produced. In large-scale production egg-laying chickens are treated far worse than chickens for slaughter. Perhaps some people will need to eat meat to treat disorders. Perhaps where other sources of food are unavailable. Or in cultures where it would be a social affront to refuse to eat what one was offered. Mechanized animal farming is a great technological achievement. Perhaps it is time to move to other technologies, including mechanized produce farming. Still wary of destructions.

Should we allow experiments on animals? Of course. But . . . Perhaps only in limited cases where harm was curtailed and the promise of saving human and other animal lives was apparent. Perhaps under severe restriction, after all other avenues had been explored. Perhaps not for the sake of knowledge alone. Or cosmetics. Perhaps we could set a high price on animal suffering and make abusers pay the costs.

Should we allow experiments on human beings? Of course not. But . . . Perhaps where humans might volunteer for tests that would not harm them but might save human lives. Perhaps on human beings who do not feel pain. Perhaps where many lives might be saved.

Are there no differences between human beings and animals, animals and plants? Of course. But . . . Perhaps not absolute differences. There are differences between one animal and another, animals and plants, one animal and another, one species of animal or plant and another, differences between human beings. All ethically relevant. All related to how they respond to and treat each other and how we are responsible for treating them. With mobile, porous, borders between one kind and another, resisting every purification.

Do stones and clouds have intrinsic value? Do animals or plants have rights? Of course not. But . . . Perhaps human beings do not have absolute or unqualified rights, even rights at all, except within institutional configurations. Above all, configurations of state power, where rights play their most critical role. Similarly, perhaps animals and plants have rights against arbitrary state appropriation. And rights against arbitrary abuse by others. Perhaps animals, plants, human beings, and all other things bear intrinsic value against arbitrary abuse. Nothing can be owned, possessed, treated without care, abused without qualification—qualifications derived from other human beings, community concerns, implications for other animals and plants, inherent in the things themselves, and more. Always but . . . ; an ethics of *perhaps* and *but*; an ethics of inclusion; plenishment; immeasurable debts and responsibilities.

In every case, ethics tells us what we should do, instituted into law, interrupted by responsibilities that exceed the boundaries of every rule. Returning us, perhaps, to Derrida's cats. How can I justify feeding the cats who live with me and not feeding all the other cats in the world who are starving? How can I justify writing this book instead of working toward justice in evil places? How can I justify living well and not giving all I have to the poor?

Perhaps I can justify none of these. Perhaps we should be wary of justification in ethics. But ethics begins in proximity, endless responsibility to those nearby. And others. I might take joy in feeding the cats who live with me, or the cats who live nearby, though I could not find all the cats in the world to feed. It is joyful and good to care for those one can care for. It is joyful and ethical to love and cherish. But it is never enough though it may be all that I can do where I am, given my local responsibilities.

I believe that this kind of responsibility, especially toward other kinds of creatures, directed from where we are exposed to others without measure, in propinquity, represents an ethic of plenishment: cherishment joined within its own impossibility, loss and disaster in joy. For each and every cat is loved and enjoyed and loves and enjoys the life it has. In kindness, in the kinds in which it participates. A love and joy directed to other cats and other places. My immeasurable responsibility toward all the cats in the world of which Derrida speaks is not without love and joy here and now, but pertains to the here and now as a responsibility from where I am, in proximity, toward others without firm boundaries and measures. Local responsibilities open outward and elsewhere beyond measure.

Among my local responsibilities are those toward myself, for I am in my proximity, exposed to myself as other beyond any other. The others are strangers but I am stranger to myself. If we give up the autonomy of the subject, we give up the privilege of the ego, the self toward whom I bear the greatest love. Sometimes hate. The self is other, always strange, among the other strangers. In this way, I work toward the good for myself among the others, find that my good demands goods for others in my vicinity, bear any responsibility by bearing many other responsibilities. But not all. All cannot be fulfilled. Cherishment resides in conflict, leads to sacrifice. But not always my sacrifice to others, not always the sacrifice of others to myself or my community. Never with justification. Cherishment and sacrifice cannot be given by rule, but give forth the possibility of rules, of ethical practice, care, and understanding. Endless responsibility in cherishment and sacrifice is plenishment toward oneself and others, from one's proximity to elsewhere, filled with endless qualifications.

One cannot cease feeding one's own cat to feed others. One cannot cease feeding oneself to feed others. One would cease to do good. Even lose the power to do good. The debt one owes beyond measure resides in one's proximity, still without measure. Plenishment is always in exposure and proximity even when we undertake debts from afar. From where we are to elsewhere, knowing that here and there are always elsewhere. In every place are debts and responsibilities in proximity, in propinquity, always from that place to elsewhere, in alterity. In exposure and proximity.

In expression. As *mimēsis*. Where we are, in our proximity, others speak, express, beyond the boundaries and rules of any language, any grammar. Human beings who do not speak our language. Infants who do not speak in words but communicate in gesture and look. Animals who reach out and respond, express themselves to other animals in gesture and song. Other living creatures, who respond sensitively to their surroundings, more sensitively than any human being, as nomadic people respond to their surroundings more acutely than literate human beings. Living creatures—human beings, animals, birds, vegetables, plants, and habitats, all changing, responding, intertwining. And other natural things, in mobile, delicate, responsive entwinings. Always from where one is to elsewhere. Exposure and proximity.

Natural, human, inhuman, and other things—individuals, species, and kinds—express and respond wherever they are in exposure and propinquity. Nothing is dead, neutral, without meaning or its own good, though some meanings and goods will never be known to human beings or others, and human beings experience these meanings and goods within their own limitations. Ethical responsibility inhabits this lived experience of propinquity as the debt of each person and thing to others in the kinds there are. Exposure and proximity express themselves in the impurity and heterogeneity of kinds.

And in the passion and transportation of love, inseparable from kinds and reproduction, from blood and impurity, from descent and genealogy. Loving kindness. Love in kindness. Heterogeneity is impurity in kind and alterity in love, throughout human experience. Kind and love—unbounded, sexual, erotic love, and all the other loves—are sites of heterogeneity: exposure and propinquity as love, in relation to individual and kind. As kindness. Not just for human beings. Not just human kinds, human heterogeneity, human impurity, human blood and genealogy. But in human experience, loving kindness is the radical experience of heterogeneity, crossing every border, liminal and intermediary. As exposure and proximity, crossing borders from one person to another, one person to an animal or thing, one gender to another, one species to another, from every place to elsewhere. Love in kindness as the intense crossing of borders in life and experience, propinquity and *mimēsis*. Intimately bound with cherishment, endless responsiveness between individual things, between one species and another, sometimes leading to death. For love is filled with danger, as are any crossings between one kind and another, filled with blood. Rapture, ecstasy, vulnerability. Plenishment as love. As kindness.

Kindness is endless crossings, liminal movements, endless joys and sorrows, exposure at the limits of the possibility of propinquity, marking the limitlessness of responsibility. Marking resistance to neutrality. Toward the other, and still others. Friends, lovers, children, animals, and things, all open out in proximity and touch, responsive from where they are to elsewhere, to other kinds. In kindness. In care and love. In propinquity. Crossing every place in blood, descent in blood, kin and kind.

Notes

General Preface to the Project

1. I recall Socrates' suggestion that knowledge, truth, and, perhaps, being itself all come as gifts from the good (Plato, *Republic*, 508–9), and his description of the indefinite dyad, which I associate with the good: "a gift of the gods" (*Philebus*, 16c): "all things . . . consist of a one and a many"; we must "come to see not merely that the one we started with is a one and an unlimited many, but also just how many it is"; must discern "the total number of forms the thing in question has intermediate between its one and its unlimited number" (16d), an intermediate number I associate with *technē*; "It is only then, when we have done that, that we may let each one of all these intermediate forms pass away into the unlimited and cease bothering about them" (16e). I understand the passing away as giving, general economy, the circulation of gifts, and understand the unlimited as the good, the earth's abundance, demanded by and insisting on the intermediate number, the intermediary abundance of kinds, circulating in and interrupting all human and natural works. I understand the good as intermediariness, giving the possibility of measures, norms, and standards, always contingent, partial, incomplete, local, at risk, in endless circulation, resisting authority. What mediation may bring to rest, intermediariness keeps in movement. The good brings movement and rest in abundance.

I understand *rest* as a diaphoric, intermediary movement. (See my *PE*, chaps. 4 and 5.) I understand the repeated *we*, here and elsewhere, as another such movement, evoking multiple and heterogeneous kinds.

2. I recall here several allusions to gifts and giving. One is the "gift of the gods" from *Philebus*, the movement from limit to unlimit touching intermediary numbers, intermediary movements, understood in terms of general and restricted economy (see nn. 1 and 5).

A second is Heidegger's portrayal of the "it gives" *(es gibt)* and giving of Being. "In the beginning of Western thinking, Being is thought, but not the 'It gives' as such. The latter withdraws in favor of the gift which It gives" (Heidegger, *TB*, 8). I understand these words to call attention to the giving rather than to the It or to Being, the gift.

In a similar vein, my third allusion, Lewis Hyde speaks of the circulation of the gift:

> a gift is a thing we do not get by our own efforts. We cannot buy it; we cannot acquire it through an act of will. It is bestowed upon us. (Hyde, *G*, ix)
>
> The only essential is this: *the gift must always move*. There are other forms of property that stand still, that mark a boundary or resist momentum, but the gift keeps going. (p. 4)

I understand the good as giving, always moving, circulating, where the works of humanity and nature strive to slow or halt the circulation by imposing limits and exclusions. In this way the thought of the good and giving is a thought of inclusion, beyond the limits of work and *technē*. *Technē* works by limits, exclusions; all choices and boundaries belong to *technē*. The thought of the good is a thought beyond the limits of *technē*, sometimes named *poiēsis*, sometimes *mimēsis*, giving in abundance, unlimiting every limit. I understand the circulation as general economy, after Bataille; as expression, after Spinoza; as saying, after Levinas. Giving the abundance of kinds as *mimēsis* and representation. As exposure in proximity.

My final allusion recalls Derrida's explorations of the aporias of the gift: the impossibility of a gift without giver or return, an impossibility that is the condition of the possibility of ethics, given, I would say, in the name of the good.

> It must not circulate, it must not be exchanged, it must not in any case be exhausted, as a gift, by the process of exchange, by the movement of circulation of the circle in the form of return to the point of departure. (Derrida, *GT*, 7)
>
> For this is the impossible that seems to give itself to be thought here: These conditions of possibility of the gift (that some "one" gives some "thing" to some "one other") designate simultaneously the conditions of the impossibility of the gift. And already we could translate this into other terms: these conditions of possibility define or produce the annulment, the annihilation, the destruction of the gift. (p. 11)
>
> One would even be tempted to say that a subject as such never gives or receives a gift. (p. 24)
>
> Not impossible but *the* impossible. The very figure of the impossible. It announces itself, gives itself to be thought as the impossible. (p. 7)

He speaks of the gift as giving time and death.

> The gift is not a gift, the gift only gives to the extent it *gives time*. The difference between a gift and every other operation or pure and simple exchange is that the gift gives time. *There where there is gift, there is time.* (p. 41)

> The gift made to me by God as he holds me in his gaze and in his hand while remaining inaccessible to me, the terribly dissymmetrical gift of the *mysterium tremendum* only allows me to respond and only rouses me to the responsibility it gives me by making a gift of death *[en me donnant la mort]*, giving the secret of death, a new experience of death. (Derrida, *GD*, 34)

I read Derrida as examining, and resisting, the countless ways in which the good—on my view, nothing at all—becomes goodness, offers boundless rewards to human subjects, perhaps European-Christian subjects. "An event gives the gift that transforms the Good into a Goodness that is forgetful of itself into a love that renounces itself" (Derrida, *GD*, 40); "Contamination, then, of the thought of essence by technology. . . . This problem concerns once more the relationship between animals and technology. This occurs in particular by means of a very problematical opposition, it seems to me, between *giving* and *taking*" (Derrida, *OS*, 10–11). The giving of the good, as I understand it, knows nothing of taking, gives without return; yet time is filled with endless appropriations and betrayals. I read Derrida's writing on gifts and giving to pursue these echoes of betrayal.

I remain with a giving from the good that is given by no subject, person, thing, or God; or given to them; that can never become goodness; but that gives responsibility for goodness everywhere. The good gives no reward, knows nothing of return, though all of time pays restitution for the giving, responding to the touch and its call. I hope to listen to the music of this call beyond the wounds of debt, resisting being's neutrality. See n. 14.

3. I think of exposure and the good in memory of Levinas, who speaks of *exposition*—exposure and expression—and of a responsibility to the other, dyadically, that grows as it is paid (Levinas, *TI* and *OB*). I hope to exceed the singularity of the other in the general economy of kinds. See n. 5.

4. I think of *we* and *us* and *they* as enigmatic, intermediary figures of kinds. I think of the *calling* and *giving* of the good. See nn. 1 and 2 on giving, n. 14 on calling.

5. Heidegger speaks of abundance *(Fülle)* (Heidegger, *TB*, 6; *OWA*, 34, 76); Levinas speaks of fecundity (Levinas, *TI*, 267–69): "my future does not enter into the logical essence of the possible. The relation with such a future, irreducible to the power over possibles, we shall call fecundity" (Levinas, *TI*, 269). I speak of the inexhaustibility and immeasurability of giving in abundance.

I think of the work of the good as occupying restricted economies, goods divided from bads, binary oppositions and exclusions, setting prices. I think of the good as interrupting every restricted economy, every totality, circulating in the general economy of excess, unlimit, unmeasure. The giving of the good is the general economy of local and contingent goods that circulate everywhere in restricted economies of kinds within immeasurable exposure. It works dyadically where things touch each other in restricted economies, frequently destructively and violently; it exceeds every measure in the intimacy and responsiveness of touch. It marks the possibility of an ecology that interrupts the restrictions of economy with abundance in the earth, for the sake of the good.

Whatever comes from the good, every gift, is local, contingent: restricted economy. Yet every restriction is contingent; every limit is limited, including totality. The good gives its abundance in ideality, in heterogeneity and multiplicity, in every place, in every kind: restricted economy. General economy interrupts totality with abundance; locality and contingency interrupt totality. The giving interrupts the gathering of being, resists neutrality, recalls the abundance and heterogeneity of precious things that touch each other and respond as a call without fulfillment.

In this way, the good resists every binary opposition, resists every measure, not as another opposition or measure, and not as another place or thing. The good is not a good, neither good nor bad, nor good and bad, nor neuter, indifferent to good and evil. It is neither transcendent nor immanent, high nor low, inside nor outside, but interrupts the choice of either/or and neither/nor, the grip of the one or the other, the authority of "or," and "and," and "neither," and "both," of "I" and "we," all belonging to restricted economies. I speak in the name of the good of the exposure borne by every creature and thing within its limits to countless others, and the responsibilities they bear to resist the injustices of every limit by an interrupting movement. I call this movement the general economy of the good. I think of nature as the general and excessive circulation of local and contingent goods exposed to other individuals and kinds giving birth to the work they do in restricted, exchange economies.

I pursue the thought of restricted and general economies found in Bataille, *AS*. (See my *PE*, chaps. 5 and 6; my *GBGA*, chap. 7; and my *GT*, chap. 12.) I understand the crossing of restricted and general economy as the giving of the good, expressed by Plato in *Philebus* as the indefinite dyad: limit joined with unlimit; limit passing away into unlimit. (See nn. 1, 2, and 6.) I speak here of general economy after Spinoza as the abundance of kinds, endless flows and streams, foldings, unfoldings, and refoldings. Always expressive. Always *mimēsis*.

6. I speak of the good in memory of Plato, but where the good provides no measure. I speak of the good interrupting measure rather than of instrumentality and teleology, think of inclusion rather than of hierarchy and exclusion. I speak of the good remembering excesses of desire, think of excesses of love and care, of dyads touching each other intimately in the flesh, of violence and destruction, rather than of rule and law. I speak of the good rather than of power, think of moving toward and away, of touching, rather than of causation. I speak of the good rather than of freedom, think of the call of conscience to work, to touch, rather than of movements without limit. I speak of the good rather than of being, think of truth as exposure and of exposure as touch. I speak of the good rather than of God, think of circulating in general, excessive economy, giving without ground or law. All these renunciations belong to work, to judgment, as we strive to build and control. But

something in this striving summons us to know that building requires sacrifice, that judgment calls for endless vigilance, that touch demands response. I think of this something as the good, something that calls us to and interrupts ideality, makes judgment possible. I think of the good in memory of disaster.

7. Whoever "we" are, philosophical echoes of the good. See n. 4.

8. Levinas speaks "Against the Philosophy of the Neuter *[Neutre]*" (Levinas, *TI*, 298), breaking with the impersonal neutrality of Being in the name of the good. Irigaray speaks against nature "in the neuter" (Irigaray, *TG*, 141). My project works against neutrality, in more ways, perhaps, than either names.

9. I have spoken of the good, after Anaximander, as injustice, for which all works are restitutions: injustice without measure. (See n. 13.) Derrida speaks of it as justice (Derrida, *FL*). Plato speaks of it repeatedly. Again, the good is not a thing, a measure, does not divide, does not exclude, but gives all things to us, places them in circulation, exposes us to them, charges us to respond.

10. Blanchot speaks of the step *(pas)* not *(pas)* beyond *(au-delà)* (and not a step) *(Le pas au-delà)*. I speak of *beyond* as incessantly traversing this *not*, this impossibility. The limits of limits (as) (not) (beyond), anything but absolute, impossible to measure.

11. I understand *betrayal* in the double sense of violation and revelation, as *mimēsis*. Gifts betray the giving, betray the good, freeze and reveal its movements: restricted and general economy. See n. 5.

12. I speak of sonance in my *RR*: the ring of representation. Levinas speaks of *la gloire de l'Infini* (Levinas, *AÊ*, 230). The sacred is another story.

13. "Kata to chreōn didonai gar auta dikēn kai tisin allēlois tēs adikias." The entire fragment from Simplicius is canonically translated as: "Into those things from which existing things have their coming into being, their passing away, too, takes place, according to what must be; for they make reparation to one another for their injustice according to the ordinance of time, as he puts it in somewhat poetical language" (Simplicius *Phys.*, 24, 18 [DK 12 B 1]) (Robinson, *EGP*, 34).

14. I speak repeatedly of *the call of the good*. I hope that those who respond to this call hear multiple echoes and reverberations, for example Heidegger's *call (Ruf)* of conscience, the disclosedness of *Dasein* as constituted by state-of-mind, understanding, falling, and discourse, summoned to its ownmost Being-guilty (Heidegger, *BT*, 313–14). Yet conscience and discourse seem to me to reinstate the privilege of humanity in the gift of language, marks of Spirit, interrupted by the good; summoning and guilt seem to me to express ethicality and the good without exposure to the responsivities they evoke. Another example is *saying* in Levinas, understood as interruption, exposure, and proximity, reinstating subjectivity, a mark of Spirit. A third is the debt for restitution in memory of the injustices that Anaximander says compose the ordinance of time.

A profusion of other reverberations: I think of the call of music, echoes of wind and rain, movements of celestial spheres, the timbres of bodies touching. I think of the sounds of life; the tones of voices and instruments; songs, carols, melodies, and cries, shouts and yells; screams and bellows and roars, screeches and shrieks of animals and birds; I think of debts and obligations, of demands to act, to strive, brought by necessity to performances, to deeds, summoned for the sake of something beyond show; of events promised, heralded, greeted, or announced; of being taken to task, obligated and indebted, evoked, cited, served by decree under the law, in the name of judgment; of naming and designation, questioning and interrogation, of being asked to respond; I recall congregation and community, calls to mingle and gather, echoing the assembling of being and language in the name of *legein* (see n. 16); to augur, foretell, most of all, perhaps, to prophesy and to divine—despite the death of God. I think of calling to work, to task, to art, to labor, to master, demanding knowledge, skill, craft, *technē*, and more, always something more, *poiēsis* or beauty. I think of callers, those who call out, those who call to enter—guests, visitors, or strangers; another memory of gathering and community. Repeated calls of interruption: welcoming, giving, generosity.

The calling of the good is all of these, and more. Here it is *expression*, bodies squeezing, saying, meaning, touching, evoking responsiveness to touch, a responsiveness that is known to human beings as responsibility in the name of, for the sake of the good, where the good gives and calls but is nothing, no thing, no being; giving and calling as interruption. As *mimēsis*.

The calling of the good is exposure and expression, corporeal movements of general and restricted economy, always resisting neutrality.

15. See the footnote on p. xiii of this general preface. In order of their anticipated production, additional volumes are planned to be *The Gift of Property, The Gift of Self, The Gift of Memory, The Gift of Life, The Gift of Work, The Gift of Love, The Gift of Strangeness, The Gift of Sacredness, The Gift of Time, The Gift of Place, The Gifts of Earth, Air, Fire, and Water, The Gift of Peace, The Gift of Evil, The Gift of Law, The Gift of Authority, The Gift of Ecstasy*, and finally, perhaps, in retrospection, *The Gift of the Good*.

16. I refer to *legein* as the gathering of being as saying in truth. With Levinas I read this gathering as forgetting the good. Being in the neuter. (See my *GTGG*.) My entire project undertakes resistance to neutrality.

17. Wherever I speak of ethics or politics I hope to speak of them together as ethics|politics, or politics|ethics, circulating in intimate, diaphoric relation, interrupting each other.

Introduction

1. "By body I understand a mode that in a certain and determinate way expresses God's essence insofar as he is considered as an extended thing" (see I, P25C). (II, D1).

2. The project here in relation to kinds together with my overarching project in relation to the good may be understood as this resistance: challenging the neu-

trality of being gathered under the rule of language and truth. Being, language, truth, and kinds are not neutral, not given in the neuter. Take arms against neutrality! Interrupt its reign! Cherish the kinds of the earth!

It is imperative to avoid the negativity of this phrase: interrupt, resist, work against neutrality!: anti-, non-neutrality. The words in English that might express this relation positively, especially in relation to truth and judgment, have been contaminated in binary relations beyond repair: unprejudiced|prejudiced, unbiased|biased, independent|dependent, nonpartisan|partisan, unfree|free, partial|impartial; linked with fair|unfair, candid|deceitful, just|unjust, objective|subjective, and so on. Among these we must refuse to choose. In the name of the good.

A set of terms linked with those just mentioned may be retrieved from Descartes's emphasis on indifference of the will and freedom from emotion, two neutralities against which I would muster forceful resistance. I have in mind the following pairs: detached|committed, uninvolved|involved, indifferent|engaged, unattached|attached, dispassionate|passionate, and so on. Here the second term can be understood to carry an ethical force denied to the first. In being called to the good, in bearing ethical responsibilities, we know that we must be committed, engaged, involved, passionate, even enraptured, enchanted, ecstatic, immersed, intent, and so on..None of these escapes contamination and betrayal. Why should we imagine, with Descartes, that they might? Yet they resist neutrality.

With this explanation, I will speak of resistance to neutrality as engagement| commitment|rapture|enchantment|ecstasy. As betrayal, *mimēsis*. In memory of kinds. In propinquity. Tyranny and cherishment toward kinds. Many find the link impossible, some distasteful.

3. See the discussion of heterogeneity in chap. 13.

4. Profit and advantage, of self or kind, appears to be the basis of Spinoza's ethics at a certain level, that pertaining to good and evil. Of which he famously says, "As far as good and evil are concerned, they also indicate nothing positive in things, considered in themselves, nor are they anything other than modes of thinking, or notions we form because we compare things to one another" (Spinoza, *Ethics*, IV, Pref.); "just and unjust, sin and merit, are extrinsic notions, not attributes that explain the nature of the Mind. But enough of this" (IV, P37n2). I forego detailed examination here of Spinoza's words of dismissal—"enough of this *[sed de his satis]*"—concerning the difficult topic of moral distinctions in relation to the natural world. (See the discussion in my *GTGG*, chap. 6.) What would be enough to say on the topic of good and evil in a work of ethics? Unless what is said here of justice and injustice, good and evil, does not pertain to what Spinoza thinks of ethics, in relation to God or the good. The same words conclude Spinoza's *Political Treatise*, where he places women under the rule of men and—as Kristeva says repeatedly— excludes women from ethics, from a democratic state. (See the discussion in my *PE*, chap. 3.) Spinoza's concluding words are striking: "But if we further reflect upon human passions, how men, in fact, generally love women merely from the passion of lust, and esteem their cleverness and wisdom in proportion to the excellence of their beauty, and also how very ill-disposed men are to suffer the women they love to show any sort of favour to others, and other facts of this kind, we shall easily see

that men and women cannot rule alike without great hurt to peace. But of this enough" (Spinoza, *PT*, 387). Again enough. As if to speak on such a hateful subject were always too much. As if to speak on ranked distinctions by kind were always too much.

5. Humanity transfigured by the curse. See chap. 1, p. 21.

6. That is, (not) (beyond). See the general preface, n. 10.

7. Additional examples:

> The more I return to myself, the more I divest myself, under the traumatic effect of persecution, of my freedom as a constituted, willful, imperialist subject, the more I discover myself to be responsible; the more just I am, the more guilty I am. I am "in myself" through the others. (Levinas, *OB*, 112)

> Judgment is pronounced upon me in the measure that it summons me to respond. Truth takes form in this response to a summons. The summons exalts the singularity precisely because it is addressed to an infinite responsibility. *The infinity of responsibility denotes not its actual immensity, but a responsibility increasing in the measure that it is assumed*; duties become greater in the measure that they are accomplished. (Levinas, *TI*, 244)

8. It is not foreign to Judeo-Christianity that infinity might belong to individuals, for example in the sight of God. It is forcefully present in Levinas that in the relation of the one singular individual to the other something infinite pertains to subjectivity, infinitely resistant to neutrality. Subjectivity, here, is present in singulars, never in kinds. Allowing Levinas, whose understanding of the infinity of the good is unmatched, to pass toward another heinousness of kinds.

> But is not the diachrony of the inspiration and expiration separated by the instant that belongs to an animality? Would animality be the openness upon the beyond essence? But perhaps animality is only the soul's still being too short of breath. In human breathing, in its everyday equality, perhaps we have to already hear the breathlessness of an inspiration that paralyzes essence, that transpierces it with an inspiration by the other, an inspiration that is already expiration, that "rends the soul"! It is the longest breath there is, spirit. Is man not the living being capable of the longest breath in inspiration, without a stopping point, and in expiration, without return? (Levinas, *OB*, 181–82)

The thought that claims infinity for singularity denies it to animals, singular or in kind, denies it to all natural creatures save Man, possibly denies it to women, whose task is hospitality in the home. "The woman is the condition for recollection, the interiority of the Home, and inhabitation" (Levinas, *TI*, 155). Perhaps for men.

Yet what is giving, generosity, if not hospitality? Toward and from all kinds without exclusion.

Chapter 1

1. References to neutrality and neutralization, in Irigaray, Levinas, and Derrida, allude in part to Husserl's Cartesian insistence that one of the traits of consciousness "of highest importance" is the neutralization of belief, essential to the being of truth. "It cancels nothing, it 'performs' nothing, it is the conscious counterpart of all performance: its *neutralization*. It lies enclosed in every 'withholding of performance,' 'setting out of action,' 'bracketing,' 'leaving postponed,' and so 'having postponed,' 'thinking oneself into' the performance, or 'merely thinking' what is performed without 'helping to bring it about' " (Husserl, *I*, par. 109, p. 282). Such a neutralization may be the unconditioned denial of ethics, repeated in the insistent demand to neutralize. Neutralize! Or be damned. De-neutralize! And be damned. Without the risk, truth and being are impossible. Be damned in the abundance of kinds!

2. Discussed in the introduction, p. 9.

3. "I am afraid we are not rid of God because we still have faith in grammar" (Nietzsche, *TI*, 483; " *'Reason' in Philosophy*").

4. See my *PE* and chap. 11 here.

5. See my discussion in my *GTGG* of Carlo Sini's view of truth, after Heidegger, a reading I take to remain in gathering, in language, given over to neutrality. Nevertheless, enchantment still:

> the *event* itself . . . is not experienced at all as mystery. . . . What is its sense? *It is experienced as en-chantment.* Its sense is enchantment.
>
> The en-chantment *knows* nothing of truth and error. For the enchantment, there is neither "wonder" nor will to knowledge (and nothing to know), no *alētheia* (revelation of the concealed), no *lēthe* (concealment of the revealed). (Sini, *IT*, 148)

In my *GTGG*, this gathering, however rapturous, is repeatedly interrupted by the flight of bats who insist on a truth of kinds unassimilable to the Same. "The enchantment, instead, is precisely the experience of the Sameness of the Other" (p. 148). "For en-chantment, to participate means to be a part, to take part, to assume *the* part, in every sense and above all in the sense of being a part, finite and perfect, as *symbolon*. In our example, it means: to be part *of* moon, to take part *in it*, to take on its countenance. For this reason, as we said, the child's looking is *made of moon*" (p. 149). Nothing echoes here otherwise. Enchantment, rapture, ecstasy without engagement.

Mollusks here interrupt the flight of bats.

6. See especially my *GTEG*, chap. 11, where I review Wittig's nominal profusion of body parts, women and goddesses, living things and movements, natural inorganic things, violences and destructions.

7. See my *IR*, chap. 5, *PE*, chap. 10, and *GTEG*, chaps. 13–16.

8. "The nature of evil is that the characters of things are mutually obstructive. Thus the depths of life require a process of selection" (Whitehead, *PR*, 340); "In the temporal world, it is the empirical fact that process entails loss: the past is present under an abstraction. But there is no reason, of any ultimate metaphysical generality, why this should be the whole story" (p. 340). Never the whole story, never any final story, in the abundance of nature, in *our* abundance in nature, *our* abundance and *yours* and *theirs*. Yet still *we* weep at violence and evil, at death and loss, in nature's abundance.

9. I am told that Arabs speak of *assabiliyah* as excessive violence for one's kind.

10. Griffin elsewhere speaks of the life, the memories, of stones. "It is said that the close study of stone will reveal traces from fires suffered thousands of years ago. These would have been natural conflagrations, waves of flame burning through forests. This fire was not anomalous but part of the cycle of life" (Griffin, *CS*, 9). Living, remembering stones, disallowing the border we may hope to define between humans and animals, or animals that suffer and animals that do not, between living and dead, kinds that matter and kinds that do not. Under the curse, in abjection. Even those who care profoundly insist on drawing the line. "Those who want to be absolutely certain that they are not causing suffering will not eat mollusks either; but somewhere between a shrimp and an oyster seems as good a place to draw the line as any, and better than most" (Singer, *AL*, pp. 178–79). And what of living, remembering stones? And spiders, who like Penelope and countless women immemorial, weave and spin? What of those cast out and down, called the kinds that do not matter? Singer insists that we should not hunt the fawn, gather the pigs to slaughter, rope in the trout by line; but we may hunt and gather mollusks and stones. Perhaps we must bear responsibility for every gathering, the violence and domination of gathering. In life and truth.

I hold mollusks and mackerel in abeyance. They will join us later on our journeys, with cows and mules and women, insisting that they will not be forgotten. In the memories of stones. Other kinds resist the gathering of every kind into what is common, into *we* and *us*.

Chapter 2

1. Phaedrus describes him again as a stranger (Plato, *Phaedrus*, 230cd), always *xenos*.

2. Discussed in my *GTGG*, chap. 2.

3. Evoking something of Derrida's *PF*. See here chaps. 6 and 7.

4. See chap. 6, p. 97, for the full quotation.

5. For example:

> we bring a dispersed plurality under a single form, seeing it all together—
> the purpose being to define so-and-so, and thus to make plain whatever
> may be chosen as the topic for exposition. (Plato, *Phaedrus*, 265d)

> Wherefore the first speech divided off a part on the left, and continued to
> make divisions, never desisting until it discovered one particular
> part. . . . The other speech conducted us to the forms . . . which lay on the
> right-hand side, and upon discovering a type of love that shared its name
> with the other but was divine, displayed it to our view and extolled it as
> the source of the greatest goods that can befall us. (266b)

6. See the discussions of *Phaedrus* in my *IR*, chap. 9 and *GTGG*, chap. 1.

7. The determination of forms has a definite place.

> What I wanted to discover at present, my dear Protarchus, was not which
> art or which form of knowledge is superior to all others in respect of being
> the greatest or the best or the most serviceable, but which devotes its
> attention to precision, exactness, and the fullest truth, though it may be
> small and of small profit—that is what we are looking for at this moment.
> (Plato, *Philebus*, 58bc)

Perhaps holding chaos at bay.

> SOCRATES: Do you want me, may I ask, to give way like a porter jostled
> and knocked about by the crowd, to fling open the doors and allow every sort
> of knowledge to stream in, the inferior mingling with the pure?
> PROTHARCHUS: I don't really see, Socrates, what harm one would suffer
> by taking all those other sorts of knowledge, providing one had the first
> sort.
> SOCRATES: Then I am to allow the whole company to stream in and be
> gathered together in a splendid Homeric mingling of the waters? (Plato,
> *Philebus*, 62de)

See the discussion of *Philebus* in my *PE*, chap. 5.

8. Moreover, young Socrates is present here (Plato, *Sophist*, 218b).

9. See my *PE*.

10. Omitted by Cornford in his translation. Hamilton and Cairns borrow Jowett's
translation. We might wonder, if Cornford does not think the method worth translating, why we should think it worth reading.

11. See my *GTGG*, chap. 2.

12. He speaks of this in both *Theaetetus* and *Phaedo*. "Try to explain what knowledge is. Never say it is beyond your power; it will not be so, if heaven wills and you take courage" (Plato, *Theaetetus*, 150d); "We must not let it enter our minds that there may be no validity in argument" (*Phaedo*, 90d–91b).

13. Property, possession, and propriety are the subjects of the next volume projected in this series, *The Gift of Property: Having the Good*. I understand kinds and property to be inseparable, proper kinds, not only in the West.

14. I have spoken in my *GTGG* of gathering truth, where gathering is something other than owning and possessing. Here I would wonder if gathering under the sign of *legein*, being gathered into language as truth, is assembling to own and possess. Owning and possessing, perhaps gathering, repudiate the neutrality of truth without the care, the debt, given from the good, the responsibility for resisting that neutrality.

15. See here chap. 3.

Chapter 3

1. Something of this appears explicitly in Whitehead, whose actual entities are, like monads. "the final real things of which the world is made up" (Whitehead, *PR*, 18); "The final facts are, all alike, actual entities; and these actual entities are drops of experience, complex and interdependent" (p. 18). Actual entities are both singulars and kinds.

> An actual entity cannot be described, even inadequately, by universals; because other actual entities do enter into the description of any one actual entity. Thus every so-called "universal" is particular in the sense of being just what it is, diverse from everything else; and every so-called "particular" is universal in the sense of entering into the description of any one actual entity. (p. 48)

The uncontainable immeasurability of the singular is expressed as an infinite multiplicity of a kind that can have indefinitely many instances. Nothing in the kind contains the abundance of its exemplifications. Nothing in the individual contains the abundance of its variety. In this sense, individual and kind are both collective, collectives of collectives. Whitehead expresses this collectivity in relation to actual entities and the societies that compose their environments.

> [A] society is, for each of its members, an environment with some elements of order in it, . . .
> But there is no society in isolation. Every society must be considered with its background of a wider environment of actual entities, . . . every society requires a social background, of which it is itself a part. In refer-

ence to any given society the world of actual entities is to be conceived as forming a background in layers of social order. (p. 90)

Infinite multiplicity and collectivity inhabit the constitution of actual entities and societies, collapsing the distinction between singular and kind, recognizing kind|ness in the nature of things.

2. I allude to *The Prose of the World*, discussed in the next chapter. I am speaking of *kind|ness* and *mimēsis*.

Chapter 4

1. First described by Foucault in terms of "the double relation of the representation to its model and to its sovereign" (p. 16); such that "it is not possible for the pure felicity of the image ever to present in a full light both the master who is representing and the sovereign who is being represented" (p. 16); later on the verge of disappearance: "If those arrangements were to disappear as they appeared, . . . then one can certainly wager that man would be erased, like a face drawn in sand at the edge of the sea" (p. 387). I have explored many of these themes elsewhere. See my *RR*, especially chap. 3.

The arrangements to which Foucault alludes pertain specifically to language: "Since man was constituted at a time when language was doomed to dispersion, will he not be dispersed when language regains its unity?" (p. 386). Here my restrictions may become more violent. Can I exclude language, words, from my discussion of order when Foucault describes the topic as the excesses of language? I can exclude language no more than I can exclude the subject of representation. Yet perhaps the exclusion is less a violence than a postponement and interruption, another gesture toward *mimēsis*. For I fear a certain violence of language, a certain dominance of words, marked by Hegel as the movement of spirit—Man—unknown to animals and, perhaps, to women and other lesser humans. I hold this linguistic mark of human spirit in abeyance.

2. In the four great forms of convenience, emulation, analogy, and sympathy.

Those things are "convenient" which come sufficiently close to one another to be in juxtaposition; . . . (Foucault, *OT*, 18)

There is something in the emulation of the reflection and the mirror: it is the means whereby things scattered through the universe can answer one another. (p. 19)

Through [analogy], all the figures in the whole universe can be drawn together. (p. 20)

Sympathy is an instance of the *Same* so strong and so insistent that it will not rest content to be merely one of the forms of likeness; . . .
    This is why sympathy is compensated for by its twin, antipathy. (pp. 23–24)

3. Of *Difference and Repetition* and *Logic of Sense*.

4. Something we have seen in Leibniz. Foucault is mindful of Pseudo-Dionysius, Johannes Scotus Erigena, and Hugh of St. Victor, who understood beauty in terms of a world filled with endless reminders and symbols of the divine. Things reflect, refer to, allude to each other; the world together with human works is filled with symbols and allegories. Everything answers to everything else, a beauty which everywhere reveals the hand of God in the world as divine maker, poet, and creator. Eternity, infinity, and perfection shine everywhere as beauty. Such a view of beauty cannot neutrally be said to be the same riveted onto itself.

5. The burden of my *GTEG*.

6. I am alluding in particular to my *RR*, where I speak of representation as the work, the ergonality, of nature. Now I would speak of expression, after Spinoza, understanding expression to pertain to things everywhere, where they touch, where they compose themselves and others in aggregates and kinds. All expressive, representational, unable to be contained, exceeding every limit.

These uncontainable movements are expressed corporeally in my *GTEG*. Here I mean to express them as movements in kinds.

7. Linnaeus and Jonston define "a descriptive order for natural history": "According to this order, every chapter dealing with a given animal should follow the following plan: name, theory, kind, species, attributes, use, and, to conclude, *Litteraria*" (Foucault, *OT*, 130). "The documents of this new history are . . . spaces in which things are juxtaposed: . . . in which, stripped of all commentary, of all enveloping language, creatures present themselves one beside another, their surfaces visible, grouped according to their common features, and thus already virtually analysed, and bearers of nothing but their own individual names" (p. 131). Individuals bear their proper names. Beyond that are kinds, always grouped, ordered, aggregated, classified. Knowledge is analysis; analysis is classification; classification is structure. All restrictions and exclusions, violent, violations. Anything but neutral.

8. Rolston asks us to respect and cherish the beauty and value of what there is, what nature has wrought, species and kinds: "In one sense, nature is indifferent to mountains, rivers, fauna, flora, forests, and grasslands. But in another sense, nature has bent toward making and remaking these projects, millions of kinds, for several billion years" (Rolston, *EEVDNW*, 81). Even here, this striking sense of cherishment of kinds can be given over to rule: "The projective system is fundamentally the most valuable phenomenon of all, though humans are its most valuable products. A shallow reading of 'valuable' here means that *humans*, when they arrive, are *able to value* the system out of which they have emerged. A deeper reading means that the *system is able to project values*, among which are humans" (Rolston, *EE*, 225). Another reading might challenge the alleged superiority of human beings in both senses, and more, might challenge the sense that any system, human or ecological, is to be preserved because it is there, good because it has arrived, resisting the future. Including wildness, wild individuals and kinds. I pursue a different

possibility, in which the things and kinds of the world evoke endless questions of fulfillment and disaster, endless questions of generation and transformation, endlessly interrupting every value. They do so in proximity and exposure, every individual and kind, facing abundance.

Another reading still might challenge the goal of value. See the discussion in this chapter after this interruption.

9. In human life, by now everywhere in the earth, expression and representation—*mimēsis*—appear in culture as cultural kinds. Genes are biological replicators; memes are cultural replicators: "unit[s] of cultural transmission, or . . . of *imitation*" (Dawkins, *SG*, 206). Transmission and replication as mobility and transformation. *Mimēsis* as repetition in endless deviation; representation as endless misrepresentation (see my *RR*, especially chap. 3). Natural selection is repetition through deviation, endless scramblings of codes of representation to promote the same kind—always different. Natural and cultural selection. Nature's *mimēsis*, iterability. (See here chap. 6.)

Natural and cultural selection express abundance as the excesses in every ordered system whereby it will undergo transformations, stabilized by adaptive strategies. General economy restricted to do work. As biological species and inorganic kinds, all undergoing transformations in producing kinds. Expressed by Whitehead as the expressiveness in every kind or society:

> [T]he problem for Nature is the production of societies which are "structured" with a high "complexity," and which are at the same time "unspecialized." In this way, intensity is mated with survival. . . .
>
> There are two ways in which structured societies have solved this problem. Both ways depend on that enhancement of the mental pole, which is a factor in intensity of experience. One way is by eliciting a massive average objectification of a nexus, while eliminating the detailed diversities of the various members of the nexus in question. This method, in fact, employs the device of blocking out unwelcome detail. . . .
>
> The second way of solving the problem is by an initiative in conceptual prehensions, i.e., in appetition. . . .
>
> Structured societies in which the second mode of solution has importance are termed "living." . . .
>
> In accordance with this doctrine of "life," the primary meaning of "life" is the origination of conceptual novelty—novelty of appetition. (Whitehead, *PR*, 101–2)

Biological diversity as natural diversity as structure: abundance as expression as kinds. Always under the curse of exclusion. Humanity does not own the curse. Abundance is given under the curse, in kinds. Still abundance, exceeding the limits of every kind. Organic and inorganic.

10. Another view on nature's values is expressed in n. 8. Here value falls under the curse.

Chapter 5

1. Deleuze and Guattari speak of *se rabattre sur,* falling back and down, folding and refolding. I read this phrase in memory of and resistance to *relever* and *aufheben.* We, and things, and kinds, and more, all fall back down upon themselves rather than rising beyond themselves, still preserving within the falling that from which we fall away. I understand becoming in kind in terms of *se rabattre sur,* becoming—deterritorialization—that always falls back and down, refolds itself into reterritorialization. To become in kind is to arise and to fall back, folding and refolding into kinds.

2. See chap. 3, p. 56.

3. See my *GTEG,* chap. 9.

4. Reminding us that Singer denies that he has any interest in pets or cute and cuddly animals (Singer, *AL,* x–xi). Only wild or daunting animals will do. Another line drawn in the sand.

5. For example, "Do not imitate a dog" (p. 274).

6. See the introduction here, pp. 8–9, 14–15, 19–22.

7. And Foucault, who concludes his responses to "Questions on Geography" with the following words: "Tactics and strategies deployed through implantations, distributions, demarcations, control of territories and organisations of domains which could well make up a sort of geopolitics. . . . One theme I would like to study in the next few years is that of the army as a matrix of organisation and knowledge; one would need to study the history of the fortress, the 'campaign,' the 'movement,' the colony, the territory. Geography must indeed necessarily lie at the heart of my concerns" (Foucault, *QG,* 77). The army and perhaps philosophy. The geography of truth. Perhaps Foucault always had his thoughts on geography, on borders, from within archaeology and genealogy.

8. Discussed in the next chapter.

9. Discussed in chap. 7.

10. Discussed in chap. 12.

Chapter 6

1. For the full quotation, see chap. 1, p. 13.

2. See the introduction, n. 8.

3. See my *GTGG.*

4. See chap. 1, p. 22, for the full quotation.

5. See my *GTEG*, chap. 11.

6. Something similar can be found in Butler:

This exclusionary matrix by which subjects are formed requires a domain of abject beings, those who are not yet "subjects," but who form the constitutive outside to the domain of the subject. (Butler, *BM*, 3)

[T]he very concept of nature needs to [be] rethought, for the concept of nature has a history, and the figuring of nature as the blank and lifeless page, as that which is, as it were, always already dead, is decidedly modern, linked perhaps to the emergence of technological means of domination. (p. 4)

Matter, materiality, corporeality, bodies—*nature*—are coded in discourse and language, subject to the workings of power, to histories of domination and abjection, oppression and exclusion. Nothing—including nature and natural kinds—is (for human beings, at least) "outside language," outside the codes and coding, the repetitions, that constitute the discourse of kinds. Nor, perhaps, is anything "inside." Language and materiality are inside and outside, anything but neutral.

7. I relegate *Geschlecht* in German and *race, kin,* and *kind* in English to a long footnote though they deserve extended consideration. Perhaps this entire project.

What do the words *Schlag, schlagen* mean? Hermann Paul's *Deutsches Wörterbuch* lists six principal areas of meaning for *der Schlag*: for the verb *schlagen* it cites six "proper" senses and ten "distant" meanings. Deriving from the Old High German and Gothic *slahan* (from which the English word "slay" also derives) and related to the modern German word *schlachten*, "to slaughter," *schlagen* means to strike a blow, to hit or beat. A *Schlag* may be the stroke of a hand, of midnight, or of the brain; the beating of wings or of a heart. *Schlagen* may be done with a hammer or a fist. God does it through his angels and his plagues; a nightingale does it with his song. One of the most prevalent senses of *schlagen* is to mint or stamp a coin. *Der Schlag* may therefore mean a particular coinage, imprint, or type: a horse dealer might refer to *einem gute Schlag Pferde*. It is in virtue of this sense that *Schlag* forms the root of . . . *das Geschlecht*. Paul lists three principal meanings for *Geschlecht* (Old High German *gislahti*). First, it translates the Latin word *genus*, being equivalent to *Gattung*: *das Geschlecht* is a group of people who share a common ancestry, especially if they constitute a part of the hereditary nobility. Of course, if the ancestry is traced back far enough we may speak of *des menschliche Geschlecht*, "humankind." Second, *das Geschlecht* may mean one generation of men and women who die to make way for a succeeding generation. Third, there are male and female *Geschlechter*, and *Geschlecht* becomes the root of many words for the things males and females have and do for the sake of the first two meanings: *Geschlechts-glied* or *-teil*, the genitals; *-trieb*, the sex drive; *-verkehr*, sexual intercourse; and so on. (Krell, *IM*, 165; quoted in Derrida, *G2*, 191–92)

Under the heading of *Geschlecht*, Derrida finds these links, echoes, and resonances, reflected in genealogy, traced in blood, as we have seen from the beginning in every classification of kinds.

Also in English, making up for the absence of gender. Paraphrased schematically from the *OED*, expressing the complexity, heterogeneity, and impurity of race, kin, and kind, all written into the language in blood.

KIN

I. Old English—kin, kynne; produce, beget; related to *genos*: generation:

1. family, race, blood relations; common descent; offspring, progeny, posterity; a group in each stage of descent; genealogy; the ancestral stock or race, family, kind, kindred; by birth or descent; kinsfolk, relatives, related by blood; kith and kin; kinsman, relative; quality of being related by birth, descent, blood, kinship, sanguinity;

2. class, group, division; large natural group of plants, animals, race; class with common attributes, species, sort, kind;

3. gender;

4. blood ties, relation; close relation, blood;

II. Old English—cine:

1. crack, chink, slit, fissure, crack in skin.

KIND

I. Old English—gecynde:

1. birth, descent, origin; birthright, birth position; place by birth, birthright; natural properties, rights, possessions, position; natural quality, disposition, nature; something's own nature, naturally, of itself; what is natural, especially sexual; nature in general, abstract, the course of things; by nature, in kind; natural state, form, condition; natural property, quality, characteristic; gender, kin; sexual organs, semen; natural, proper way, action, manner; character determining class or membership, specific qualities;

2. class, group, division of things; race, natural group of animals or plants with common origin, descent; class of same sex; subdivision of race, common descent, family, class, tribe; offspring, brood, progeny, descendants; generation; descent, genealogy; family, ancestral race, stock; class of individuals or objects with common properties; each element of Eucharist; kind of—plurality; in kind—proper payment, exchange, repayment, restitution.

II. Old English—gecynde:

1. natural, native; implanted by nature, innate, inherent; proper, appropriate, fitting; belonging by right of birth, descent, inheritance; native (country or language); lawful, rightful (heir); native, character, status, by birth; related by kinship, family, people;

2. of good birth, nature, disposition; well-born, well-bred, gentle, generous; good kind, good of kind, good qualities; well-disposed, gentle, sympathetic, benevolent, generous, liberal; favorably disposed, bearing good will; benevolence, friendliness; affectionate, loving, fond, intimate; agreeable, pleasant, winsome; grateful, thankful;

3. kindly.

RACE

I. Old English—*ræse*:

1. run, running, rush; course, path, way; journey, voyage; regular movement, daily movement, deviation; course of time, course of events, course of history, course of life; impact, blow; current, flow, movement of water; portion of time or space, space of time, a while; reach, channel of river; path of shuttle in weaving; circular path of horse in driving machinery; space of revolution of wheel;

   , 2. competition of running, riding, sailing, contest of speed, time; bet on competition;

3. competition, match, bout, conflict, contest, event, game, marathon, meet, meeting, regatta, round robin, run, tournament, tourney;

4. speed, flash, zoom, sprint, dash, gallop, jog, run, speed.

II. French *rasse* (1512), Italian *razza*:

1. group of persons, animals, plants of common descent, origin; offspring, posterity, children, descendants, breeding; generation; house, family, kin; tribe, nation, people, common stock; several tribes, common ethnic stock; one of great divisions of humanity; breed, stock of animals, plants, subspecies; stud, herd; genus, species, kind, variety; one of great divisions of living creatures; class, kind—animate or inanimate (race of heaven, race of gods); stock, family, class, kin; belonging to people or stock; qualities, dispositions of kind; set, class, group in common; one of sexes; line, descent, of office; one of three kingdoms of nature; class of wine; speech, writing, style, manner;

2. people, breed, clan, class, family, household, relatives, stock, tribe, nation;

3. cut, slit, mark, scratch (see verb).

III. Old English: *Rase*:

4. heart, liver, lungs of calf;

5. mark down face of horse, dog;

6. rhizome of ginger;

7. of white in brick (see 5);

8. scrape, shave; ships low in water;

9. measure (vs. full measure);

10. to run a race, compete; to move swiftly, animate or inanimate; bring off (as in bout); to make move swiftly; to lose by racing; to suspend before racing;

11. to impart nature of parent to offspring;

12. to scratch, tear, cut, slash; ornamentally; cut a way, pierce, penetrate; slash with tusks (boars); scrape out, erase; alter by erasure; level with ground (raze);

13. to tear, scratch, pluck.

Class, kin, kind, race, stock, nation, gender; linked with nature and humanity; bound to the battle, the stamp, the trace, and its erasure: *eidos, genos, mimēsis.* Supplemented by tearing and the contest of life and being, as if always over others in their kind. Resisted in kind for the sake of the good, in immeasurable abundance.

Kin, kind, race. Not just words. Anything but neutral.

8. See my *GTGG.*

9. See my *RR*, chap. 8; *IJ*, chap. 7; *PE*, chap. 7; *GB*, Int. and chap. 6; *GTGG*, int.

10. "[A]ls Hören der Stimme des Freundes, den jedes Dasein bei sich trägt" (Heidegger, *SZ*, p. 163).

11. As Derrida suggests. See the next chapter, p. 113.

12. See Derrida, *SM*, where he takes up these questions explicitly in relation to Marx.

13. More on *mimēsis* in the next two chapters.

Chapter 7

1. Further examples:

> The origin of the call that comes from nowhere, an origin in any case that is not yet a divine or human "subject," institutes a responsibility that is to be found at the root of all ulterior responsibilities (moral, juridical, political), and of every categorical imperative. To say of this responsibility, and even of this friendship, that it is not "human," no more than it is "divine," does not come down to saying that it is simply inhuman. (Derrida, *EW*, 276)

> [D]oes the animal hear the call that originates responsibility? does it question? Moreover, can the call heard by *Dasein* come originally to or from the animal? Is there an advent of the animal? Can the voice of the friend be that of an animal? Is friendship possible for the animal or between animals? Like Aristotle, Heidegger would say: no. Do we have a responsibility toward the living in general? The answer is still "no," and this may be because the question is formed, asked in such a way that the answer must necessarily be "no" according to the whole canonized or hegemonic discourse of Western metaphysics or religions, including the most original forms that this discourse might assume today, for example, in Heidegger or Levinas.
>
> I am not recalling this in order to start a support group for vegetarianism, ecologism, or for the societies for the protection of animals— which is something I might also want to do, and something which would lead us to the center of the subject. By following this necessity, I am trying

especially to underscore the *sacrificial* structure of the discourses to which I am referring. I don't know if "sacrificial structure" is the most accurate expression. In any case, it is a matter of discerning a place left open, in the very structure of these discourses (which are also "cultures") for a noncriminal putting to death. Such are the executions of ingestion, incorporation, or introjection of the corpse. (p. 278)

If we are to respond to the call of animals and other creatures of the earth to be treated with responsibility, we must understand and underscore the sacrificial structure—eating, consuming, devouring, destroying, stockpiling, making our own— that constitutes our culture as Human.

2. He describes six rules of disciplinary mechanisms:

> *The rule of minimum quantity.*
> *The rule of sufficient ideality.*
> *The rule of lateral effects.*
> *The rule of perfect certainty.*
> *The rule of common truth.*
> *The rule of optimal specification.* (Foucault, *DP*, 94–98)

3. See the discussion here in chap. 1, pp. 19–25.

4. See Milton, *RMDED*, who argues that prohibitions concerning what may or may not be eaten mark cultural borders between Us and Them, Real Men and others. Sacrifice and curse always define The Human abjectly.

5. See the discussion in chap. 12.

6. No beautiful death. See Lyotard, *D*, Result.

Chapter 8

1. I am alluding to Foucault's suggestion that value is the sacrifice of goods within nature's generosity. See here chap. 4, pp. 104–7.

2. Other guidelines to plenishment in the earth can be found in chaps. 10 and 14.

3. See chap. 6, n. 6, for the genealogy and kindlred|ness of race, kin, and kind.

4. The full quotation:

> A black feminist ideology, first and foremost, thus declares the visibility of black women. It acknowledges the fact that two innate and inerasable traits, being both black and female, constitute our special status in American society. Second, black feminism assets self-determination as essential.... Third, a black feminist ideology fundamentally challenges the interstructure of the oppressions of racism, sexism, and classism both in the dominant society and within movements for liberation....

Finally, a black feminist ideology presumes an image of black women as powerful, independent subjects. By concentrating on our multiple oppressions, scholarly descriptions have confounded our ability to discover and appreciate the ways in which black women are not victims. (King, *MJMC*, 312)

5. Dropping the diaphoric bar. Kindredness and kindness toward the abundance of kinds in the earth.

6. See the introduction here, pp. 8–9. Universality and exaltation in Wittig express what in kinds is more than common, resist owning and possessing the identities of kinds even by their members as a claim of privilege and authority.

7. Catharine MacKinnon argues, as I read her, that in a society organized around the heterosexual domination of women, women get it coming and going among all the practices of liberation. I read Gates as arguing that something similar appears in postsubject theory: another view in which blacks get it coming and going. In the name of universality.

8. Balibar calls racism a humanism, with a qualification. I recall the humanism of sacrifice.

[R]acism is unquestionably *a philosophy of history*, and, above all, *this philosophy is itself a humanism.* . . . I mean a theoretical humanism.

Racism is a philosophy of history, or better yet a historiosophy, by which I mean a philosophy that *merges* with an interpretation of history, but makes history the consequence of a "secret" hidden and revealed to men about their own nature and birth; a philosophy that *reveals the invisible cause* of the destiny of societies and peoples, ignorance of which accounts for degeneration or for the historical power of evil. (Balibar, *PU*, 287)

Chapter 9

1. Translated by Van Den Abbeele as "Reality entails the differend") (Lyotard, *DPD*, p. 50). I take Lyotard to mean that nature, reality, is made up of *différends*, of strange, heterogeneous, and multiple kinds.

2. Before the rise of the nation state, Africa intimately knew the presence of strangers.

For the Tallensi, the status of the stranger who comes in from outside their society varies with time and circumstances. He may be regarded as a virtual enemy at the outset; but may at once or later be accepted as a welcome or at least tolerated guest. To be able to stay permanently, he must be given status in the host's domestic group and be thus brought into the community's kinship sphere or into the quasi-kinship sphere of adherence to a common ancestor cult. (Fortes, *S*, 233)

Strangers in Africa, like strangers elsewhere, were and are exceptionally strange, touching the abundance of boundaries marked as strangeness.

> Strangers in African societies, like strangers everywhere, are as socially ambiguous as the word "stranger" implies. Alien, intruder, interloper, foreigner, *novus homo*, newcomer, immigrant, guest, outsider, outlander, and so on—all are convenient labels that social groups habitually apply to persons who, by reasons of custom, language, or social role, stand on the margin of society. (Shack and Skinner, *SAS*, 1)

At the margins, inside and out, of every social kin and kind, strangers mark the ambiguity and impurity of every boundary, every threshold. In Africa, however, expressing the liminality of boundaries, multiple impurities in every purification, liminal rituals exist to bring strangers into the kinship sphere.

> Africa is replete with examples of individuals and groups who formed settled communities of occupational specialists in societies other than their own. . . . It is not inconceivable that in the formative stages of communities of African strangers, the subjects were, to use Turner's phrase, "liminal entities," or better still, "liminaries." (Levine, *SAS*, 40)

At least did so before colonialism.

> [I]n so many of the new states of Africa and Asia following independence. In many instances, Guests have been redefined as Intruders; Newcomers of long standing have been turned into Marginal Men; and most dramatically, Sojourners have been transformed into Inner Enemies, and subjected to harassment, expulsion, and even assassination. (Levine, *SAS*, 35)

Throughout this remarkable history of limins, thresholds, and outsiders, women are always strangers. And others. Exogamy insists on strangeness in blood.

> [A] newly married wife is described as a "stranger" *(saan)* in her husband's house. So, it is said, she must be treated with special consideration. . . . By degrees, as she becomes accustomed *(malem)* to her husband's family, and in particular to her mother-in-law, as she becomes incorporated in its economic and ritual activities, perhaps in some months, perhaps only after she has borne a child, and thus becomes a mother in her conjugal family, she stops being regarded as a *saan* and becomes a member of the family *(yidem)*. Nevertheless, there is always a trace of feeling that a wife is never wholly free from stranger-hood. (Fortes, *S*, 230)

A wife is never wholly free from strangeness. And perhaps a husband, a man, and others. If all are strangers, some have strangeness visited upon them, defining them as intruders, outsiders even where dwelling on the inside, subject to harassment, expulsion, and death. A profound consequence of post-colonialism, for some. But perhaps always a possibility, a lived reality, for others.

As if the strangeness of strangers in their kind posed fundamental questions of ethics and politics, as if the ethical possibility of exposure to strangeness opened the possibility of a politics that respected strangers; as if proximity, vulnerability, and exposure were the prevailing conditions of life and being.

3. As Spinoza says, we do not know what bodies can do. To which the third volume of this project is devoted. See my *GTEG*. Here, I speak less of what bodies can do than of what kinds may be and to the responsibilities they evoke.

4. I retain the French to mark the strangeness of *le différend*, at least in English.

5. Discussed here in chap. 6.

6. And wildness. See chaps. 4 and 12, p. 76 and p. 200.

7. Again and again, most recently in relation to HIV and AIDS.

8. See my *GTEG*. Here the emphasis is on the strangeness of kinds.

9. In chap. 13.

Chapter 10

1. A pragmatist ethics depends on calculation and reflection in the midst of contingency and variability. In ethical terms, this means acknowledging disaster.

> Ends are, in fact, literally endless, forever coming into existence as new activities occasion new consequences. "Endless ends" is a way of saying that there are no ends—that is no fixed self-enclosed finalities. (Dewey, *HNC*, 232)
>
> The object thought of [desired as good] and the outcome *never* agree. (p. 252).

Habits and principles must change with changing circumstances and outcomes. On one side, this means openness to contingency and variation. On the other side, it means responding to the harm that precious goods and values bring to pass. The good imagined and sought is never the good achieved, sometimes with disastrous results. Dewey's pragmatism may not reach far enough toward sacrificing sacrifice, may not be vigilant enough toward the disastrous possibilities of its own reflections. If any ethical view has been so vigilant.

2. Some critical observations:

> [O]ne of the most important features of the whole Earth image is the vantage point from which it is obtained: from the outside. We have left the Earth in order to get a better view, in order to see it all at once. (Garb, *PE*, 265)

> We were once surrounded by our world, experiencing it with all our senses, participating in it with devout attention to its details—but we have left the cathedral. (p. 266)

I would recall Descartes's great architectural projects and Kant's tower that fails to reach heaven. Cathedrals tower before us as well as around us. Perhaps the whole earth image is another grand project encompassing a totality spread before us. God's view, reminding us of Leibniz (see chap. 3, pp. 52–57). "We now possess . . . the 'God's eye view' of Earth, where nothing is hidden" (p. 266). Or think we do.

> Feminists (and postmodernists in general) have become wary of complete pictures, of single unifying viewpoints from which everything can be seen all at once. (p. 269)

> Yet the whole Earth image was brought to light and is still being used by those who rebel *against* what is destructive in the Western relationship to the Earth: by peace activists, environmentalists, and proponents of a new Earth-based spirituality. . . . The image, they claim, shows us the incredible beauty of the Earth. (p. 275)

We rebel against domination and destruction with a unified figure of beauty and abundance. I respond that beauty and abundance are anything but unified, anything but total, pure. Recalling the prose of the world, without God. Everything mirroring everything else, expressing the totality of God's love for the world, everywhere crossing, expressing, touching, responding to other things, in abundance without totality, an abundance of heterogeneities and impurities, of kinds. In kinds. Endless exposure and responsibility.

3. Reminding us, perhaps, of Derrida's words on the sublime: "why is the sublime large and not small?" (Derrida, *TP*, 136); why great rather than trivial? Why is excess anything at all, excess of value in the very large and the very small, and everywhere between. Impure.

4. Anticipating chap. 14. With exuberance!

Chapter 11

1. From *The Homeric Hymns*, trans. Thelma Sargent (New York: Norton), 1973. p. 79.

2. See chap. 2, n. 13.

3. See chap. 8, p. 135.

Chapter 12

1. See chap. 4, pp. 104–7, for the full quotation and extended discussion.

2. Reading Beauvoir, *SS*, as insisting on freedom.

3. Understanding this death as sacrificing sacrificing against any absolute authority.

4. And tribal peoples have been repeatedly denied rights under law.

5. I wonder how it is possible to present a rigorous argument except from premises taken for granted in relation to rights and values—premises Serres hopes to challenge. Historically, arguments to establish ethical premises are conflicted and controversial, anything but rigorous. Perhaps what we need, as many ecologists argue, is a fable that may enable us to break away from the limits of our understanding of ethical arguments.

6. This ambiguity toward finality persists in Kant where he recognizes the supreme finality of nature as culture: humanity as freedom.

> [M]an is the final purpose of creation, since without him the chain of mutually subordinated purposes would not be complete as regards its ground. Only in man, and only in him as a subject of morality, do we meet with unconditioned legislation in respect of purposes, which therefore alone renders him capable of being a final purpose, to which the whole of nature is teleologically subordinated. (Kant, *CJ*, §84, p. 286)

> The production of the aptitude of a rational being for arbitrary purposes in general (consequently in his freedom) is *culture*. Therefore, culture alone can be the ultimate purpose which we have cause for ascribing to nature in respect to the human race (not man's earthly happiness or the fact that he is the chief instrument of instituting order and harmony in irrational nature external to himself). (Kant, *CJ*, §83, p. 281)

He ranks the natural world accordingly, and the human world, cultural and political. Another fascism, in the name of humanism and culture. "But all culture is not adequate to this ultimate purpose of nature" (p. 281); "Skill cannot be developed in the human race except by means of inequality among men" (p. 282). Domination is the condition of freedom, under law. "Splendid misery" (p. 282).

7. No doubt these words ring differently in English from their French counterparts.

8. Kant agrees with Hume that "The Negroes of Africa have by nature no feeling that rises above the trifling" (Kant, *OBS*, 110). In Hume's words: "I am apt to suspect the negroes to be naturally inferior to the whites. There scarcely ever was

a civilized nation of that complexion, nor even any individual eminent either in action or speculation. No ingenious manufactures amongst them, no arts, no sciences" (Hume, *ONC*, 252n).

9. The following selections are from Oelschlaeger, *Postmodern Environmental Ethics*, representative examples of a possibility.

10. And with King for whom the natural is absolutely social. See here chap. 11.

11. Also:

> The late John Fire Lame Deer . . . comments . . . that although the whites . . . imagine earth, rocks, water, and wind to be dead, they nevertheless "are very much alive." . . .
> . . . "You ask stones for aid to find things which are lost or missing. Stones can give warning of an enemy, of approaching misfortune." Butterflies, coyotes, grasshoppers, eagles, owls, deer, especially elk and bear all talk and possess and convey power. "You have to listen to all these creatures, listen with your mind. They have secrets to tell." (Callicott, *TAIWEA*, 200; quoted from Erodes, *LD*, 108–9, 101, 124)

12. See my *RR*, especially chap. 1.

Chapter 13

1. Discussed in chap. 9.

2. See chap. 2, n. 13.

3. I am speaking of the principle of ontological parity, which I have written of throughout most of my career. I now understand it as an ethical principle. As does Buddhism. As I understand Buddhism.

4. Explicated as follows:

> Monks, there is a not-born, a no-become, a not-made, a not-compounded. Monks, if that unborn, not-become, not-made, not-compounded were not, there would be apparently no escape from this here that is born, become, made, compounded.
> But since, monks, there is an unborn . . . therefore the escape from this here is born, become . . . is apparent. (*Udēna: Verses of Uplift*; in Woodward, *MAPC*, 98)

> The passage gives a clear indication that reality has two facets lodged in the selfsame ground of existence (p. 235).

Endless facets, I would say, abundant kinds.

5. In the beautiful language of the texts themselves:

Nagarjuna expressed what this insight means for a *bodhisattva*.

> The essential nature of all bodhisattvas is a great
> compassionate heart, and all living beings are the
> object of its compassion.

Shantideva put it like this:

> I should dispel the misery of others
> Because it is suffering, just like my own,
> And I should benefit others
> Because they are living things, just like myself
> . . . .
> I hope for nothing in return.
> (Batchelor, *ESS*, 6; quoted from Nagarjuna, *ES*; Shantideva, *B*)

6. In Korean as well as Greek, recalling Anaximander.

> From the time of ploughing and sowing until the food reaches your mouth
> and the clothes your body, not only do men and oxen suffer great pains
> in producing them, but countless insects are also killed and injured. It is
> improper to benefit in this way from the hardships of others. . . . A very
> heavy debt is incurred through wearing fine clothes and eating fine foods.
> (Batchelor, *ESS*, 8; quoted from Ya Un Sunim)

See the general preface, n. 11.

7. In other words:

> Once you see what it is all about, you really want to be very careful about
> what you do and say. You can have no intention to live life at the expense
> of any other creature. One does not feel that one's life is so much more
> important than anyone else's. One begins to feel the freedom and the
> lightness in that harmony with nature rather than the heaviness of exploi-
> tation of nature for personal gain. When you open the mind to the truth,
> then you realize there is nothing to fear. What arises passes away, what is
> born dies, and is not self—so that our sense of being caught in an identity
> with this human body fades out. We don't see ourselves as some isolated,
> alienated entity lost in a mysterious and frightening universe. We don't
> feel overwhelmed by it, trying to find a little piece of it that we can grasp
> and feel safe with, because we feel at peace with it. Then we have merged
> with the Truth. (Batchelor, *ESS*, 15; quoted from Ajahn Sumedho)

8. Reminding us of God's Christian world. See here chap. 3, pp. 49–57.

9. Turning elsewhere, from Asia to Africa, for another ethical thought of abundance. And *mimēsis*.

> So, for the African, living according to the moral law means living according to his nature, composed as it is of contradictory elements but complementary life forces. Thus he gives stuff to the stuff of the universe and tightens the threads of the tissue of life. (Senghor, *N*, 50)

> This, then, is Africa's lesson in aesthetics: art does not consist in photographing nature but in taking it, like the hunter when he reproduces the call of the hunted animal, like a separated couple, or two lovers, calling to each other in their desire to be reunited. The call is not the simple reproduction of the cry of the Other; it is a call of complementarity, a *song*; a call of harmony to the harmony of union that enriches by increasing *being*. We call it pure harmony. (p. 53)

Not, perhaps, without contamination, giving as taking. Or with sufficient attention to invisibility and forgetting, supplementarity rather than complementarity. Yet within the song of being is responsibility given as a call. In kinds.

Bibliography

Abbott, Sally. "The Origins of God in the Blood of the Lamb" *[OGBL]*. In Diamond and Orenstein, eds., *Reweaving the World*.

Abram, David. *The Spell of the Sensuous: Perception and Language in a More-Than-Human World [SS]*. New York: Pantheon, 1996.

Acker, Kathy. "Against Ordinary Language: The Language of the Body" *[AOL]*. In Kroker and Kroker, eds., *Last Sex*.

Ackerman, Robert John. *Heterogeneities: Race, Gender, Class, Nation, and State [H]*. Amherst: University of Massachusetts Press, 1996.

Adams, Carol J. *The Sexual Politics of Meat [SPM]*. New York: Continuum, 1992.

Addelson, Kathryn Pyne. *Impure Thoughts [IT]*. Philadelphia: Temple University Press, 1991.

———. "The Man of Professional Wisdom" *[MPW]*. In *Impure Thoughts*.

Agamben, Giorgio. *Language and Death: The Place of Negativity [LD]*. Minneapolis: University of Minnesota Press, 1991.

Allen, Paula Gunn. *The Sacred Hoop: Recovering the Feminine in American Indian Traditions [SH]*. Boston: Beacon, 1986.

Ames, Roger T. "Putting the *Te* Back into Taoism" *[PTBT]*. In Callicott and Ames, eds., *Nature in Asian Traditions of Thought*.

Andersen, Margaret L., and Patricia Hill Collins, eds. *Race, Class, and Gender: An Anthology [RCG]*. 2nd ed. Belmont, Calif.: Wadsworth, 1995.

Andolsen, Barbara Hilkert, Christine E. Gudorf, and Mary D. Pellauer, eds. *Women's Consciousness, Women's Conscience [WCWC]*. New York: Winston, 1985.

Appelbaum, David. *The Interpenetrating Reality: Bringing the Body to Touch [IR]*. New York: Lang, 1988.

Appiah, Kwame Anthony. "Racisms" *[R]*. In Goldberg, ed., *Anatomy of Racism*.

Apter, Andrew. *Black Critics & Kings: The Hermeneutics of Power in Yoruba Society [BCK]*. Chicago: University of Chicago Press, 1992.

Aquinas, Thomas. *Basic Writings of St. Thomas Aquinas [BWTA]*. Ed. Anton C. Pegis. 2 vols. New York: Random House, 1945.

———. *Summa Theologica [ST]*. Trans. Fathers of the English Dominican Province. London: Burns, Oates & Washbourne, 1912–36.

Arendt, Hannah. *Eichmann in Jerusalem: A Report on the Banality of Evil [EJ]*. Rev. and enl. ed. New York: Viking, 1964.

———. *The Human Condition [HC]*. Chicago: University of Chicago Press, 1958.

Arens, W., and I. Karp, eds. *Creativity of Power [CP]*. Washington, D.C., and London: Smithsonian Press, 1989.

Aristotle. *The Basic Works of Aristotle [BWA]*. Ed. Richard McKeon. New York: Random House, 1941.

———. *The Complete Works of Aristotle [CWA]*. Ed. Jonathan Barnes. 2 vols. Princeton: Princeton University Press, 1984. All quotations from Aristotle are from this edition unless otherwise indicated.

———. *Poetics [P]*. Reprinted in part in Ross, ed., *Art and Its Significance*. From *Basic Works of Aristotle*.

Augustine. *Basic Writings of Saint Augustine [BWA]*. Ed. and int. Whitney J. Oates. New York: Random House, 1948.

———. *The City of God [CG]*. In *Basic Writings of Saint Augustine*.

Bacon, Francis. *Novum Organum [NO]*. In Burtt, ed., *English Philosophers from Bacon to Mill*.

Badiner, Allan Hunt, ed. *Dharma Gaia: A Harvest of Essays in Buddhism and Ecology [DG]*. Berkeley: Parallax Press, 1990.

Bakhtin, Mikhail Mikhailovich. *Discourse in the Novel [DN]*. Reprinted in part in Ross, ed., *Art and Its Significance*. From *Dialogic Imagination*. Ed. Michael Holquist. Trans. Caryl Emerson and Michael Holquist. Austin: University of Texas Press, 1981.

Balibar, Etienne. "Paradoxes of Universality" *[PU]*. In Goldberg, ed., *Anatomy of Racism*.

Bar On, Bat-Ami, ed. *Modern Engendering: Critical Feminist Readings in Modern Western Philosophy [ME]*. Albany: State University of New York Press, 1994.

Barnard, Kathryn E., and T. Berry Brazelton, eds. *Touch: The Foundation of Experience [T]*. National Center for Clinical Infant Programs. Madison, Conn.: International Universities Press, 1990.

Barthes, Roland. *The Pleasure of the Text [PT]*. Trans. Richard Miller. New York: Hill and Wang, 1975.

Bataille, Georges. *The Accursed Share: An Essay on General Economy [AS]*. Trans. Richard Hurley. 2 vols. New York: Zone Books, 1988 and 1993. Translation of *La Part maudite, L'Histoire de l'érotisme*, and *La Souveraineté* (*Consumption [1]; The History of Eroticism [2]; Sovereignty [3]*). In Georges Bataille, *Oeuvres Complètes*. Paris: Gallimard, 1976.

———. *L'Expérience intérieure [EI]*. Paris: Gallimard, 1954.

———. *Méthode de Méditation [MM]*. In *L'Expérience intérieure*. Quoted in Derrida, "From Restricted to General Economy."

Batchelor, Martine. "Even the Stones Smile: Selections from the Scriptures" *[ESS]*. In Batchelor and Brown, eds., *Buddhism and Ecology*.

———. "Buddhist Economics Reconsidered" *[BER]*. In Badiner, ed., *Dharma Gaia*.

———. "The Sands of the Ganges" *[SG]*. In Batchelor and Brown, eds., *Buddhism and Ecology*.

Batchelor, Martine, and Kerry Brown, eds. *Buddhism and Ecology [BE]*. New York: Cassell Publishers, 1992.

Baudrillard, Jean. *Forget Foucault [FF]*. New York: Semiotext(e), 1987.

Beauvoir, Simone de. *The Ethics of Ambiguity [EA]*. Trans. Bernard Frechtman. New York: Citadel Press, 1991.

———. *The Second Sex [SS]*. Trans. H. M. Parshley. New York: Knopf, 1971.

Benjamin, Walter. *Erfahrung und Armut [EA]*. Passages quoted in Derrida, "Letter to Peter Eisenman."

———. "On Language as Such and on the Language of Man" *[LSLM]*. In *Reflections*.

———. *Reflections: Essays, Aphorisms, Autobiographical Writings [R]*. Trans. Edmund Jephcott. New York: Schocken, 1978.

———. "The Work of Art in the Age of Its Technical Reproducibility" *[WAATR]*. Reprinted in part in Ross, ed., *Art and Its Significance*. Selections from "The Work of Art in the Age of Mechanical Reproduction." Trans. Harry Zohn. In *Illuminations*. New York: Harcourt Brace & World, 1968.

Berman, Morris. *The Reenchantment of the World [RW]*. Ithaca, N.Y.: Cornell University Press, 1981.

Bernal, Martin. *Black Athena: The Afroasiatic Roots of Classical Civilization, Volume 1: The Fabrication of Ancient Greece 1785–1985 [BA]*. New Brunswick: Rutgers University Press, 1987.

Bhabha, Homi K. "Interrogating Identity: The Postcolonial Prerogative" *[II]*. In Goldberg, ed., *Anatomy of Racism*.

Birch, Thomas H. "The Incarceration of Wildness: Wilderness Areas as Prisons" *[IW]*. In Oelschlaeger, ed., *Postmodern Environmental Ethics*.

Blake, William. *The Book of Urizen [BU]*. Ed. and comm. Kay Parkhurst Easson and Roger R. Easson. Boulder: Shambhala, 1978.

Bookchin, Murray. *The Ecology of Freedom [EF]*. Palo Alto, Calif.: Cheshire Books, 1982.

———. "Social Ecology versus 'Deep Ecology': A Challenge to the Ecology Movement" *[SEDE]*. In *Green Perspectives, Newsletter of the Green Program Project* 4–5.

Bordo, Susan. "The Cartesian Masculinization of Thought and the Seventeenth-Century Flight from the Feminine" *[CMT]*. In Bar On, ed., *Modern Engendering*.

Bormann, F. Herbert, and Stephen R. Kellert, eds. *Ecology, Economics, Ethics: The Broken Circle [EEE]*. New Haven: Yale University Press, 1991.

Bowden, Ross. "Sorcery, Illness and Social Control in Kwoma Society" *[SISC]*. In Stephen, ed., *Sorcerer and Witch*.

Buber, Martin. *I and Thou [IT]*. Trans. R. G. Smith. New York: Scribner's, 1927.

Bullough, Edward. " 'Psychical Distance' as a Factor in Art and as an Aesthetic Principle" *[PD]*. Reprinted in Ross, ed., *Art and Its Significance*. Originally published in *British Journal of Psychology* (1912): 87–98.

Burtt, Edwin A., ed. *The English Philosophers from Bacon to Mill [EPBM]*. New York: Modern Library, 1959.

Butler, Judith. *Bodies That Matter: On the Discursive Limits of "Sex" [BM]*. New York: Routledge, 1993.

———. *Gender Trouble: Feminism and the Subversion of Identity [GT]*. New York: Routledge, 1990.

Callicott, J. Baird. *In Defense of a Land Ethic [DL]*. Albany: State University of New York Press, 1989.

———. "Traditional American Indian and Western European Attitudes Toward Nature: An Overview" *[TAIWEA]*. In Oelschlaeger, ed., *Postmodern Environmental Ethics*.

Callicott, J. Baird, and Roger T. Ames, eds. *Nature in Asian Traditions of Thought: Essays in Environmental Philosophy [NATT]*. Albany: State University of New York Press, 1989.

Capra, Fritjof, and Charlene Spretnak. *Green Politics: The Global Promise [GP]*. New York: Dutton, 1984.

Caputo, John D. *Against Ethics: Contributions to a Poetics of Obligation with Constant Reference to Deconstruction [AE]*. Bloomington: Indiana University Press, 1993.

Card, Claudia, ed. *Feminist Ethics [FE]*. Lawrence: University Press of Kansas, 1991.

Céline, Louis-Ferdinand. *Journey to the End of the Night [JEN]*. Trans. John H. P. Marks. Boston: Little, Brown, 1934.

Cheal, David. *The Gift Economy [GE]*. New York: Routledge, 1988.

Cheney, Jim. "Eco-feminism and Deep Ecology" *[EDE]*. *Environmental Ethics* 9, no. 2 (Summer 1987): 115–45.

———. "Postmodern Environmental Ethics: Ethics as Bioregional Narrative" *[PMEE]*. In Oelschlaeger, ed., *Postmodern Environmental Ethics*.

Christ, Carol P. "Reverence for Life: The Need for a Sense of Finitude" *[RL]*. In Cooey, Farmer, and Ross, eds., *Embodied Love*.

———. "Spiritual Quest and Women's Experience" *[SQWE]*. In Christ and Plaskow, eds., *Womanspirit Rising*.

Christ, Carol P., and Judith Plaskow, eds. *Womanspirit Rising [WR]*. New York: Harper & Row, 1979.

Cixous, Hélène. "Laugh of the Medusa" *[LM]*. In Marks and Courtivron, eds., *New French Feminisms*.

Cixous, Hélène, and Catherine Clément. *The Newly Born Woman [NBW]*. Trans. Betsy Wing. Int. Sandra M. Gilbert. Minneapolis: University of Minnesota Press, 1975.

Clark, Cedric X. "Some Implications of Nkrumah's Consciencism for Alternative Coordinates in NonEuropean Causality" *[SINC]*. In Ruch and Anyanwu, eds., *African Philosophy*.

Clément, Catherine. "The Guilty Ones" *[GO]*. In Cixous and Clément, *Newly Born Woman*.

Clifford, James. "On Collecting Art and Culture" *[CAC]*. Reprinted in Ross, ed., *Art and Its Significance*. From Russell Ferguson et al., eds. *Out There: Marginalization and Contemporary Cultures*. New York: New Museum of Contemporary Art and Cambridge: MIT Press, 1990, 141–46, 151–65.

Cobb, Jr., John. "Christian Existence in a World of Limits" *[CEWL]*. In Oelschlaeger, ed., *Postmodern Environmental Ethics*.

Cobham, Rhonda, and Merle Collins, eds. *Watchers and Seekers: Creative Writing by Black Women in Britain [WS]*. London: Women's Press, 1987.

Codiga, Doug. "Zen Practice and a Sense of Place" *[ZPSP]*. In Badiner, ed., *Dharma Gaia*.

Cole, Eve Browning, and Susan Coultrap-McQuin, eds. *Explorations in Feminist Ethics: Theory and Practice [EFE]*. Bloomington: Indiana University Press, 1992.

Coleridge, Samuel Taylor. *Biographia Literaria [BL]*. Ed. J. Shawcross. London: Oxford University Press, 1949.

Collingwood, R. G. *The Principles of Art [PA]*. Oxford: Oxford University Press, 1972.

Comstock, Gary. "Pigs and Piety: A Theocentric Perspective on Food Animals" *[PP]*. *Between the Species*, 8, no. 3 (Summer 1992): 121–35.

Cooey, Paula M. "The Word Become Flesh: Woman's Body, Language, and Value" *[WF]*. In Cooey, Farmer, and Ross, eds., *Embodied Love*.

Cooey, Paula M., Sharon A. Farmer, and Mary Ellen Ross, eds. *Embodied Love: Sensuality and Relationship as Feminist Values [EL]*. San Francisco: Harper and Row, 1987.

Cook, Francis H. "The Jewel Net of Indra" *[JNI]*. In Callicott and Ames, eds., *Nature in Asian Traditions of Thought*.

Cooper, David E., and Joy A. Palmer, eds. *The Environment in Question: Ethics and Global Issues [EQ]*. New York: Routledge, 1992.

Cornell, Drucilla. *Beyond Accommodation: Ethical Feminism, Deconstruction, and the Law [BA]*. New York: Routledge, 1991.

———. *The Imaginary Domain: Abortion, Pornography and Sexual Harassment [ID]*. New York: Routledge, 1995.

———. *The Philosophy of the Limit [PL]*. New York: Routledge, 1992.

———. *Transformations: Recollective Imagination and Sexual Difference [T]*. New York: Routledge, 1993.

Cornell, Drucilla, Michel Rosenfeld, and David Gray Carlson, eds. *Deconstruction and the Possibility of Justice [DPJ]*. New York: Routledge, Chapman and Hall, 1992.

Cose, Ellis. *A Nation of Strangers [NS]*. New York: William Morrow and Co., 1992.

Curtin, Deane. "Toward an Ecological Ethic of Care" *[TEEC]*. In Warren, ed., *Hypatia* 6, no. 1 (Spring 1991): 60–74.

Curtiss, Susan. *Genie: A Psycholinguistic Study of a Modern-Day "Wild Child" [G]* New York: Academic Press, 1977.

Daly, Mary. "After the Death of God the Father: Women's Liberation and the Transformation of Christian Consciousness" *[ADGF]*. In Christ and Plaskow, eds., *Womanspirit Rising*.

———. *Gyn/Ecology: The Metaethics of Radical Feminism [G/E]*. Boston: Beacon Press, 1990.

Danto, Arthur C. "Approaching the End of Art" *[AEA]*. In *State of the Art*.

———. *The State of the Art [SA]*. New York: Prentice Hall, 1987.

———. *Transfiguration of the Commonplace: A Philosophy of Art [TC]*. Cambridge: Harvard University Press, 1981.

Dawkins, Richard. *The Selfish Gene [SG]*. Oxford: Oxford University Press, 1976.

de Silva, Lily. "The Hills Wherein My Soul Delights: Exploring the Stories and Teachings" *[HWSD]*. In Batchelor and Brown, eds., *Buddhism and Ecology*.

de Waal, Frans. *Good Natured: The Origins of Right and Wrong in Humans and Other Animals [GN]*. Cambridge: Harvard University Press, 1996.

Delacampagne, Christian. "Racism and the West: From Praxis to Logos" *[RW]*. In Goldberg, ed., *Anatomy of Racism*.

Deleuze, Gilles. *Difference and Repetition [DR]*. Trans. Paul Patton. New York: Columbia University Press, 1994. Translation of *Différence et répétition*. Paris: P.U.F., 1968.

———. *The Logic of Sense [LS]*. Trans. Mark Lester with Charles Stivale. New York: Columbia University Press, 1990. Translation of *Logique du sens*. Paris: Editions de Minuit, 1969.

Deleuze, Gilles, and Félix Guattari. *Anti-Oedipus: Capitalism and Schizophrenia [A-O]*. Trans. Robert Hurley, Mark Seem, and Helen R. Lane. Minneapolis: University of Minnesota Press, 1983.

———. *A Thousand Plateaus: Capitalism and Schizophrenia [TP]*. Trans. Brian Massumi. Minneapolis: University of Minnesota Press, 1987.

———. *What Is Philosophy? [WP]*. Trans. Hugh Tomlinson and Graham Burchell. New York: Columbia University Press, 1994.

Deloria, Jr., Vine. *God Is Red [GR]*. New York: Dell, 1973.

Derrida, Jacques. "Cogito and the History of Madness" *[CHM]*. In *Writing and Difference*.

———. *Dissemination [D]*. Trans. and int. Barbara Johnson. Chicago: University of Chicago Press, 1981.

———. "Economimesis" *[E]*. *Diacritics* 11, no. 2 (June 1981): 3–25.

———. " 'Eating Well,' or the Calculation of the Subject" *[EW]*. Trans. Peter Connor and Avital Ronell. In *Points*.

———. "Force of Law: The 'Mystical Foundation of Authority' " *[FL]*. In Cornell, Rosenfeld, and Carlson, eds., *Deconstruction and the Possibility of Justice*. Reprinted from *Cardozo Law Review* 11, nos. 5–6 (July/August 1991): 919–1045.

———. "From Restricted to General Economy: A Hegelianism without Reserve" *[FRGE]*. In *Writing and Difference*.

———. "Geschlecht: Sexual Difference, Ontological Difference" *[G1]*. *Research in Phenomenology* 13 (1983): 65–83.

———. "*Geschlecht* II: Heidegger's Hand" *[G2]*. Trans. John P. Leavey, Jr. In Sallis, ed., *Deconstruction in Philosophy: The Texts of Jacques Derrida*.

———. *The Gift of Death [GD]*. Trans. David Wills. Chicago: University of Chicago Press, 1994.

———. *Given Time [GT]*. Trans. Peggy Kamuf. Chicago: University of Chicago Press, 1992.

———. "Heidegger's Ear: Philopolemology (*Geschlecht* IV)" *[G4]*. In Sallis, ed., *Reading Heidegger*. Bloomington: Indiana University Press, 1993.

———. "Letter to Peter Eisenman" *[LPE]*. Reprinted in Ross, ed., *Art and Its Significance*. From *Assemblage* 12: 7–13.

———. *Margins of Philosophy [MP]*. Trans. Alan Bass. Chicago: University of Chicago Press, 1982.

———. *Of Spirit: Heidegger and the Question [OS]*. Trans. Geoffrey Bennington and Rachel Bowlby. Chicago: University of Chicago Press, 1989.

———. "Parergon" *[P]*. Reprinted in part in Ross, ed., *Art and Its Significance*.

———. "Passe-Partout" *[P-P]*. Reprinted in Ross, ed., *Art and Its Significance*. Introduction to *Truth in Painting*.

———. "Plato's Pharmacy" *[PP]*. From *Dissemination*.

———. *Points . . . : Interviews, 1974–94 [P. . .]*. Trans. Peggy Kamuf and others. Stanford, Calif.: Stanford University Press, 1995.

———. "The Politics of Friendship" *[PF]*. *The Journal of Philosophy* 85 (November 1988): 632–44.

———. "Restitutions" *[R]*. Reprinted in part in Ross, ed., *Art and Its Significance*. From *Truth in Painting*.

———. *Specters of Marx: The State of the Debt, The Work of Mourning, and the New International [SM]*. Trans. Peggy Kamuf. Int. Bernd Magnus and Stephen Cullenberg. New York: Routledge, 1994.

———. *The Truth in Painting [TP]*. Trans. G. Bennington and I. McLeod. Chicago: University of Chicago Press, 1987.

———. "Violence and Metaphysics: An Essay on the Thought of Emmanuel Levinas" *[VM]*. In *Writing and Difference*.

———. "White Mythology: Metaphor in the Text of Philosophy" *[WM]*. In *Margins of Philosophy*.

————. *Writing and Difference [WD]*. Trans. Alan Bass. Chicago: University of Chicago Press, 1978.

Descartes, René. *Discourse on the Method of Rightly Conducting the Reason and Seeking Truth in the Sciences [DM]*. In *Philosophical Writings of Descartes*, vol. 1.

————. *Early Writings [EW]*. In *Philosophical Writings of Descartes*, vol. 1.

————. *Meditations [M]*. In *Philosophical Writings of Descartes*, vol. 2.

————. *Objections and Replies [OR]*. In *Philosophical Writings of Descartes*, vol. 2.

————. *Optics [O]*. In *Philosophical Writings of Descartes*, vol. 1.

————. *The Passions of the Soul [PS]*. In *Philosophical Writings of Descartes*, vol. 1.

————. *The Philosophical Writings of Descartes [PWD]*. Trans. John Cottingham, Robert Stoothoff, and Dugald Murdoch. 2 vols. Cambridge: Cambridge University Press, 1985.

————. *Principles of Philosophy [PP]*. In *Philosophical Writings of Descartes*, vol. 1.

————. *Rules for the Direction of the Mind [RDM]*. In *Philosophical Writings of Descartes*, vol. 1.

————. *Treatise on Man [TM]*. In *Philosophical Writings of Descartes*, vol. 1.

————. *The World [W]*. In *Philosophical Writings of Descartes*, vol. 1.

Devall, Bill, and George Sessions. *Deep Ecology: Living as if Nature Mattered [DE]*. Salt Lake City: Peregrene Smith, 1985.

Devi, Mahasweta, *Imaginary Maps: Three Stories [IM]*. Trans. Gayatri Chakravorty Spivak. New York: Routledge, 1995.

Dewey, John. *Art and Experience [AE]*. New York: Putnam, 1934. Reprinted in part in Ross, ed., *Art and Its Significance*.

————. "Body and Mind" *[BM]*. In *Philosophy and Civilization*.

————. "Context and Thought" *[CT]*. In *Experience, Nature, and Freedom*.

————. *Experience and Nature [EN]*. 2nd ed. New York: Dover, 1958.

————. *Experience, Nature, and Freedom [ENF]*. Ed. and int. Richard J. Bernstein. Indianapolis: Library of Liberal Arts, 1960.

————. *Human Nature and Conduct [HNC]*. New York: Holt, 1922.

————. *Logic: The Theory of Inquiry [L]*. New York: Henry Holt & Co., 1938.

————. "Nature in Experience" *[NE]*. In *Experience, Nature, and Freedom*.

————. "The Need for a Recovery of Philosophy" *[NRP]*. In *Experience, Nature, and Freedom*.

————. *Philosophy and Civilization [PC].* New York: Minton, Balch, 1931.

————. *Quest for Certainty [QC].* New York: Minton, Balch, 1929.

————. *Theory of Valuation [TV].* Chicago: University of Chicago Press, 1939.

Diamond, Irene. "Babies, Heroic Experts, and a Poisoned Earth" *[BHEPE].* In Diamond and Orenstein, eds., *Reweaving the World.*

Diamond, Irene, and Gloria Feman Orenstein, eds. *Reweaving the World: The Emergence of Ecofeminism [RW].* San Francisco: Sierra Club Books, 1990.

Dimen, Muriel. "Power, Sexuality, and Intimacy" *[PSI].* In Jaggar and Bordo, eds., *Gender/Body/Knowledge.*

Dixon, Vernon J. "World Views and Research Methodology" *[WVRM].* In King, Dixon, and Nobles, eds., *African Philosophy.*

Dorter, Kenneth: *Plato's* Phaedo: *An Interpretation [PP].* Toronto: University of Toronto Press, 1982.

Dostoevsky, Fyodor. *The Brothers Karamazov [BK].* Trans. Constance Garnett. New York: Modern Library, 1950.

Dryzek, John S. "Green Reason: Communicative Ethics for the Biosphere" *[GR].* In Oelschlaeger, ed., *Postmodern Environmental Ethics.*

————. *Rational Ecology: Environment and Political Economy [RE].* New York: Blackwell, 1987.

Du Bois, W. E. B. *A W. E. B. Du Bois Reader [WEBDR].* Ed. Andrew G. Paschal. New York: Macmillan, 1971.

————. "The Concept of Race" *[CR].* In Hord and Lee, eds., *I Am Because We Are.*

————. "The Conservation of Races" *[CR].* In *Du Bois Reader.*

duBois, Page. *Sowing the Body: Psychoanalysis and Ancient Representations of Women [SB].* Chicago: University of Chicago Press, 1988.

————. *Torture and Truth [TT].* New York: Routledge, 1991.

Duerr, Hans Peter. *Dreamtime: Concerning the Boundary between Wilderness and Civilization [D].* Trans. Felicitas Goodman. Oxford: Blackwell, 1985.

Dworkin, Andrea. *Intercourse [I].* New York: Free Press, 1987.

Dworkin, Ronald. "Feminists and Abortion" *[FA]. New York Review of Books* 40, no. 11 (June 10, 1993): 27–29.

————. *Law's Empire [LE].* Cambridge: Harvard University Press, 1986.

Dworkin. Review of MacKinnon, *Only Words [OW]. The New York Review of Books* 40, no. 17 (October 21, 1993): 36–42.

Ecker, Gisela, ed. *Feminist Aesthetics [FA]*. Trans. Harriet Anderson. Boston: Beacon Press, 1985.

Eckersley, Robyn. *Environmentalism and Political Theory: Toward an Ecocentric Approach [EPT]*. Albany, N.Y.: State University of New York, 1992.

Ehrenfeld, David. *The Arrogance of Humanism [AH]*. New York: Oxford University Press, 1978.

El Sadaawi, Nawal. *The Hidden Face of Eve: Women in the Arab World [HFE]*. Trans. Sherif Hetata. Boston: Beacon Press, 1980.

Eliade, Mircea. *Shamanism: Archaic Techniques of Ecstacy [S]*. Princeton: Princeton University Press, 1972.

Erodes, Richard. *Lame Deer: Seeker of Visions [LD]*. New York: Simon & Schuster, 1976.

Euripides. *Hecuba [H]*. Trans. E. P. Coleridge. In Oates and O'Neill, eds., *Complete Greek Drama*.

Fanon, Frantz. *Black Skin, White Masks [BSWM]*. Trans. Charles Lam Markmann. New York: Grove Press, 1967.

―――. *Wretched of the Earth [WE]*. Trans. Constance Farrington. Pref. Jean-Paul Sartre. New York: Grove Press, 1965.

Feng, Yu-lan. *A History of Chinese Philosophy [HCP]*. Trans. Derk Bodde. Princeton: University of Princeton Press, 1952–53.

Ferry, Luc. *The New Ecological Order [NEO]*. Trans. Carol Volk. Chicago: University of Chicago Press, 1995.

Feyerabend, Paul. *Against Method: Outline of an Anarchistic Theory of Knowledge [AM]*. Atlantic Highlands, N.J.: Humanities Press, 1975.

Fortes, Meyer. "Strangers" *[S]*. In Fortes and Patterson, *Studies in African Social Anthropology*.

Fortes, Meyer, and Patterson, Sheila. *Studies in African Social Anthropology [SASA]*. New York: Academic Press, 1975.

Foucault, Michel. *Archaeology of Knowledge [AK]*. Trans. A. M. Sheridan-Smith. New York: Pantheon, 1981.

―――. *The Care of the Self [CS]*. Trans. Robert Hurley. New York: Pantheon, 1986.

―――. *Discipline and Punish: The Birth of the Prison [DP]*. Trans. Alan Sheridan. New York: Vintage, 1979.

―――. *Folie et déraison: Histoire de la folie à la l'âge classique [FD]*. Paris: Plon, 1961.

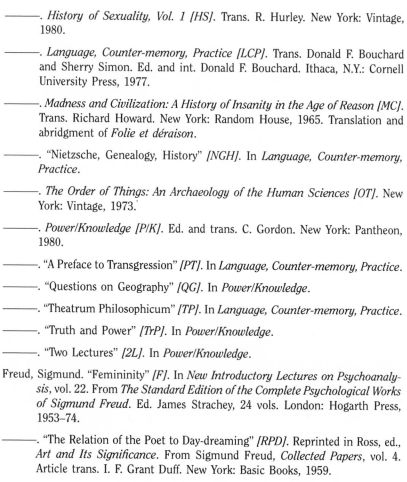

————. *History of Sexuality, Vol. 1 [HS]*. Trans. R. Hurley. New York: Vintage, 1980.

————. *Language, Counter-memory, Practice [LCP]*. Trans. Donald F. Bouchard and Sherry Simon. Ed. and int. Donald F. Bouchard. Ithaca, N.Y.: Cornell University Press, 1977.

————. *Madness and Civilization: A History of Insanity in the Age of Reason [MC]*. Trans. Richard Howard. New York: Random House, 1965. Translation and abridgment of *Folie et déraison*.

————. "Nietzsche, Genealogy, History" *[NGH]*. In *Language, Counter-memory, Practice*.

————. *The Order of Things: An Archaeology of the Human Sciences [OT]*. New York: Vintage, 1973.

————. *Power/Knowledge [P/K]*. Ed. and trans. C. Gordon. New York: Pantheon, 1980.

————. "A Preface to Transgression" *[PT]*. In *Language, Counter-memory, Practice*.

————. "Questions on Geography" *[QG]*. In *Power/Knowledge*.

————. "Theatrum Philosophicum" *[TP]*. In *Language, Counter-memory, Practice*.

————. "Truth and Power" *[TrP]*. In *Power/Knowledge*.

————. "Two Lectures" *[2L]*. In *Power/Knowledge*.

Freud, Sigmund. "Femininity" *[F]*. In *New Introductory Lectures on Psychoanalysis*, vol. 22. From *The Standard Edition of the Complete Psychological Works of Sigmund Freud*. Ed. James Strachey, 24 vols. London: Hogarth Press, 1953–74.

————. "The Relation of the Poet to Day-dreaming" *[RPD]*. Reprinted in Ross, ed., *Art and Its Significance*. From Sigmund Freud, *Collected Papers*, vol. 4. Article trans. I. F. Grant Duff. New York: Basic Books, 1959.

Frodeman, Robert. "Radical Environmentalism and the Political Roots of Postmodernism: Differences that Make a Difference" *[REPRP]*. In Oelschlaeger, ed., *Postmodern Environmental Ethics*.

Fry, Tony, and Anne-Marie Willis. "Aboriginal Art: Symptom or Success?" *[AA]*. Reprinted in part in Ross, ed., *Art and Its Significance*. From *Art in America* (July 1989): 111–16, 159–61.

Fuller, Steve. *Controversial Science: From Content to Contention [CS]*. Albany: State University of New York Press, 1993.

————. *Philosophy of Science and Its Discontents [PSD]*. Boulder, Colo.: Westview Press, 1989.

————. *Social Epistemology [SE]*. Bloomington and Indianapolis: Indiana University Press, 1988.

Gadamer, Hans-Georg. *Truth and Method [TM]*. New York: Seabury Press, 1975.

Gallop, David. *Plato:* Phaedo *[PP]*. Oxford: Clarendon Press, 1975.

Gallop, Jane. *Thinking Through the Body [TTB]*. New York: Columbia University Press, 1988.

Gamble, George, and James Bond, eds. *Race and Intelligence [RI]*. American Anthropologist, 1971.

Garb, Yaakov Jerome. "Perspective or Escape? Ecofeminist Musings on Contemporary Earth Imagery" *[PE]*. In Diamond and Orenstein, eds., *Reweaving the World*.

Gates, Jr., Henry Louis. "Critical Remarks" *[CR]*. In Goldberg, ed., *Anatomy of Racism*.

Gates, Jr., Henry Louis, ed. *"Race," Writing, and Difference [RWD]*. Chicago: University of Chicago Press, 1986.

Gilbert, Bil. "Crows by Far and Wide, But There's No Place Like Home" *[CFW]*. *Smithsonian* 23, no. 5 (August 1992): 101–11.

Gilead, Amihud. *The Platonic Odyssey: A Philosophical-Literary Inquiry into the* Phaedo *[PO]*. Amsterdam: Rodopi, 1994.

Gilligan, Carol. *In a Different Voice: Psychological Theory and Women's Development [IDV]*. Cambridge: Harvard University Press, 1982.

Godway, Eleanor M., and Geraldine Finn, eds. *Who Is This "We"?: Absence of Community [WW]*. Montréal: Black Rose Books, 1994.

Goldberg, David Theo, ed. *Anatomy of Racism [AR]*. Minneapolis: University of Minnesota Press, 1990.

Golding, Sue. "The Excess" *[E]*. In Kroker and Kroker, eds., *Last Sex*.

Goodman, Nelson. *Languages of Art: An Approach to a Theory of Symbols [LA]*. 2nd ed. Indianapolis: Hackett, 1976.

———. *Ways of Worldmaking [WW]*. Indianapolis: Hackett, 1978.

Goosens, William K. "Underlying Trait Terms" *[UTT]*. In Schwartz, ed., *Naming, Necessity, and Natural Kinds*.

Gottlieb, Alma. "Witches, Kings, and the Sacrifice of Identity or The Power of Paradox and the Paradox of Power among the Beng of Ivory Coast" *[WKS]*. In Arens and Karp, eds., *Creativity of Power*.

Göttner-Abendroth, Heide. "Nine Principles of a Matriarchal Aesthetics" *[MA]*. Trans. Harriet Anderson. Reprinted in Ross, ed., *Art and Its Significance*. From Ecker, ed., *Feminist Aesthetics*.

Graves, Robert. *The Greek Myths [GM]*. Baltimore: Penguin, 1955.

Griffin, Susan. *A Chorus of Stones [CS]*. New York: Doubleday, 1992.

————. *Pornography and Silence [PS]*. New York: Harper & Row, 1981.

————. *Woman and Nature: The Roaring Inside Her [WN]*. New York: Harper & Row, 1978.

Grosz, Elizabeth. *Volatile Bodies: Toward a Corporeal Feminism [VB]*. Bloomington: Indiana University Press, 1994

Guidieri, R. "Les sociétés primitives aujourd'hui" *[SPA]*. In *Philosopher: les interrogations contemporarines*. Ed. Ch. Delacampagne and R. Maggiori. Paris: Fayard, 1980.

Guy-Sheftall, Beverly, ed. *Words of Fire: An Anthology of African-American Feminist Thought [WF]*. New York: New Press, 1995.

Habermas, Jürgen. *Communication and the Evolution of Society [CES]*. Ed. T. McCarthy. Boston: Beacon Press, 1979.

Hallen, Barry. "Phenomenology and the Exposition of African Traditional Thought" *[PEATT]*. In *Proceedings of the Seminar on African Philosophy/La Philosophie Africaine*. Ed. Claude Sumner. Addis Ababa: Chamber Printing House, 1980.

Hallen, B., and J. O. Sodipo. *Knowledge, Belief and Witchcraft: Analytic Experiments in African Philosophy [KBW]*. London: Ethnographica, 1986.

Hamilton-Grierson, P. J. "Strangers" *[S]*. In *Encyclopaedia of Religion and Ethics*. Ed J. Hastings. Edinburgh: T. & T. Clark, 1921. Vol. 11: 883–96.

Harman, Lesley D. *The Modern Stranger [MS]*. Amsterdam: Mouton de Gruyter, 1988.

Haraway, Donna. *Simians, Cyborgs, and Women: The Reinvention of Nature [SCW]*. New York: Routledge, 1991.

Harding, Sandra. "The Curious Coincidence of Feminine and African Moralities: Challenges for Feminist Theory" *[CCFAM]*. In Kittay and Meyers, eds., *Women and Moral Theory*.

————. "The Instability of the Analytical Categories of Feminist Theory" *[IACFT]*. *Signs*, 11, no. 4 (Summer 1986): 645–64.

————. *The Science Question in Feminism [SQF]*. Ithaca, N.Y.: Cornell University Press, 1986.

————. *Whose Science? Whose Knowledge? Thinking from Women's Lives [WSWK]*. Ithaca, N.Y.: Cornell University Press, 1991.

Hargrove, Eugene C. *Foundations of Environmental Ethics [FEE]*. Englewood Cliffs, N.J.: Prentice Hall, 1989.

Hargrove, Eugene C., ed. *Religion and Environmental Crisis [REC]*. Athens, Ga.: University of Georgia Press, 1986.

Harris, Leonard. "Postmodernism and Utopia, an Unholy Alliance" *[PU]*. In Hord and Lee, eds., *I Am Because We Are*.

Harrison, Beverly Wildung. "Our Right to Choose" *[RC]*. In Andolsen, Gudorf, and Pellauer, eds., *Women's Consciousness, Women's Conscience*.

Hegel, G. W. F. *Aesthetics: Lectures on Fine Art [A]*. Trans. T. M. Knox. London: Oxford University Press, 1975. Introduction reprinted in part in *Art and Its Significance* as "Philosophy of Fine Art" *[PFA]*.

―――. *Jenenser Realphilosophie I, Der Vorlesungen von 1803–1804 [JR1]*. Ed. J. Hoffmeister. Leibzig: 1932. Quoted and translated in Agamben, *Language and Death*.

―――. *Jenenser Realphilosophie II, Die Vorlesungen von 1803–1804 [JR2]*. Ed. J. Hoffmeister. Leipzig: 1932. Quoted and translated in Agamben, *Language and Death*.

―――. *The Logic of Hegel, translated from the Encyclopaedia of the Philosophical Sciences [EL]*. Trans. William Wallace. Oxford: Oxford University Press, 1892.

―――. *The Phenomenology of Mind [PM]*. Trans. and int. James Baillie. London: George Allen & Unwin, 1910.

Heidegger, Martin. "The Anaximander Fragment" *[AF]*. In *Early Greek Thinking*.

―――. *Basic Writings [BW]*. Ed. David Farrell Krell. New York: Harper & Row, 1977.

―――. *Being and Time [BT]*. Trans. John Macquarrie and Edward Robinson. Translation of *Sein und Zeit [SZ]*. New York: Harper & Row, 1962.

―――. *Discourse on Thinking: A Translation of* Gelassenheit *[DT]*. Trans. John M. Anderson and E. Hans Freund. New York: Harper & Row, 1966.

―――. *Early Greek Thinking [EGT]*. Trans. D. F. Krell and F. A. Capuzzi. New York: Harper & Row, 1984.

―――. *Identity and Difference [ID]*. Trans. and int. Joan Stambaugh. New York: Harper & Row, 1969.

―――. *Introduction to Metaphysics [IM]*. Trans. Ralph Manheim. Garden City, N.Y.: Doubleday, 1961.

―――. "Language" *[L]*. In *Poetry, Language, Thought*.

―――. "Language in the Poem" *[LP]*. In *On the Way to Language*.

―――. "Letter on Humanism" *[LH]*. In *Basic Writings*.

―――. "Martin Heidegger interrogé par *Der Spiegel*. Réponses et questions sur l'histoire et la politique" (Martin Heidegger interviewed by *Der Spiegel*: Responses and questions on history and politics.) Trans. William J. Richardson S. J. as " 'Only a God Can Save Us': The *Spiegel* Interview." In Sheehan, ed., *Heidegger, the Man and the Thinker*.

―――. "The Nature of Language" *[NL]*. In *On the Way to Language*.

———. "On the Being and Conception of *Physis* in Aristotle's *Physics* B.1" *[OBCP]*. Trans. T. J. Sheehan. *Man and World* 9, no. 3 (August 1976): 219–70.

———. "On the Essence of Truth" *[OET]*. In *Basic Writings*.

———. *On the Way to Language [OWL]*. Trans. Peter D. Hertz. New York: Harper & Row, 1971.

———. *On Time and Being [OTB]*. Trans. Joan Stambaugh. New York: Harper & Row, 1972.

———. "The Onto-theo-logical Constitution of Metaphysics" *[OTLCM]*. In *Identity and Difference*.

———. "The Origin of the Work of Art" *[OWA]*. Reprinted in part in Ross, ed., *Art and Its Significance*. From *Poetry, Language, Thought*.

———. *Poetry, Language, Thought [PLT]*. Trans. Albert Hofstadter. New York: Harper & Row, 1971.

———. "The Question Concerning Technology" *[QT]*. In *Basic Writings*.

———. *The Question Concerning Technology and Other Essays [QTOE]*. Trans. William Lovitt. New York: Harper & Row, 1977.

———. "Time and Being" *[TB]*. In *On Time and Being*.

———. *Was ist das—die Philosophie [WP]*, 1955. Quoted in Derrida, "Heidegger's Ear."

———. "The Way to Language" *[WL]*. In *On the Way to Language*.

———. "What Calls for Thinking?" *[WCT]*. In *Basic Writings*.

Heller, Morton A. and William Schiff, eds. *The Psychology of Touch [PT]*. Hillsdale, N.J.: Lawrence Erlbaum Associates, 1991.

Hester, Jr., Randolph T. "Sacred Structures and Everyday Life: A Return to Manteo, North Carolina" *[SSEL]*. In Seamon, ed., *Dwelling, Seeing, and Designing*.

Hix, H. L. *Spirits Hovering over the Ashes: Legacies of Postmodern Theory [SHOA]*. Albany: State University of New York Press, 1995.

Hoagland, Sarah Lucia. "Lesbian Ethics and Female Agency" *[LEFA]*. In Cole and Coultrap-McQuin, eds., *Explorations in Feminist Ethics*.

———. "Some Thoughts about 'Caring' " *[STC]*. In Card, ed., *Feminist Ethics*.

Hobbes, Thomas. *Complete Works [CW]*. Ed. William Molesworth. English Works, 11 vols, 1839. Latin Works, 5 vols., 1845.

———. *Elements of Philosophy [EOP]*. In *Complete Works*, vol. 4.

———. *Leviathan [L]*. In *Complete Works*, vol. 1.

Hölderlin, Friedrich. *Friedrich Hölderlin Poems and Fragments [FHPF]*. Trans. Michael Hamburger. Ann Arbor: University of Michigan Press, 1966.

———. "Patmos" *[P]*. In *Friedrich Hölderlin Poems and Fragments.*

Homann, Margaret. *Bearing the Word: Language and Female Experience in Nineteenth-Century Women's Writing [BW]*. Chicago: University of Chicago Press, 1986.

Hord, Fred Lee (Mzee Lasana Okpara), and Jonathan Scott Lee, eds. *I Am Because We Are: Readings in Black Philosophy [IABWA]*. Amherst: University of Massachusetts, 1995.

Hume, David. *An Enquiry Concerning Human Understanding [EHU]*. New York: Prometheus, 1988.

———. "Of the Standard of Taste" *[OST]*. Reprinted in Ross, ed., *Art and Its Significance.*

———. "On National Characters" *[ONC]*. In T. H. Green and T. H. Grose, eds., *Philosophical Works [PW]*. Vol. 3. Aalen: Scientia Verlag, 1964.

———. *A Treatise of Human Nature [T]*. London: Oxford University Press, 1888.

Husserl, Edmund. *Ideas: General Introduction to Pure Phenomenology [I]*. Trans. W. R. Boyce Gibson. New York: Collier Books, 1962.

Hyde, Lewis. *The Gift: Imagination and the Erotic Life of Property [G]*. New York: Random House, 1979.

Illich, Ivan. *Gender [G]*. New York: Pantheon, 1982.

———. "Toward a History of Gender" *[GHG]*. *Feminist Issues* 3, no. 1 (Spring 1983). Includes symposium on his work.

Inada, Kenneth K. "Environmental Problematics" *[EP]*. In Callicott and Ames, eds., *Nature in Asian Traditions of Thought.*

Irigaray, Luce. "Any Theory of the 'Subject' has Always Been Appropriated by the 'Masculine'" *[ATS]*. In *Speculum of the Other Woman.*

———. "The Culture of Difference" *[CD]*. In *Je, tu, nous.*

———. *An Ethics of Sexual Difference [ESD]*. Trans. Carolyn Burke and Gillian C. Gill. Ithaca, N.Y.: Cornell University Press, 1993. Translation of *Éthique de la Différence sexuelle [ÉDS]*. Paris: Minuit, 1984.

———. "The Fecundity of the Caress: A Reading of Levinas, *Totality and Infinity*, 'Phenomenology of Eros'" *[FC]*. In *Ethics of Sexual Difference.*

———. "He Risks Who Risks Life Itself" *[HR]*. In *Irigaray Reader.*

———. "The Invisible of the Flesh: A Reading of Merleau-Ponty, *The Visible and the Invisible*, 'The Intertwining—The Chiasm'" *[IF]*. In *Ethics of Sexual Difference.*

———. *The Irigaray Reader [IR]*. Trans. Seán Hand. Ed. and int. Margaret Whitford. Oxford: Blackwell, 1991.

———. "Je—Luce Irigaray" *[J]*. Ed. and trans. Elizabeth Hirsh and Gaëton Brechotte. Interview in *Hypatia* 10, no. 2 (Spring 1995): 93–114.

———. *Je, tu, nous: Toward a Culture of Difference [JTN]*. Trans. Alison Martin. New York: Routledge, 1993.

———. *Marine Lover of Friedrich Nietzsche [ML]*. Trans. Gillian C. Gill. New York: Columbia University Press, 1991.

———. "The 'Mechanics' of Fluids" *[MF]*. In *This Sex Which Is Not One*.

———. *"La Mystérique" [M]*. In *Speculum of the Other Woman*.

———. "The Necessity for Sexuate Rights" *[NSR]*. In *Irigaray Reader*.

———. *L'oubli de l'air: Chez Martin Heidegger [OA]*. Paris: Minuit, 1983.

———. "The Power of Discourse and the Subordination of the Feminine" *[PDSF]*. In *This Sex Which Is Not One*.

———. "Questions" *[Q]*. In *Irigaray Reader*.

———. "Questions to Emmanuel Levinas" *[QEL]*. In *Irigaray Reader*.

———. "Sexual Difference" *[SD]*. In *Irigaray Reader*.

———. *Speculum of the Other Woman [SOW]*. Trans. Gillian C. Gill. Ithaca, N.Y.: Cornell University Press, 1985. Translation of *Speculum de l'autre femme*. Paris: Minuit, 1974.

———. *This Sex Which Is Not One [SWNO]*. Trans. Catherine Porter. Ithaca, N.Y.: Cornell University Press, 1985.

———. "This Sex Which Is Not One" *[TSWNO]*. In *This Sex Which Is Not One*.

———. "The Three *Genres*" *[TG]*. In *Irigaray Reader*.

———. "Volume-Fluidity" *[VF]*. Translation of "L'incontourable volume" *(Volume without Contour)*. In *Speculum of the Other Woman*.

———. "When Our Lips Speak Together" *[WOLST]*. In *This Sex Which Is Not One*.

———. "Why Define Sexed Rights?" *[WDSR]*. In *Je, tu, nous*.

———. "Women on the Market" *[WM]*. In *This Sex Which Is Not One*.

Isasi-Diaz, Ada Maria. "Toward an Understanding of *Feminismo Hispano* in the U.S.A." *[FH]*. In Andolsen, Gudorf, and Pellauer, eds., *Women's Consciousness, Women's Conscience*.

Jackson, Wes, et al., eds. *Meeting the Expectations of the Land [MEL]*. San Francisco: North Point Press, 1984.

Jacobs, Jane. *Systems of Survival: A Dialogue on the Moral Foundations of Commerce and Politics [SS]*. New York: Random House, 1993.

Jacoby, Karl. "Slaves by Nature? Domestic Animals and Human Slaves" *[SN]*. *Slavery & Abolition: A Journal of Slave and Post-Slave Studies* (April 1994): 89–97.

Jaggar, Alison M., and Susan R. Bordo, eds. *Gender/Body/Knowledge: Feminist Reconstructions of Being and Knowing [GBK]*. New Brunswick: Rutgers University Press, 1989.

James, William. *Essays in Radical Empiricism [ERE]*. New York: Longman's Green, 1912.

Johnson, Mark. *The Body in the Mind: The Bodily Basis of Meaning, Imagination, and Reason [BM]*. Chicago: University of Chicago Press, 1987.

Jonas, Hans. "De la Gnose au Principe Responsabilité: Entretien avec Hans Jonas" *[GPR]. Esprit* 171 (May 1991): 5–21.

―――. *The Imperative of Responsibility: In Search of an Ethics for the Technological Age. [IR]*. Chicago: University of Chicago Press, 1984.

Jowett, Donna. "Origins, Occupations, and the Proximity of the Heighbour" *[OOPN]*. In Godway and Finn, eds., *Who Is This "We"?*

Jung, Carl Gustav. *Modern Man in Search of a Soul [MMSS]*. Trans. W. S. Dell and Cary F. Baynes. New York: Harcourt Brace Jovanovich, 1955.

―――. "Psychology and Literature" *[PL]*. Reprinted in Ross, ed., *Art and Its Significance*. From *Modern Man in Search of a Soul*.

Jussawalla, Adil. *Missing Person [MP]*. Bombay: Clearing House, 1976.

Kafka, Franz. *The Complete Stories [CS]*. Ed. Nahum N. Glatzer. New York: Schocken, 1971.

―――. "In the Penal Colony" *[IPC]*. In Kafka, *Complete Stories*.

Kant, Immanuel. *The Conflict of the Faculties; Der Streit der Fakultäten [CF]*. Trans. Mary J. Gregor. New York: Abaris, 1979.

―――. *Critique of Judgment [CJ]*. Trans. J. H. Bernard. New York: Hafner, 1951. Translation of *Kritik der Urteilskraft*. In *Kritik der Urteilskraft und Schriften zur Naturphilosophie*. Wiesbaden: Insel-Verlag Zweigstelle, 1957.

―――. *Critique of Practical Reason [CPrR]*. From *Kant's Critique of Practical Reason and Other Works on the Theory of Ethics*. Trans. T. K. Abbott. London: Longman's Green, 1954.

―――. *Critique of Pure Reason [CPR]*. Trans. J. M. D. Meiklejohn. Buffalo: Prometheus, 1990. Trans. Norman Kemp Smith *[CPR (NKS)]*. New York: St. Martin's, 1956. Translation of *Kritik der reinen Vernunft [KRV]*. 2 vols. Berlin: Deutsche Bibliothek, 1936.

―――. *Fundamental Principles of the Metaphysics of Morals [FPMM]*. In *Kant's Critique of Practical Reason and Other Works on the Theory of Ethics*.

―――. *Lectures on Ethics [LE]*. Trans. L. Infield. New York: Harper & Row, 1963.

―――. *The Metaphysical Principles of Virtue [MPV]*. Indianapolis: Bobbs-Merrill, 1968.

———. *Observations on the Beautiful and the Sublime [OBS]*. Trans. John T. Goldthwait. Berkeley: University of California Press, 1960.

Katz, David. *The World of Touch [WT]*. Trans. Lester E. Krueger. Hillsdale, N.J.: Lawrence Erlbaum Associates, 1989.

Katz, Eric. "The Call of the Wild: The Struggle against Domination and the Technological Fix of Nature" *[CW]*. In Oelschlaeger, ed., *Postmodern Environmental Ethics*.

Keller, Mara Lynn. "The Eleusinian Mysteries: Ancient Nature Religion of Demeter and Persephone" *[EM]*. In Diamond and Orenstein, eds., *Reweaving the World*.

Kheel, Marti. "Ecofeminism and Deep Ecology: Reflections on Identity and Difference" *[EDE]*. In Diamond and Orenstein, eds., *Reweaving the World*.

———. "The Liberation of Nature: A Circular Affair" *[LN]*. *Environmental Ethics* 7, no. 2 (Summer 1985): 135–50.

Kierkegaard, Søren. *Either/Or [E/O]*. Trans. David F. Swenson and Lillian Marvin Swenson. Rev. Howard A. Johnson. 2 vols. Garden City, N.Y.: Doubleday, 1959.

———. *Fear and Trembling/The Sickness unto Death [FT]*. Trans. W. Lowrie. Garden City, N.Y.: Doubleday, 1954.

King, Deborah K. "Multiple Jeopardy, Multiple Consciousness: The Context of a Black Feminist Ideology" *[MJMC]*. In Guy-Sheftall, ed., *Words of Fire*.

King, Lewis M. "On the Nature of a Creative World" *[ONCW]*. In Ruch and Anyanwu, eds., *African Philosophy*.

King, Lewis M., Vernon J. Dixon, and Wade W. Nobles, eds. *African Philosophy: Assumptions & Paradigms for Research on Black Persons [AP]*. Los Angeles: Charles R. Drew Postgraduate Medical School, 1976. Fanon Research and Development Center Publication, Area 8, no. 2.

King, Roger J. H. "Caring about Nature: Feminist Ethics and the Environment" *[CN]*. In Warren, ed., *Hypatia* 6, no. 1 (Spring 1991): 75–89.

King, Ynestra. "The Ecology of Feminism and the Feminism of Ecology" *[EFFE]*. In Plant, ed., *Healing the Wounds*.

———. "Healing the Wounds: Feminism, Ecology, and the Nature/Culture Dualism" *[HW]*. In Diamond and Orenstein, ed., *Reweaving the World*.

Kirkham, Richard L. *Theories of Truth: A Critical Introduction [TT]*. Cambridge, Mass.: MIT Press, 1992.

Kittay, Eva Feder, and Diana T. Meyers, eds. *Women and Moral Theory [WMT]*. Totowa, N.J.: Rowman & Littlefield, 1987.

Kokole, Omari H. "The Political Economy of the African Environment" *[PEAE]*. In Westra and Wenz, eds., *Faces of Environmental Racism: Confronting Issues of Global Justice*.

Krell, David Farrell. *Daimon Life: Heidegger and Life-Philosophy [DL]*. Bloomington: Indiana University Press, 1992.

———. *Intimations of Mortality [IM]*. University Park: Pennsylvania State University Press, 1986.

Kristeva, Julia. *Black Sun: Depression and Melancholia [BS]*. Trans. Leon S. Roudiez. New York: Columbia University Press, 1989.

———. *Desire in Language: A Semiotic Approach to Literature and Art [DL]*. Trans. Leon S. Roudiez. New York: Columbia University Press, 1980.

———. *The Kristeva Reader [KR]*. Ed. Toril Moi. Trans. Alice Jardine and Harry Blake. New York: Columbia University Press, 1986.

———. *Powers of Horror: An Essay on Abjection [PH]*. Trans. Leon S. Roudiez. New York: Columbia University Press, 1982.

———. "Stabat Mater" *[SM]*. In *Kristeva Reader*.

———. *Strangers to Ourselves [SO]*. Trans. Leon S. Roudiez. New York: Columbia University Press, 1991.

———. "Women's Time" *[WT]*. In *Kristeva Reader*. Published as "Le temps des femmes." *Cahiers de recherche de sciences des textes et documents* 5 (Winter 1979).

Kroker, Arthur, and Marilouise Kroker, eds. *The Last Sex: Feminism and Outlaw Bodies [LS]*. New York: St. Martin's, 1993.

Lacan, Jacques. *Feminine Sexuality [FS]*. Ed. Juliet Mitchell and Jacqueline Rose. Trans. Jacqueline Rose. New York: Norton, 1985.

———. "God and the *Jouissance* of ~~The~~ Woman" *[GJW]*. In *Feminine Sexuality*.

LaChapelle, Dolores. *Earth Wisdom [EW]*. San Diego: Guild of Tudors, 1978.

Lacoue-Labarthe, Philippe. *The Subject of Philosophy [SP]*. Trans. Thomas Trezise, Hugh J. Silverman, Gary M. Cole, Timothy D. Bent, Karen McPherson, and Claudette Sartiliot. Ed. Thomas Trezise. Minneapolis: University of Minnesota Press, 1993; translation of *Le Sujet de la philosophie [Sp]*. Paris: Aubier-Flammarion, 1979.

LaFleur, William. "Sattva—Enlightenment for Plants and Trees" *[S]*. In Badiner, ed., *Dharma Gaia*.

Lahar, Stephanie. "Ecofeminist Theory and Grassroots Politics" *[ETGP]*. In Warren, ed., *Hypatia* 6, no. 1 (Spring 1991): 28–45.

Langer, Susanne K. *Feeling and Form: A Theory of Art [FF]*. New York: Scribner's, 1953.

Leibniz, G. W. F. "The Exigency to Exist in Essences: Principle of Plenitude" *[EEE]*. In *Leibniz Selections*.

———. *Leibniz Selections [LS].* Ed. P. Wiener. New York: Scribner's, 1951. All references to Leibniz are from this edition.

———. "The Monadology" *[M].* In *Leibniz Selections.*

Leopold, Aldo. *A Sand County Almanac [SCA].* New York: Ballantine Books, 1970.

Levinas, Emmanuel. *The Levinas Reader [LR].* Ed. Seán Hand. Oxford: Blackwell, 1989.

———. "Martin Buber and the Theory of Knowledge" *[MBTK].* In *Levinas Reader.*

———. *Otherwise than Being or Beyond Essence [OB].* Trans. Alfonso Lingis. The Hague: Martinus Nijhoff, 1978. Translation of *Autrement qu'être ou au-delà de l'essence [AÊ].* The Hague: Martinus Nijhoff, 1974.

———. "Reality and Its Shadow" *[RS].* Trans. Alphonso Lingis. In *Levinas Reader.*

———. *Totality and Infinity [TI].* Trans. Alfonso Lingis. Pittsburgh: Duquesne University Press, 1969.

———. "The Transcendence of Words" *[TW].* Trans. Seán Hand. In *Levinas Reader.*

Levine, Donald N. "Simmel at a Distance: On the History and Systematics of the Sociology of the Stranger" *[SD].* In Shack & Skinner, eds., *Strangers in African Societies.*

Lévi-Strauss, Claude. *The Elementary Structure of Kinship [ESK].* Trans. James Harle Bell, John Richard von Sturmer, and Rodney Needham. Boston: Beacon Press, 1969.

Liddell, Henry George, and Robert Scott. *An Intermediate Greek-English Lexicon, Founded upon the Seventh Edition of Liddell and Scott's Greek-English Lexicon [IGEL].* Oxford: Oxford University Press, 1991.

Lingis, Alphonso. *Foreign Bodies [FB].* New York: Routledge, 1994.

Linsky, Leonard, ed. *Semantics and the Philosophy of Language [SPL].* Urbana: University of Illinois Press. 1952.

Locke, John. *An Essay Concerning Human Understanding [E].* Ed. Alexander Campbell Fraser. New York: Dover, 1959.

Lorde, Audre. "Age, Race, Class, and Sex: Women Redefining Difference" *[ARCS].* In Andersen and Collins, eds., *Race, Class, and Gender.*

Lovelock, James. *Gaia: A New Look at Life on Earth [G].* Oxford: Oxford University Press, 1979.

Lowrie, Robert H. *Primitive Religion [PR].* New York: Boni and Liveright, 1924.

Lugones, Marìa C. "On the Logic of Pluralist Feminism" *[OLPF].* In Card, ed., *Feminist Ethics.*

————. "Playfulness, 'World'-Travelling, and Loving Perception" *[PWTLP]*. *Hypatia* 2, no. 2 (Summer 1987): 3–20.

Lyotard, Jean-François. *Le Différend [D]*. Paris: Minuit, 1983.

————. *The Differend: Phrases in Dispute [DPD]*. Trans. Georges Van Den Abbeele. Minneapolis: University of Minnesota Press, 1988.

————. "Europe, the Jew, and the Book" *[EJB]*. In *Political Writings*.

————. "German Guilt" *[GG]*. In *Political Writings*.

————. "The Grip *(Mainmise)*" *[G]*. In *Political Writings*.

————. *Heidegger and "the jews" [HJ]*. Trans. A. Michel and M. Roberts. Minneapolis: University of Minnesota Press, 1990.

————. "Heidegger and 'the jews': A Conference in Vienna and Freiburg" *["HJ"]*. In *Political Writings*.

————. *The Inhuman: Reflections on Time [I]*. Trans. Geoffrey Bennington and Rachel Bowlby. Stanford: Stanford University Press, 1991.

————. *The Lyotard Reader [LR]*. Ed. Andrew Benjamin. Oxford: Blackwell, 1989.

————. *"Oikos" [O]*. In *Political Writings*.

————. *Peregrinations [P]*. New York: Columbia University Press, 1988.

————. *Political Writings [PW]*. Trans. Bill Readings and Kevin Paul Geiman. Minneapolis: University of Minnesota Press, 1993.

————. *The Postmodern Condition: A Report on Knowledge [PMC]*. Trans. Geoff Bennington and Brian Massumi. Minneapolis: University of Minnesota Press, 1984.

————. "The Sign of History" *[SH]*. In *Lyotard Reader*.

————. "What Is Postmodernism?" *[WPM?]*. Reprinted in part in Ross, ed., *Art and Its Significance*. From *Postmodern Condition*.

Lyotard, Jean-François, and Jean-Loup Thébaud. *Just Gaming [JG]*. Trans. Wlad Godzich. Minneapolis: University of Minnesota Press, 1985.

MacKinnon, Catharine A. "Feminism, Marxism, Method, and the State: An Agenda for Theory" *[FMMS1]*. *Signs* 7, no. 3 (Spring 1982): 515–44.

————. "Feminism, Marxism, Method, and the State: Toward Feminist Jurisprudence" *[FMMS2]*. *Signs* 8, no. 4 (1982): 635–58.

————. *Feminism Unmodified: Discourses on Life and Law [FU]*. Cambridge: Harvard University Press, 1987.

————. *Only Words [OW]*. Cambridge: Harvard University Press, 1993.

———. "Sexuality" *[S]*. Chapter 7 in *Toward a Feminist Theory of the State*.

———. *Toward a Feminist Theory of the State [TFTS]*. Cambridge: Harvard University Press, 1989.

———. "Toward Feminist Jurisprudence" *[TFJ]*. Chapter 13 in *Toward a Feminist Theory of the State*.

Manes, Christopher. *Green Rage: Radical Environmentalism and the Unmaking of Civilization [GRF]*. Boston: Little, Brown and Co., 1990.

———. "Nature and Silence" *[NS]*. In Oelschlaeger, ed., *Postmodern Environmental Ethics*.

Marks, Elaine, and Isabelle Courtivron, eds. *New French Feminisms: An Anthology [NFF]*. New York: Schocken, 1981.

Mauss, Marcel. *The Gift: Forms and Functions of Exchange in Archaic Societies [G]*. Trans. Ian Cunnison. Glenco: Free Press, 1954. Also *The Gift: The Form and Reason for Exchange in Archaic Societies*. Trans. W. D. Halls. London: Routledge, 1990.

Maw, Joan, and John Picton, eds. *Concepts of the Body/Self in Africa [CBS]*. Vienna: Afro-Pub, 1992.

Mbiti, John S. *African Religions and Philosophy [ARP]*. London: Heinemann Educational Books, 1969.

McIntosh, Peggy. "White Privilege and Male Privilege: A Personal Account of Coming to See Correspondences through Work in Women's Studies" *[WPMP]*. In Andersen and Collins, eds., *Race, Class, and Gender*.

McLaughlin, Andrew. *Regarding Nature: Industrialism and Deep Ecology [RN]*. Albany: State University of New York Press, 1993.

Meiling, Jin. "Strangers on a Hostile Landscape" *[SHL]*. In Cobham and Collins, eds., *Watchers and Seekers*.

Merchant, Carolyn. *The Death of Nature: Women, Ecology, and the Scientific Revolution [DN]*. New York: Harper & Row, 1980.

———. *Radical Ecology: The Search for a Livable World [RE]*. New York: Routledge, 1992.

Merleau-Ponty, Maurice. *Eye and Mind [EM]*. Trans. Carleton Dallery. Reprinted in part in Ross, ed., *Art and Its Significance*. From *Primacy of Perception*, 282–98.

———. *Phenomenology of Perception [PhP]*. Trans. Colin Smith. London: Routledge & Kegan Paul, 1962.

———. *The Primacy of Perception [PrP]*. Ed. James M. Edie. Evanston: Northwestern University Press, 1964.

————. *The Visible and the Invisible [VI]*. Ed. Claude Lefort. Trans. Alphonso Lingis. Evanston: Northwestern University Press, 1968.

Meyer, Christine, and Faith Moosang, eds. *Living with the Land: Communities Restoring the Earth [LL]*. Gabriola Island, B.C.: New Society Publishers, 1992.

Mill, John Stuart. *On Liberty; with The Subjection of Women and Chapters on Socialism [L]*. New York: Cambridge University Press, 1989.

————. *Utilitarianism and Other Essays [U]*. New York: Penguin, 1987.

Milton, Katharine. "Real Men Don't Eat Deer" *[RMDED]*. *Discover* 18, no. 6 (June 1997): 46–53.

Morgan, Robin, ed. *Sisterhood Is Powerful: An Anthology of Writings from the Women's Liberation Movement [SP]*. New York: Random House, 1970.

Mote, Frederick W. *Intellectual Foundations of China [IFC]*. New York: Alfred A. Knopf, 1971.

Mudimbe, V. Y. *The Invention of Africa [IA]*. Reprinted in part in Ross, ed., *Art and Its Significance*. From *Invention of Africa: Gnosis, Philosophy, and the Order of Knowledge*. Bloomington: Indiana University Press, 1988.

Naess, Arne. *Ecology, Community and Lifestyle: Outline of an Ecosophy [ECL]*. Trans. David Rothenberg. Cambridge: Cambridge University Press, 1989.

————. "The Shallow and the Deep: Long Range Ecology Movement," *Inquiry* 16 (1973): 95–100.

Nagarjuna. *Elegant Sayings [ES]*. Ed. Sakya Pandit. Emeryville, Calif.: Dharma Publishing, 1977.

Nagel, Thomas. *Moral Questions [MQ]*. Cambridge: Cambridge University Press, 1979.

Nancy, Jean-Luc. *The Inoperative Community [IC]*. Trans. P. Connor, L. Garbus, M. Holland, and S. Sawhney. Minneapolis: University of Minnesota Press, 1991.

Nash, Roderick. *The Rights of Nature [RN]*. Madison: University of Wisconsin, Press, 1989.

————. *Wilderness and the American Mind [WAM]*. 3rd ed. New Haven: Yale University Press, 1982.

Neihardt, John G. *Black Elk Speaks [BES]*. Lincoln: University of Nebraska Press, 1993.

Nietzsche, Friedrich. *The Antichrist [A]*. In *Portable Nietzsche*.

————. "Attempt at a Self-Criticism" *[ASC]*. In *Basic Writings*. Reprinted in Ross, ed., *Art and Its Significance*.

——. *Basic Writings of Nietzsche [BWN]*. Trans. Walter Kaufmann. New York: Random House, Modern Library Giant, 1968.

——. *Beyond Good and Evil [BGE]*. In *Basic Writings*.

——. *Birth of Tragedy [BT]*. In *Basic Writings*. Reprinted in part in Ross, ed., *Art and Its Significance*.

——. *Ecce Homo [EH]*. In *Basic Writings*.

——. *The Gay Science [GS]*. Trans. with comm. Walter Kaufman. New York: Vintage, 1974.

——. *The Portable Nietzsche [PN]*. Ed. and trans. Walter Kaufmann. New York: Viking Press, 1954.

——. *Seventy-Five Aphorisms from Five Volumes [75A]*. In *Basic Writings*. From *Dawn [D]; Gay Science [GS]; Human, All-Too-Human [H]; Mixed Opinions and Maxims [MOM]; The Wanderer and His Shadow [WS]*.

——. *Thus Spake Zarathustra [Z]*. In *Basic Writings*.

——. *Twilight of the Idols [TI]*. In *Portable Nietzsche*.

——. *The Will to Power [WP]*. Ed. Walter Kaufmann. Trans. Robert Hollingdale and Walter Kaufmann. New York: Vintage, 1968.

Nodding, Nel. *Caring: A Feminine Approach to Ethics and Moral Education [C]*. Berkeley: University of California Press, 1984.

Nussbaum, Martha. *The Fragility of Goodness [FG]*. Cambridge: Cambridge University Press, 1986.

——. *Love's Knowledge: Essays on Philosophy and Literature [LK]*. New York: Oxford University Press, 1990.

——. *Poetic Justice: The Literary Imagination and Public Life [PJ]*. Boston, Mass.: Beacon Press, 1995.

——. *The Therapy of Desire: Theory and Practice in Hellenistic Ethics [TD]*. Princeton, N.J.: Princeton University Press, 1994.

——. *Women, Culture, and Development: A Study of Human Capabilities [WCD]*. Oxford: Clarendon Press, 1995.

Oates, W. J., and E. O'Neill, eds. *The Complete Greek Drama [CGD]*. New York: Random House, 1938.

Oelschlaeger, Max, ed. *The Wilderness Condition: Essays on Environment and Civilziation [WC]*. San Francisco: Sierra Club Books, 1992.

——. *Postmodern Environmental Ethics [PMEE]*. Albany: State University of New York Press, 1995.

Omolade, Barbara. "Hearts of Darkness" *[HD]*. In Guy-Sheftall, ed., *Words of Fire*.

Ophuls, William. *Ecology and the Politics of Scarcity [EPS]*. San Francisco: W. H. Freeman, 1977

Osoro, R. *The African Identity in Crisis [AIC]*. Hudsonville, Mich.: Bayana Publishers, 1993.

Outlaw, Lucius. *Philosophy, Ethnicity, and Race: The Alfred B. Stiernotte Lectures in Philosophy [PER]*. Hamden, Conn.: Quinnipiac College, 1989.

————. "Philosophy, Ethnicity, and Race" *[PER]*. In Hord and Lee, eds., *I Am Because We Are*.

————. "Toward a Critical Theory of 'Race' " *[TCTR]*. In Goldberg, ed., *Anatomy of Racism*.

Owens, Craig. "The Discourse of Others: Feminists and Postmodernism" *[DO]*. Reprinted in Ross, ed., *Art and Its Significance*.

Pagels, Elaine H. "What Became of God the Mother? Conflicting Images of God in Early Christianity" *[WBGM]*. In Christ and Plaskow, eds., *Womanspirit Rising*.

Parrinder, Geoffrey. *Witchcraft: European and African [WEA]*. London: Faber and Faber, 1970.

Peirce, Charles Sanders. *The Collected Papers of Charles Sanders Peirce [CP]*. 6 vols. Ed. Charles Hartshorne and Paul Weiss. Cambridge: Harvard University Press, 1931–35.

————. *The Philosophical Writings of Peirce [PP]*. Ed. Justus Buchler. New York: Dover, 1955.

Picton, John. "Masks and Identities in Ebira Culture" *[MIEC]*. In Maw and Picton, eds., *Concepts of the Body/Self in Africa*.

Plant, Christopher, and Judith Plant, eds. *Green Business: Hope or Hoax? [GB]*. Gabriola Island, B.C.: New Society Publishers, 1991.

Plant, Judith, ed. *Healing the Wounds: The Power of Ecological Feminism [HW]*. Philadelphia: New Society Publishers, 1989.

Plato. *The Collected Dialogues of Plato [CDP]*. Ed. Edith Hamilton and Huntington Cairns. Princeton: Princeton University Press, 1961. All quotations from Plato are from this edition unless otherwise indicated.

————. *Phaedo [PP]*. Ed., with int., and notes by John Burnet. London: Oxford University Press, 1963.

————. *Phaedo*. Trans. Harold North Fowler. Loeb Classical Library. Cambridge: Harvard University Press, 1914. All Greek passages from *Phaedo* are from this edition.

————. *Phaedo*. Trans. Benjamin Jowett. In *The Dialogues of Plato*. New York: Random House, 1920.

———. *Phaedrus*. Trans. Harold North Fowler. Loeb Classical Library. Cambridge: Harvard University Press, 1914. All Greek passages from *Phaedrus* are from this edition.

———. *Protagoras*. Trans. Benjamin Jowett, 3rd ed. London: Oxford University Press, 1982.

———. *Symposium*. Reprinted in part in Ross, ed., *Art and Its Significance*. From *The Dialogues of Plato*. Trans. Benjamin Jowett, 3rd ed. London: Oxford University Press, 1982. All quotations in English from *Symposium* are from this edition.

———. *Symposium*. Trans. W. R. M. Lamb. Loeb Classical Library. Cambridge: Harvard University Press, 1925. All Greek passages from *Symposium* are from this edition.

Quigley, Peter. "Rethinking Resistance: Environmentalism, Literature, and Poststructural Theory" *[RR]*. In Oelschlaeger, ed., *Postmodern Environmental Ethics*.

Quine, Willard Van Ormine. "Natural Kinds" *[NK]*. In Schwartz, ed., *Naming, Necessity, and Natural Kinds*.

———. *Word and Object [WO]*. Cambridge: MIT Press, 1960.

Rachels, James. "Why Animals Have a Right to Liberty" *[WARL]*. In Regan and Singer, eds., *Animal Rights and Human Obligations*.

Randall, Jr., John Herman. *Aristotle [A]*. New York: Columbia University Press, 1960.

———. *Plato: Dramatist of the Life of Reason [P]*. New York: Columbia University Press, 1970.

Rawls, John. *A Theory of Justice [TJ]*. Cambridge: Belknap Press of Harvard University, 1971.

Reed, A. W. *Myths and Legends of Australia [MLA]*. Sydney: A. H. and A. W. Reed, 1971.

Regan, Tom. *The Case for Animal Rights [CAR]*. Berkeley: University of California Press, 1983.

Regan, Tom, and Peter Singer, eds. *Animal Rights and Human Obligations [ARHO]*. 2nd ed. Englewood Cliffs, N.J.: Prentice Hall, 1989.

Rigterink, Roger J. "Warning: The Surgeon Moralist Has Determined That Claims of Rights Can Be Detrimental to Everyone's Interests" *[W]*. In Cole and Coultrap-McQuin, eds., *Explorations in Feminist Ethics*.

Roach, Catherine. "Loving Your Mother: On the Woman-Nature Relationship" *[LM]*. In Warren, ed., *Hypatia* 6, no. 1 (Spring 1991): 46–59.

Robinson, John Manley. *An Introduction to Early Greek Philosophy [EGP]*. Boston: Houghton Mifflin, 1968. All Greek fragments are quoted from this edition unless otherwise indicated.

Rolston, III, Holmes. *Environmental Ethics: Duties to and Values in the Natural World [EE]*. Philadelphia: Temple University Press, 1988.

———. "Environmental Ethics: Values in and Duties to the Natural World" *[EEVDNW]*. In Bormann and Kellert, eds., *Broken Circle*.

Rorty, Richard. *Consequences of Pragmatism [CP]*. Minneapolis: University of Minnesota Press, 1982.

———. "Philosophy in America Today" *[PAT]*. In *Consequences of Pragmatism*.

Ross, Stephen David. *The Gift of Beauty: The Good as Art [GBGA]*. Albany: State University of New York Press, 1996.

———. *The Gift of Touch: Embodying the Good [GTEG]*. Albany: State University of New York Press, 1998.

———. *The Gift of Truth: Gathering the Good [GTGG]*. Albany: State University of New York Press, 1997.

———. *Ideals and Responsibilities: Ethical Judgment and Social Identity [IR]*, Belmont, Calif.: Wadsworth, 1998.

———. *Inexhaustibility and Human Being: An Essay on Locality [IHB]*. New York: Fordham University Press, 1989.

———. *Injustice and Restitution: The Ordinance of Time [IR]*. Albany: State University of New York Press, 1993.

———. *Learning and Discovery [LD]*. New York: Gordon and Breach, 1981.

———. *The Limits of Language [LL]*. New York: Fordham University Press, 1993.

———. *Locality and Practical Judgment: Charity and Sacrifice [LPJ]*. New York: Fordham University Press, 1994.

———. *Metaphysical Aporia and Philosophical Heresy [MAPH]*. Albany: State University of New York Press, 1989

———. *Perspective in Whitehead's Metaphysics [PWM]*. Albany: State University of New York Press, 1983.

———. *Plenishment in the Earth: An Ethic of Inclusion [PE]*. Albany: State University of New York, 1995.

———. *The Ring of Representation [RR]*. Albany: State University of New York Press, 1992.

———. *A Theory of Art: Inexhaustibility by Contrast [TA]*. Albany: State University of New York Press, 1983.

———. "Translation as Transgression" *[TT]*. In *Translation Perspectives*, vol. 5. Ed. D. J. Schmidt. Binghamton: Binghamton University, 1990.

Ross, Stephen David, ed., *Art and Its Significance: An Anthology of Aesthetic Theory [AIS]*. 3rd ed. Albany: State University of New York Press, 1994.

Ruch, E. A., and K. C. Anyanwu, eds. *African Philosophy: An Introduction to the Main Philosophical Trends in Contemporary Africa [AP]*. Rome: Catholic Book Agency, 1984.

Ruether, Rosemary. *New Woman, New Earth [NWNE]*. New York: Seabury Press, 1975.

Sacks, Oliver. *The Man Who Mistook His Wife for a Hat and Other Clinical Tales*, published in four volumes as *Awakenings [A]*; *A Leg to Stand On [LSO]*; *The Man Who Mistook His Wife for a Hat and Other Clinical Tales [MMWH]*; and *Seeing Voices [SV]*. New York: Quality Paperback Book Club, 1990.

Salleh, Ariel. "Class, Race, and Gender Discourse in the Ecofeminism/Deep Ecology Debate" *[CRGD]*. In Oelschlaeger, ed., *Postmodern Environmental Ethics*.

Sallis, John, ed. *Deconstruction in Philosophy: The Texts of Jacques Derrida [DP]*. Chicago: University of Chicago Press, 1987.

———. *Reading Heidegger: Commemorations [RH]*. Bloomington: Indiana University Press, 1993.

Salomon, Charlotte. *Charlotte: Life or Theater? An Autobiographical Play by Charlotte Salomon [CLT]*. Trans. Leila Vennewitz. Int. Judith Herzberg. New York: Viking Press, 1981.

———. *Leven? of Theater? Life? or Theatre? [L?T?]*. Int. Judith C. E. Belinfante, Christine Fisher-Defoy, and Ad Petersen. Amsterdam: Joods Historisch Museum, 1992.

Sartre, Jean-Paul. *Nausea [N]*. Trans. Lloyd Alexander. New York: New Directions, 1964.

Schapiro, Meyer. "The Still Life as a Personal Object" *[SLPO]*. In Marianne M. Simmel, ed., *Reach of the Mind: Essays in Memory of Kurt Goldstein*. New York: Springer Publishing Company, 1968. Discussed in Derrida, "Restitutions," in *Truth in Painting*.

Scheper-Hughes, Nancy. "Vernacular Sexism: An Anthropological Response to Ivan Illich" *[VS]*. In *Feminist Issues* 3, no. 1 (Spring 1983): 28–36.

Scherer, Donald, and Tom Attig, eds. *Ethics and the Environment [EE]*. Englewood Cliffs, N.J.: Prentice Hall, 1983.

Schor, Naomi. "This Essentialism Which Is Not One: Coming to Grips with Irigaray" *[TEWNO]*. *Differences: A Journal of Feminist Cultural Studies* 2, no. 1 (Summer 1989): 38–58.

Schumacher, E. F. *Small Is Beautiful: Economics as if People Mattered [SB]*. New York: Harper & Row, 1973.

Schutte, Ofelia. *Cultural Identity and Social Liberation in Latin American Thought [CISL]*. Albany: State University of New York Press, 1993.

Schutz, Alfred. "The Stranger: An Essay in Social Psychology" *[S]*. *American Journal of Sociology* 49, no. 6 (1944): 499–507.

———. "The Homecomer" *[H]*. *American Journal of Sociology* 60, no. 5 (1945): 369–76.

Schwartz, Stephen P., ed. *Naming, Necessity, and Natural Kinds [NNNK]*. Ithaca, N.Y.: Cornell University Press, 1977.

Scott, Charles E. *The* Question *of Ethics: Nietzsche, Foucault, Heidegger [QE]*. Bloomington: Indiana University Press, 1990.

Seamon, David, ed. *Dwelling, Seeing, and Designing [DSD]*. Albany: State University of New York Press, 1993.

Seed, John, Joanna Macy, Pat Fleming, and Arne Naess. *Thinking Like a Mountain: Toward a Council of All Beings [TLM]*. Philadelphia: New Society Publishers, 1988.

Selfe, Lorna. *Nadia: A Case Study of Extraordinary Drawing Ability in an Autistic Child [N]*. New York and London: Harcourt Brace Jovanovich, 1977.

Sen, Amartya. "More Than 100 Million Women Are Missing" *[MMWM]*. *New York Review of Books* (December 20, 1990): 61–66.

Senghor, Léopold Sédar. "Negritude: A Humanism of the Twentieth Century" *[N]*. In Hord and Lee, eds., *I Am Because We Are.*

Serequeberhan, Tsenay. *African Philosophy: The Essential Readings [AP]*. New York: Paragon House, 1991.

Serres, Michel. *The Natural Contract [NC]*. Trans. Elizabeth MacArthur and William Paulson. Ann Arbor: University of Michigan Press, 1995.

Sessions, Robert. "Deep Ecology versus Ecofeminism: Healthy Differences or Incompatible Philosophies?" *[DEE]*. In Warren, ed., *Hypatia* 6, no. 1 (Spring 1991): 90–107.

Shack, William A. "Open Systems and Closed Boundaries: The Ritual Process of Stranger Relations in New African States" *[OSCB]*. In Shack and Skinner, eds., *Strangers in African Societies.*

Shack, William A., and Elliott P. Skinner, eds. *Strangers in African Societies [SAS]*. Berkeley: University of California Press, 1979.

Shantideva, *Bodhicaryavatara [B]* 8:114. Trans. Stephen Batchelor. *A Guide to the Bodhisattva's Way of Life [GBWL]*. Dharamsala, India: Library of Tibetan Works and Archives, 1979.

Sheehan, Thomas, ed. *Heidegger, the Man and the Thinker [HMT]*. Chicago: Precedent Publishing, 1981.

Shepard, Paul. *Nature and Madness [NM]*. San Franciso: Sierra Club Books, 1982.

Shiva, Vandana. "Development as a New Project of Western Patriarchy" *[DNPWP]*. In Diamond and Orenstein, eds., *Reweaving the World*.

———. *Staying Alive [SA]*. London: Zed, 1989.

Silko, Leslie Marmon. *Ceremony [C]*. New York: New American Library, 1977.

Sillah, Memuna M. "Bundu Trap" *[BT]*. *Natural History* (August 1996): 42–53.

Simmel, Georg. "The Stranger" *[S]*. In Donald N. Levine, *On Individuality and Social Forms*. Chicago: University of Chicago Press, 1971.

Singer, Linda. "Defusing the Canon: Feminist Rereading and Textual Politics" *[DC]*. In *Erotic Welfare: Sexual Theory and Politics in the Age of Epidemic*. Ed. and int. Judith Butler and Maureen MacGrogan. New York: Routledge, 1993.

Singer, Peter. *Animal Liberation: A New Ethics for Our Treatment of Animals [AL]*. New York: Avon, 1975.

Sini, Carlo. *Images of Truth: From Sign to Symbol [IT]*. Trans. Massimo Verdicchio. Atlantic Highlands, N.J.: Humanities Press, 1993.

Slicer, Deborah. "Your Daughter or Your Dog" *[DD]*. In Warren, ed., *Hypatia* 6, no. 1 (Spring 1991): 108–23.

Smith, Mick. "Cheney and the Myth of Postmodernism" *[CMP]*. In Oelschlaeger, ed., *Postmodern Environmental Ethics*.

Sophocles. *Oedipus the King [OK], Antigone [A], Oedipus at Colonus [OC]*. All trans. R. C. Jebb. In Oates and O'Neill, eds., *Complete Greek Drama*.

Sorabji, Richard. "Aristotle on Demarcating the Five Senses" *[ADFS]*. *Philosophical Review* 80: 55–79.

Soyinka, Wole. *Art, Dialogue, and Outrage: Essays on Literature and Culture [ADO]*. New York: Pantheon, 1994.

Spelman, Elizabeth V. *Inessential Woman: Problems of Exclusion in Feminist Thought [IW]*. Boston: Beacon Press, 1988.

Spiegel, Marjorie. *The Dreaded Comparison: Human and Animal Slavery [DC]*. Rev. ed. New York: Mirror Books, 1996.

Spinoza, Benedict de. *Collected Works of Spinoza [CWS]*. Vol. 1. 2nd printing with corr. Ed. and trans. Edwin Curley. Princeton: Princeton University Press, 1988.

———. *Descartes' Principles of Philosophy [DPP]*. In *Collected Works*, vol. 1.

———. *Ethics [E]*. In *Collected Works*, vol. 1.

———. *Ethics [EG]*. Trans. William Hale White. Rev. Amelia Hutchinson Stirling. Ed. and int. James Gutmann. New York: Hafner, 1949.

————. *A Political Treatise [PT]*. Trans. and int. R. H. M. Elwes. New York: Dover, 1951.

Spretnak, Charlene. *The Spiritual Dimension of Green Politics [SDGP]*. Santa Fe, N.M.: Bear and Co., 1986.

Starhawk [Miriam Simos]. "Ethics and Justice in Goddess Religion" *[EJGR]*. In Andolsen, Gudorf, and Pellauer, eds., *Women's Consciousness, Women's Conscience*.

————. "Witchcraft and Women's Culture" *[WWC]*. In Christ and Plaskow, eds., *Womanspirit Rising*.

Stephen, Michele. "Contrasting Images of Power" *[CIP]*. In Stephen ed., *Sorcerer and Witch*.

————. "Master of Souls: The Mekeo Sorcerer" *[MS]*. In Stephen ed., *Sorcerer and Witch*.

Stephen, Michele, ed. *Sorcerer and Witch in Melanesia [SWM]*. New Brunswick, N.J.: Rutgers University Press, 1987.

Stone, Christopher D. *Earth and Other Ethics [EOE]*. New York: Harper & Row, 1987.

————. "Moral Pluralism and the Course of Environmental Ethics" *[MPCEE]*. In Oelschlaeger, ed., *Postmodern Environmental Ethics*.

Strawson, Peter F. *Individuals: An Essay in Descriptive Metaphysics [I]*. Garden City, N.Y.: Doubleday & Co., 1959.

Sumner, Claude. *The Source of African Philosophy: The Ethiopian Philosophy of Man [SAP]*. Stuttgart: Franz Steiner Verlag Wiesbaden GMBH, 1986.

Swift, Jonathan. *Gulliver's Travels and Other Writings [GT]*. Int. Louis A. Landa. Boston: Houghton Mifflin, 1960.

Tannen, Deborah. *You Just Don't Understand: Women and Men in Conversation [YJDU]*. New York: Ballantine, 1990.

Tarski, Alfred. "The Semantic Conception of Truth" *[SCT]*. *Philosophy and Phenomenological Research* 4:341–76 (1944). Reprinted in Linsky, ed., *Semantics and the Philosophy of Language*. All page references to Linsky.

Taylor, Paul. *Respect for Nature: A Theory of Environmental Ethics [RN]*. Princeton: Princeton University Press, 1986.

Tellenbach, Hubertus, and Bin Kimura. "The Japanese Concept of 'Nature' " *[JCN]*. In Callicott and Ames, eds., *Nature in Asian Traditions of Thought*.

Theroux, Paul. "Self-Propelled" *[SP]*. *The New York Times Magazine* (April 25, 1993): 22–24.

Thomas, Elizabeth Marshall. "Reflections (Lions)" *[L]*. *The New Yorker* (October 15, 1990): 78–101.

Thompson, Robert Farris. *Flash of the Spirit; African and Afro-American Art and Philosophy [FS]*. New York: Vintage, 1984.

Tolstoy, Leo. *What Is Art? [WA]*. Reprinted in part in Ross, ed., *Art and Its Significance*.

Trinh, T. Minh-ha. *Woman, Native, Other: Writing Postcoloniality and Feminism [WNO]*. Indianapolis: Indiana University Press, 1989.

Trumbull, H. C. *The Threshold Covenant [TC]*. New York: Scribner's, 1896.

Tu Wei-ming. "The Continuity of Nature: Chinese Visions of Nature" *[CN]*. In Callicott and Ames, eds., *Nature in Asian Traditions of Thought*.

Turner, Victor. *The Ritual Process [RP]*. Chicago: Aldine, 1969.

Tyler, Edward B. *Primitive Culture [PC]*. New York: Holt and Co., 1889.

Valiente, Doreen. *Witchcraft for Tomorrow [WT]*. Custer, Wash.: Phoenix, 1987.

Vattimo, Gianni. *The End of Modernity [EM]*. Trans. J. R. Snyder. Cambridge: Polity Press, 1988.

Warren, Karen J. "Feminism and Ecology: Making Connections" *[FEMC]. Environmental Ethics* 9, no. 1 (Spring 1987): 3–20

———. "The Promise and Power of Ecological Feminism" *[PPEF]. Environmental Ethics* 12, no. 2 (Summer 1990): 125–46.

Warren, Karen J., ed. *Hypatia* 6, no. 1 (Spring 1991). Special Issue on Ecological Feminism.

Warren, Karen J., and Jim Cheney. "Ecological Feminism and Ecosystem Ecology" *[EFEE]*. In Warren, ed., *Hypatia* 6, no. 1 (Spring 1991): 179–97.

Weber, Renée, "A Philosophical Perspective on Touch" *[PPT]*. In Barnard and Brazelton, eds., *Touch*.

Wenders, William. *Wings of Desire [WD]*. Screenplay by Wenders and Peter Handke. 1988.

Wenz, Peter S. "Just Garbage" *[JG]*. In Westra and Wenz, eds., *Faces of Environmental Racism: Confronting Issues of Global Justice*.

West, Cornel. *Keeping Faith: Philosophy and Race in America [KP]*. New York: Routledge, 1993.

———. "Race Matters" *[RM]*. In Andersen and Collins, eds., *Race, Class, and Gender*.

Weston, Anthony. "Before Environmental Ethics" *[BEE]*. In Oelschlaeger, ed., *Postmodern Environmental Ethics*.

Westra, Laura, and Peter S. Wenz, eds. *Faces of Environmental Racism: Confronting Issues of Global Justice [FER]*. Lanham, Md.: Rowman & Littlefield, 1995.

Whitehead, Alfred North. *Adventures of Ideas [AI]*. New York: Macmillan, 1933.

———. *Modes of Thought [MT]*. New York: Capricorn, 1938.

———. *Process and Reality [PR]*. Corrected edition. Ed. D. R. Griffin and D. W. Sherburne. New York: Free Press, 1978.

———. *Science in the Modern World [SMW]*. New York: Macmillan, 1925.

Wilcox, Finn, and Jeremiah Gorsline, eds. *Working the Woods, Working the Sea [WW]*. Port Townsend, Wash.: Empty Bowl, 1986.

Wilson, Edward O. *The Diversity of Life [DL]*. Cambridge: Harvard University Press, 1992.

Wittgenstein, Ludwig. *The Blue and Brown Books [BB]*. New York: Harper & Row, 1958.

———. *Philosophical Investigations [PI]*. Trans. G. E. M. Anscombe. Oxford: Blackwell, 1963.

———. *Tractatus Logico-Philosophicus [TLP]*. Trans. D. F. Pears and B. F. McGuinness. London: Routledge & Kegan Paul, 1961.

Wittig, Monique. "The Category of Sex" *[CS]*. In *Straight Mind*.

———. *The Lesbian Body [LB]*. Trans. David Le Vay. Boston: Beacon, 1973. Translation of *Le Corps Lesbien [CL]*. Paris: Minuit, 1973.

———. "The Mark of Gender" *[MG]*. In *Straight Mind*

———. "One Is Not Born a Woman" *[OBW]*. In *Straight Mind*.

———. "The Straight Mind" *[SM]*. In *Straight Mind*.

———. *The Straight Mind and Other Essays [SME]*. Boston: Beacon Press, 1992.

Woodward, F. L., trans. *The Minor Antholoties of the Pali Canon [MAPC]*. London: Geoffrey Cumberlege, 1948.

Worster, Donald. *Rivers of Empire [RE]*. New York: Pantheon, 1985.

Zack, Naomi. *Bachelors of Science: Seventeenth-Century Identity, Then and Now [BS]*. Philadelphia: Temple University Press, 1996.

Zimmerman, Michael E. "Quantum Theory, Intrinsic Value, and Panentheism" *[QTIVP]*. In Oelschlaeger, ed., *Postmodern Environmental Ethics*.

Index